GO!
with Microsoft® Office

Access 2003
Brief

GO! with Microsoft® Office

Access 2003

Brief

Linda Foster-Turpen

Shelley Gaskin, Series Editor

PEARSON Prentice Hall

Upper Saddle River, New Jersey

Library of Congress Cataloging-in-Publication Data

Foster-Turpen, Linda.
Go! with Microsoft Office Access 2003 : brief / Linda Foster-Turpen.
p. cm. — (Go! with Microsoft Office 2003)
ISBN 0-13-143428-4 (alk. paper)
1. Microsoft Office. 2. Microsoft Access. 3. Business—Computer programs. 4. Database management. I. Title. II. Series. HF5548.4.M525 F67 2003 005.75'65—dc22
2003018376

Vice President and Publisher: Natalie E. Anderson
Executive Acquisitions Editor: Jodi McPherson
Marketing Manager: Emily Williams Knight
Marketing Assistant: Nicole Beaudry
Associate Director IT Product Development: Melonie Salvati
Senior Project Manager, Editorial: Mike Ruel
Project Manager, Supplements: Melissa Edwards
Senior Media Project Manager: Cathi Profitko
Editorial Assistants: Jasmine Slowik, Jodi Bolognese, Alana Meyers
Manager, Production: Gail Steier de Acevedo
Senior Project Manager, Production: Tim Tate
Manufacturing Buyer: Tim Tate
Design Manager: Maria Lange
Art Director: Pat Smythe
Cover Designer: Brian Salisbury
Cover Photo: Steve Bloom/Getty Images, Inc.
Interior Designer: Quorum Creative Services
Full Service Composition: Black Dot Group
Printer/Binder: Von Hoffmann Corporation
Cover Printer: Phoenix Color Corporation

Credits and acknowledgments borrowed from other sources and reproduced, with permission, in this textbook appear below or on the appropriate page within the text.

PEARSON
Prentice Hall

10 9 8 7 6 5 4 3 2 1
ISBN 0-13-143428-4

I would like to dedicate this book to my awesome family. I want to thank my husband, Dave Alumbaugh, who always lets me be exactly who I am; my kids, Michael, Jordan, and Ceara, who give me hope and my drive for everything that I do; my mom, who never gives up; and my dad, who has been my light, my rock, and one of my best friends every day that I can remember. I love you all and . . . thanks for putting up with me.

—Linda Foster-Turpen

This book is dedicated to my students, who inspire me every day, and to my husband, Fred Gaskin.

—Shelley Gaskin

Microsoft® Office Specialist Approved Courseware

What does this logo mean?

It means this courseware has been approved by the Microsoft® Office Specialist Program to be among the finest available for learning **Microsoft® Office Word 2003, Microsoft® Office Excel 2003, Microsoft® Office PowerPoint® 2003,** and **Microsoft® Office Access 2003.** It also means that upon completion of this courseware, you may be prepared to take an exam for Microsoft Office Specialist qualification.

What is a Microsoft Office Specialist?

A Microsoft Office Specialist is an individual who has passed exams for certifying his or her skills in one or more of the Microsoft Office desktop applications such as Microsoft Word, Microsoft Excel, Microsoft PowerPoint, Microsoft Outlook, Microsoft Access, or Microsoft Project. The Microsoft Office Specialist Program typically offers certification exams at the "Specialist" and "Expert" skill levels.* The Microsoft Office Specialist Program is the only program approved by Microsoft for testing proficiency in Microsoft Office desktop applications and Microsoft Project. This testing program can be a valuable asset in any job search or career advancement.

More Information:

To learn more about becoming a Microsoft Office Specialist, visit **www.microsoft.com/officespecialist**

To learn about other Microsoft Office Specialist approved courseware from Pearson Education, visit **www.prenhall.com/phit**

*The availability of Microsoft Office Specialist certification exams varies by application, application version, and language. Visit www.microsoft.com/officespecialist for exam availability.

GO!

Series for Microsoft® Office System 2003

Series Editor: Shelley Gaskin

Office
Getting Started
Brief
Intermediate
Advanced

Word
Brief
Volume 1
Volume 2
Comprehensive

Excel
Brief
Volume 1
Volume 2
Comprehensive

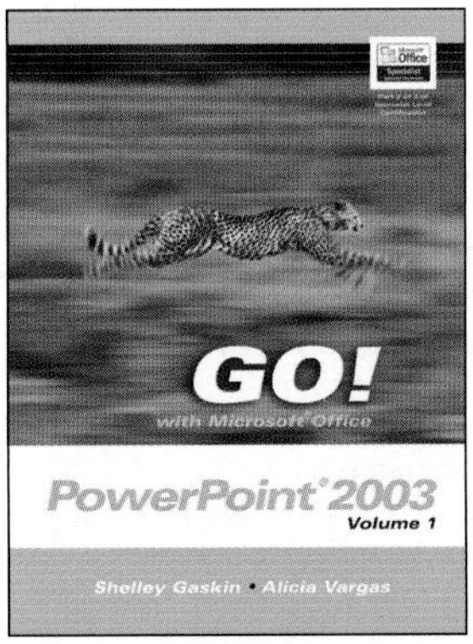

PowerPoint
Brief
Volume 1
Volume 2
Comprehensive

Access
Brief
Volume 1
Volume 2
Comprehensive

GO! Series Reviewers

We would like to thank the following "Super Reviewers" for both their subject matter expertise and attention to detail from the instructors' perspective. Your time, effort, hard work, and diligence has helped us create the best books in the world. Prentice Hall and your author partners thank you:

Rocky Belcher	Sinclair CC
Judy Cameron	Spokane CC
Gail Cope	Sinclair CC
Larry Farrer	Guilford Tech CC
Janet Enck	Columbus State CC
Susan Fry	Boise State
Lewis Hall	Riverside CC
Jeff Howard	Finger Lakes CC
Jason Hu	Pasadena City College
Michele Hulett	Southwestern Missouri State U.
Donna Madsen	Kirkwood CC
Cheryl Reindl-Johnson	Sinclair CC
Jan Spaar	Spokane CC
Mary Ann Zlotow	College of DuPage

We would also like to thank our valuable student reviewers who bring us vital input from those who will someday study from our books:

Nicholas J. Bene	Southwestern Missouri State U.
Anup Jonathan	Southwestern Missouri State U.
Kimber Miller	Pasadena City College
Kelly Moline	Southwestern Missouri State U.
Adam Morris	Southwestern Missouri State U.
Robert Murphy	Southwestern Missouri State U.
Drucilla Owenby	Southwestern Missouri State U.
Vince Withee	Southwestern Missouri State U.

Finally, we have been lucky to have so many of you respond to review our chapter manuscripts. You have given us tremendous feedback and helped make a fantastic series. We could not have done it without you.

Abraham, Reni	Houston CC
Agatston, Ann	Agatston Consulting
Alejandro, Manuel	Southwest Texas Junior College
Ali, Farha	Lander University
Anik, Mazhar	Tiffin University
Armstrong, Gary	Shippensburg University
Bagui, Sikha	Univ. West Florida
Belton, Linda	Springfield Tech. Com College
Bennett, Judith	Sam Houston State University
Bishop, Frances	DeVry Institute- Alpharetta (ATL)
Branigan, Dave	DeVry University
Bray, Patricia	Allegany College of Maryland
Buehler, Lesley	Ohlone College
Buell, C	Central Oregon CC
Byars, Pat	Brookhaven College
Cacace, Rich	Pensacola Jr. College
Cadenhead, Charles	Brookhaven College
Calhoun, Ric	Gordon College
Carriker, Sandra	North Shore CC
Challa, Chandrashekar	Virginia State University
Chamlou, Afsaneh	NOVA Alexandria
Chapman, Pam	Wabaunsee CC
Christensen, Dan	Iowa Western CC
Conroy-Link, Janet	Holy Family College
Cosgrove, Janet	Northwestern CT Community Technical College
Cox, Rollie	Madison Area Technical College
Crawford, Hiram	Olive Harvey College
Danno, John	DeVry University/ Keller Graduate School
Davis, Phillip Md.	Del Mar College
Doroshow, Mike	Eastfield College
Douglas, Gretchen	SUNY Cortland
Driskel, Loretta	Niagara CC
Duckwiler, Carol	Wabaunsee CC
Duncan, Mimi	University of Missouri-St. Louis
Duvall, Annette	Albuquerque Technical Vocational Institute

Reviewers continues

Ecklund, Paula	Duke University
Edmondson, Jeremy	Mount Pisgah School
Erickson, John	University of South Dakota
Falkenstein, Todd	Indiana University East
Fite, Beverly	Amarillo College
Foltz, Brian	East Carolina University
Friedrichsen, Lisa	Johnson County CC
Fustos, Janos	Metro State
Gallup, Jeanette	Blinn College
Gentry, Barb	Parkland College
Gerace, Karin	St. Angela Merici School
Gerace, Tom	Tulane University
Ghajar, Homa	Oklahoma State University
Gifford, Steve	Northwest Iowa CC
Gregoryk, Kerry	Virginia Commonwealth State University
Griggs, Debra	Bellevue CC
Grimm, Carol	Palm Beach CC
Helms, Liz	Columbus State CC
Hernandez, Leticia	TCI College of Technology
Hogan, Pat	Cape Fear CC
Horvath, Carrie	Albertus Magnus College
Howard, Chris	DeVry University
Huckabay, Jamie	Austin CC
Hunt, Laura	Tulsa CC
Jacob, Sherry	Jefferson CC
Jacobs, Duane	Salt Lake CC
Johnson, Kathy	Wright College
Jones, Stacey	Benedict College
Kasai, Susumu	Salt Lake CC
Keen, Debby	Univ. of Kentucky
Kirk, Colleen	Mercy College
Kliston, Linda	Broward CC
Kramer, Ed	Northern Virginia CC
Laird, Jeff	Northeast State CC
Lange, David	Grand Valley State
LaPointe, Deb	Albuquerque TVI
Lenhart, Sheryl	Terra CC
Letavec, Chris	University of Cincinnati
Lightner, Renee	Broward CC
Lindberg, Martha	Minnesota State University
Linge, Richard	Arizona Western College
Loizeaux, Barbara	Westchester CC
Lopez, Don	Clovis- State Center CC District
Low, Willy Hui	Joliet Junior College
Lowe, Rita	Harold Washington College
Lucas, Vickie	Broward CC
Lynam, Linda	Central Missouri State University
Machuca, Wayne	College of the Sequoias
Madison, Dana	Clarion University
Maguire, Trish	Eastern New Mexico University
Malkan, Rajiv	Montgomery College
Manning, David	Northern Kentucky University
Marghitu, Daniela	Auburn University
Marks, Suzanne	Bellevue CC
Marquez, Juanita	El Centro College
Marucco, Toni	Lincoln Land CC
Mason, Lynn	Lubbock Christian University
Matutis, Audrone	Houston CC
McCannon, Melinda (Mindy)	Gordon College
McClure, Darlean	College of Sequoias
McCue, Stacy	Harrisburg Area CC
McEntire-Orbach, Teresa	Middlesex County College
McManus, Illyana	Grossmont College
Menking, Rick	Hardin-Simmons University
Meredith, Mary	U. of Louisiana at Lafayette
Mermelstein, Lisa	Baruch College
Metos, Linda	Salt Lake CC
Meurer, Daniel	University of Cincinnati
Monk, Ellen	University of Delaware
Morris, Nancy	Hudson Valley CC
Nadas, Erika	Wright College
Nadelman, Cindi	New England College
Ncube, Cathy	University of West Florida
Nicholls, Doreen	Mohawk Valley CC
Orr, Claudia	New Mexico State University
Otieno, Derek	DeVry University
Otton, Diana Hill	Chesapeake College
Oxendale, Lucia	West Virginia Institute of Technology
Paiano, Frank	Southwestern College
Proietti, Kathleen	Northern Essex CC
Pusins, Delores	HCCC
Reeves, Karen	High Point University
Rhue, Shelly	DeVry University
Richards, Karen	Maplewoods CC
Ross, Dianne	Univ. of Louisiana in Lafayette
Rousseau, Mary	Broward CC
Sams, Todd	University of Cincinnati
Sandoval, Everett	Reedley College
Sardone, Nancy	Seton Hall University
Scafide, Jean	Mississippi Gulf Coast CC
Scheeren, Judy	Westmoreland County CC
Schneider, Sol	Sam Houston State University
Scroggins, Michael	Southwest Missouri State University
Sever, Suzanne	Northwest Arkansas CC
Sheridan, Rick	California State University-Chico
Sinha, Atin	Albany State University
Smith, T. Michael	Austin CC
Smith, Tammy	Tompkins Cortland CC
Stefanelli, Greg	Carroll CC
Steiner, Ester	New Mexico State University
Sterling, Janet	Houston CC
Stroup, Tracey	Pasadena City College
Sullivan, Angela	Joliet Junior College
Szurek, Joseph	University of Pittsburgh at Greensburg
Taylor, Michael	Seattle Central CC
Thangiah, Sam	Slippery Rock University
Thompson-Sellers, Ingrid	Georgia Perimeter College
Tomasi, Erik	Baruch College
Toreson, Karen	Shoreline CC
Turgeon, Cheryl	Asnuntuck CC
Turpen, Linda	Albuquerque TVI
Upshaw, Susan	Del Mar College
Vargas, Tony	El Paso CC
Vicars, Mitzi	Hampton University
Vitrano, Mary Ellen	Palm Beach CC
Wahila, Lori	Tompkins Cortland CC
Wavle, Sharon	Tompkins Cortland CC
White, Bruce	Quinnipiac University
Willer, Ann	Solano CC
Williams, Mark	Lane CC
Wimberly, Leanne	International Academy of Design and Technology
Worthington, Paula	NOVA Woodbridge
Yauney, Annette	Herkimer CCC
Zavala, Ben	Webster Tech

About the Authors/Acknowledgments

About Linda Foster-Turpen

Linda Foster-Turpen is an instructor in Computer Information Systems at Albuquerque TVI in Albuquerque, New Mexico, where she teaches and has developed computer applications courses. Linda received her B.B.A. in Accounting as well as her M.B.A. in MIS and M.B.A. in Accounting from the University of New Mexico. She has developed new courses for her college including courses in Intranets/Extranets, Management Information Systems, and Distance Learning courses in introductory computer applications and Microsoft Access.

In addition to teaching and authoring, Linda likes to hike and backpack with her family. She lives in Corrales, New Mexico, with her husband Dave, her three children, Michael, Jordan, and Ceara, and their animals.

Acknowledgments from Linda Foster-Turpen

I would like to thank everyone at Prentice Hall (and beyond) who was involved with the production of this book. To my reviewers, your input and feedback were appreciated more than you could know. I would not want to write a book without you! To my technical editors, Jan Snyder and Mary Pascarella, thank you for your attention to detail and for your comments and suggestions during the writing of this book. A big thank you to Emily Knight in Marketing, Gail Steier de Acevedo and Tim Tate in Production, and Pat Smythe and Maria Lange in Design for your contributions. To the series editor, Shelley Gaskin, thank you for your wonderful vision for this book and the entire *GO! Series*. Your ideas and inspiration were the basis for this whole project from its inception. To the Editorial Project Manager, Mike Ruel, thanks for making sure all of my ducks were always in a row, and to the Executive Editor, Jodi McPherson, thank you for your faith and confidence in me from the beginning. A huge thanks to my students, you are the reason these books are written! I would also like to thank my colleagues at TVI for giving me a sounding board from which I could bounce ideas or just vent my frustrations. Any book takes a team of people, and I was most fortunate to have all of you on mine. I also want to thank God for . . . everything.

About Shelley Gaskin

Shelley Gaskin, Series Editor, is a professor of business and computer technology at Pasadena City College in Pasadena, California. She holds a master's degree in business education from Northern Illinois University and a doctorate in adult and community education from Ball State University. Dr. Gaskin has 15 years of experience in the computer industry with several Fortune 500 companies and has developed and written training materials for custom systems applications in both the public and private sector. She is also the author of books on Microsoft Outlook and word processing.

Acknowledgments from Shelley Gaskin

Many talented individuals worked to produce this book, and I thank them for their continuous support. My Executive Acquisitions Editor, Jodi McPherson, gave me much latitude to experiment with new things. Editorial Project Manager Mike Ruel worked with me through each stage of writing and production. Emily Knight and the Prentice Hall Marketing team worked with me throughout this process to make sure both instructors and students are informed about the benefits of using this series. Also, very big thanks and appreciation goes to Prentice Hall's top-notch Production and Design team: Associate Director Product Development Melonie Salvati, Manager of Production Gail Steier de Acevedo, Senior Production Project Manager and Manufacturing Buyer Tim Tate, Design Manager Maria Lange, Art Director Pat Smythe, Interior Designer Quorum Creative Services, and Cover Designer Brian Salisbury.

Thanks to all!
Shelley Gaskin, Series Editor

Why I Wrote This Series

Dear Professor,

If you are like me, you are frantically busy trying to implement new course delivery methods (e.g., online) while also maintaining your regular campus schedule of classes and academic responsibilities. I developed this series for colleagues like you, who are long on commitment and expertise but short on time and assistance.

The primary goal of the ***GO! Series***, aside from the obvious one of teaching **Microsoft® Office 2003** concepts and skills, is ease of implementation using any delivery method—traditional, self-paced, or online.

There are no lengthy passages of text; instead, bits of expository text are woven into the steps at the teachable moment. This is the point at which the student has a context within which he or she can understand the concept. A scenario-like approach is used in a manner that makes sense, but it does not attempt to have the student "pretend" to be someone else.

A key feature of this series is the use of Microsoft procedural syntax. That is, steps begin with where the action is to take place, followed by the action itself. This prevents the student from doing the right thing in the wrong place!

The *GO! Series* is written with all of your everyday classroom realities in mind. For example, in each project, the student is instructed to insert his or her name in a footer and to save the document with his or her name. Thus, unidentified printouts do not show up at the printer nor do unidentified documents get stored on the hard drives.

Finally, an overriding consideration is that the student is not always working in a classroom with a teacher. Students frequently work at home or in a lab staffed only with instructional aides. Thus, the instruction must be error-free, clearly written, and logically arranged.

My students enjoy learning the Microsoft Office software. The goal of the instruction in the *GO! Series* is to provide students with the skills to solve business problems using the computer as a tool, for both themselves and the organizations for which they might be employed.

Thank you for using the ***GO! Series for Microsoft® Office System 2003*** for your students.

Regards,

Shelley Gaskin

Shelley Gaskin, Series Editor

Preface

Philosophy

Our overall philosophy is ease of implementation for the instructor, whether instruction is via lecture, lab, online, or partially self-paced. Right from the start, the *GO! Series* was created with constant input from professors just like you. You've told us what works, how you teach, and what we can do to make your classroom time problem free, creative, and smooth running—to allow you to concentrate on not what you are teaching from but who you are teaching to—your students. We feel that we have succeeded with the *GO! Series*. Our aim is to make this instruction high quality in both content and presentation, and the classroom management aids complete—an instructor could begin teaching the course with only 15 minutes advance notice. An instructor could leave the classroom or computer lab; students would know exactly how to proceed in the text, know exactly what to produce to demonstrate mastery of the objectives, and feel that they had achieved success in their learning. Indeed, this philosophy is essential for real-world use in today's diverse educational environment.

How did we do it?

- All steps utilize **Microsoft Procedural Syntax**. The *GO! Series* puts students where they need to be, before instructing them what to do. For example, instead of instructing students to "Save the file," we go a few steps further and phrase the instruction as "On the **Menu** bar, click **File**, then select **Save As**."
- A unique teaching system (packaged together in one easy to use **Instructor's Edition** binder set) that enables you to teach anywhere you have to—online, lab, lecture, self-paced, and so forth. The supplements are designed to save you time:
  - ***Expert Demonstration Document***—A new project that mirrors the learning objectives of the in-chapter project, with a full demonstration script for you to give a lecture overview quickly and clearly.
  - ***Chapter Assignment Sheets***—A sheet listing all the assignments for the chapter. An instructor can quickly insert his or her name, course information, due dates, and points.
  - ***Custom Assignment Tags***—These cutout tags include a brief list of common errors that students could make on each project, with check boxes so instructors don't have to keep writing the same error description over and over! These tags serve a dual purpose: The student can do a final check to make sure all the listed items are correct, and the instructor can check off the items that need to be corrected.

- ***Highlighted Overlays***—These are printed and transparent overlays that the instructor lays over the student's assignment paper to see at a glance if the student changed what he or she needed to. Coupled with the Custom Assignment Tags, this creates a "grading and scoring system" that is easy for the instructor to implement.
- ***Point Counted Chapter Production Test***—Working hand-in-hand with the Expert Demonstration Document, this is a final test for the student to demonstrate mastery of the objectives.

Goals of the GO! Series

The goals of the *GO! Series* are as follows:

- Make it *easy for the instructor to implement* in any instructional setting through high-quality content and instructional aids and provide the student with a valuable, interesting, important, satisfying, and clearly defined learning experience.
- Enable true diverse delivery for today's diverse audience. The *GO! Series* employs various instructional techniques that address the needs of all types of students in all types of delivery modes.
- Provide *turn-key implementation* in the following instructional settings:
    - Traditional computer classroom—Students experience a mix of lecture and lab.
    - Online instruction—Students complete instruction at a remote location and submit assignments to the instructor electronically—questions answered by instructor through electronic queries.
    - Partially self-paced, individualized instruction—Students meet with an instructor for part of the class, and complete part of the class in a lab setting.
    - Completely self-paced, individualized instruction—Students complete all instruction in an instructor-staffed lab setting.
    - Independent self-paced, individualized instruction—Students complete all instruction in a campus lab staffed with instructional aides.
- Teach—*to maximize the moment*. The *GO! Series* is based on the Teachable Moment Theory. There are no long passages of text; instead, concepts are woven into the steps at the teachable moment. Students always know what they need to do and where to do it.

Pedagogical Approach

The *GO! Series* uses an instructional system approach that incorporates three elements:

- *Steps are written in* ***Microsoft Procedural Syntax***, which prevents the student from doing the right thing but in the wrong place. This makes it easy for the instructor to teach instead of untangle. It tells the student where to go first, then what to do. For example—"On the File Menu, click Properties."
- *Instructional strategies* including five new, unique ancillary pieces to support the instructor experience. The foundation of the instructional strategies is performance based instruction that is constructed in a manner that makes it *easy for the instructor* to demonstrate the content with the GO Series Expert Demonstration Document, guide the practice by using our many end-of-chapter projects with varying guidance levels, and assess the level of mastery with tools such as our Point Counted Production Test and Custom Assignment Tags.
- *A physical design* that makes it *easy for the instructor* to answer the question, "What do they have to do?" and makes it easy for the student to answer the question, "What do I have to do?" Most importantly, you told us what was needed in the design. We held several focus groups throughout the country where we showed ***you*** our design drafts and let you tell us what you thought of them. We revised our design based on your input to be functional and support the classroom experience. For example, you told us that a common problem is students not realizing where a project ends. So, we added an "END. You have completed the Project" at the close of every project.

Microsoft Procedural Syntax

Do you ever do something right but in the wrong place?

That's why we've written the *GO! Series* step text using Microsoft procedural syntax. That is, the student is informed where the action should take place before describing the action to take. For example, "On the menu bar, click File," versus "Click File on the menu bar." This prevents the student from doing the right thing in the wrong place. This means that step text usually begins with a preposition—a locator—rather than a verb. Other texts often misunderstand the theory of performance-based instruction and frequently attempt to begin steps with a verb. In fact, the objectives should begin with a verb, not the steps.

The use of Microsoft procedural syntax is one of the key reasons that the *GO! Series* eases the burden for the instructor. The instructor spends less time untangling students' unnecessary actions and more time assisting students with real questions. No longer will students become frustrated and say "But I did what it said!" only to discover that, indeed, they *did* do "what it said" but in the wrong place!

Chapter Organization—Color-Coded Projects

All of the chapters in every *GO! Series* book are organized around interesting projects. Within each chapter, all of the instructional activities will cluster around these projects without any long passages of text for the student to read. Thus, every instructional activity contributes to the completion of the project to which it is associated. Students learn skills to solve real business problems; they don't waste time learning every feature the software has. The end-of-chapter material consists of additional projects with varying levels of difficulty.

The chapters are based on the following basic hierarchy:

Project Name

Objective Name (begins with a verb)

Activity Name (begins with a gerund)

Numbered Steps (begins with a preposition or a verb using Microsoft Procedural Syntax.)

Project Name→ **Project 1A Exploring Outlook 2003**

Objective Name→ **Objective 1**
Start Outlook and Identify Outlook Window Elements

Activity Name→ **Activity 1.1** Starting Outlook

Numbered Steps→ 1 On the Windows taskbar, click the Start button, determine from your instructor or lab coordinator where the Microsoft Office Outlook 2003 program is located on your system, and then click Microsoft Office Outlook 2003.

A project will have a number of objectives associated with it, and the objectives, in turn, will have one or more activities associated with them. Each activity will have a series of numbered steps. To further enhance understanding, each project, and its objectives and numbered steps, is color coded for fast, easy recognition.

In-Chapter Boxes and Elements

Within every chapter there are helpful boxes and in-line notes that aid the students in their mastery of the performance objectives. Plus, each box has a specific title—"Does Your Notes Button Look Different?" or "To Open the New Appointment Window." Our GO! Series Focus Groups told us to add box titles that indicate the information being covered in the box, and we listened!

Alert!

Does Your Notes Button Look Different?

The size of the monitor and screen resolution set on your computer controls the number of larger module buttons that appear at the bottom of the Navigation pane.

Alert! boxes do just that—they alert students to a common pitfall or spot where trouble may be encountered.

Another Way

To Open the New Appointment Window

You can create a new appointment window using one of the following techniques:

- On the menu bar, click File, point to New, and click Appointment.
- On the Calendar Standard toolbar, click the New Appointment button.

Another Way boxes explain simply "another way" of going about a task or shortcuts for saving time.

Note — Server Connection Dialog Box

If a message displays indicating that a connection to the server could not be established, click OK. Even without a mail server connection, you can still use the personal information management features of Outlook.

Notes highlight additional information pertaining to a task.

More Knowledge — Creating New Folders

A module does not have to be active in order to create new folders within it. From the Create New Folder text box, you can change the type of items that the new folder will contain and then select any location in which to place the new folder. Additionally, it is easy to move a folder created in one location to a different location.

More Knowledge is a more detailed look at a topic or task.

Organization of the GO! Series

The *GO! Series for Microsoft® Office System 2003* includes several different combinations of texts to best suit your needs.

- **Word, Excel, Access, and PowerPoint 2003** are available in the following editions:
    - **Brief:** Chapters 1–3 (1–4 for Word 2003)
    - **Volume 1:** Chapters 1–6
~ Microsoft Office Specialist Certification
    - **Volume 2:** Chapters 7–12 (7–8 for PowerPoint 2003)
    - **Comprehensive:** Chapters 1–12 (1–8 for PowerPoint 2003)
~ Microsoft Office Expert Certification for Word and Excel 2003.
- Additionally, the *GO! Series* is available in four combined **Office 2003** texts:
    - **Microsoft® Office 2003 Getting Started** contains the Windows XP Introduction and first chapter from each application (Word, Excel, Access, and PowerPoint).
    - **Microsoft® Office 2003 Brief** contains Chapters 1–3 of Excel, Access, and PowerPoint, and Chapters 1–4 of Word. Four additional supplementary "Getting Started" books are included (Internet Explorer, Computer Concepts, Windows XP, and Outlook 2003).
    - **Microsoft® Office 2003 Intermediate** contains Chapters 4–8 of Excel, Access, and PowerPoint, and Chapters 5–8 of Word.
    - **Microsoft® Office 2003 Advanced** version picks up where the Intermediate leaves off, covering advanced topics for the individual applications. This version contains Chapters 9–12 of Word, Excel, and Access.

Microsoft Office Specialist Certification

Microsoft® Office™ Specialist Approved Courseware

The *GO! Series* has been approved by Microsoft for use in preparing for the Microsoft Office Specialist exams. The Microsoft Office Specialist program is globally recognized as the standard for demonstrating desktop skills with the Microsoft Office System of business productivity applications (Microsoft Word, Microsoft Excel, Microsoft Access, Microsoft PowerPoint, and Microsoft Outlook). With Microsoft Office Specialist certification, thousands of people have demonstrated increased productivity and have proved their ability to utilize the advanced functionality of these Microsoft applications.

Instructor and Student Resources

Instructor's Resource Center and Instructor's Edition

The *GO! Series* was designed for you—instructors who are long on commitment and short on time. *We asked you how you use our books and supplements and how we can make it easier for you and save you valuable time.* We listened to what you told us and created this Instructor's Resource Center for you—different from anything you have ever had access to from other texts and publishers.

What is the Instructor's Edition?

1) Instructor's Edition

New from Prentice Hall, exclusively for the *GO! Series*, the Instructor's Edition contains the entire book, wrapped with vital margin notes—things like objectives, a list of the files needed for the chapter, teaching tips, Microsoft Office Specialist objectives covered, and MORE! Below is a sample of the many helpful elements in the Instructor's Edition.

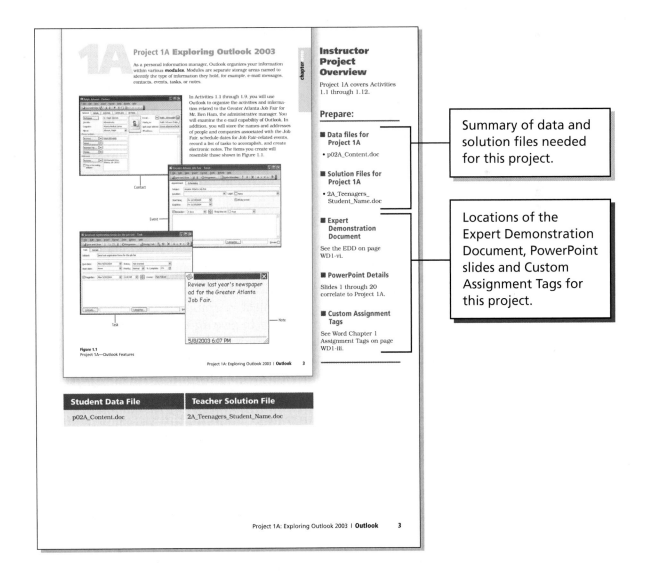

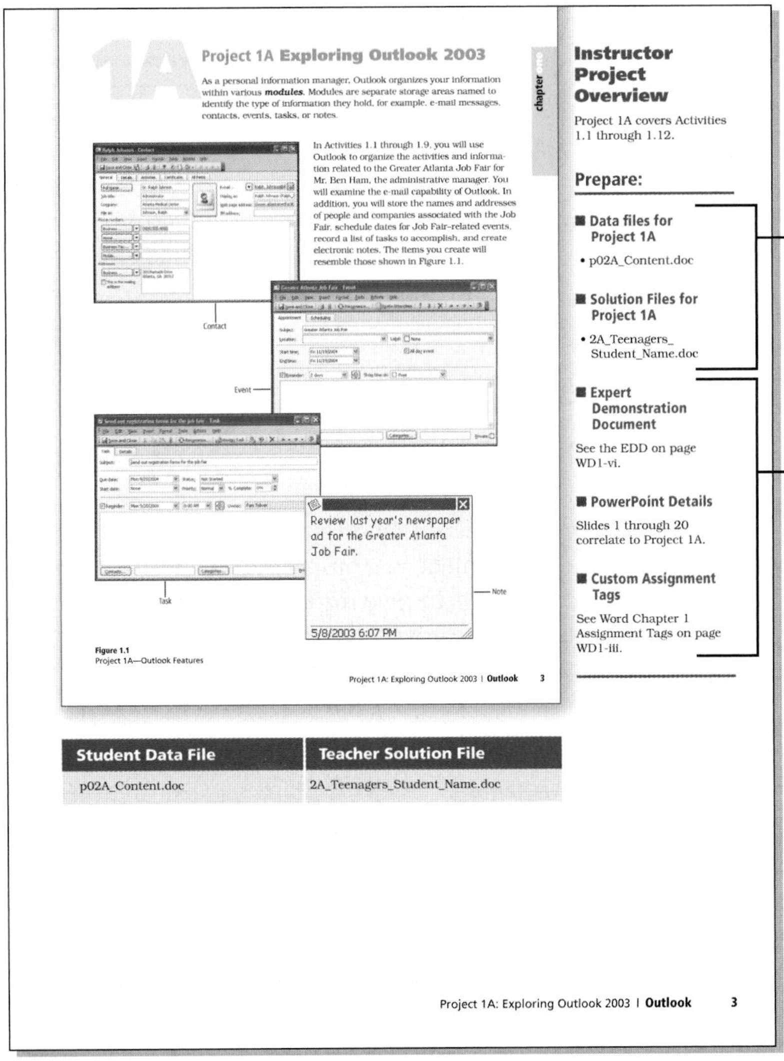
1A

Project 1A **Exploring Outlook 2003**

As a personal information manager, Outlook organizes your information within various **modules**. Modules are separate storage areas named to identify the type of information they hold, for example, e-mail messages, contacts, events, tasks, or notes.

In Activities 1.1 through 1.9, you will use Outlook to organize the activities and information related to the Greater Atlanta Job Fair for Mr. Ben Ham, the administrative manager. You will examine the e-mail capability of Outlook. In addition, you will store the names and addresses of people and companies associated with the Job Fair, schedule dates for Job Fair-related events, record a list of tasks to accomplish, and create electronic notes. The items you create will resemble those shown in Figure 1.1.

Figure 1.1
Project 1A—Outlook Features

Project 1A: Exploring Outlook 2003 | **Outlook** 3

Instructor Project Overview

Project 1A covers Activities 1.1 through 1.12.

Prepare:

- **Data files for Project 1A**
  - p02A_Content.doc
- **Solution Files for Project 1A**
  - 2A_Teenagers_Student_Name.doc
- **Expert Demonstration Document**

  See the EDD on page WD1-vi.
- **PowerPoint Details**

  Slides 1 through 20 correlate to Project 1A.
- **Custom Assignment Tags**

  See Word Chapter 1 Assignment Tags on page WD1-iii.

Student Data File	Teacher Solution File
p02A_Content.doc	2A_Teenagers_Student_Name.doc

Project 1A: Exploring Outlook 2003 | **Outlook** 3

Summary of data and solution files needed for this project.

Locations of the Expert Demonstration Document, PowerPoint slides and Custom Assignment Tags for this project.

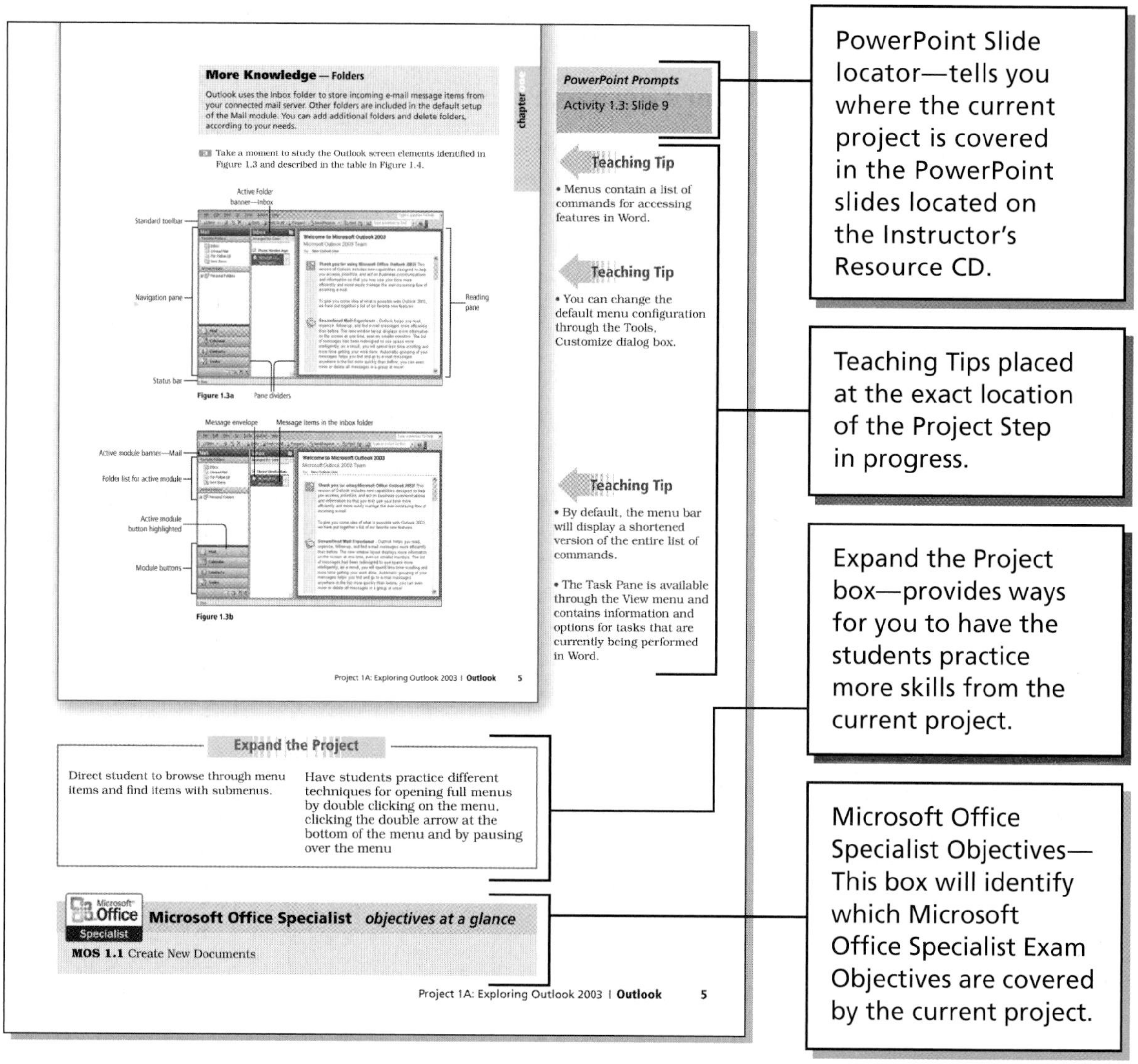

The Instructor's Edition also contains printed copies of these supplement materials *unique* to the *GO! Series*:

- ***Expert Demonstration Document (EDD)***—A mirror image of each in-chapter project, accompanied by a brief script. The instructor can use it to give an expert demonstration of each objective that will be covered in the chapter, without having to use one of the chapter's projects. This EDD also prevents students from "working ahead during the presentation," as they do not have access to this document/project.
- ***Chapter Assignment Sheets***—With a sheet listing all the assignments for the chapter, the instructor can quickly insert his or her name, course information, due dates, and points.
- ***Custom Assignment Tags***—These cutout tags include a brief list of common errors that students could make on each project, with check boxes so instructors don't have to keep writing the same error description over and over! These tags serve a dual purpose: The student can do a final check to make sure all the listed items are correct, and the instructor can check off the items that need to be corrected.

- ***Highlighted Overlays***—These are printed and transparent overlays that the instructor lays over the student's assignment paper to see at a glance if the student changed what he or she needed to. Coupled with the Custom Assignment Tags, this creates a "grading and scoring system" that is easy for the instructor to implement.
- ***Point Counted Chapter Production Test***—Working hand-in-hand with the EDD, this is a final test for the student to demonstrate mastery of the objectives.

2) Enhanced Instructor's Resource CD-ROM

The Instructor's Resource CD-ROM is an interactive library of assets and links. The Instructor's Resource CD-ROM writes custom "index" pages that can be used as the foundation of a class presentation or online lecture. By navigating through the CD-ROM, you can collect the materials that are most relevant to your interests, edit them to create powerful class lectures, copy them to your own computer's hard drive, and/or upload them to an online course management system.

The new and improved Prentice Hall Instructor's Resource CD-ROM includes tools you expect from a Prentice Hall text:

- The Instructor's Manual in Word and PDF formats—includes solutions to all questions and exercises from the book and Companion Website
- Multiple, customizable PowerPoint slide presentations for each chapter
- Data and Solution Files
- Complete Test Bank
- Image library of all figures from the text
- TestGen Software with QuizMaster
  - TestGen is a test generator that lets you view and easily edit test bank questions, transfer them to tests, and print in a variety of formats suitable to your teaching situation. The program also offers many options for organizing and displaying test banks and tests. A built-in random number and text generator makes it ideal for creating multiple versions of tests that involve calculations and provides more possible test items than test bank questions. Powerful search and sort functions let you easily locate questions and arrange them in the order you prefer.
  - QuizMaster allows students to take tests created with TestGen on a local area network. The QuizMaster utility built into TestGen lets instructors view student records and print a variety of reports. Building tests is easy with TestGen, and exams can be easily uploaded into WebCT, Blackboard, and CourseCompass.

3) Instructor's Edition CD-ROM

The Instructor's Edition CD-ROM contains PDF versions of the Instructor's Edition as well as Word versions of the *GO! Series* unique supplements for easy instructor customization.

Training and Assessment—www2.phgenit.com/support

Prentice Hall offers performance-based training and assessment in one product—Train&Assess IT. The training component offers computer-based training that a student can use to preview, learn, and review Microsoft Office application skills. Web or CD-ROM delivered, Train IT offers interactive, multimedia, computer-based training to augment classroom learning. Built-in prescriptive testing suggests a study path based not only on student test results but also on the specific textbook chosen for the course.

The assessment component offers computer-based testing that shares the same user interface as Train IT and is used to evaluate a student's knowledge about specific topics in Word, Excel, Access, PowerPoint, Outlook, the Internet, and Computing Concepts. It does this in a task-oriented environment to demonstrate proficiency as well as comprehension of the topics by the students. More extensive than the testing in Train IT, Assess IT offers more administrative features for the instructor and additional questions for the student.

Assess IT also allows professors to test students out of a course, place students in appropriate courses, and evaluate skill sets.

Companion Website @ www.prenhall.com/go

This text is accompanied by a Companion Website at www.prenhall.com/go. Features of this new site include an interactive study guide, downloadable supplements, online end-of-chapter materials, additional practice projects, Web resource links, and technology updates and bonus chapters on the latest trends and hottest topics in information technology. All links to Web exercises will be constantly updated to ensure accuracy for students.

CourseCompass—www.coursecompass.com

CourseCompass is a dynamic, interactive online course-management tool powered exclusively for Pearson Education by Blackboard. This exciting product allows you to teach market-leading Pearson Education content in an easy-to-use, customizable format.

Blackboard—www.prenhall.com/blackboard

Prentice Hall's abundant online content, combined with Blackboard's popular tools and interface, result in robust Web-based courses that are easy to implement, manage, and use—taking your courses to new heights in student interaction and learning.

WebCT—www.prenhall.com/webct

Course-management tools within WebCT include page tracking, progress tracking, class and student management, gradebook, communication, calendar, reporting tools, and more. Gold Level Customer Support, available exclusively to adopters of Prentice Hall courses, is provided free-of-charge on adoption and provides you with priority assistance, training discounts, and dedicated technical support.

TechTV—www.techtv.com

TechTV is the San Francisco-based cable network that showcases the smart, edgy, and unexpected side of technology. By telling stories through the prism of technology, TechTV provides programming that celebrates its viewers' passion, creativity, and lifestyle.

TechTV's programming falls into three categories:

1. **Help and Information**, with shows like *The Screen Savers*, TechTV's daily live variety show featuring everything from guest interviews and celebrities to product advice and demos; *Tech Live*, featuring the latest news on the industry's most important people, companies, products, and issues; and *Call for Help*, a live help and how-to show providing computing tips and live viewer questions.
2. **Cool Docs**, with shows like *The Tech Of...*, a series that goes behind the scenes of modern life and shows you the technology that makes things tick; *Performance*, an investigation into how technology and science are molding the perfect athlete; and *Future Fighting Machines*, a fascinating look at the technology and tactics of warfare.
3. **Outrageous Fun**, with shows like *X-Play*, exploring the latest and greatest in videogaming; and *Unscrewed* with Martin Sargent, a new late-night series showcasing the darker, funnier world of technology.

For more information, log onto www.techtv.com or contact your local cable or satellite provider to get TechTV in your area.

Visual Walk-Through

Project-based Instruction
Students do not practice features of the application; they create real projects that they will need in the real world. Projects are color coded for easy reference.

Word 2003

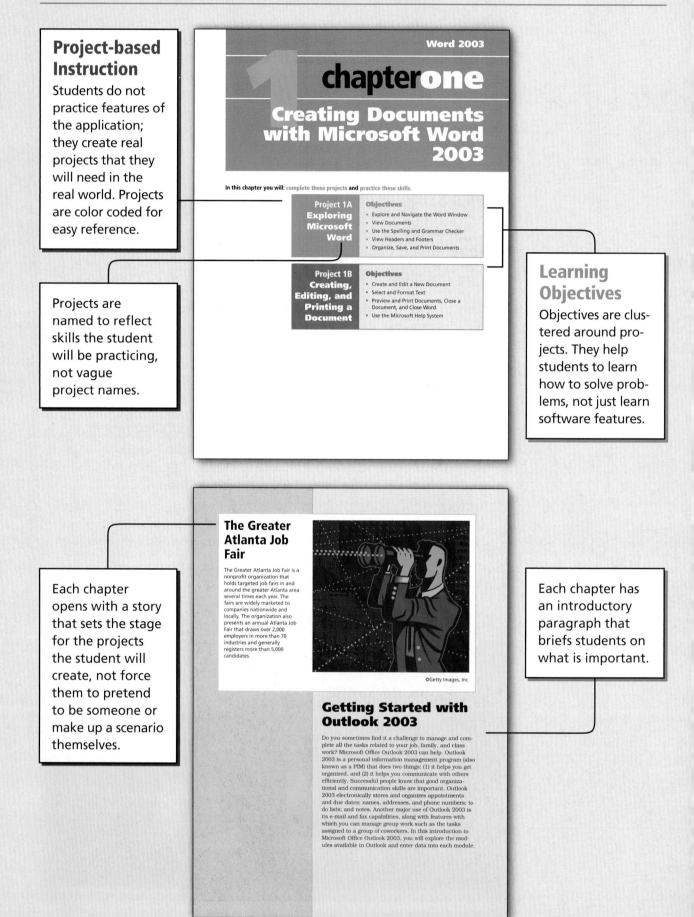

chapterone
Creating Documents with Microsoft Word 2003

In this chapter you will: complete these projects **and** practice these skills.

Project	Objectives
Project 1A **Exploring Microsoft Word**	• Explore and Navigate the Word Window • View Documents • Use the Spelling and Grammar Checker • View Headers and Footers • Organize, Save, and Print Documents
Project 1B **Creating, Editing, and Printing a Document**	• Create and Edit a New Document • Select and Format Text • Preview and Print Documents, Close a Document, and Close Word • Use the Microsoft Help System

Projects are named to reflect skills the student will be practicing, not vague project names.

Learning Objectives
Objectives are clustered around projects. They help students to learn how to solve problems, not just learn software features.

Each chapter opens with a story that sets the stage for the projects the student will create, not force them to pretend to be someone or make up a scenario themselves.

The Greater Atlanta Job Fair

The Greater Atlanta Job Fair is a nonprofit organization that holds targeted job fairs in and around the greater Atlanta area several times each year. The fairs are widely marketed to companies nationwide and locally. The organization also presents an annual Atlanta Job Fair that draws over 2,000 employers in more than 70 industries and generally registers more than 5,000 candidates.

©Getty Images, Inc.

Each chapter has an introductory paragraph that briefs students on what is important.

Getting Started with Outlook 2003

Do you sometimes find it a challenge to manage and complete all the tasks related to your job, family, and class work? Microsoft Office Outlook 2003 can help. Outlook 2003 is a personal information management program (also known as a PIM) that does two things: (1) it helps you get organized, and (2) it helps you communicate with others efficiently. Successful people know that good organizational and communication skills are important. Outlook 2003 electronically stores and organizes appointments and due dates; names, addresses, and phone numbers; to do lists; and notes. Another major use of Outlook 2003 is its e-mail and fax capabilities, along with features with which you can manage group work such as the tasks assigned to a group of coworkers. In this introduction to Microsoft Office Outlook 2003, you will explore the modules available in Outlook and enter data into each module.

Visual Summary

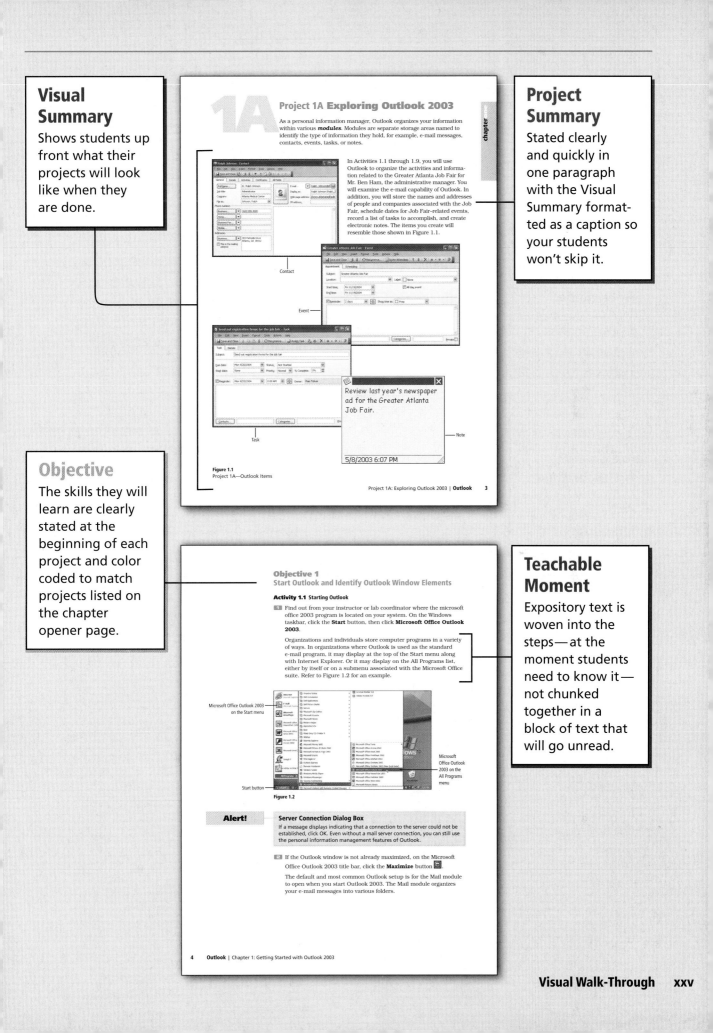

Shows students up front what their projects will look like when they are done.

Project Summary

Stated clearly and quickly in one paragraph with the Visual Summary formatted as a caption so your students won't skip it.

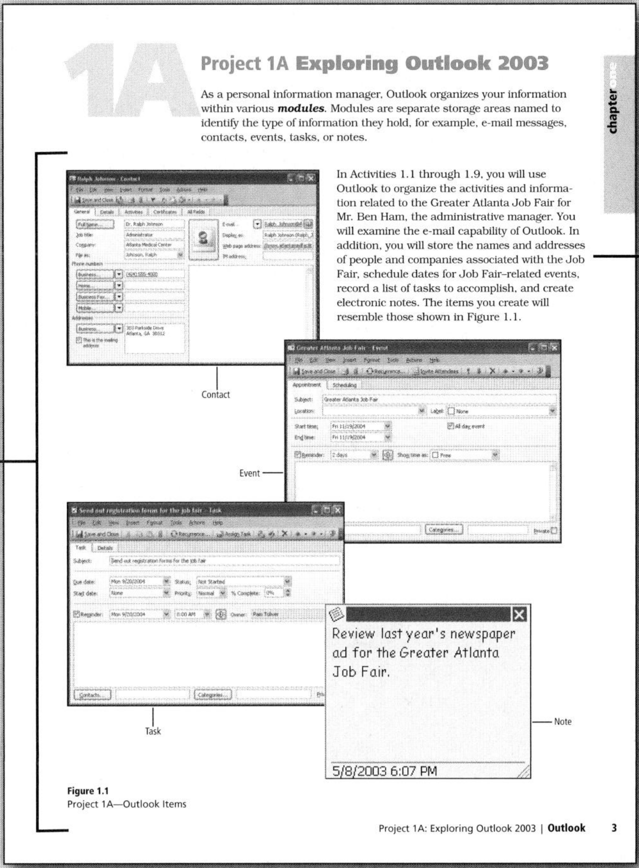

chapter one

1A

Project 1A Exploring Outlook 2003

As a personal information manager, Outlook organizes your information within various ***modules***. Modules are separate storage areas named to identify the type of information they hold, for example, e-mail messages, contacts, events, tasks, or notes.

In Activities 1.1 through 1.9, you will use Outlook to organize the activities and information related to the Greater Atlanta Job Fair for Mr. Ben Ham, the administrative manager. You will examine the e-mail capability of Outlook. In addition, you will store the names and addresses of people and companies associated with the Job Fair, schedule dates for Job Fair–related events, record a list of tasks to accomplish, and create electronic notes. The items you create will resemble those shown in Figure 1.1.

Figure 1.1
Project 1A—Outlook Items

Project 1A: Exploring Outlook 2003 | **Outlook** 3

Objective

The skills they will learn are clearly stated at the beginning of each project and color coded to match projects listed on the chapter opener page.

Teachable Moment

Expository text is woven into the steps—at the moment students need to know it—not chunked together in a block of text that will go unread.

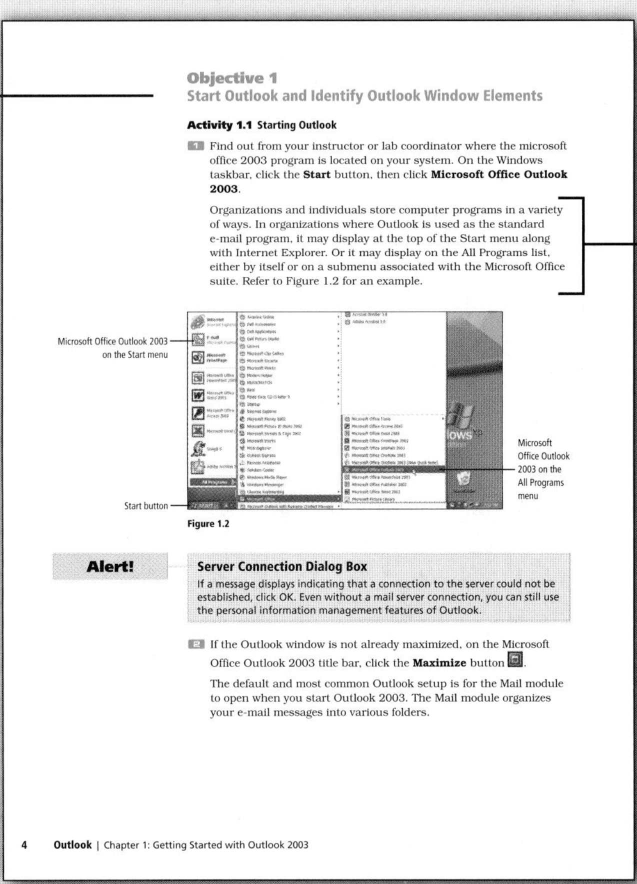

Objective 1
Start Outlook and Identify Outlook Window Elements

Activity 1.1 Starting Outlook

1. Find out from your instructor or lab coordinator where the microsoft office 2003 program is located on your system. On the Windows taskbar, click the **Start** button, then click **Microsoft Office Outlook 2003**.

   Organizations and individuals store computer programs in a variety of ways. In organizations where Outlook is used as the standard e-mail program, it may display at the top of the Start menu along with Internet Explorer. Or it may display on the All Programs list, either by itself or on a submenu associated with the Microsoft Office suite. Refer to Figure 1.2 for an example.

Figure 1.2

Alert!

Server Connection Dialog Box
If a message displays indicating that a connection to the server could not be established, click OK. Even without a mail server connection, you can still use the personal information management features of Outlook.

2. If the Outlook window is not already maximized, on the Microsoft Office Outlook 2003 title bar, click the **Maximize** button.

   The default and most common Outlook setup is for the Mail module to open when you start Outlook 2003. The Mail module organizes your e-mail messages into various folders.

4 **Outlook** | Chapter 1: Getting Started with Outlook 2003

Steps

Color coded to the current project, easy to read, and not too many to confuse the student or too few to be meaningless.

Microsoft Procedural Syntax

All steps are written in Microsoft Procedural Syntax in order to put the student in the right place at the right time.

Sequential Page Numbering

No more confusing letters and abbreviations.

End of Project Icon

All projects in the *GO! Series* have clearly identifiable end points, useful in self-paced or online environments.

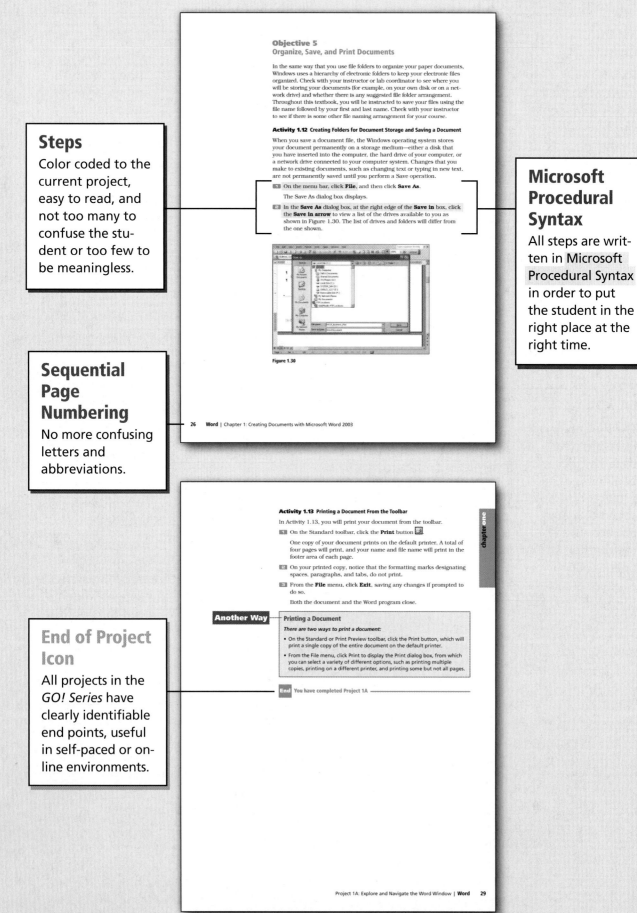

Objective 5
Organize, Save, and Print Documents

In the same way that you use file folders to organize your paper documents, Windows uses a hierarchy of electronic folders to keep your electronic files organized. Check with your instructor or lab coordinator to see where you will be storing your documents (for example, on your own disk or on a network drive) and whether there is any suggested file folder arrangement. Throughout this textbook, you will be instructed to save your files using the file name followed by your first and last name. Check with your instructor to see if there is some other file naming arrangement for your course.

Activity 1.12 Creating Folders for Document Storage and Saving a Document

When you save a document file, the Windows operating system stores your document permanently on a storage medium—either a disk that you have inserted into the computer, the hard drive of your computer, or a network drive connected to your computer system. Changes that you make to existing documents, such as changing text or typing in new text, are not permanently saved until you perform a Save operation.

1. On the menu bar, click **File**, and then click **Save As**.

   The Save As dialog box displays.

2. In the **Save As** dialog box, at the right edge of the **Save in** box, click the **Save in arrow** to view a list of the drives available to you as shown in Figure 1.30. The list of drives and folders will differ from the one shown.

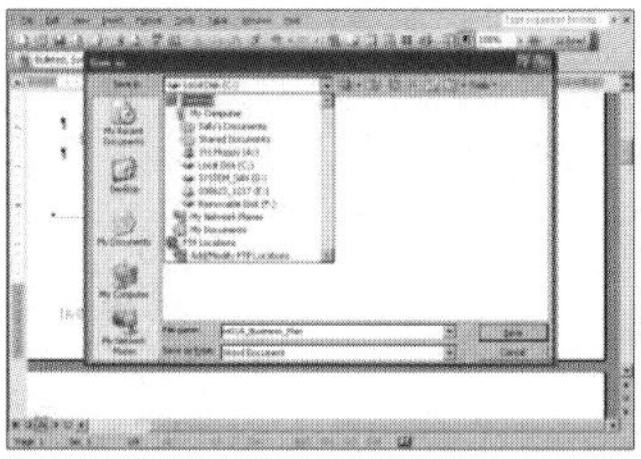

Figure 1.30

26 **Word** | Chapter 1: Creating Documents with Microsoft Word 2003

Activity 1.13 Printing a Document From the Toolbar

In Activity 1.13, you will print your document from the toolbar.

1. On the Standard toolbar, click the **Print** button.

   One copy of your document prints on the default printer. A total of four pages will print, and your name and file name will print in the footer area of each page.

2. On your printed copy, notice that the formatting marks designating spaces, paragraphs, and tabs, do not print.

3. From the **File** menu, click **Exit**, saving any changes if prompted to do so.

   Both the document and the Word program close.

chapter one

Another Way

Printing a Document

There are two ways to print a document:

- On the Standard or Print Preview toolbar, click the Print button, which will print a single copy of the entire document on the default printer.
- From the File menu, click Print to display the Print dialog box, from which you can select a variety of different options, such as printing multiple copies, printing on a different printer, and printing some but not all pages.

End You have completed Project 1A

Project 1A: Explore and Navigate the Word Window | **Word** 29

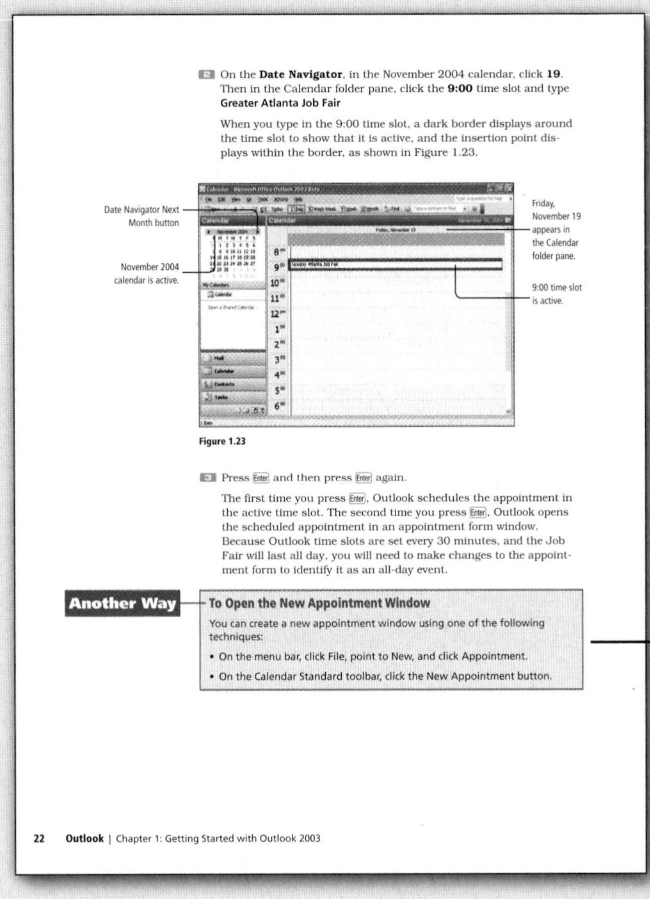

2 On the **Date Navigator**, in the November 2004 calendar, click **19**. Then in the Calendar folder pane, click the **9:00** time slot and type **Greater Atlanta Job Fair**

When you type in the 9:00 time slot, a dark border displays around the time slot to show that it is active, and the insertion point displays within the border, as shown in Figure 1.23.

Figure 1.23

3 Press Enter and then press Enter again.

The first time you press Enter, Outlook schedules the appointment in the active time slot. The second time you press Enter, Outlook opens the scheduled appointment in an appointment form window. Because Outlook time slots are set every 30 minutes, and the Job Fair will last all day, you will need to make changes to the appointment form to identify it as an all-day event.

Another Way

To Open the New Appointment Window

You can create a new appointment window using one of the following techniques:

- On the menu bar, click File, point to New, and click Appointment.
- On the Calendar Standard toolbar, click the New Appointment button.

22 **Outlook** | Chapter 1: Getting Started with Outlook 2003

Alert box

Draws students' attention to make sure they aren't getting too far off course.

Another Way box

Shows students other ways of doing tasks.

More Knowledge box

Expands on a topic by going deeper into the material.

Note box

Points out important items to remember.

End-of-Chapter Material

Take your pick… Skills Assessment, Performance Assessment, or Mastery Assessment. Real-world projects with high, medium, or low guidance levels.

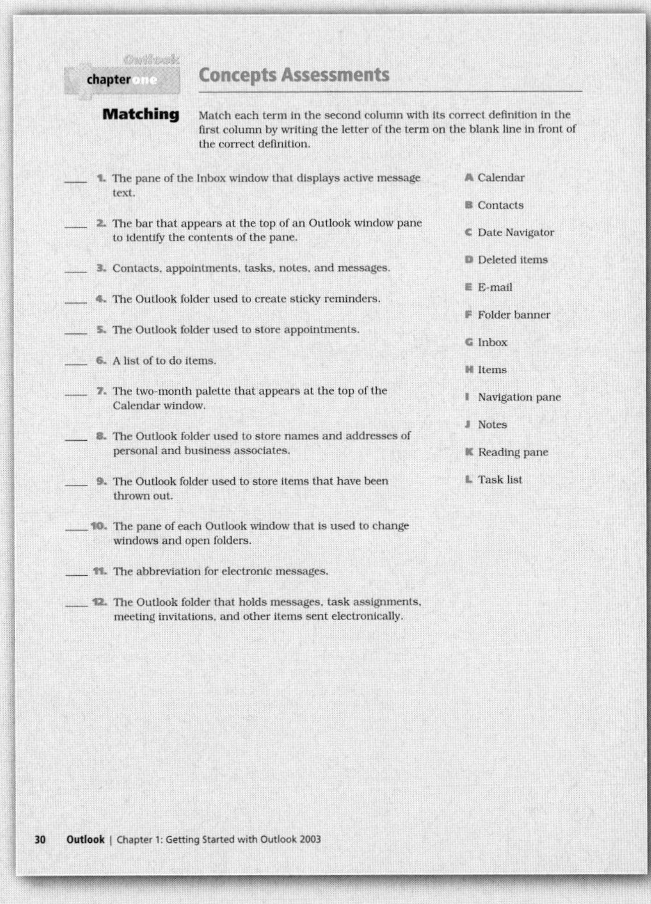

Outlook chapter one

Concepts Assessments

Matching Match each term in the second column with its correct definition in the first column by writing the letter of the term on the blank line in front of the correct definition.

___ 1. The pane of the Inbox window that displays active message text.

___ 2. The bar that appears at the top of an Outlook window pane to identify the contents of the pane.

___ 3. Contacts, appointments, tasks, notes, and messages.

___ 4. The Outlook folder used to create sticky reminders.

___ 5. The Outlook folder used to store appointments.

___ 6. A list of to do items.

___ 7. The two-month palette that appears at the top of the Calendar window.

___ 8. The Outlook folder used to store names and addresses of personal and business associates.

___ 9. The Outlook folder used to store items that have been thrown out.

___ 10. The pane of each Outlook window that is used to change windows and open folders.

___ 11. The abbreviation for electronic messages.

___ 12. The Outlook folder that holds messages, task assignments, meeting invitations, and other items sent electronically.

A Calendar
B Contacts
C Date Navigator
D Deleted items
E E-mail
F Folder banner
G Inbox
H Items
I Navigation pane
J Notes
K Reading pane
L Task list

30 **Outlook** | Chapter 1: Getting Started with Outlook 2003

Objectives List

Each project in the GO! Series end-of-chapter section starts with a list of the objectives covered, in order to easily find the exercises you need to hone your skills.

Outlook chapter one

Performance Assessments

Project 1D—Creating Folders for College Fairs

Objectives: *Start Outlook and Create Outlook Folders.*

The fairs for Mercer College and Georgia Tech have been set for April 2005. As a result, you need to create folders to hold vendor information for the fairs. When you have created the contact folders for these two fairs, your Contacts list will appear as in Figure 1.35.

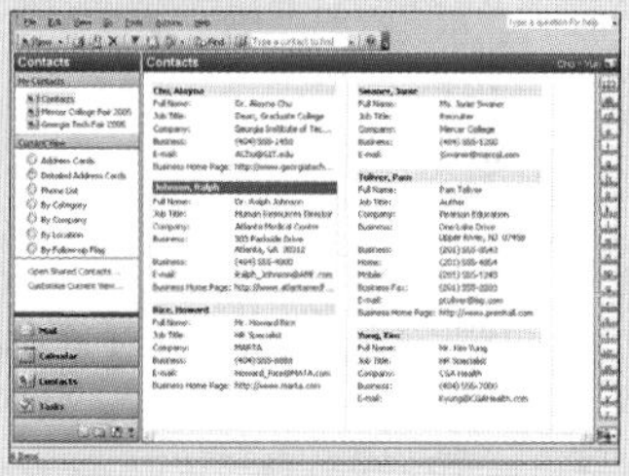

Figure 1.35

1. Start Outlook, open the **Contacts** module, open the main **Contacts** folder, and on the menu bar, click **File**, point to **Folder**, and click **New Folder** to open the **Create New Folder** dialog box.
2. In the **Name** text box, type **Mercer College Fair 2005** ensure that **Contact Items** appears in the **Folder contains** text box, and click **OK**.
3. Repeat the procedures in Steps 1 and 2 to create another contacts folder named **Georgia Tech Fair 2005**

End You have completed Project 1D

Project 1D: Creating Folders for College Fairs | **Outlook** 35

End of Each Project Clearly Marked

Groups of steps that the student performs; the guided practice in order to master the learning objective.

On the Internet

In this section, students are directed to go out to the Internet for independent study.

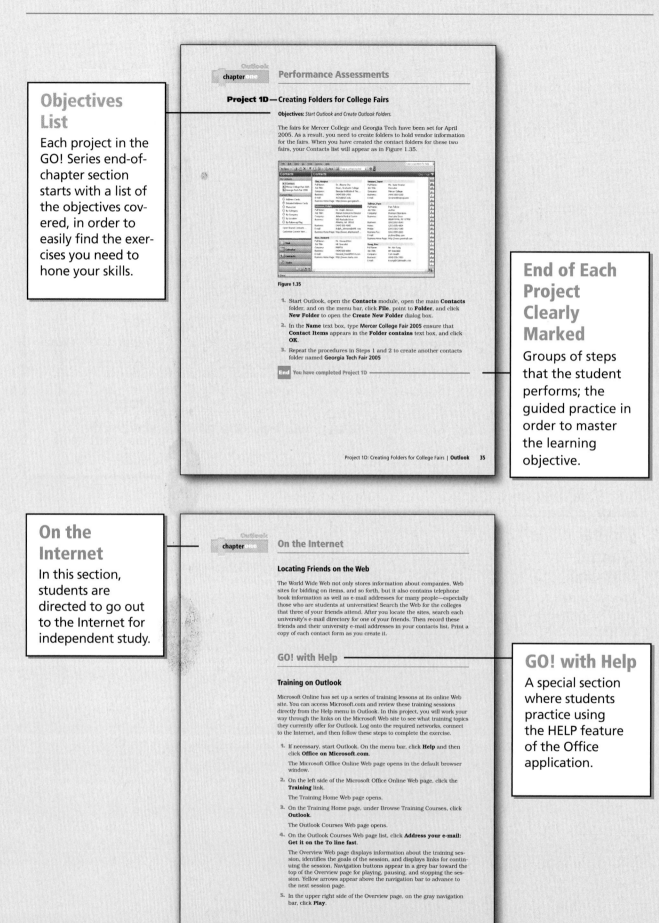

Outlook chapter one

On the Internet

Locating Friends on the Web

The World Wide Web not only stores information about companies, Web sites for bidding on items, and so forth, but it also contains telephone book information as well as e-mail addresses for many people—especially those who are students at universities! Search the Web for the colleges that three of your friends attend. After you locate the sites, search each university's e-mail directory for one of your friends. Then record these friends and their university e-mail addresses in your contacts list. Print a copy of each contact form as you create it.

GO! with Help

Training on Outlook

Microsoft Online has set up a series of training lessons at its online Web site. You can access Microsoft.com and review these training sessions directly from the Help menu in Outlook. In this project, you will work your way through the links on the Microsoft Web site to see what training topics they currently offer for Outlook. Log onto the required networks, connect to the Internet, and then follow these steps to complete the exercise.

1. If necessary, start Outlook. On the menu bar, click **Help** and then click **Office on Microsoft.com**.

   The Microsoft Office Online Web page opens in the default browser window.
2. On the left side of the Microsoft Office Online Web page, click the **Training** link.

   The Training Home Web page opens.
3. On the Training Home page, under Browse Training Courses, click **Outlook**.

   The Outlook Courses Web page opens.
4. On the Outlook Courses Web page list, click **Address your e-mail: Get it on the To line fast**.

   The Overview Web page displays information about the training session, identifies the goals of the session, and displays links for continuing the session. Navigation buttons appear in a grey bar toward the top of the Overview page for playing, pausing, and stopping the session. Yellow arrows appear above the navigation bar to advance to the next session page.
5. In the upper right side of the Overview page, on the gray navigation bar, click **Play**.

GO! with Help | **Outlook** 41

GO! with Help

A special section where students practice using the HELP feature of the Office application.

Contents in Brief

Table of Contents

1 chapterone

Getting Started with Access Databases and Tables

In this chapter, you will: complete these projects **and** practice these skills.

Project 1A **Opening and Viewing a Database**	**Objectives** • Rename a Database • Start Access, Open an Existing Database, and View Database Objects
Project 1B Creating a Database	**Objectives** • Create a New Database • Create a New Table • Create a Primary Key and Add Records to a Table • Close and Save a Table • Open a Table • Modify the Table Design • Print a Table • Edit Records in a Table • Sort Records • Navigate to Records in a Table • Close and Save a Database • Use the Access Help System

Lake Michigan City College

Lake Michigan City College is located along the lakefront of Chicago—one of the nation's most exciting cities. The college serves its large and diverse student body and makes positive contributions to the community through relevant curricula, partnerships with businesses and nonprofit organizations, and learning experiences that allow students to be full participants in the global community. The college offers three associate degrees in 20 academic areas, adult education programs, and continuing education offerings on campus, at satellite locations, and online.

Getting Started with Access Databases and Tables

Do you have a collection of things that you like, such as a coin collection, stamp collection, recipe collection, or collection of your favorite music CDs? Do you have an address book with the names, addresses, and phone numbers of your friends, business associates, and family members? If you collect something, chances are you have made an attempt to keep track of and organize the items in your collection. If you have an address book, you have probably wished it were better organized. A computer program like Microsoft Access can help you organize and keep track of information.

For example, assume you have a large collection of music CDs. You could organize your CDs into a database because your CDs are a collection of related items. By organizing your CDs in a database, you would be able to find the CDs by various categories that you define. If the information in your address book were placed in a database, you could produce a list of all your friends and family members who have birthdays in the month of April. In this chapter, you will see how useful a database program like Access can be.

1A Project 1A Computer Club

Data refers to facts about people, events, things, or ideas. A ***database*** is a collection of data related to a particular topic or purpose. Data that has been organized in a useful manner is referred to as ***information***. Examples of data that could be in a database include the titles and artists of all the CDs in a collection or the names and addresses of all the students in an organization. Microsoft Office Access 2003 is a database program that you can use to create and work with information in databases. Databases, like the ones you will work with in Access, include not only the data, but also tools for organizing the data in a way that is useful to you.

In Activities 1.1 through 1.8, you will create a new folder where you will store your projects. Then you will copy a database to your folder and rename the database so you can use it to complete the steps in this project. In this project, you will open a database and view information about the Club Events sponsored by the Computer Club at Lake Michigan City College. See Figure 1.1. In addition to the Event Name and the date of the event, the information includes the name of the Event Coordinator and the type of event.

Club Events

Event#	*Event Name*	*Date*	*Event Type*	*Coordinator*
01	New Member Social	08/15	Social	Jordan Williams
02	Bi-Monthly Meeting	08/15	Meeting	Annette Jacobson
03	Bi-Monthly Meeting	09/1	Meeting	Annette Jacobson
04	Making Access work for	09/10	Training	Mike Franklin
05	Introduction to Outlook	09/16	Training	Mike Franklin
06	Bi-Monthly Meeting	09/15	Meeting	Annette Jacobson
07	Bi-Monthly Meeting	10/1	Meeting	Annette Jacobson
08	Bi-Monthly Meeting	10/15	Meeting	Annette Jacobson
09	Bi-Monthly Meeting	11/1	Meeting	Annette Jacobson
10	Bi-Monthly Meeting	11/15	Meeting	Annette Jacobson
11	Bi-Monthly Meeting	12/1	Meeting	Annette Jacobson
12	Annual Party	12/10	Social	Linda Turpen
13	Project 1A	11/18	Training	Firstname Lastname

Thursday, October 16, 2003 *Page 1 of 1*

Figure 1.1
Project 1A—Computer Club

Objective 1
Rename a Database

To complete the projects in the chapters, you will locate the student files that accompany this textbook and copy them to the drive and folder where you are storing your projects. Databases that you copy to your storage location must be renamed so you can differentiate them from the data files that accompany this book. In this activity, you will learn how to do this.

Activity 1.1 Renaming a Database

1. Using the **My Computer** feature of your Windows operating system, navigate to the drive where you will be storing your projects for this book, for example, Removable Disk (D:) drive.

2. On the menu bar, click **File**, point to **New**, and then click **Folder**.

   A new folder is created, the words *New Folder* display highlighted in the folder's name box, and the insertion point is blinking. Recall that within Windows, highlighted text will be replaced by your typing.

3. Type **Chapter 1** and then press Enter.

4. Navigate to the location where the student files that accompany this textbook are located, and then click once to select the file **a01A_ComputerClub**.

> **Note — Using File Extensions**
>
> ***Access databases use a .mdb extension.***
>
> The computer that you are using may be set such that file extensions display. If so, this file name will display as a01A_ComputerClub.mdb. The .mdb extension indicates that this file is a Microsoft database file.

5. Move the mouse pointer over the selected file name and then right-click to display a shortcut menu. On the displayed shortcut menu, click **Copy**.

6. Navigate to and open the **Chapter 1** folder you created in Step 3. Right-click to display a shortcut menu and then click **Paste**.

   The database file is copied to your folder and is selected.

7 Move your mouse pointer over the selected file name, right-click to display the shortcut menu, and then on the shortcut menu, click **Rename**. As shown in Figure 1.2, and using your own first and last name, type **1A_ComputerClub_Firstname_Lastname**

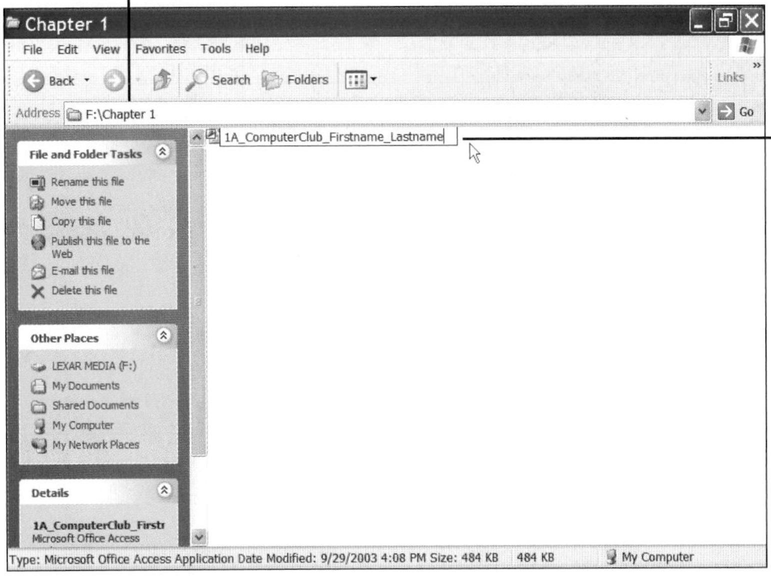

Figure 1.2

8 Press Enter to save the new file name. If the *Confirm File Rename* message displays, click **Yes**. Be sure that the file name is still selected (highlighted), pause your mouse pointer over the selected name, and then right-click to display the shortcut menu.

Note — Naming Files

Use underscores instead of spaces.

The Microsoft Windows operating system recognizes file names with spaces. However, some Internet file transfer programs do not. To facilitate sending your files over the Internet using a course management system, in this textbook you will be instructed to save files using an underscore rather than a space. On your keyboard, the underscore key is the shift of the hyphen key, to the right of the zero key.

9 On the displayed shortcut menu, click **Properties**.

The Properties dialog box with the database name in the title bar displays. The databases provided with this book have a Read-only attribute that protects them from being altered. To use a database, you must first save the database to the location where you are storing your files, rename the database, and then remove the Read-only attribute so you can make changes to the database.

10 At the bottom of the dialog box, click to clear the check mark next to **Read-only**. See Figure 1.3.

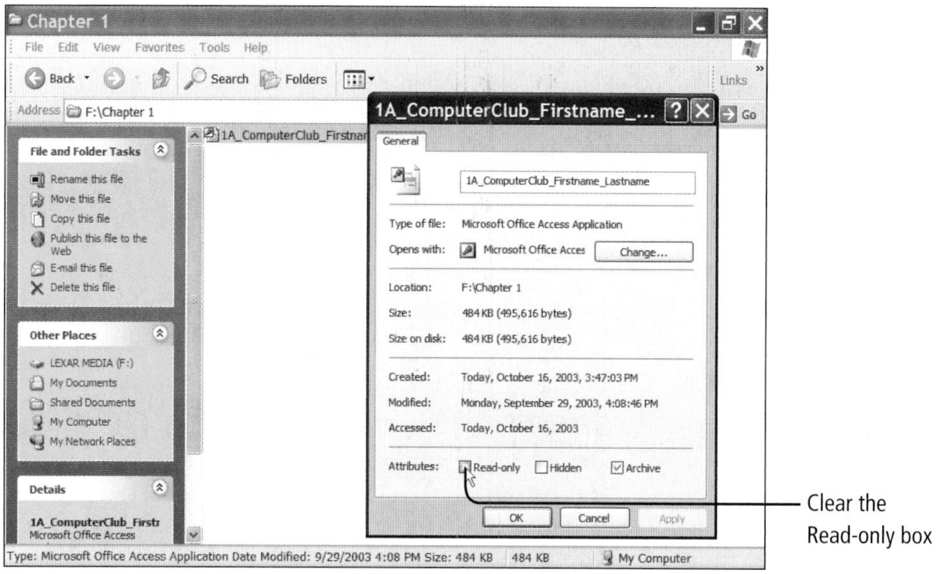

Figure 1.3

11 Click **OK** to close the dialog box.

12 **Close** the **My Computer** window.

You may want to mark or otherwise make a note of this section for future reference when you need to retrieve, copy, and rename additional databases for use in this textbook.

Objective 2
Start Access, Open an Existing Database, and View Database Objects

Activity 1.2 Starting Access and Opening an Existing Database

Data that is organized in a format of horizontal rows and vertical columns is called a ***table***. A table is the foundation on which an Access database is built. In the following activity, you will view a table within a database.

1 On the left side of the Windows taskbar, click the **Start** button 
.

The Start menu displays.

2 On the computer you are using, determine where the Access program is located and point to **Microsoft Office Access 2003**.

Organizations and individuals store computer programs in a variety of ways. The Access program might be located under All Programs or Microsoft Office or some other arrangement. See Figure 1.4 for an example.

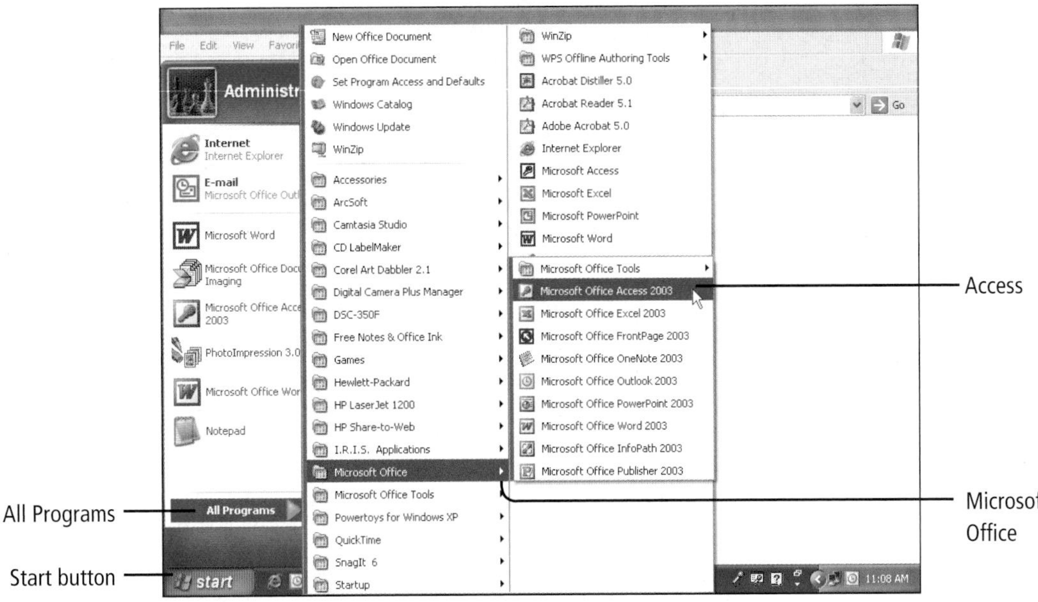

Figure 1.4

3 Click once to open the **Access** program.

The Access program opens. Across the upper portion of the Access window is the title bar, a menu bar, and the Database toolbar. The main window is divided into two sections—the ***task pane*** on the right and a blank gray area on the left. The task pane is a window within a Microsoft Office application that provides commonly used commands. Its location and small size allow you to use these commands while working in your database. A database, when opened, will display in the gray area. See Figure 1.5.

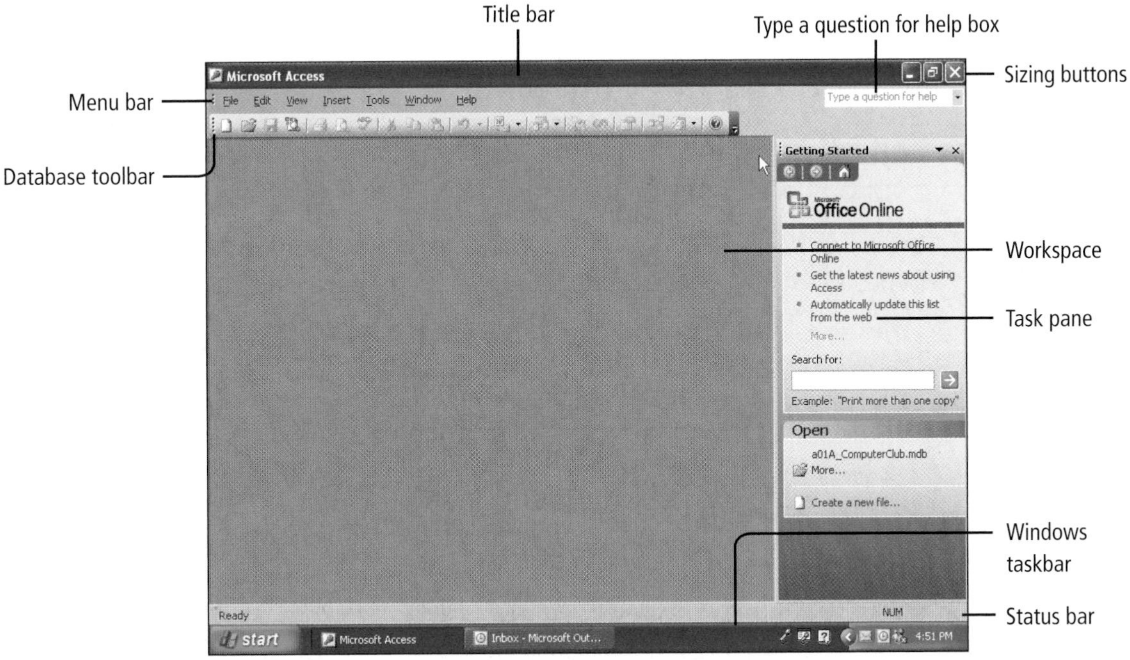

Figure 1.5

Note — Comparing Programs

Access opens the program only.

You may have used Microsoft Word, which opens and displays a blank document, or Microsoft Excel, which opens and displays a blank workbook. Access, however, does not open a blank database—it opens the program only.

4 Take a moment to study the elements of the Access window as shown in Figure 1.5 and as described in the table in Figure 1.6.

Elements of the Access Window

Element	Description
Title bar	Displays the name of the program.
Sizing buttons	Enable you to minimize, maximize, restore, and close the Access window.
Type a question for help box	Allows you to access the Microsoft Access Help feature by typing a question.
Menu bar	Contains the menus of Access commands. Display a menu by clicking on its name in the menu bar.
Database toolbar	Contains a row of buttons that provide a one-click method to perform the most common commands in Access.
Task pane	Displays commonly used commands.
Status bar	Displays information about the task you are working on.
Windows taskbar	Displays the Start button and buttons indicating active windows.
Workspace	Gray area where an open database displays.

Figure 1.6

5 On the Database toolbar, pause your mouse pointer over the **Open** button .

When you position the mouse pointer over a button, Access displays the button's name in a box called a ***ScreenTip***. You should see the ScreenTip *Open*.

6 On the menu bar, click **File**.

The File menu displays. When you display a menu in Access, either the short menu, shown in Figure 1.7, or the full menu, shown in Figure 1.8, displays.

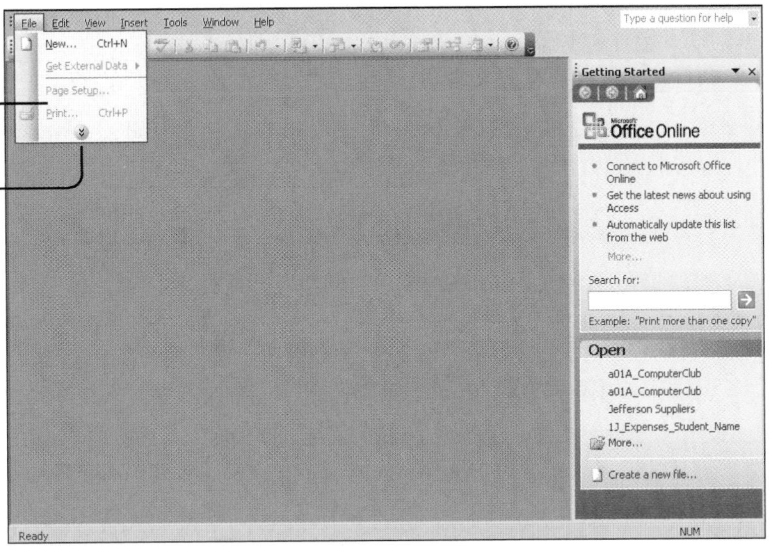

Figure 1.7

The short menu will display fully after a few seconds. Alternatively, you can click the small double arrow at the bottom of the short menu to display the full menu.

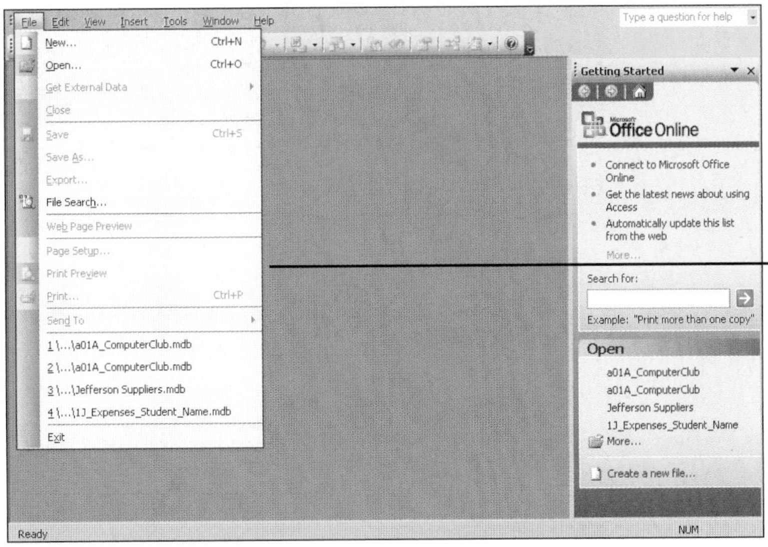

Figure 1.8

More Knowledge — Displaying the Full Menu

Select the Always show full menus *option.*

If you do not see the short version of the File menu as shown in Figure 1.7, your system has been set so that full menus always display. Many individuals prefer the full menu display. To set a system to always display the full menu, display the Tools menu, click Customize, and then click the Options tab. Select (place a check mark in) the Always show full menus check box. Click Close.

7 On the displayed **File** menu, click **Open**.

The Open dialog box displays.

8 Click the **Look in arrow** shown in Figure 1.9 and then navigate to the location where you are storing your projects for this chapter.

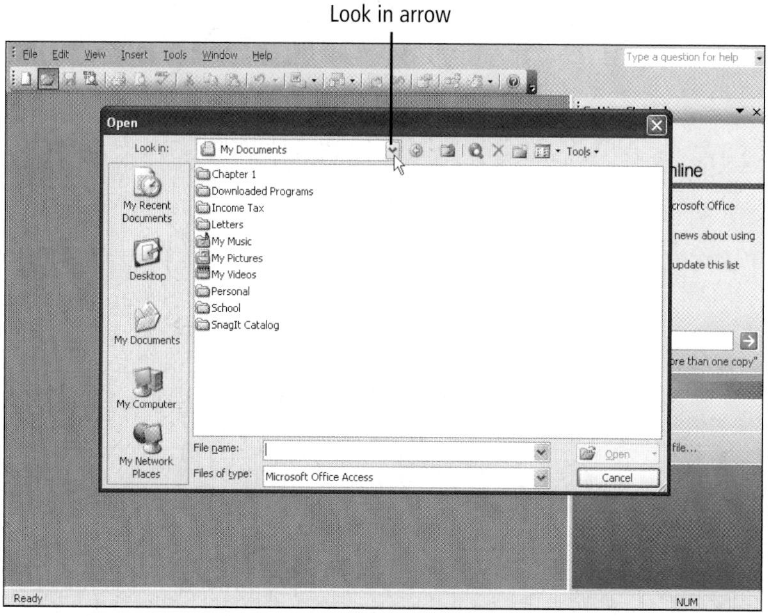

Figure 1.9

9 Locate the database file that you saved and renamed with your name in Activity 1.1. Click the **1A_ComputerClub_Firstname_Lastname** database file once to select it, and then, in the lower right corner, click the **Open** button. Alternatively, you can double-click the name of the database.

10 If the message in Figure 1.10, or similar message, displays on your screen, click **Yes**.

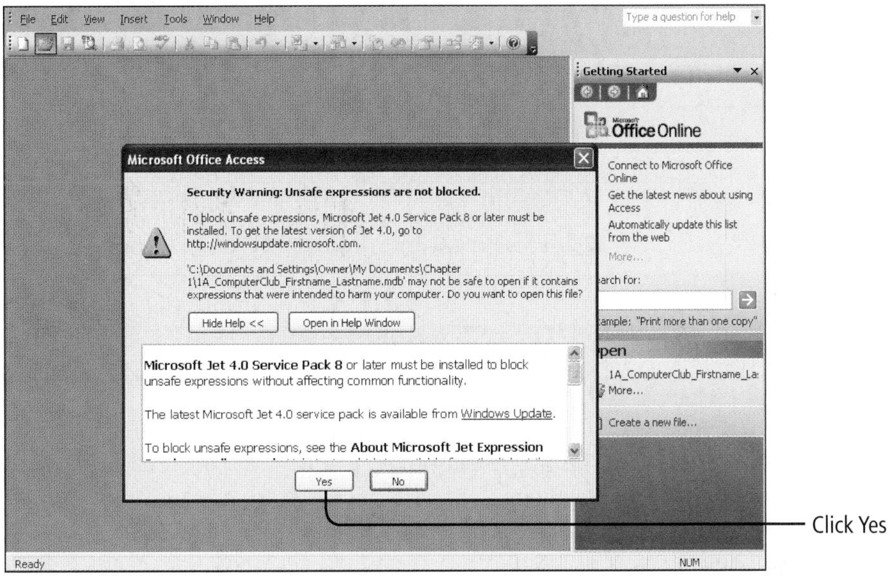

Figure 1.10

11 If another Security Warning message displays, click **Open**.

The ComputerClub Database window opens, as shown in Figure 1.11.

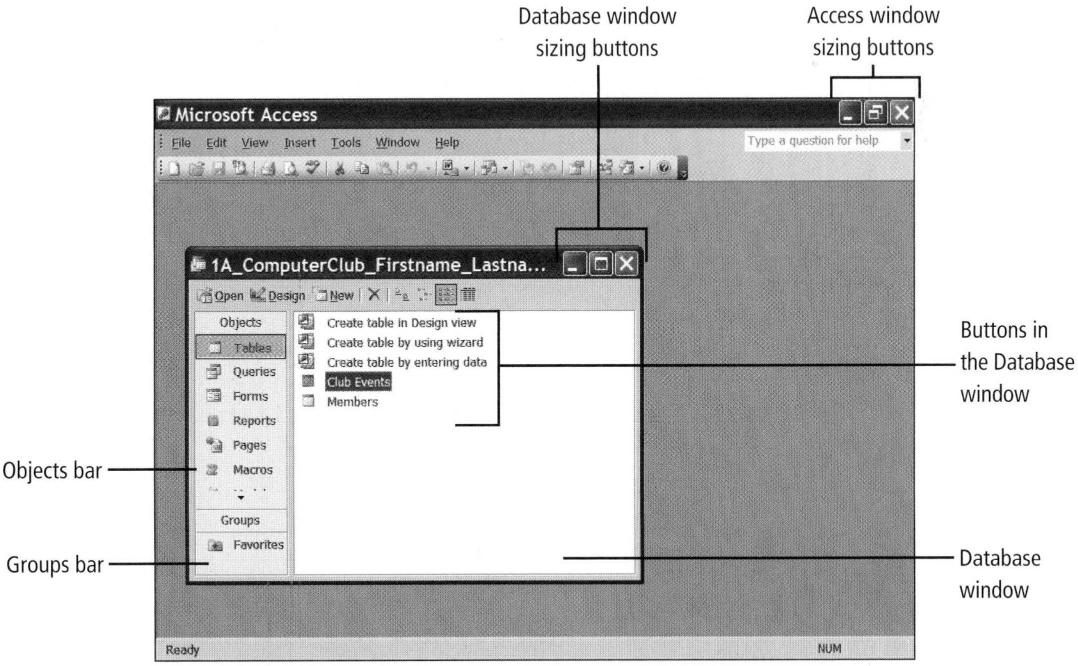

Figure 1.11

Activity 1.3 Viewing the Database Window

The ***Database window*** displays when a database is open. The ***Objects bar*** on the left side of the Database window has buttons—called ***objects***—that you can work with in Access. Objects are the primary components of an Access database.

Just one object—***Tables***—actually *stores* your data; the other objects are used to organize, manage, and manipulate the data. Recall that a table is a collection of data organized in a format of columns and rows. One or more tables can be used to store data in a database.

1 Take a moment to study the elements of the Database window shown in Figure 1.11 and described in the table in Figure 1.12.

Elements of the Database Window

Element	Description
Database window	Displays when a database is open and allows you to access all the database objects.
Objects bar	Contains buttons that activate the objects (tools) of a database.
Groups bar	Contains shortcuts to different types of database objects.
Database window sizing buttons	Enables you to minimize, maximize, and close the Database window.
Buttons in the Database window	Activate commands related to the selected database object.

Figure 1.12

2 In the extreme upper right corner of your screen, locate the **Type a question for help** box. Just above that box, click the Access window's **Minimize** button. See Figure 1.11.

The Access window is minimized and displays as a button on the Windows taskbar at the lower edge of your screen. See Figure 1.13.

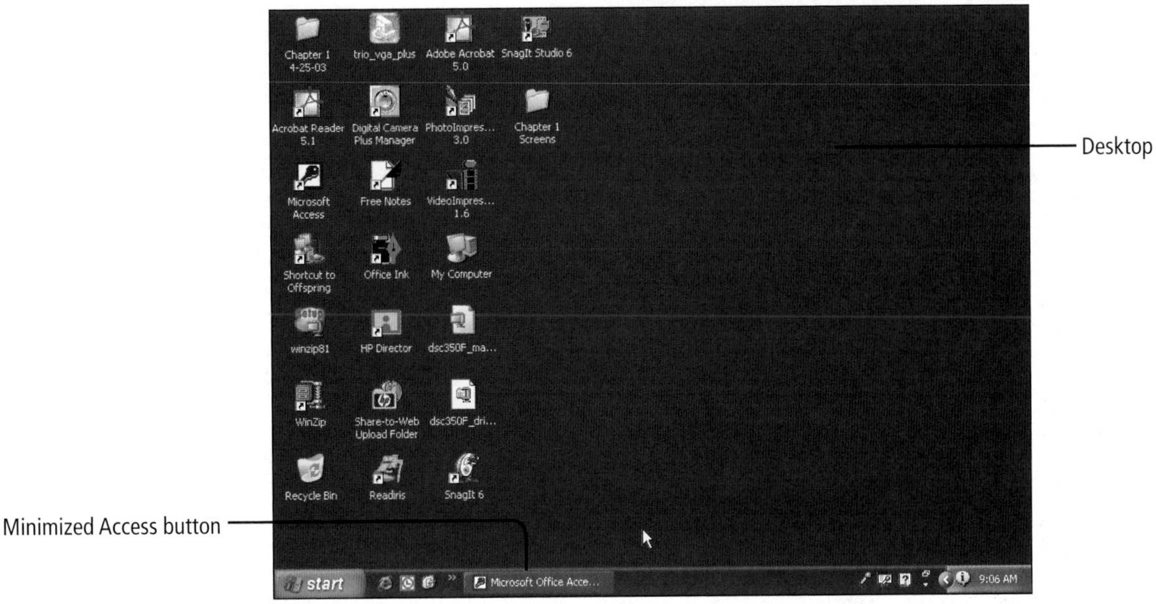

Figure 1.13

3 On the Windows taskbar, click **Microsoft Access**.

The Access window and Database window are restored. Minimizing windows in this manner enables you to view your Desktop.

4 Look at the Database window (the smaller window) and notice that it also has a set of sizing buttons at the right edge of its title bar. Click its **Maximize** button.

The Database window fills the entire gray workspace within the Access window. The Database window's title bar no longer displays—the name of the database displays instead on the main title bar enclosed in square brackets. See Figure 1.14.

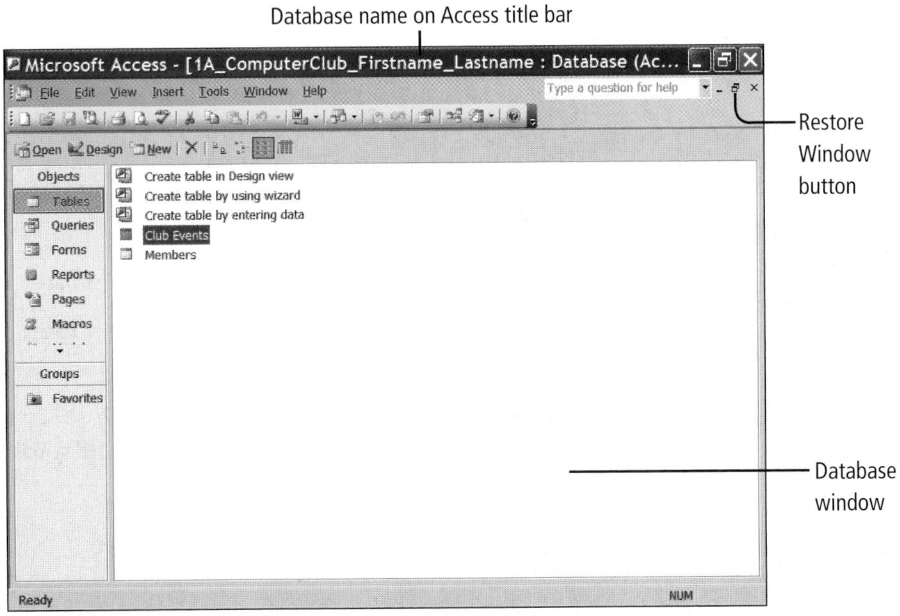

Figure 1.14

5 To the right of the **Type a question for help** box, click the small **Restore Window** button. See Figure 1.14.

The Database window is restored to its original size and position, as shown in Figure 1.11. You can see that the Database window is a separate window that can be manipulated like other windows.

Note — Sizing the Database Window

Maximize to fill the gray area.

You have seen that the Database window can be maximized to fill the gray area, or left in its original size, which is smaller and contained within the gray area. Many Access users prefer keeping the Database window smaller than the gray area of the Access window. This visually separates the Objects bar and the other parts of the Database window from features that are part of the larger Access window.

6 On the Objects bar, notice that *Tables* is selected. With the Tables object selected, point to, but do not click, each of the remaining objects one by one.

The Computer Club Database window displays seven objects: Tables, Queries, Forms, Reports, Pages, Macros, and Modules. Each of these objects is used by Access to manage the information stored in the Computer Club database. As you progress in your study of Access, you will learn more about each of these objects.

Activity 1.4 Opening a Table

Recall that tables are the foundation of your Access database because that is where the data is stored. Each table in an Access database stores data about only one subject. For example, in the Computer Club database, the Club Events table stores data about individual club events and the Members table stores data about the Club's members.

1 On the Objects bar, if necessary, click **Tables** to select it.

Notice that to the right of the Objects bar, three command icons display followed by the names of two tables. The command icons provide three different methods for creating a new table. Following the command icons, the names of the tables that have been created and saved as part of the Computer Club database display. There are two tables in this database, the *Club Events* table and the *Members* table.

2 Click the **Club Events** table once to select it if necessary, and then, just above the Objects bar, click the **Open** button. Alternatively, you can double-click the table name to open it.

The table opens, as shown in Figure 1.15. Here you can see the data organized in a format of columns and rows.

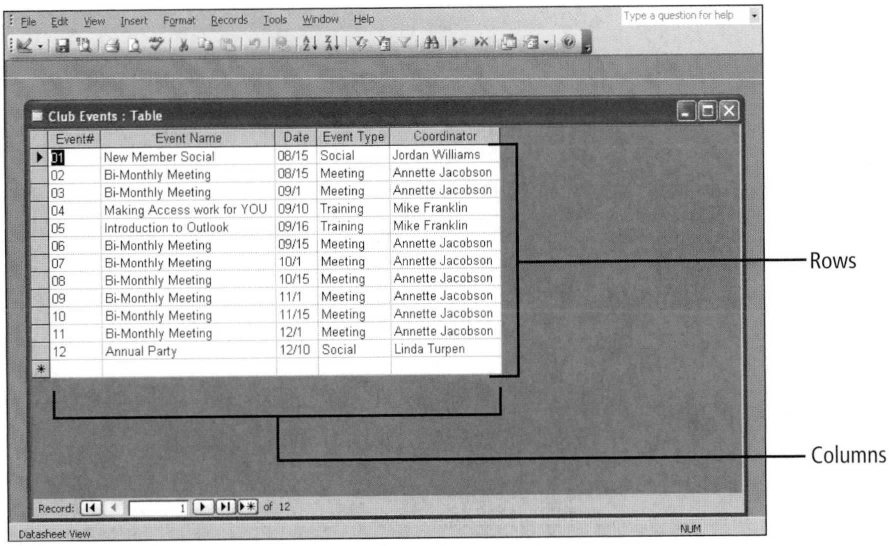

Figure 1.15

3. Along the left side of the open table, move your mouse pointer until it displays as a right-pointing arrow, as shown in Figure 1.16.

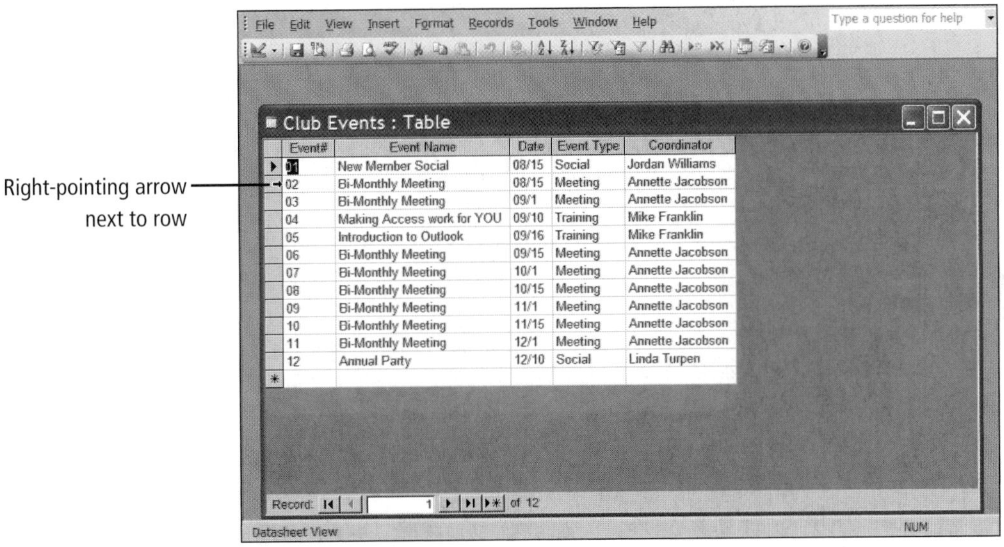

Figure 1.16

4 Pause the arrow pointer at the row containing the event *Annual Party* and click once.

The row containing the information for the Annual Party is highlighted in black. Each horizontal row of a table stores all of the information about one database item. You can see that, in the Club Events table, each event has a separate row in the database table. The information in a row is referred to as a ***record***.

5 Use the technique you just used in Step 4 to find and select the record for the training event **Introduction to Outlook**.

6 Across the top of the table, move your mouse pointer over the words *Event Type* until it becomes a down arrow, and then click once to select the column. See Figure 1.17.

Each record contains information located in vertical columns, called ***fields***, which describe the record. For example, in the Club Events table, each event (record) has the following fields: Event#, Event Name, Date, Event Type, and Coordinator.

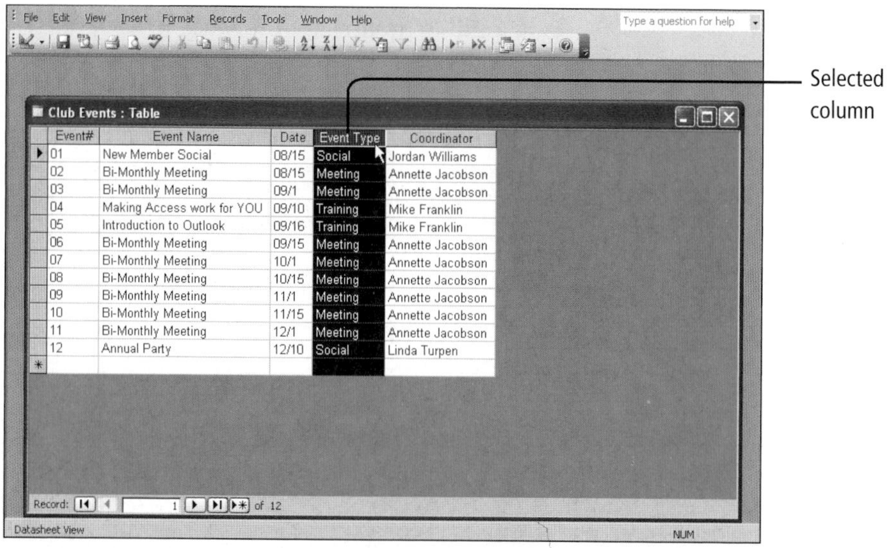

Figure 1.17

7 Use your mouse pointer to select the column representing the **Coordinator** field. Take a moment to look at the other column names in the table to familiarize yourself with these *fields*.

8 In the last row of the table, click once in the **Event#** field under the last record in the table. See Figure 1.18.

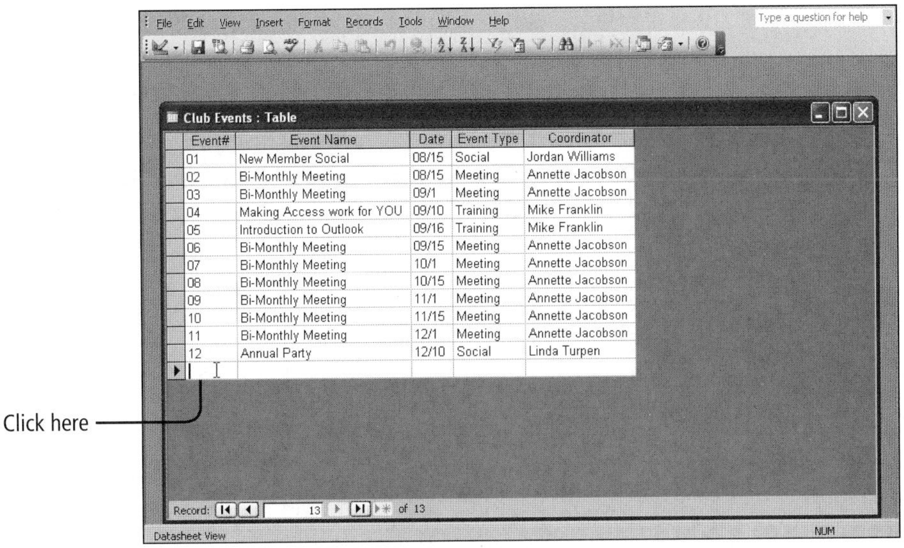

Figure 1.18

9 In the **Event#** field type **13**

10 Notice the pencil image in the gray box to the left. See Figure 1.19.

In the ***row selector***—the small gray box at the left end of a row—a small pencil image displays in the row in which a new record is being entered. The pencil image in the row selector indicates that the information in this record is in the process of being entered and has not yet been saved.

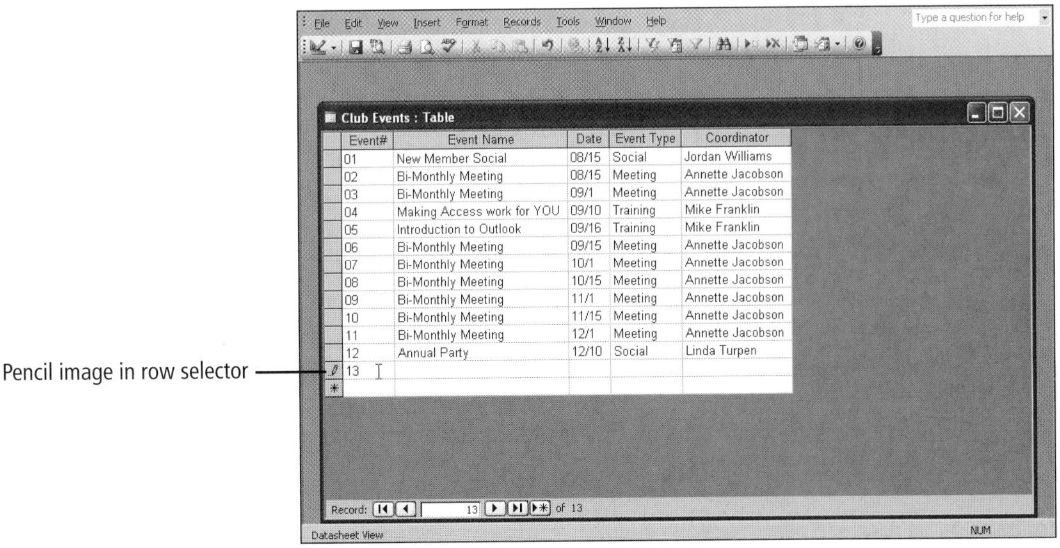

Figure 1.19

11 Press [Tab] once.

The insertion point is blinking in the next field to the right, which is the *Event Name* field.

12 In the **Event Name** field, type **Project 1A** and then press [Tab].

13 In the **Date** field, type **11/18** and then press [Tab].

14 In the **Event Type** field, type **Training** and then press [Tab] to move to the **Coordinator** field. Using your own first and last name, in the **Coordinator** field, type **Firstname Lastname**

15 Press either [Enter] or [Tab] on your keyboard to save the record.

The pencil image no longer displays, indicating that the record is saved. Compare your screen to Figure 1.20.

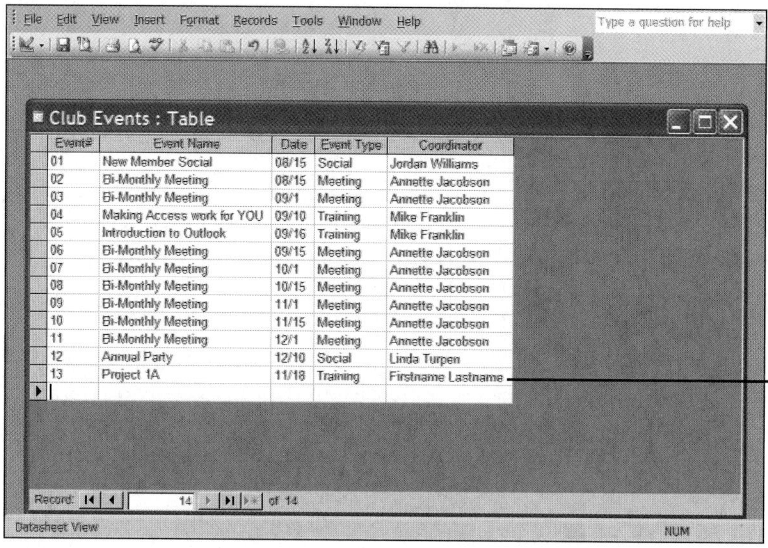

File Edit View Insert Format Records Tools Window Help
Type a question for help
Club Events : Table
Event# Event Name Date Event Type Coordinator
01 New Member Social 08/15 Social Jordan Williams
02 Bi-Monthly Meeting 08/15 Meeting Annette Jacobson
03 Bi-Monthly Meeting 09/1 Meeting Annette Jacobson
04 Making Access work for YOU 09/10 Training Mike Franklin
05 Introduction to Outlook 09/16 Training Mike Franklin
06 Bi-Monthly Meeting 09/15 Meeting Annette Jacobson
07 Bi-Monthly Meeting 10/1 Meeting Annette Jacobson
08 Bi-Monthly Meeting 10/15 Meeting Annette Jacobson
09 Bi-Monthly Meeting 11/1 Meeting Annette Jacobson
10 Bi-Monthly Meeting 11/15 Meeting Annette Jacobson
11 Bi-Monthly Meeting 12/1 Meeting Annette Jacobson
12 Annual Party 12/10 Social Linda Turpen
13 Project 1A 11/18 Training Firstname Lastname
Record: 14 of 14
Datasheet View
NUM

Record with your name

Figure 1.20

Activity 1.5 Viewing a Table

The Tables database object has four ***views***. A view is a way of looking at something such as a table or form. As you work with tables of data, there are two ways to look at tables that are particularly useful—the Datasheet view, which is currently displayed on your screen, and the Design view.

In the previous activity, you opened the Club Events table in the Datasheet view. The Datasheet view displays all the records in a table in a format of columns (fields) and rows (records).

1 On the Table Datasheet toolbar, locate the **View** button, as shown in Figure 1.21.

Its picture, displaying a ruler, a pencil, and a protractor, indicates that clicking the button will switch the display to the Design view of the table. This button will change depending on the current view to allow you to switch back and forth between ***Design view*** and ***Datasheet view***.

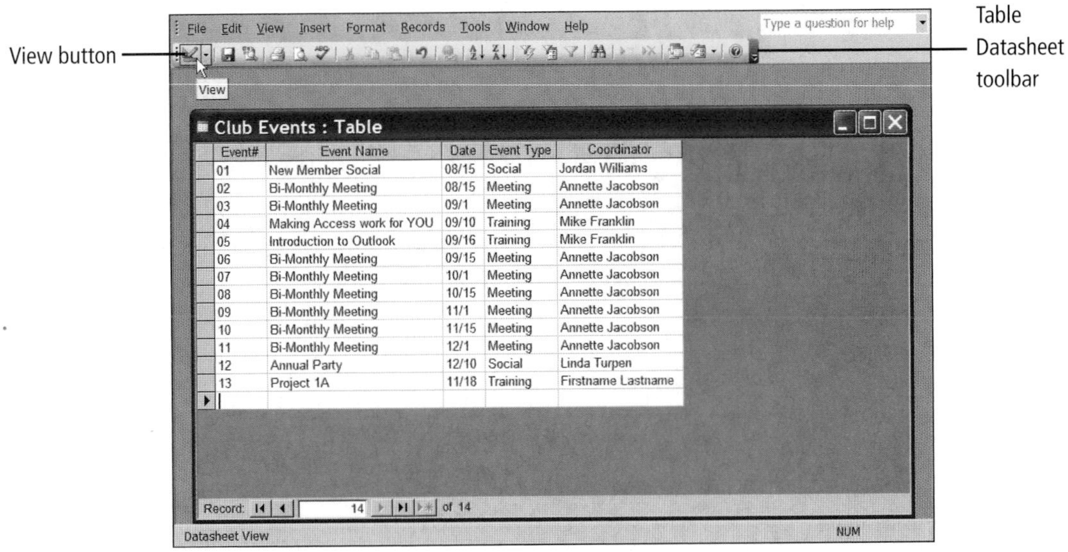

Figure 1.21

2 Click the **View** button.

The Design view of the table displays. Notice that in Design view, you do not see the names of the club events—or other information contained in the records. You see only the names of the fields, such as *Event Name* and *Coordinator*. In this view, you can change the design of the table—that is, the way each field displays its associated data.

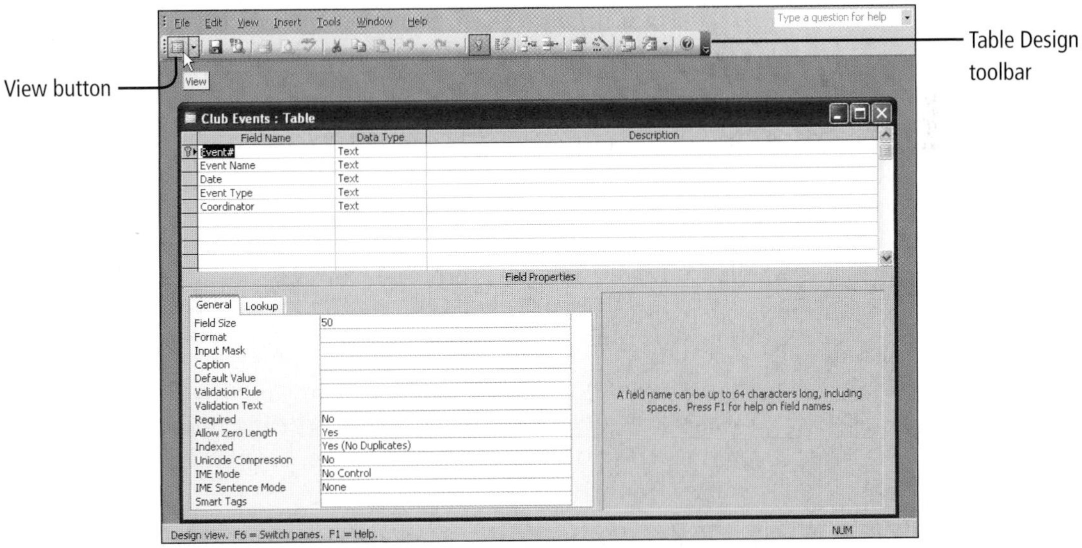

Figure 1.22

3 On the Table Design toolbar, locate the **View** button. See Figure 1.22.

Now the View button displays as a small table—or datasheet. This picture on the View button indicates that clicking the button will return you to the Datasheet (table) view.

4 Click the **View** button.

The table redisplays in Datasheet view. Recall that the Datasheet view of a table displays the individual records in horizontal rows and the field names at the top of each column. Thus, the View button displays as [icon] when you are in the Datasheet view and as [icon] when you are in the Design view—indicating which view will be displayed when you click the button.

5 In the upper right corner of the Table window, click the **Close** button [icon] to close the table. See Figure 1.23.

The Database window displays.

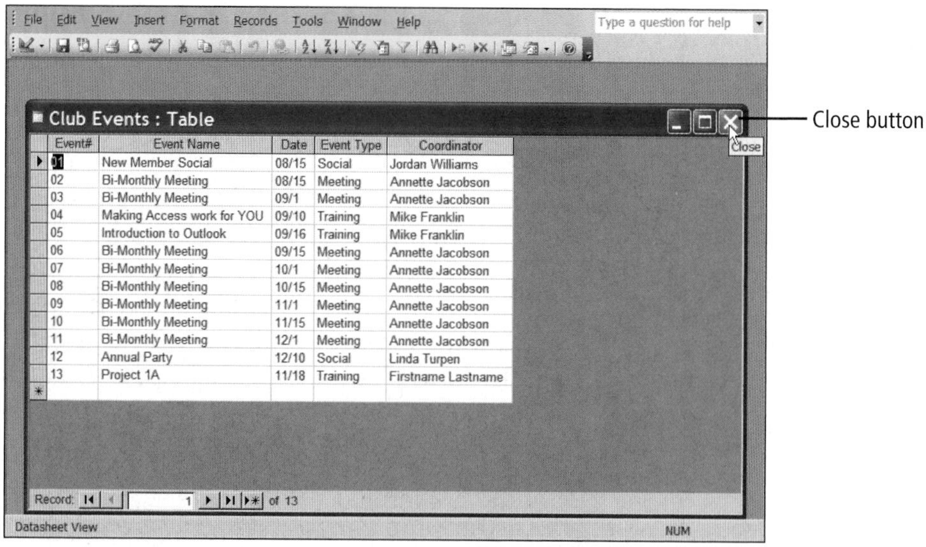

Figure 1.23

Activity 1.6 Viewing a Query

The second object on the Objects bar is *Queries*. To ***query*** is to ask a question. The Queries object is a tool with which you can ask questions about the data stored in the Tables objects.

For example, you could use the Queries object to ask how many Club Events are social events. Locating specific information in a database, such as the number of social events, is referred to as ***extracting*** information from the database.

1 On the Objects bar, click **Queries**.

The Database window displays two command icons that can be used to create a new query. They are followed by one query that has been created and saved as part of the Computer Club database. Later, you will create and save your own queries.

2 Double-click the **Social Events Query**. Alternatively, you can right-click the query name, and then click Open on the displayed shortcut menu, or click once to select the query and then click the Open button [Open] in the Database window.

When a query is opened, Access *runs*—processes—the query and displays the results. The results of the query will display only selected information from the table.

3 Look at the records that display as a result of this query.

The number of records in the query result is less that the number of records in the original table because certain ***criteria***—specifications that determine what records will be displayed—were entered as part of the query. For example, this query was created to locate the names of all the events in the table that are Social Events. Notice that two records display—New Member Social and Annual Party. See Figure 1.24.

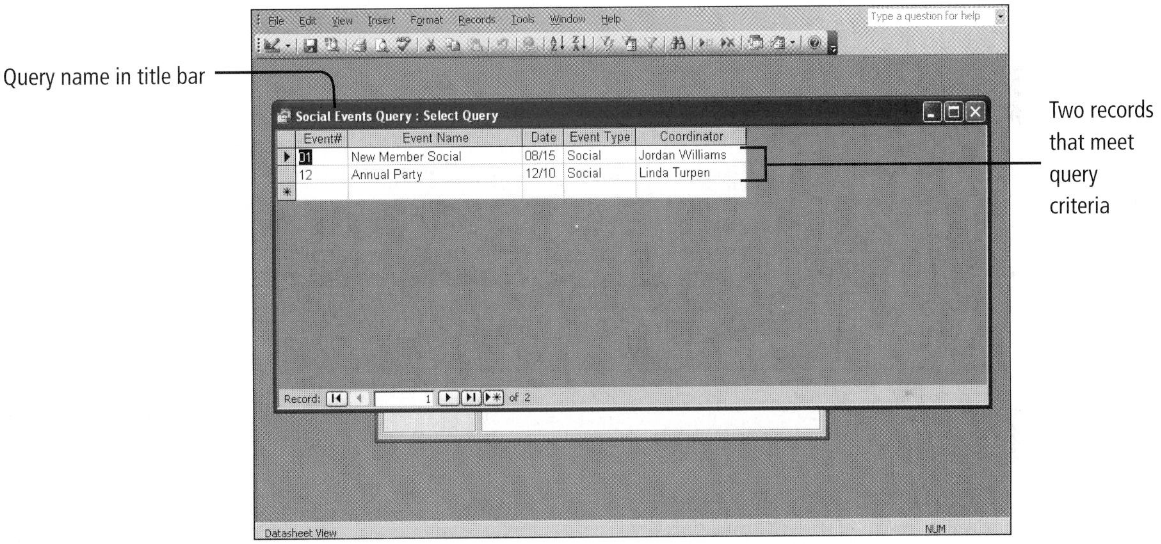

Figure 1.24

4 In the upper right corner of the query window, click the **Close** button [X].

The Database window displays.

Activity 1.7 Viewing a Form

Forms, the third object on the Objects bar, provides an alternative method to both enter and display data in the Tables object. The records that display in a form are the same records that are in the table, with one difference: forms can be designed to display only one record at a time.

1 On the Objects bar, click **Forms**.

To the right of the Objects bar, two command icons for creating a new form display, followed by a form that has been created and saved as part of the Computer Club database. Thus far, only one form, the Club Events form, has been created for this database.

2 Double-click the **Club Events** form.

The Club Events form displays with fields filled in with the data representing the first record in the database. See Figure 1.25.

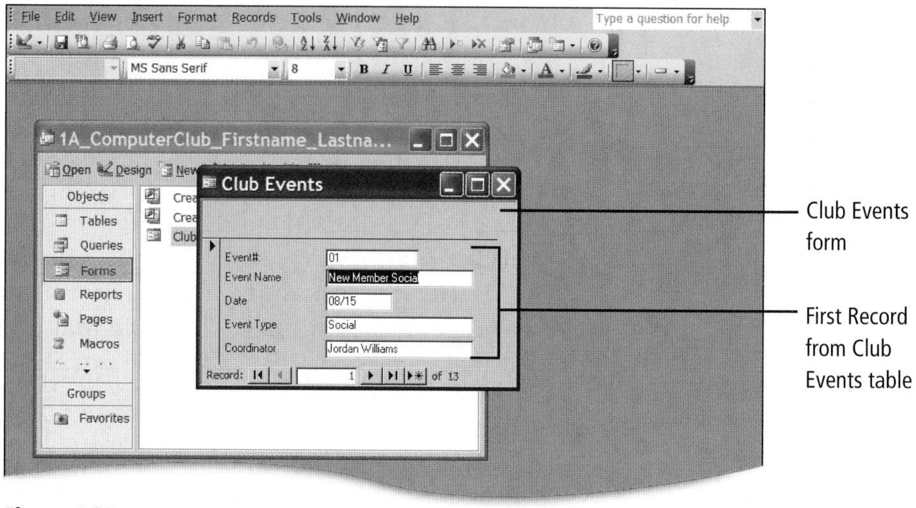

Figure 1.25

3 At the lower edge of the form, click the **Next Record** button until you see the 12th record—the Annual Party event—displayed in the form. See Figure 1.26.

As you click the Next Record button, notice how each individual record in the table of Club Events displays in the window.

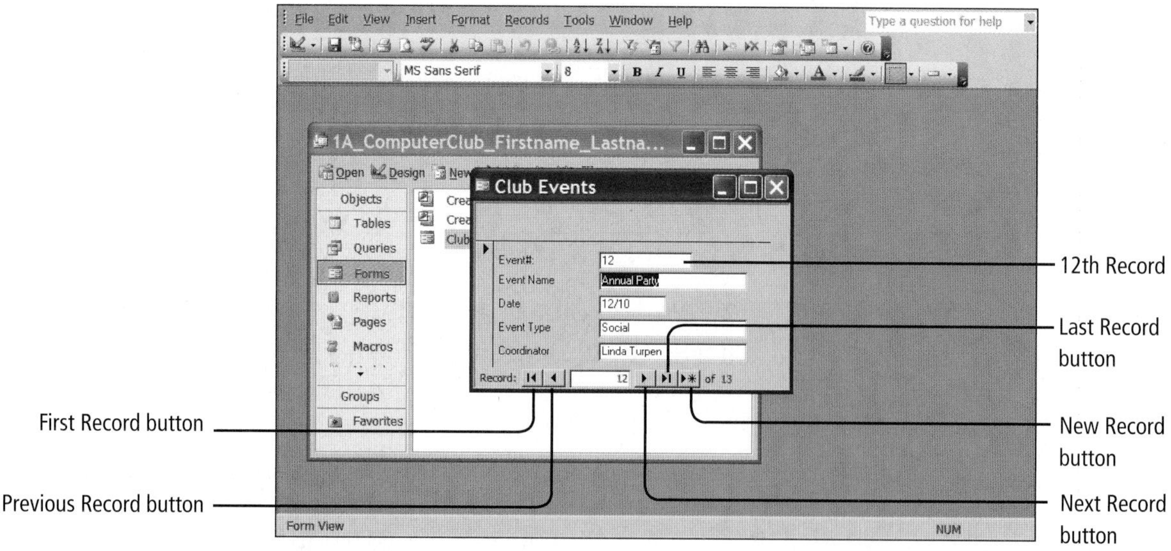

Figure 1.26

4 In the upper right corner of the Club Events form window, click the **Close** button to close the form. The Database window displays.

Activity 1.8 Viewing and Printing a Report

The fourth button on the Objects bar is *Reports*. A ***report*** is a database object that displays the fields and records from the table (or query) in an easy-to-read format suitable for printing. Reports are created to summarize information in a database in a professional-looking manner.

1 On the Objects bar, click **Reports**. See Figure 1.27.

To the right of the Objects bar, command icons for creating a new report display, followed by a report that has been created and saved as part of the Computer Club database. Thus far, only one report, the Club Events report, has been created for this database.

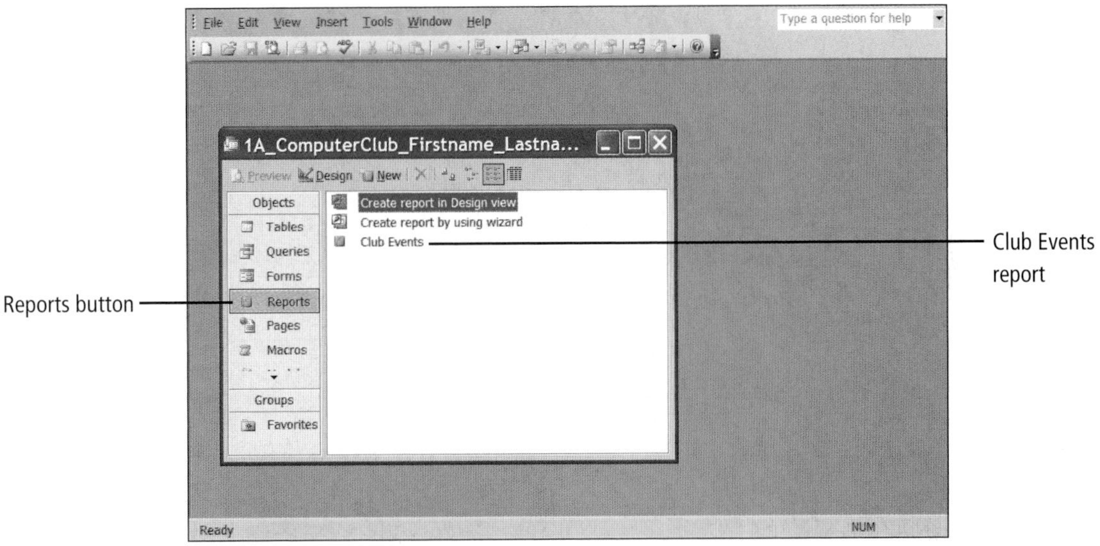

Figure 1.27

2 Double-click the **Club Events** report.

The Club Events report displays, as shown in Figure 1.28.

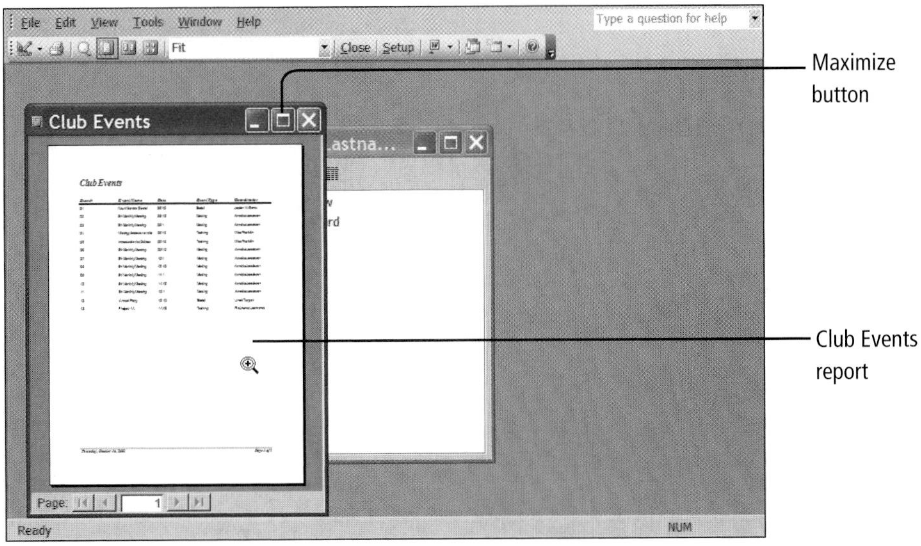

Figure 1.28

3 In the upper right corner of the Club Events report window, click the **Maximize** button.

The window is maximized on your screen.

4 On the toolbar, pause the mouse pointer over the word *Fit* and see the ScreenTip *Zoom.*

To ***zoom*** means to make the page view larger or smaller. ***Fit*** means that an entire page of the report will display on your screen at one time giving you an overall view of what the printed pages will look like.

5 On the toolbar, click the **Zoom arrow** and then, from the displayed list, click **100%**. See Figure 1.29.

Zooming to 100% displays the report in the approximate size it will be when it is printed.

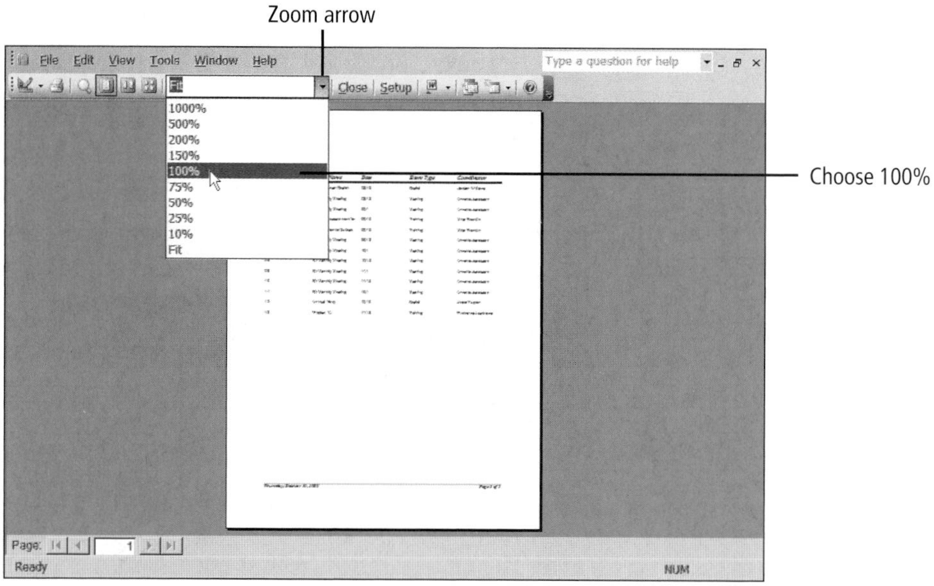

Figure 1.29

6 In the displayed report page, locate the record **Project 1A**. You may need to use the vertical scroll bar in the window to see this record. See Figure 1.30.

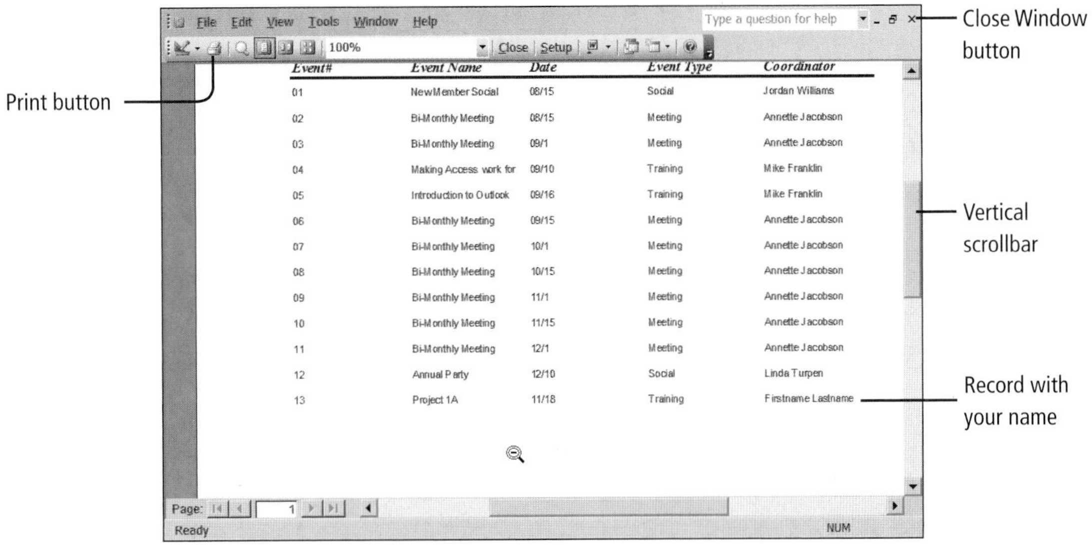
Print button
Close Window button
Vertical scrollbar
Record with your name
File Edit View Tools Window Help
Type a question for help
100%
Close Setup
Event# Event Name Date Event Type Coordinator
01 New Member Social 08/15 Social Jordan Williams
02 Bi-Monthly Meeting 08/15 Meeting Annette Jacobson
03 Bi-Monthly Meeting 09/1 Meeting Annette Jacobson
04 Making Access work for 09/10 Training Mike Franklin
05 Introduction to Outlook 09/16 Training Mike Franklin
06 Bi-Monthly Meeting 09/15 Meeting Annette Jacobson
07 Bi-Monthly Meeting 10/1 Meeting Annette Jacobson
08 Bi-Monthly Meeting 10/15 Meeting Annette Jacobson
09 Bi-Monthly Meeting 11/1 Meeting Annette Jacobson
10 Bi-Monthly Meeting 11/15 Meeting Annette Jacobson
11 Bi-Monthly Meeting 12/1 Meeting Annette Jacobson
12 Annual Party 12/10 Social Linda Turpen
13 Project 1A 11/18 Training Firstname Lastname
Page: 1
Ready
NUM

Figure 1.30

Notice that on your screen, the report displays as if it were printed on a piece of paper. A report is designed to be a professional-looking document that you can print.

A report is generated each time you open it and displays up-to-date information. For example, this report was created before you opened the database, but the record you added with your name now displays in the report.

7 On the toolbar, click the **Print** button. See Figure 1.30.

The Club Events report prints.

8 In the upper right corner of the report window, click the **Close Window** button to close the report.

The Database window displays.

9 To the right of the **Type a question for help** box, click the small **Restore Window** button to restore the Database window to its previous size. See Figure 1.31.

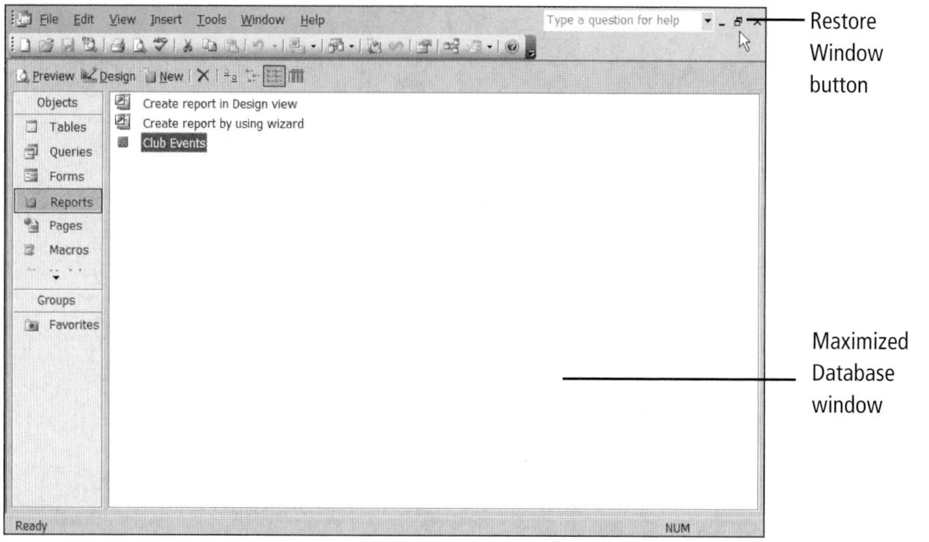

Figure 1.31

10 In the Database window, click the **Close** button to close the Computer Club database. See Figure 1.32.

The Computer Club database closes. The Access program remains open. As you advance in your studies of Access, you will learn about the remaining objects on the Objects bar: Pages, Macros, and Modules.

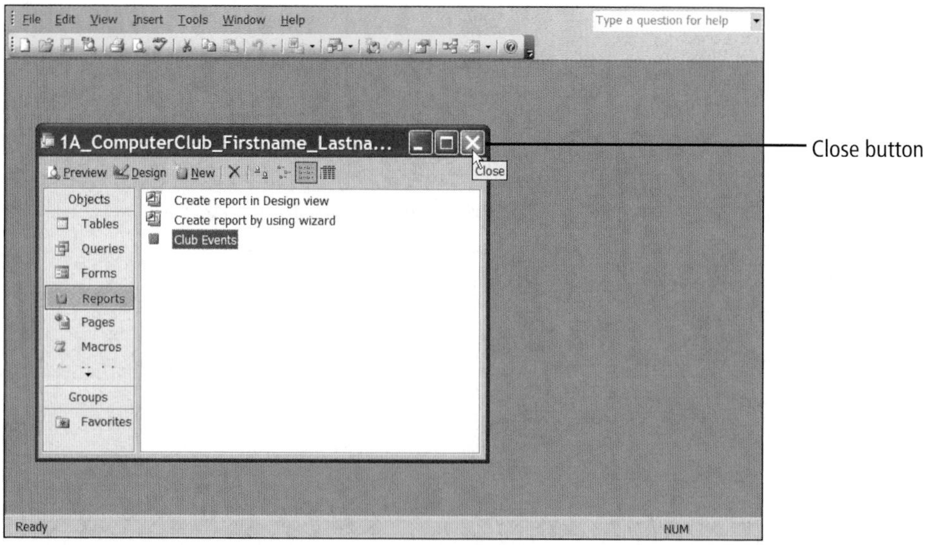

Figure 1.32

End **You have completed Project 1A**

one

1B Project 1B School

In the previous project, you opened an existing database. The Tables object and some of the other object tools used for viewing and manipulating the database were already created. In this project, you will begin a new database and create the table yourself.

In Activities 1.9 through 1.27 you will create a new database for the Distance Learning Department at Lake Michigan City College. The database will have one table that will store student records. Your student table object will look like Figure 1.33. You will save the database as *1B_School_Firstname_Lastname*.

1B Students Firstname Lastname 10/16/2003

Student#	Last Name	First Name	Address	City	Postal Code	Balance	First Term Atten
23895	Jackson	Robert	2320 Aldrich Circle	Chicago	60605	$46.00	SP01
45689	Jackson	Laura	1967 Arizona St.	Chicago	60605	$65.00	FA02
54783	Williams	Pat	62 Cockatiel Lane	Chicago	60605	$42.00	SP03
63257	Apodaca	Allen	679 Martinique Pl.	Chicago	60605	$32.00	SU03
64589	Metheny	Elizabeth	10225 Fairview	Chicago	60605	$15.00	FA02
95140	Vaughn	Sydney	2105 Waldo Ave.	Chicago	60605	$56.00	FA03
95874	Van Wegan	Michaela	100 Quantico Ave.	Chicago	60605	$25.00	FA99
96312	Berstein	Krista	136 South Street	Chicago	60605	$12.00	FA00

Page 1

Figure 1.33

Objective 3
Create a New Database

Activity 1.9 Creating a New Database

In this activity you will create a new database. There are two methods to create a new Access database:

- Create a new database using a wizard (an Access tool that walks you step-by-step through a process).
- Create a new blank database—which is more flexible because you can add each object separately.

Regardless of which method you use, you will have to name and save the database before you can create any objects such as tables, queries, forms, or reports. Think of a database file as a container that stores the database objects—tables, queries, forms, reports, and so forth—that you create and add to the database.

1 If necessary, start Access and close any open databases.

2 On the Database toolbar, click the **New** button.

The New File task pane displays on the right. See Figure 1.34. Recall that the task pane is a window within a Microsoft Office application that provides commonly used commands related to the current task.

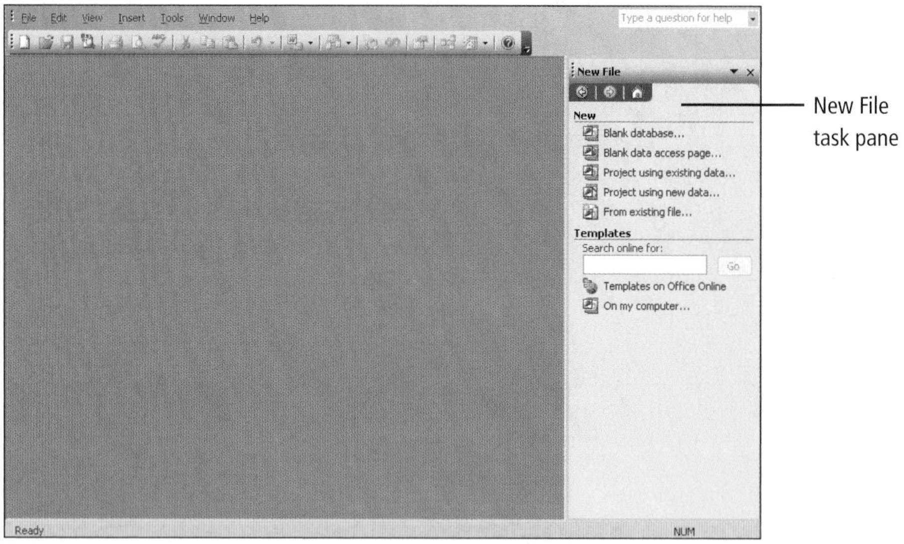

Figure 1.34

3 In the task pane, under **New**, click **Blank database**.

The File New Database dialog box displays.

4 In the **Save in** box, click the **Save in arrow** (the arrow at the right edge of the Save in box) to view a list of the drives available to you.

5 If necessary, navigate to your Chapter 1 folder where you are storing your projects.

6 Clear any text in the **File name** box and then, using your own information, type **1B_School_Firstname_Lastname**

7 In the lower right corner of the dialog box, click **Create**.

The School database is created and the Database window displays with the new database name indicated in the title bar of the Database window.

Objective 4
Create a New Table

When you buy a new address book, it is not very useful until you fill it with names, addresses, and phone numbers. Likewise, a new database is not useful until you ***populate***, or fill, a table with data.

In the next activity, you will create a table in Design view and then add the table's fields.

Activity 1.10 Adding Fields to a Table

Recall that fields, located in columns, contain the information that describes each record in your database. The columnar fields describe the records in a table. For example, in the Club Events table you viewed earlier in Project 1A, there were fields for the *Event Name*, *Event Type*, and so forth. These fields provided information about the records in the table.

1 In the Database window, double-click the command icon **Create table in Design view**. See Figure 1.35. Alternatively, right-click the command icon and click Open on the displayed shortcut menu.

The Design view of the new table displays and the title bar indicates *Table1*: Because you have not yet named or saved this table, it has the default name *Table1*. The word *Table* after the colon indicates that this database object is a table. The insertion point is blinking in the first Field Name box, indicating that Access is ready for you to type the first field name. See Figure 1.36.

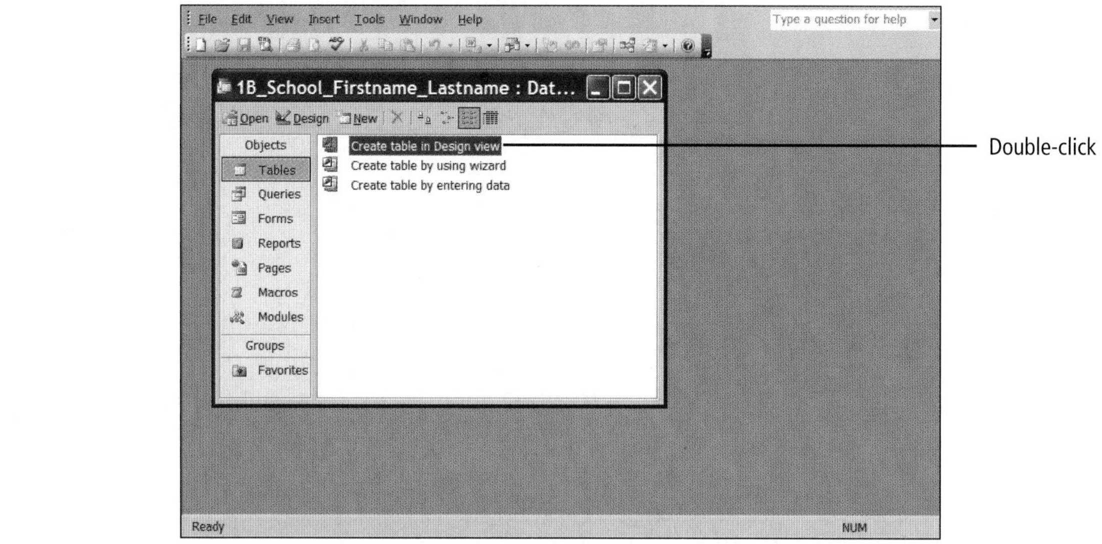

Figure 1.35

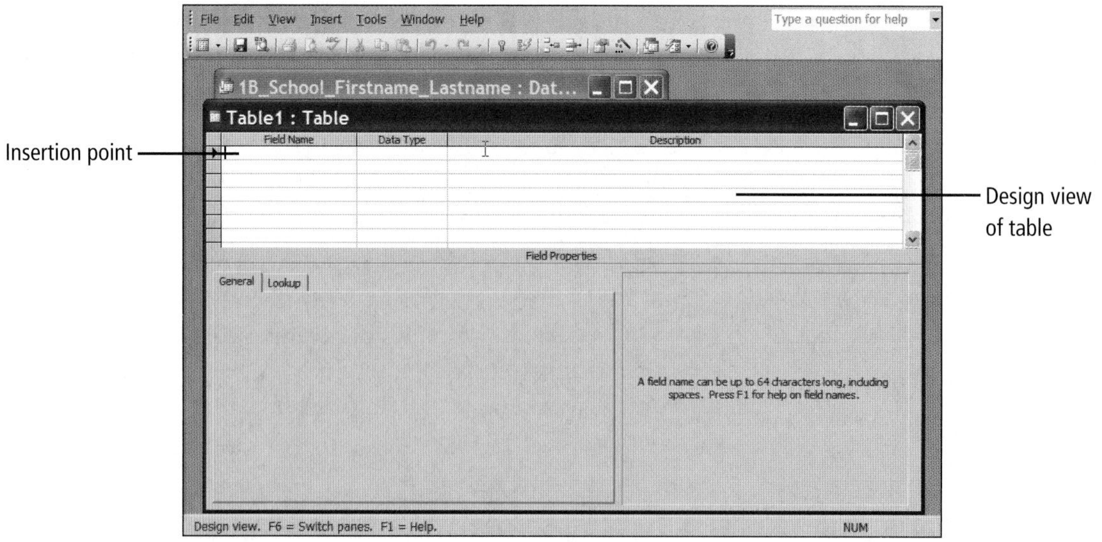

Figure 1.36

2 In the first **Field Name** box, refer to Figure 1.37 and then type **Student#**

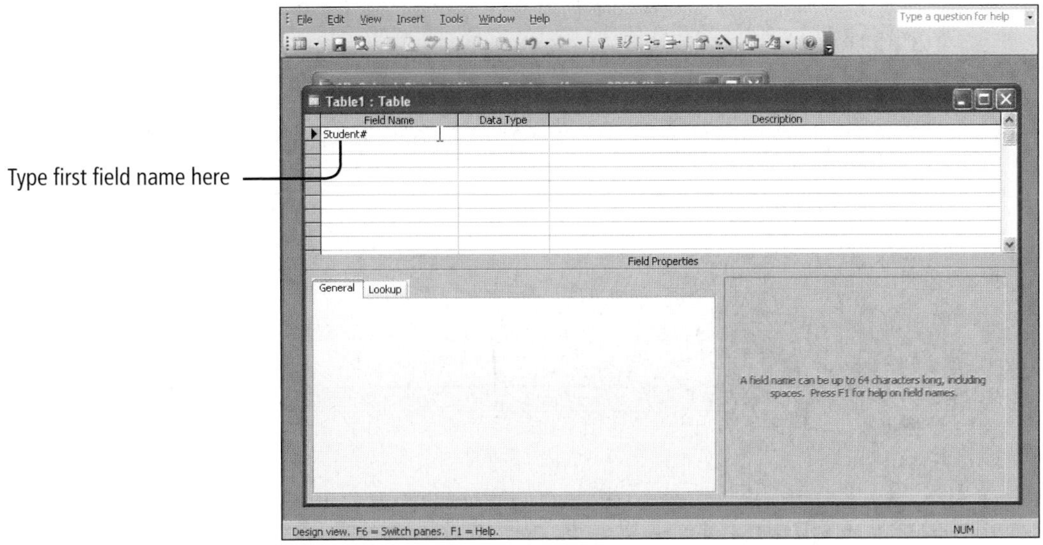

Figure 1.37

3 Press Tab to move the insertion point to the **Data Type** column.

The insertion point is blinking in the Data Type column and *Text* displays and is selected. At the right end of the box, an arrow displays. Notice that this arrow does not display until you click in this box. Some Access features become available in this manner—when a specific location is selected.

Data type specifies how Access organizes and stores data in a field. For example, if you define a field's data type as *Text*, any character can be typed as data in the field. If you define a field's data type as *Number*, only numbers can be typed as data in the field.

4 Click the **Data Type arrow** to display a list of data types. From the displayed list, click **Text** to accept the default data type. See Figure 1.38.

This field will contain a student number for each individual record. Although the student number contains only numbers—no letters or characters—it is customary to define such a number as *Text* rather than *Number*. Because the numbers are used only as a way to identify students—and not used for mathematical calculations—they function more like text.

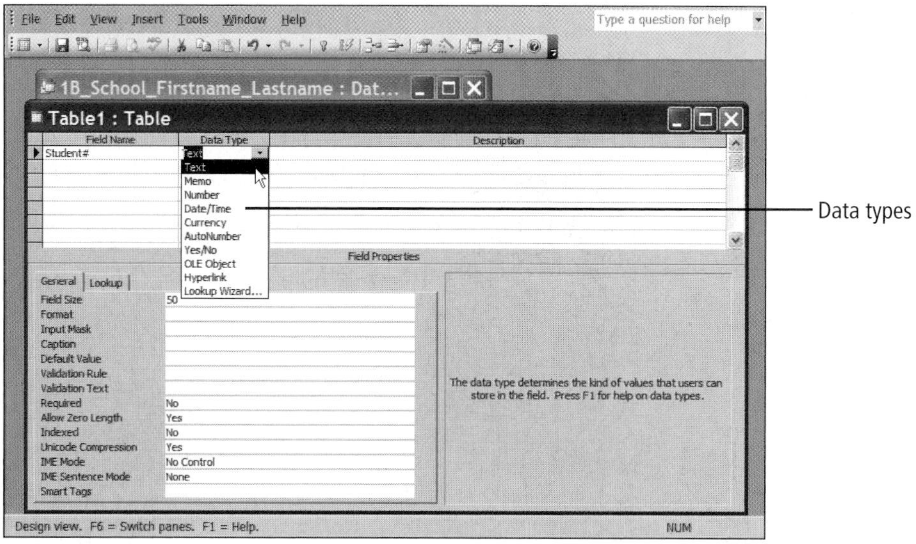

Figure 1.38

5 Press Tab to move the insertion point to the **Description** column.

Descriptions for fields in a table are not required. Include a description if the Field Name does not provide an obvious description of the field. In this instance, the field name *Student#* is self-explanatory, so no additional description is necessary.

6 Press Tab again to move the insertion point down and prepare to enter the next field name.

7 Using the technique you just practiced, add the fields shown in the Figure 1.39.

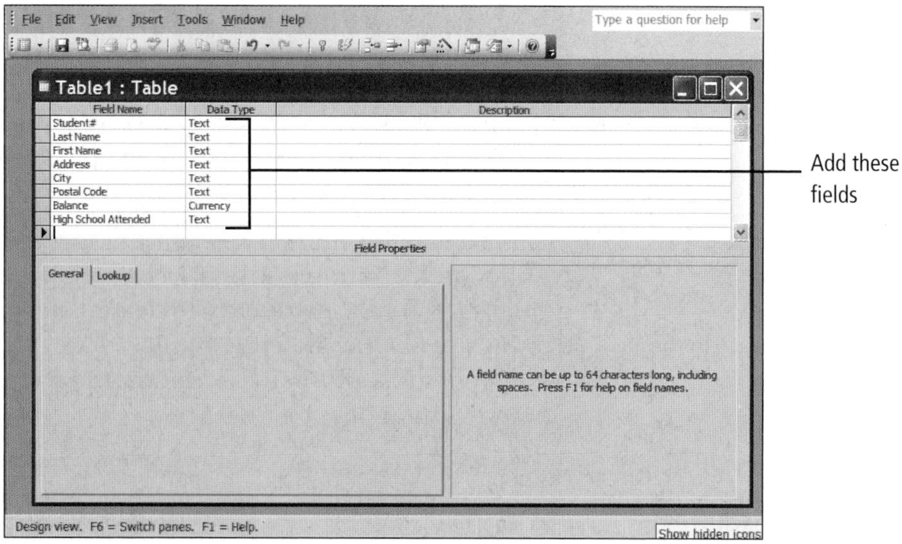

Figure 1.39

Another Way

Creating a New Table in a Database

There are three ways to create a new table in a database:

- Create a table in Design view by creating and naming the fields (columns).
- Create a table using a wizard, a process that helps you, step-by-step, to create the table.
- Create a table by typing data directly into an empty table in the Datasheet view, creating the column (field) names as you do so.

Activity 1.11 Switching Between Views

By naming and defining the data types for the fields, you have determined the number and type of pieces of information that you will have for each student's record in your database. In this activity, you will add the student records to the database. You will use the method of typing records directly into the Datasheet view of the table. You will learn other ways to enter records as your study of Access progresses.

1 On the Table Design toolbar, click the **View** button, as shown in Figure 1.40.

A message displays indicating that you must save the table before this action can be completed. See Figure 1.41.

View button

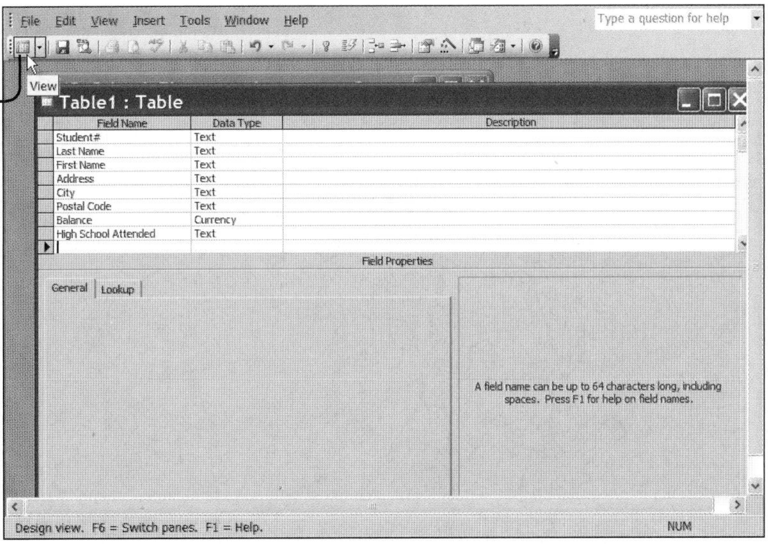

Figure 1.40

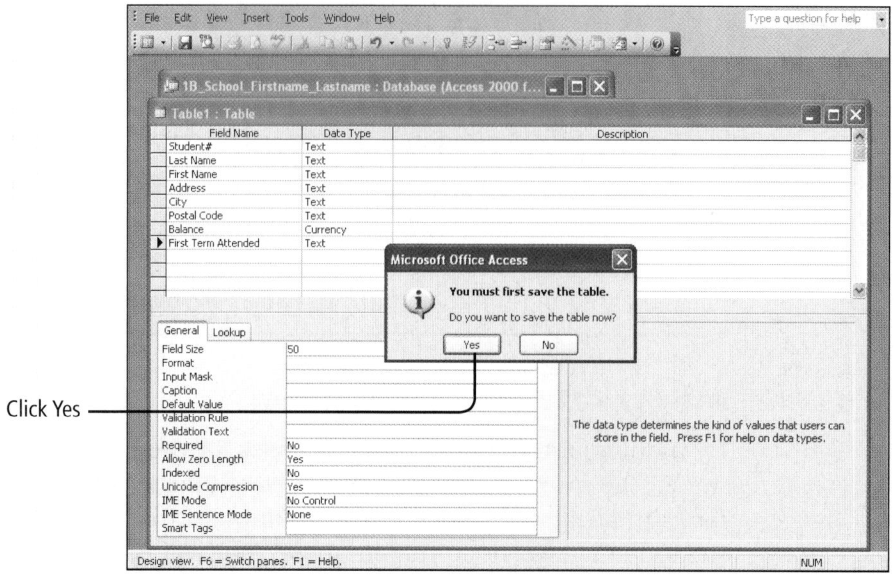

Figure 1.41

2 Click **Yes**.

3 In the displayed **Save As** dialog box, in the **Table Name** box, use your own first and last name and type **1B Students Firstname Lastname** and then click **OK**.

The message *There is no primary key defined* displays.

4 Click **No**.

The Datasheet view displays. You will add a primary key to the table in the next activity.

Note — Varying Toolbar Names

Toolbar name changes depending on view.

In Access, the name used to refer to the toolbar changes, depending on the current view of the database object. When a table is displayed in the Design view, the toolbar below the menu bar is referred to as the Table Design toolbar.

Objective 5
Create a Primary Key and Add Records to a Table

A ***primary key*** is a field that uniquely identifies a record in a table. For example, in a college registration system, your student number uniquely identifies you—no other student at the college has your exact student number. Two students at your college could have the exact same name, for example, *David Michaels*, but each would have a different and unique student number. Designating a field as a primary key ensures that you do not enter the same record more than once, because primary keys do not permit duplicate entries within the database.

Activity 1.12 Creating a Primary Key in a Table

If Access creates a primary key for you, as it prompted you to do in the previous activity, Access will add an additional field with a Data Type of

AutoNumber. AutoNumber assigns a number to each record as it is entered into the database. AutoNumber fields are convenient as a primary key for a database where the records have no unique field—such as the CDs in your CD collection. When each record in your table already has a unique number, such as a Student#, you will want to define that as your primary key.

1. On the Table Datasheet toolbar, click the **View** button to switch to the Design view of your Students table.

   When a table is displayed in the Datasheet view, the toolbar is referred to as the *Table Datasheet toolbar*.

2. Click to position the insertion point anywhere in the Field Name for **Student#**.

3. On the toolbar, click the **Primary Key** button, as shown in Figure 1.42.

   The Primary Key image displays to the left of the Student# field.

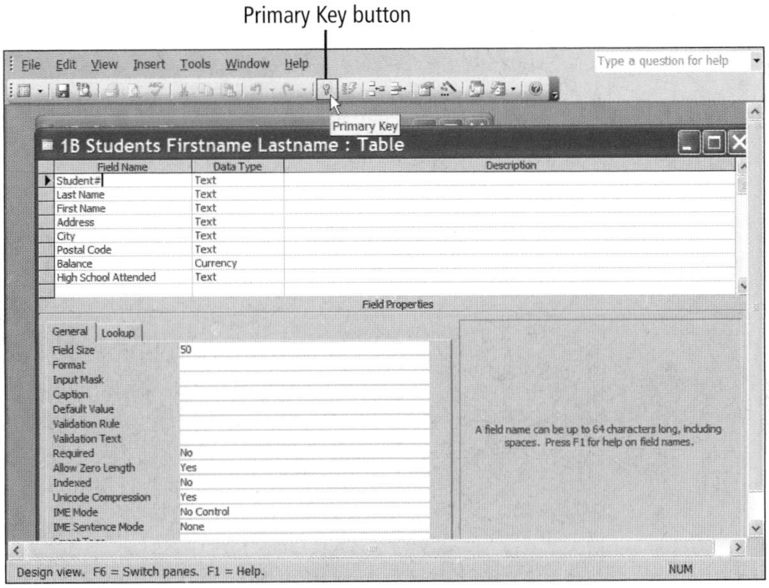

Figure 1.42

Alert!

Does Your Screen Differ?

If you attached the Primary Key to the wrong Field Name, move to the toolbar and then click the Primary Key button again. The Primary Key image will be removed and you can click the correct field name.

4. On the toolbar, click the **View** button to switch back to the Datasheet view. When prompted, click **Yes** to save the change you have made to the table.

Activity 1.13 Adding Records to a Table

1. With your table in Datasheet view, make sure your insertion point is in the **Student#** column and then type **54783**
2. Press Tab to move to the **Last Name** column and then type **Williams**
3. Press Tab, and then, in the **First Name** column, type **Pat**
4. Continue in this manner until the remainder of the information for Pat Williams is entered as the first record in the Students table shown in Figure 1.43. Press Tab after you enter the information for each column.

> ## **Note — Entering Currency Data**
>
> ***Type only the whole number.***
>
> When you enter the information in the Balance column, you only need to type in the whole number, for example, 42, for the Balance in the Pat Williams record. After you press Tab, Access will add the dollar sign, decimal point, and two decimal places to the entry in that column. The reason for this is that the Balance field has a data type of Currency.

As you type, do not be alarmed if it appears that your entries will not fit into the columns in the table. The widths of the columns in the figure have been adjusted so that you can view the data that is to be entered.

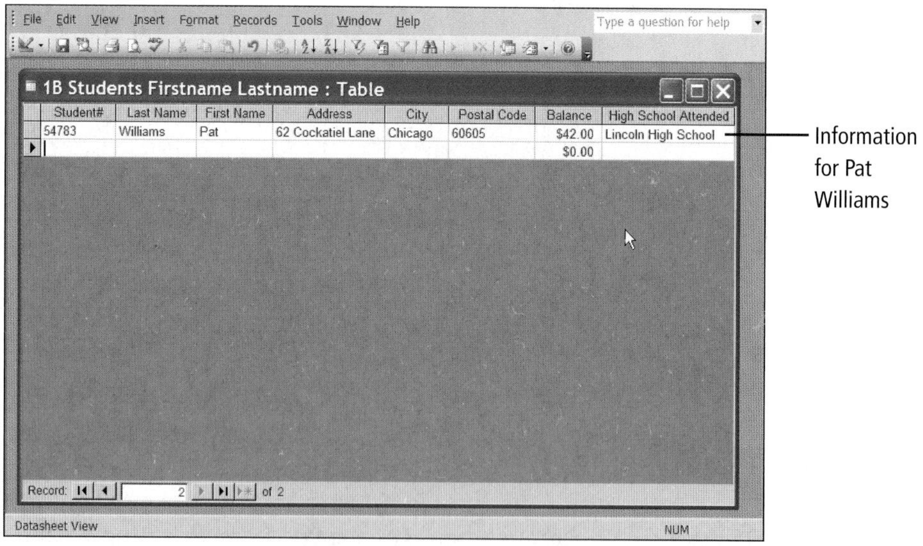

Figure 1.43

5 Continue entering the remaining seven records shown in Figure 1.44.

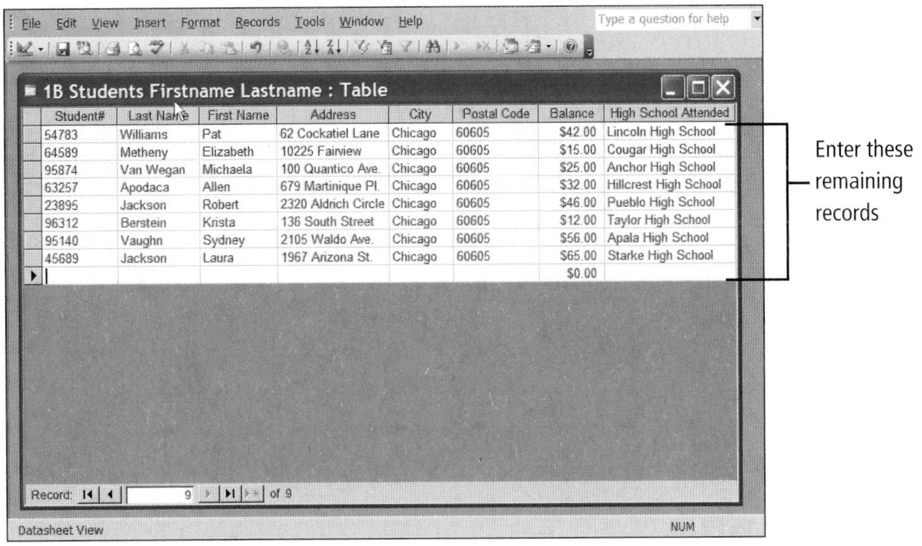

Student#	Last Name	First Name	Address	City	Postal Code	Balance	High School Attended
54783	Williams	Pat	62 Cockatiel Lane	Chicago	60605	$42.00	Lincoln High School
64589	Metheny	Elizabeth	10225 Fairview	Chicago	60605	$15.00	Cougar High School
95874	Van Wegan	Michaela	100 Quantico Ave.	Chicago	60605	$25.00	Anchor High School
63257	Apodaca	Allen	679 Martinique Pl.	Chicago	60605	$32.00	Hillcrest High School
23895	Jackson	Robert	2320 Aldrich Circle	Chicago	60605	$46.00	Pueblo High School
96312	Berstein	Krista	136 South Street	Chicago	60605	$12.00	Taylor High School
95140	Vaughn	Sydney	2105 Waldo Ave.	Chicago	60605	$56.00	Apala High School
45689	Jackson	Laura	1967 Arizona St.	Chicago	60605	$65.00	Starke High School
						$0.00	

Figure 1.44

Objective 6
Close and Save a Table

When you close a table object, Access saves any additions or changes you made to the records or fields. You do not have to initiate a Save operation.

Activity 1.14 Closing and Saving a Table

1 In the upper right corner of the Table window, click the **Close** button [X]. See Figure 1.45.

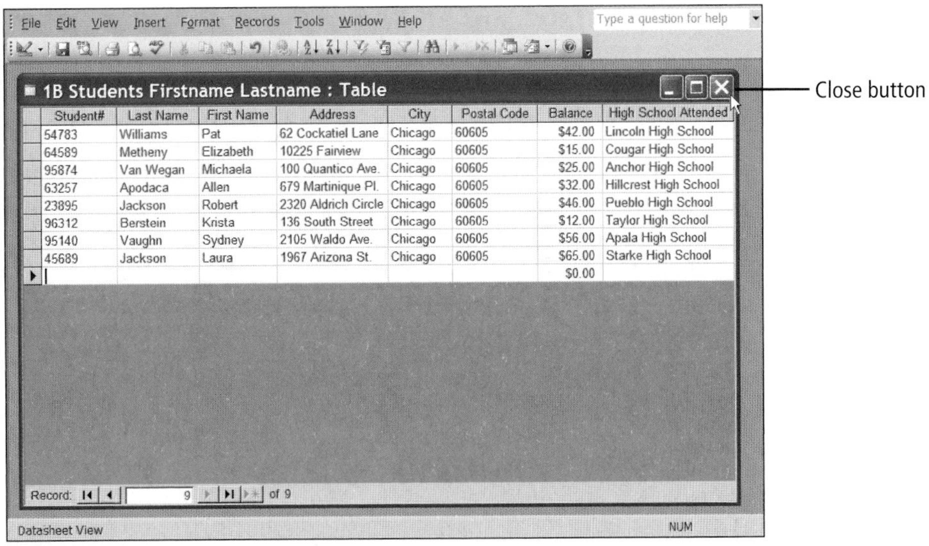

Student#	Last Name	First Name	Address	City	Postal Code	Balance	High School Attended
54783	Williams	Pat	62 Cockatiel Lane	Chicago	60605	$42.00	Lincoln High School
64589	Metheny	Elizabeth	10225 Fairview	Chicago	60605	$15.00	Cougar High School
95874	Van Wegan	Michaela	100 Quantico Ave.	Chicago	60605	$25.00	Anchor High School
63257	Apodaca	Allen	679 Martinique Pl.	Chicago	60605	$32.00	Hillcrest High School
23895	Jackson	Robert	2320 Aldrich Circle	Chicago	60605	$46.00	Pueblo High School
96312	Berstein	Krista	136 South Street	Chicago	60605	$12.00	Taylor High School
95140	Vaughn	Sydney	2105 Waldo Ave.	Chicago	60605	$56.00	Apala High School
45689	Jackson	Laura	1967 Arizona St.	Chicago	60605	$65.00	Starke High School
						$0.00	

Figure 1.45

The table is closed and the records you entered are saved. Your Students table displays in the Database window. See Figure 1.46.

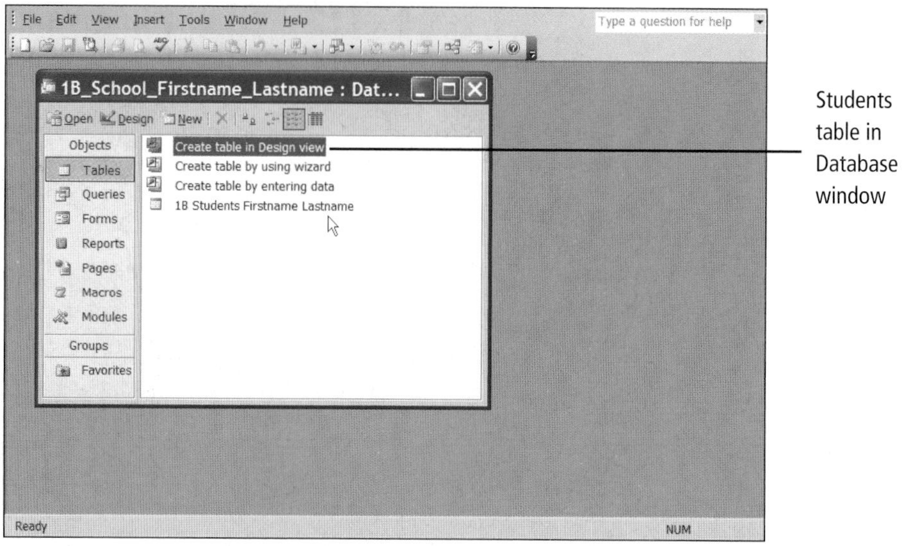

Figure 1.46

Objective 7
Open a Table

There are multiple ways to perform tasks in Access. You can open a table in Design view or Datasheet view, depending on what action you want to perform on the table. For example, if you want to view, add, delete, or modify records, use the Datasheet view. If you want to view, add, delete, or modify the field information (such as field name), use the Design view.

Activity 1.15 Opening a Table

1. In the Database window, double-click your **1B Students** table.

   The table opens in Datasheet view, but the records do not display in the same order in which you entered them. Rather, Access has placed the records in sequential order according to the Primary key field.

2. Click the **Close** button in the upper right corner of the table window to close the table.

   The Database window displays.

3. If necessary, click your **1B Students** table once to select it, and then just above the Objects bar, click the **Open** button in the Database window.

   The table opens again in Datasheet view. This is another method to open a table in the Datasheet view.

4. In the upper right corner of the table window, click the **Close** button to close the table and display the Database window.

5 Open the table in Design view by clicking your **1B Students** table once (it may already be selected), and then clicking the **Design** button  in the area above the Objects bar. See Figure 1.47. Alternatively, you can right-click the table name and then click Design View from the displayed shortcut menu.

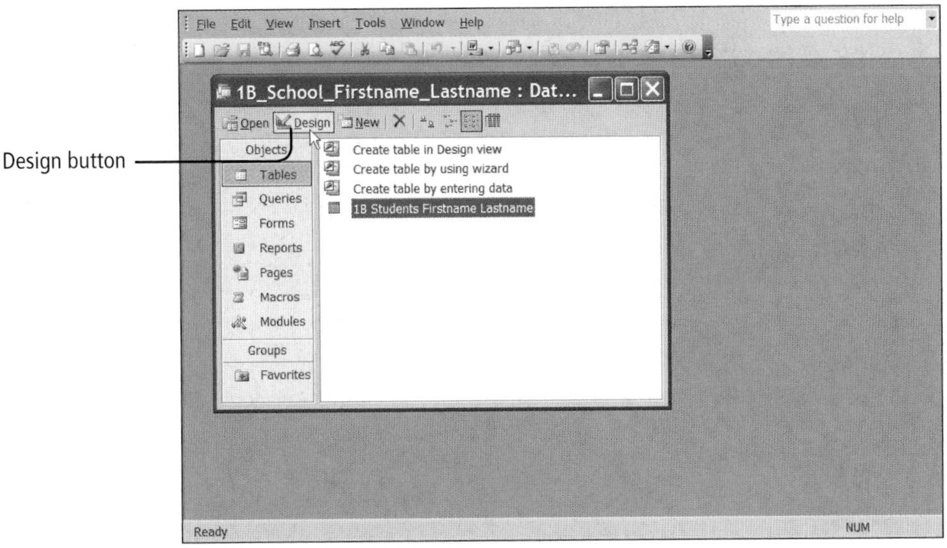

Figure 1.47

6 Leave the table open in Design view for the next activity.

Objective 8
Modify the Table Design

An early consideration when creating a new table is the number and content of the fields in the table. This is referred to as the table's ***design***. For example, when setting up an address book database, you will want to have fields for name, address, home phone number, and so forth. After you begin entering records, you might realize that you should have included a field for a cell phone number, too. Fortunately, Access lets you add or delete fields at any time.

Activity 1.16 Deleting Fields

If you decide that a field in your database is no longer useful to you, you can delete that field from the table.

1 In the Design view of your **1B Students** table**,** position your mouse pointer in the row selector at the far left, next to **High School Attended** field.

The pointer changes to a right-pointing arrow. See Figure 1.48.

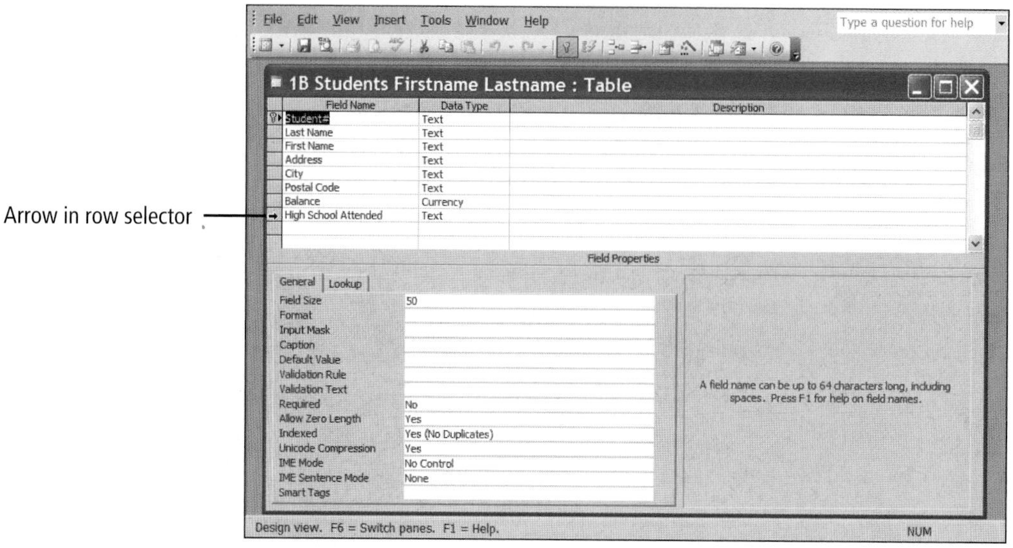

Figure 1.48

2 Click to select the row **High School Attended** and then press [Delete].

A message displays asking whether or not you want to permanently delete the field. See Figure 1.49.

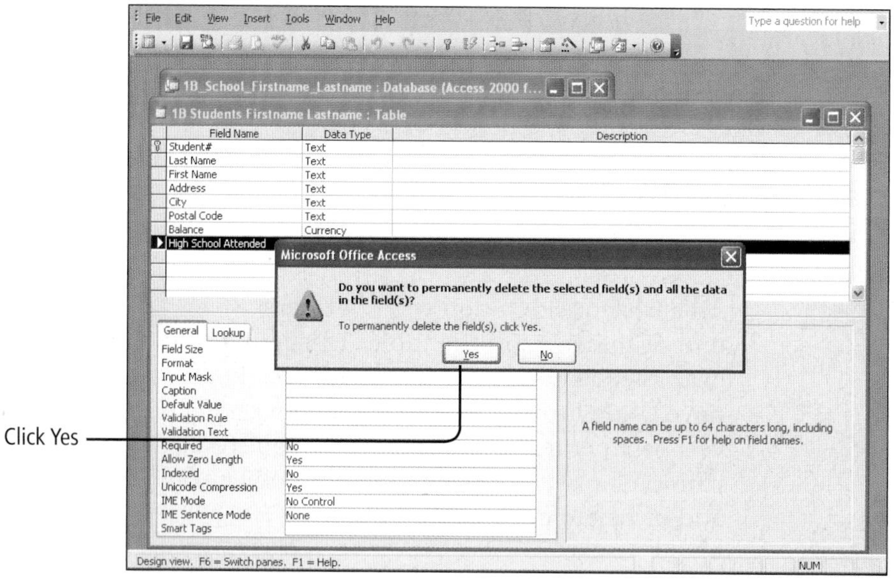

Figure 1.49

3 Click **Yes** to delete the field.

The High School Attended field is deleted. Deleting the field also deletes any data in the field of each record. Later, you could add the field back if you decide to do so, but you would have to re-enter the field's data for each record.

4 Pause your mouse pointer in the title bar area of the table and right-click. On the displayed shortcut menu, click **Datasheet view**, and when prompted, click **Yes** to save the table. This is another way to switch back to Datasheet view.

The High School Attended field no longer displays in the Datasheet view of the table.

5 On the toolbar, click the **View** button to switch back to Design view.

Activity 1.17 Adding Fields

If you decide to add a field to the table, you can add the field and then, for each record, enter data into the field.

1 At the bottom of the list of fields, click in the next available **Field Name** box, type **First Term Attended** and then press Tab two times.

The default text data type is accepted and the description column is left empty.

2 Use any method to switch back to Datasheet view, and when prompted, click **Yes** to save the table. Notice the new column for the field you just added.

3 For each record, enter the information shown in Figure 1.50 for the **First Term Attended** field.

> **Note — Using Long Column Headings**
>
> *Adjust them later.*
>
> The column heading for the First Term Attended field may not display entirely. You will adjust this in a later step.

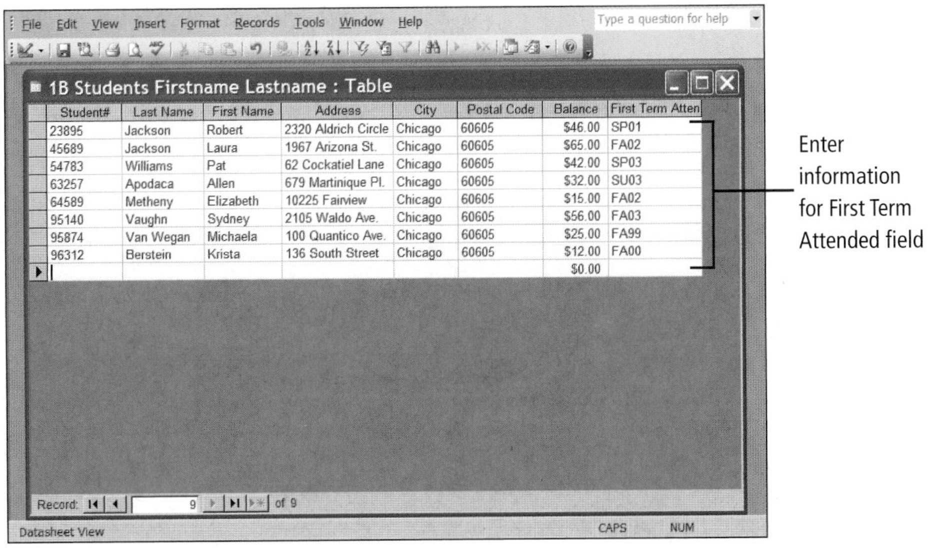

Figure 1.50

Objective 9
Print a Table

There are multiple ways to print objects in Access. The quickest way to print a database table is to click the Print button on the Database toolbar. This will print one complete copy of the table on the default printer. If you want to print anything other than one complete copy, for example, multiple copies or only selected pages, or to select a different printer, you must initiate the Print command from the File menu.

Activity 1.18 Printing a Table

Although a printed table is not as professional or formal looking as a report, there are times when you may want to print your table in this manner as a quick reference or for proofreading.

1. If necessary, open your **1B Students** table in the Datasheet view.
2. On the toolbar, locate but do not click the **Print** button.

   You could print the table without opening the table by selecting the table from the Database window, and then clicking the Print button on the toolbar. This method does not offer you an opportunity to change anything about the way the table prints.

3. With your **1B Students** table still open, display the **File** menu and then click **Print**.

   The Print dialog box displays. Here you can make changes to your print settings. See Figure 1.51.

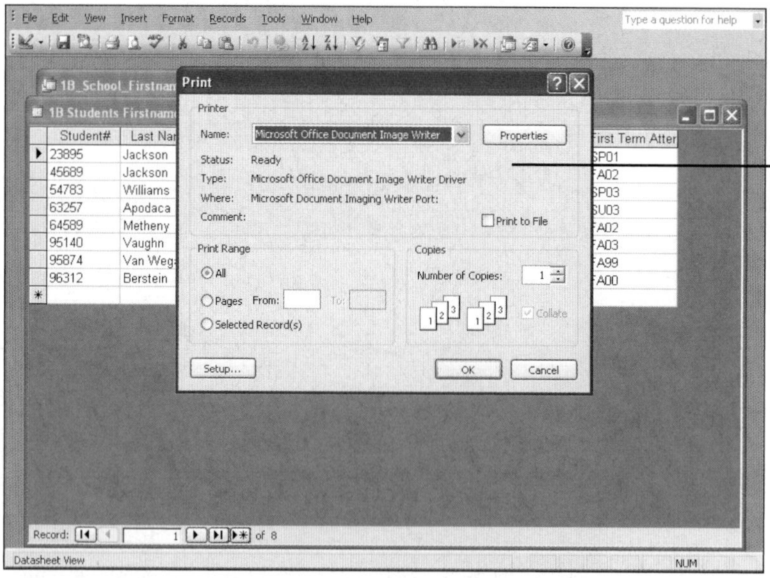

Print dialog box

Figure 1.51

4 In the upper right corner next to the printer name, click the **Properties** button.

The Properties dialog box displays. See Figure 1.52. Because the settings for printer models vary, your Properties box may display differently than that shown in the figure.

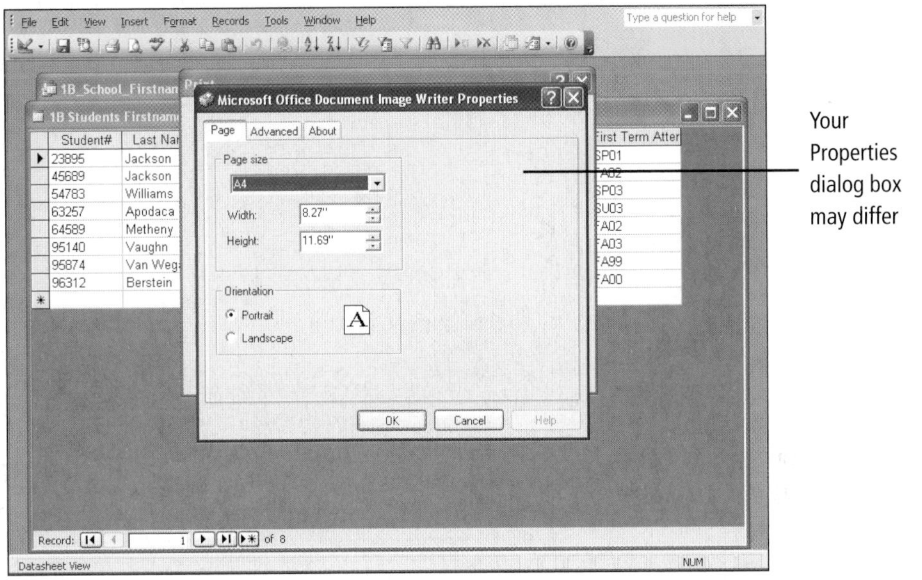

Figure 1.52

By default, Access prints in ***Portrait orientation***—the printed page is taller than it is high. An alternate orientation is ***Landscape orientation***—the printed page is wider than it is tall.

5 Locate and then click **Landscape**. See Figure 1.53. The properties for printer models vary somewhat. You may have to locate the Landscape orientation on a different tab of your printer Properties dialog box, and thus your screen will differ from the figure shown.

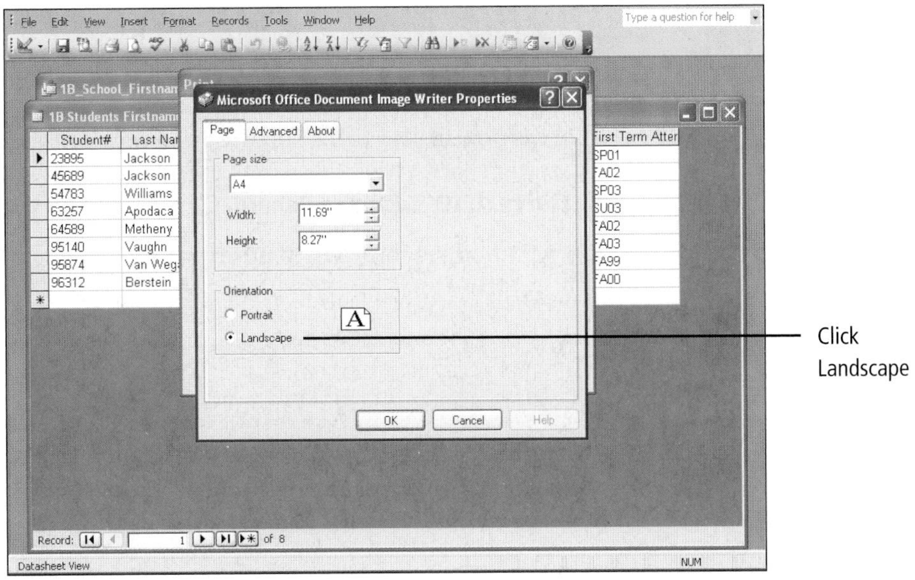

Figure 1.53

6 Click the **OK** button.

7 In the lower left corner of the **Print** dialog box, click the **Setup** button.

The Page Setup dialog box displays with margins set to 1 inch on the Top, Bottom, Left, and Right of the page. See Figure 1.54.

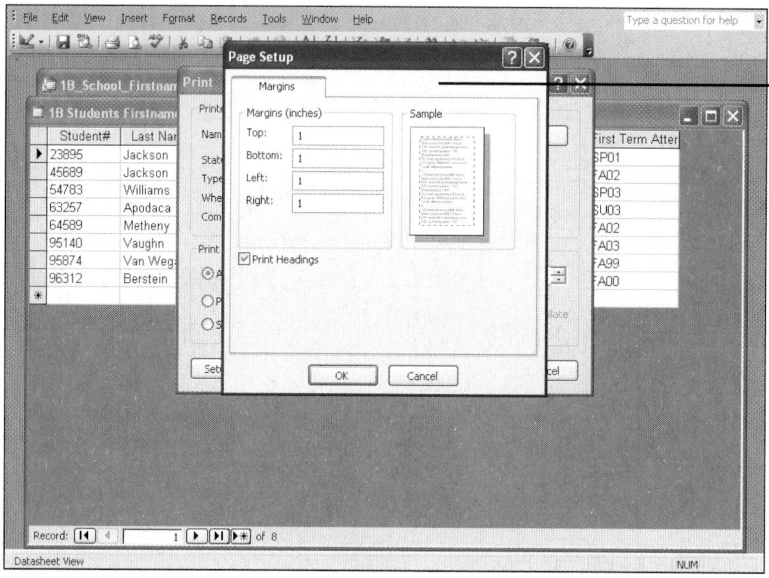

Figure 1.54

8 Click **OK** to accept the default settings.

9 In the Print dialog box, click **OK**.

Your table prints, and your name is printed at the top of the page in the table name.

Objective 10
Edit Records in a Table

When necessary, you will edit (change) the information in a record. For example, you may realize that you made an error when you entered the information in the table, or the information has changed.

Activity 1.19 Editing a Record

1 Make sure your **1B Students** table is open in Datasheet view.

2 Locate the record for **Pat Williams**. In the **Address** field, click to position the insertion point to the right of *62*. See Figure 1.55.

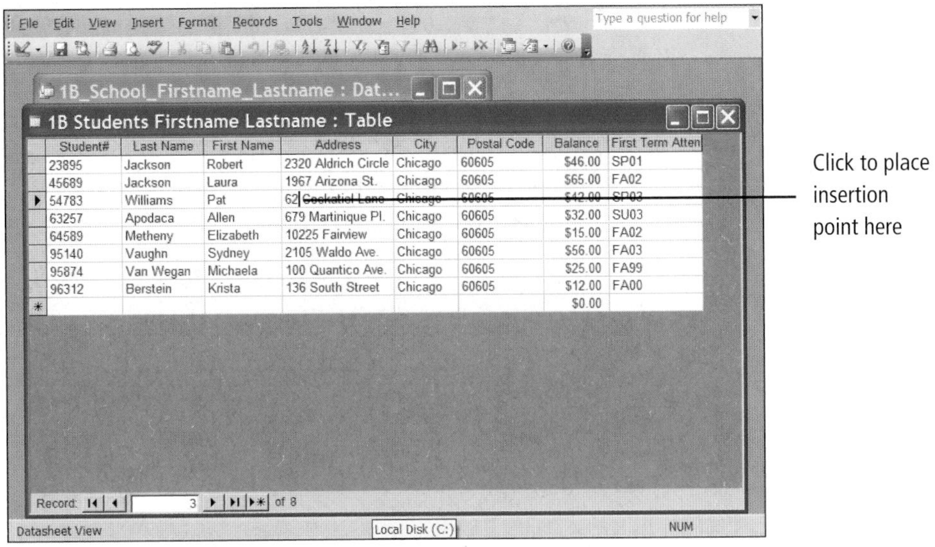

Figure 1.55

3 Type **5** and then press [Tab].

The address for Pat Williams is changed to *625 Cockatiel Lane*. Leave the Students table open.

Activity 1.20 Deleting a Record

Keeping a database up to date means that you may have to delete records when they are no longer needed. In this activity, you will delete the record for Sydney Vaughn, which was mistakenly included in the Students table—she is not a student.

1 Be sure your **1B Students** table is open in Datasheet view.

2 Locate the record for **Sydney Vaughn**, position the mouse pointer in the row selector for Sydney Vaughn's record until it takes the shape of a right-pointing arrow, and then click to select the row.

The entire record is selected. See Figure 1.56.

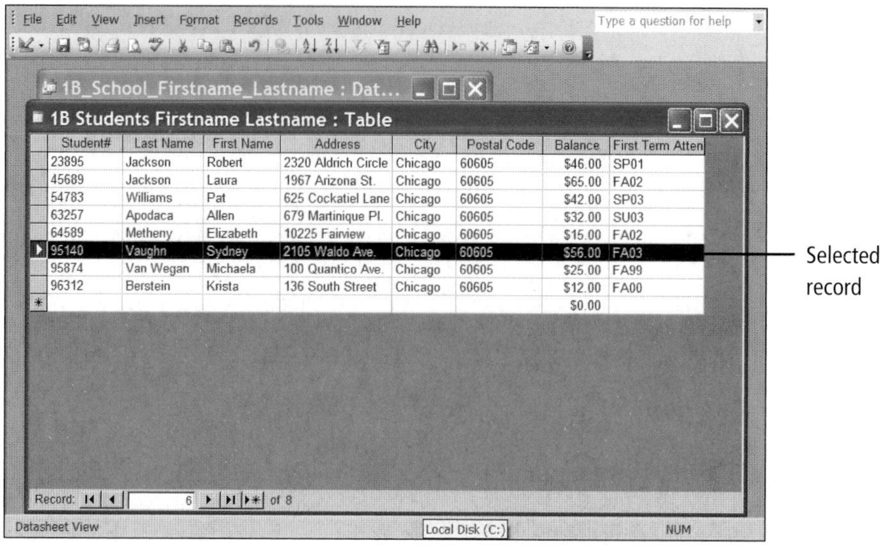

Figure 1.56

3. On the toolbar click the **Delete Record** button. Alternatively, you could press Delete on the keyboard.

   A message displays alerting you that you are about to delete a record. If you click Yes and delete the record, you cannot use the Undo button to reverse the action. If you delete a record by mistake, you will have to re-create the record.

4. Click **Yes** to delete the record.

   The record is deleted from the 1B Students table.

Activity 1.21 Resizing Columns and Rows

You can adjust the size of columns and rows in a table. Sometimes this is necessary to get a better view of the data. Column widths and row heights are adjusted by dragging the borders between the columns or rows. Reducing the column width allows you to display more fields on your screen at one time. Increasing the width of a column allows you to view data that is too long to display in the column.

Adjusting the size of columns and rows does not change the data contained in the table's records. It changes only your *view* of the data.

1. Be sure your **1B Students** table is open in Datasheet view.

2. In the gray row of column headings, pause your mouse pointer over the vertical line between the **Address** column and the **City** column until it becomes a double-headed arrow, as shown in Figure 1.57.

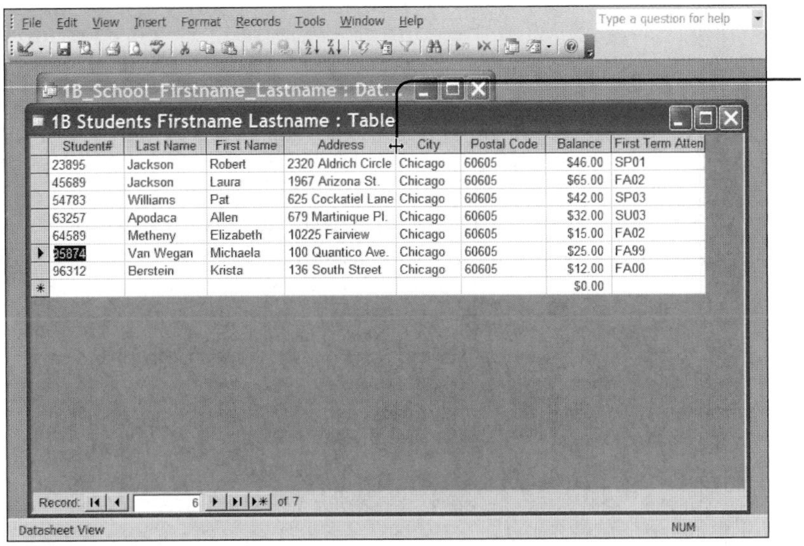

Figure 1.57

3 Press and hold the left mouse button and drag the line in between the columns to the right approximately 0.5 inch. The measurement need not be precise; use your eye to judge this. Release the mouse button.

The column's width is increased.

4 In the gray column headings, point to the vertical bar between the **Address** column heading and the **City** column heading until the double-headed arrow displays, and then double-click.

Access adjusts the width of the Address column to accommodate the widest entry in the column. Use this as a quick method to adjust columns to accommodate the widest entry in a column.

5 In the row of column headings, pause the mouse pointer over the **Student#** column heading until the mouse pointer becomes a downward-pointing black arrow. Then drag to the right until all of the columns are selected. See Figure 1.58.

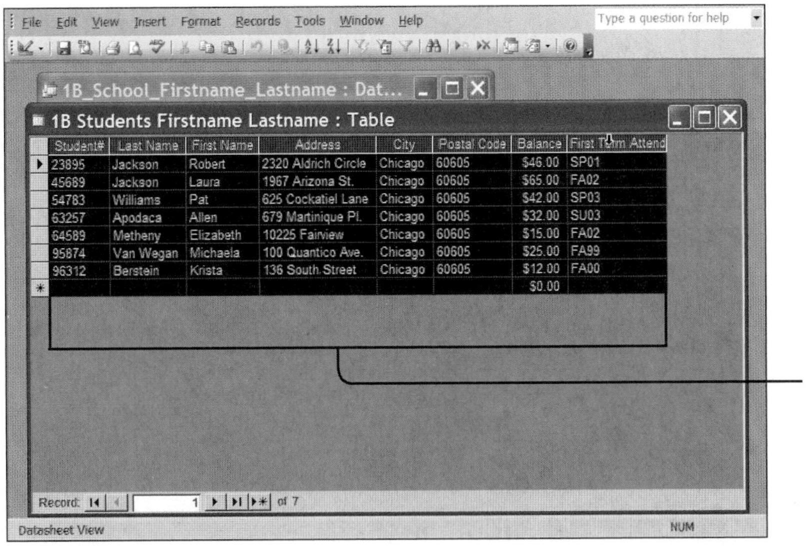

Figure 1.58

6 With the columns selected, pause your mouse pointer over the vertical line between any of the column headings until the mouse pointer takes the shape of a double-headed arrow, and then double-click.

All of the columns are resized to accommodate the widest entry in each column. In some instances, the widest entry is the column heading, for example, *First Term Attended*. Use this method as a quick way to adjust the widths of several columns at once.

7 Click anywhere in the table to deselect the table.

8 To adjust row height, point to the horizontal line between the second and third record until the double-headed arrow displays. See Figure 1.59.

Pause mouse pointer here

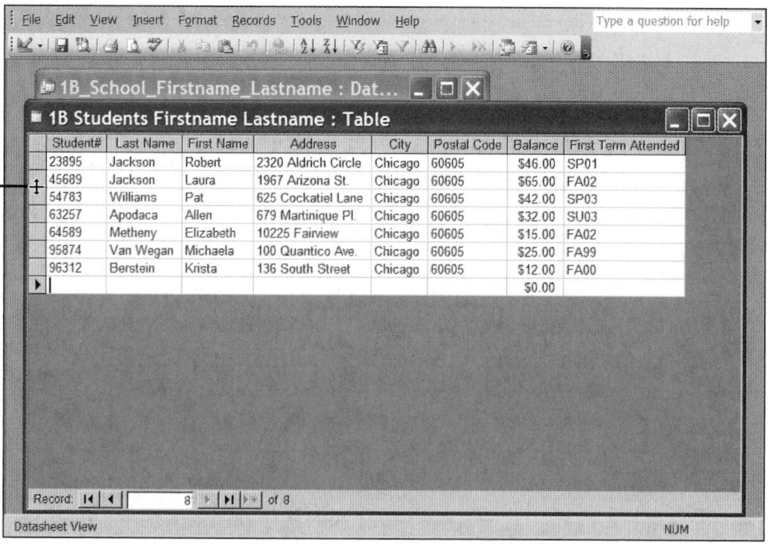

Figure 1.59

9 Drag the horizontal line down approximately 0.5 inch. The exact measurement is not important. Use your eye to judge the distance. Release the mouse button.

The height of all of the rows is increased by the same amount. Adjusting the row height enables you to see long names that may have wrapped to two lines in a column—and still have many columns visible on the screen.

10 On the menu bar, click **Format** and then click **Row Height**.

The Row Height dialog box displays. Here you can return row heights to their default setting or enter a precise number for the height of the row.

11 Select the **Standard Height** check box and then click **OK**. See Figure 1.60.

The height of all rows is restored to the default setting. Use this dialog box to set the rows to any height.

Standard Height check box

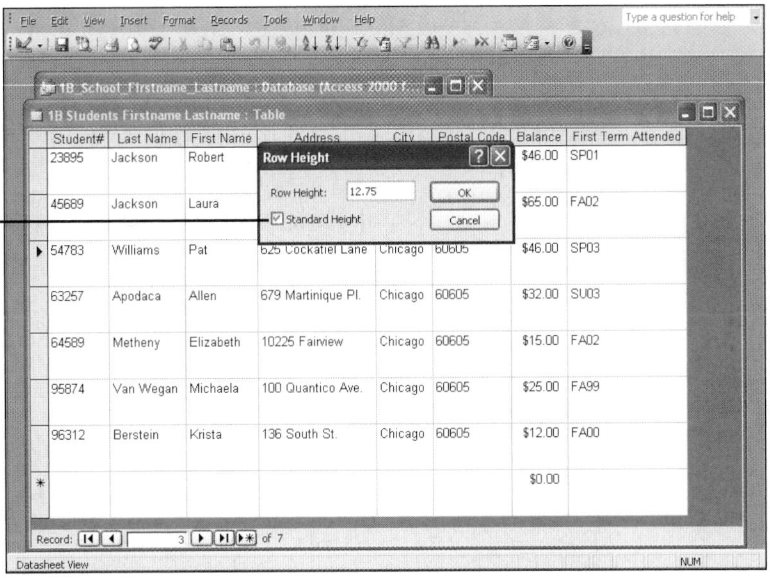

Figure 1.60

Activity 1.22 Hiding Columns

When a table contains many fields (columns), you can temporarily hide one or more columns so that you can get a better view of other columns.

1 Click to position your insertion point anywhere in the **City** column, display the **Format** menu, and then click **Hide Columns**.

The City column is hidden from view, and the columns to the right of the City column shift to the left. Hidden columns and the data that they contain are not deleted—they are merely hidden from view.

2 From the **Format** menu, click **Unhide Columns**. See Figure 1.61.

The Unhide Columns dialog box displays. All of the columns except the City column are checked, indicating that they are in view.

Unhide Columns option on Format menu

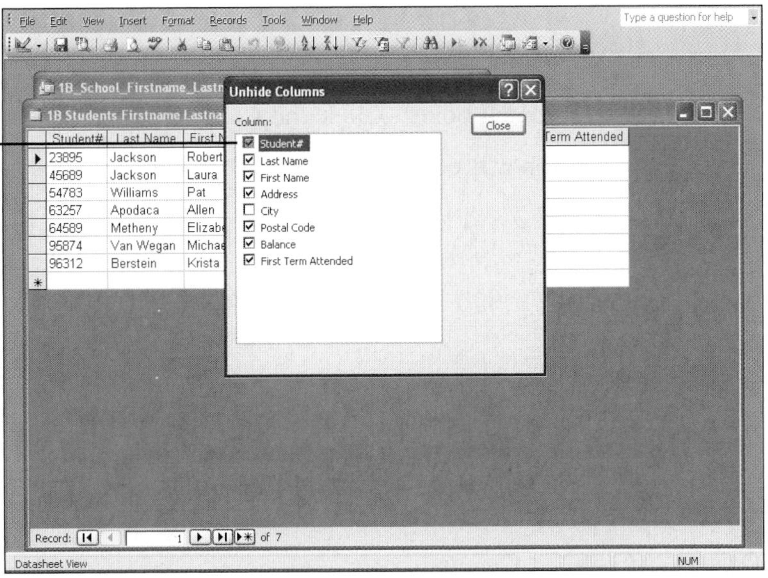

Figure 1.61

3 Select the **City** check box and then click the **Close** button.

The City column returns to view.

4 Click the column heading **City**, press and hold Shift, and then click the column heading **Balance**.

The City, Postal Code, and Balance columns are selected.

You can hide two or more *adjacent* columns (columns that are next to each other) at one time. If you select a column and then select another column while holding Shift, those columns are selected in addition to any columns between them.

5 With the three columns selected, display the **Format** menu, and then click **Hide Columns**. See Figure 1.62.

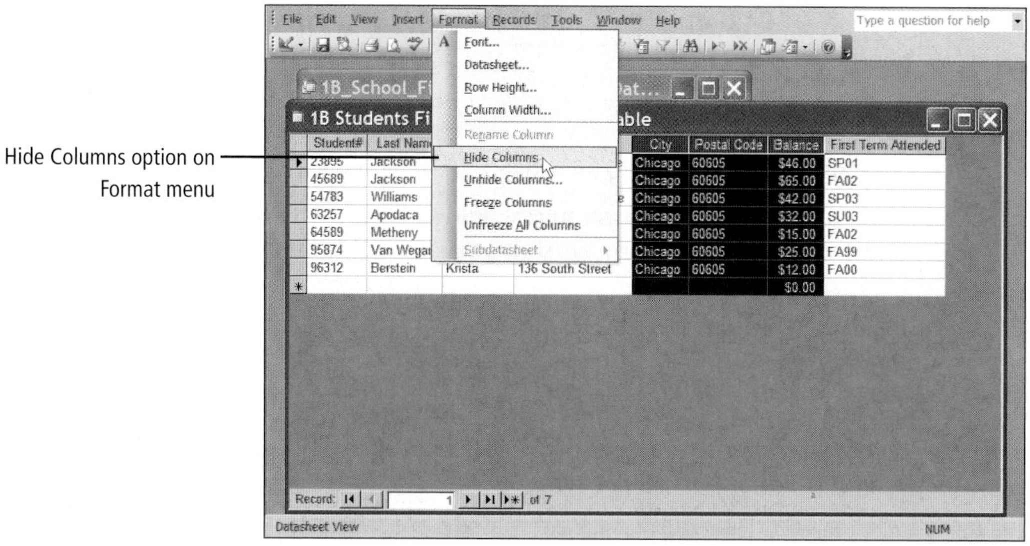

Figure 1.62

The City, Postal Code, and Balance columns are hidden.

6 To unhide the columns, display the **Format** menu, click **Unhide Columns**, and then select the **City**, **Postal Code**, and the **Balance** check boxes. Click the **Close** button.

The three columns are returned to view in your 1B Students table.

Objective 11
Sort Records

Sorting records in a table is the process of rearranging records in a specific order. For example, you could sort the names in your address book database alphabetically by each person's last name, or you could sort your CD collection database by the date of purchase.

Activity 1.23 Sorting Records in a Table

Information stored in an Access table can be sorted in either ***ascending order*** or ***descending order***. Ascending order sorts text alphabetically (A to Z) and sorts numbers from the lowest number to the highest number. Descending order sorts text in reverse alphabetic order (Z to A) and sorts numbers from the highest number to the lowest.

1 Be sure your **1B Students** table is open in the Datasheet view.

2 Click anywhere in the **Last Name** column and then on the toolbar click the **Sort Ascending** button. See Figure 1.63.

The records are sorted in ascending order according to each Student's Last Name.

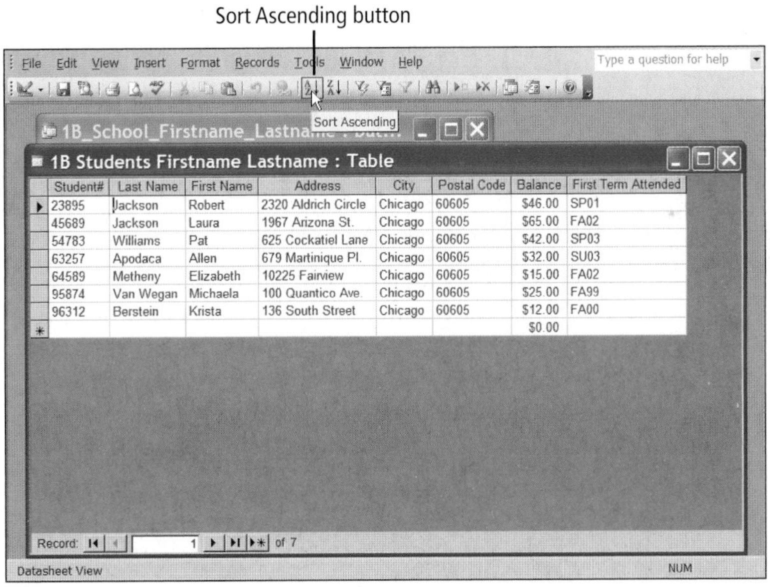

Figure 1.63

3 Click anywhere in the **First Name** column and then on the toolbar click the **Sort Ascending** button.

The records are sorted in ascending order according to each student's First Name.

4 Click the column heading **Last Name**, press and hold Shift, and then click the column heading **First Name**.

Both the Last Name column and the First Name column are selected.

Information in an Access table can be sorted using more than one field. For example, data can be sorted by the ***primary sort field***—the field that Access sorts by initially—and then, for any records having an identical primary sort field, records are sorted further by the ***secondary sort field***—the field that Access uses to sort records that have matching primary sort fields.

5 On the toolbar, click the **Sort Ascending** button.

The records are sorted alphabetically by Last Name. Within records that have identical last names, for example, *Jackson*, the records are sorted alphabetically by First Name.

Access sorts the records consecutively from left to right, meaning any fields that you want to sort *must* be adjacent to each other, and your primary sort field (*Last Name* in this example) must be to the left of the secondary sort field (*First Name* in this example).

6 Look at the two records for which the last name is **Jackson**.

Notice that those two records are also sorted alphabetically by First Name—Laura comes before Robert.

7 On the menu bar, click **Records** and then click **Remove Filter/Sort**.

You can return your records to the original sort order at any time by selecting Remove Filter/Sort from the Records menu. In this instance, the original sort order is by primary key.

8 Leave your **1B Students** table open for the next activity.

Objective 12
Navigate to Records in a Table

The Students table that you created has only seven records, and you can see all of them on the screen. Most Access tables, however, contain many records—more than you can see on the screen at one time. Access provides several tools to help you navigate (move) among records in a table. For example, you can move the insertion point to the last record in a table or to the first record in a table, or move up one record at a time or down one record at a time.

Activity 1.24 Navigating Among Records Using the Navigation Area

Figure 1.64 illustrates the navigation functions in the navigation area of a table.

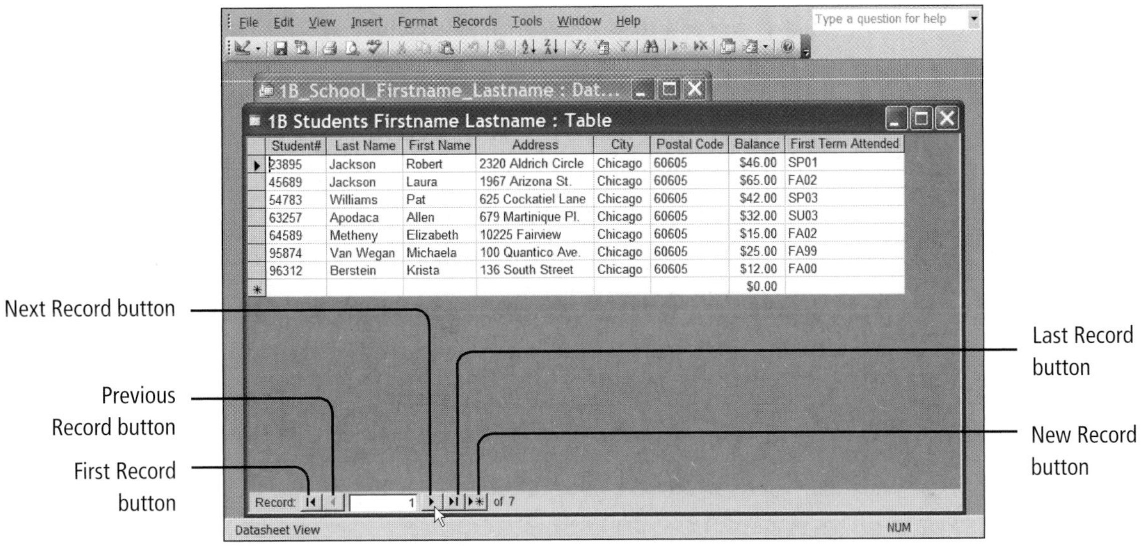

Figure 1.64

1. If necessary, open your **1B Students** table in Datasheet view.
2. Click anywhere in the first record of the table.
3. In the navigation area, click the **Next Record** button. See Figure 1.64.

   Depending on the field in which your insertion point was located, the next record in the table is selected, in the same field.
4. In the navigation area, click the **Last Record** button. See Figure 1.64.

   The last record in the table is selected.
5. Experiment with the different navigation buttons as shown in Figure 1.64.

Activity 1.25 Navigating Among Records Using the Keyboard

You can also navigate among records in a table using the keyboard. Figure 1.65 lists the keystrokes and the resulting movement.

Key Combinations for Navigating a Table

Keystroke	Movement
↑	Moves the selection up one record at a time.
↓	Moves the selection down one record at a time.
Page Up	Moves the selection up one screen at a time.
PageDown	Moves the selection down one screen at a time.
Ctrl + Home	Moves the selection to the first field in the table.
Ctrl + End	Moves the selection to the last field in the table.

Figure 1.65

1 If necessary, open your **1B Students** table in Datasheet view and click anywhere in any record except the last record.

2 Press [↓].

The selection moves down one record.

3 Experiment with the different navigation keystrokes.

4 Click the **Close** button [X] in the table window to close the **1B Students** table. Click **Yes** if you are prompted to save changes to the design of your table.

The Database window displays.

Objective 13
Close and Save a Database

When you close an Access table, any changes are saved automatically. At the end of your Access session, close your database and then close Access.

Activity 1.26 Closing and Saving a Database

1 In the smaller Database window, click the **Close** button [X].

The database closes. The Access program remains open. See Figure 1.66.

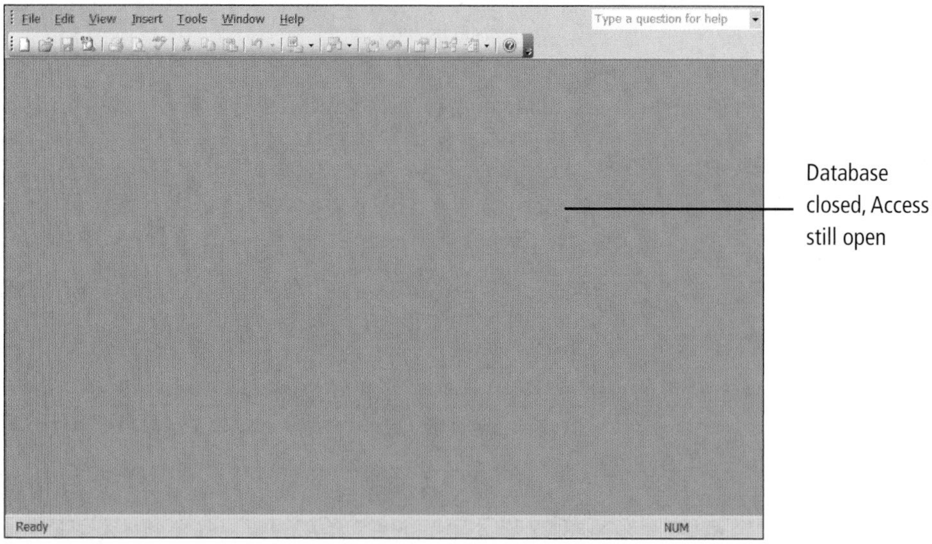

Figure 1.66

2 On the title bar of the Access window, click the **Close** button [X] to close the Access program.

Objective 14
Use the Access Help System

Access contains a Help feature designed to assist you when performing a task in Access or if you would like more information about a particular topic in Access. There are multiple ways to use the Help feature in Access, including the Office Assistant, and the Type a question for help box.

Activity 1.27 Using the Access Help System

The Office Assistant is an animated figure that displays to assist you with a task.

1. Start Access. On the menu bar, click **Help** and then click **Show the Office Assistant**.

   The Office Assistant character displays. The animated character may be a paperclip, or some other character.

2. Double-click the Office Assistant to display the **What would you like to do?** box.

3. With *Type your question here and then click Search* highlighted, type **How do I get help?** and then click **Search**.

4. In the **Search Results** task pane, click **About getting help while you work**. You may have to use the vertical scroll bar to see this topic.

   The Microsoft Access Help window displays with hyperlinks (usually in blue text) listed. Clicking on these hyperlinks will link you to additional information about the topic.

5. Click on the links that display and you will see the description of each of these expanded in the area below the link. For example, click **Microsoft Press** to expand the topic and then click it again to collapse it.

6 After viewing the Help topics, click the **Close** button ☒ to close the Help window. See Figure 1.67.

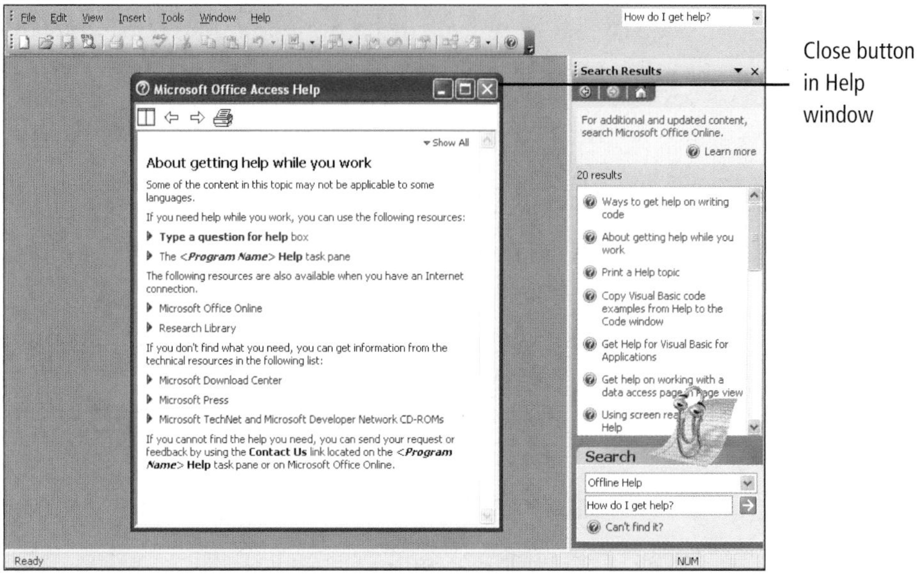

Figure 1.67

7 In the upper right corner of the Access window, locate the **Type a question for help** box and click it. See Figure 1.68.

The text in the box is selected.

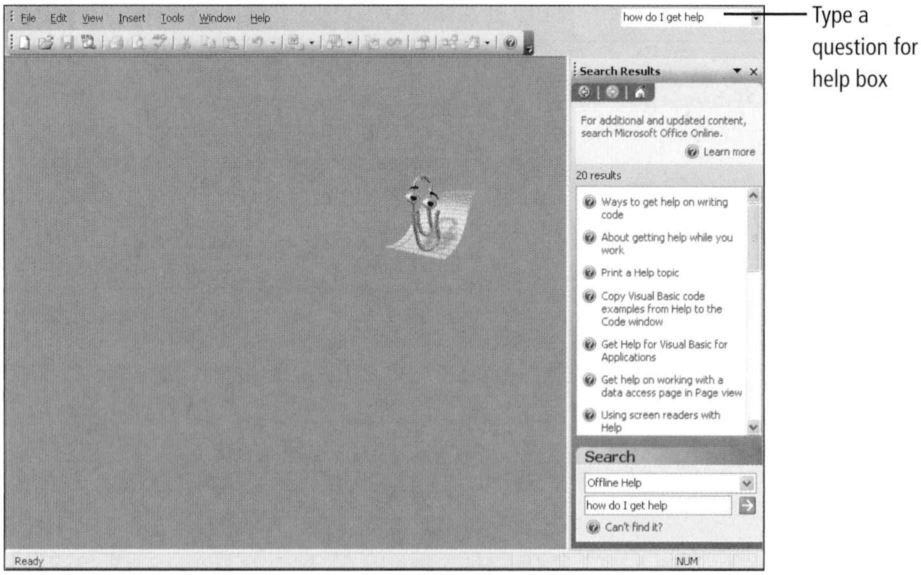

Figure 1.68

8 In the **Type a question for help** box, type **table**

9 Press Enter and click **About creating a table (MDB)**.

A window containing information about creating a table displays. See Figure 1.69. Keywords, identified in a different color, display additional information when they are clicked.

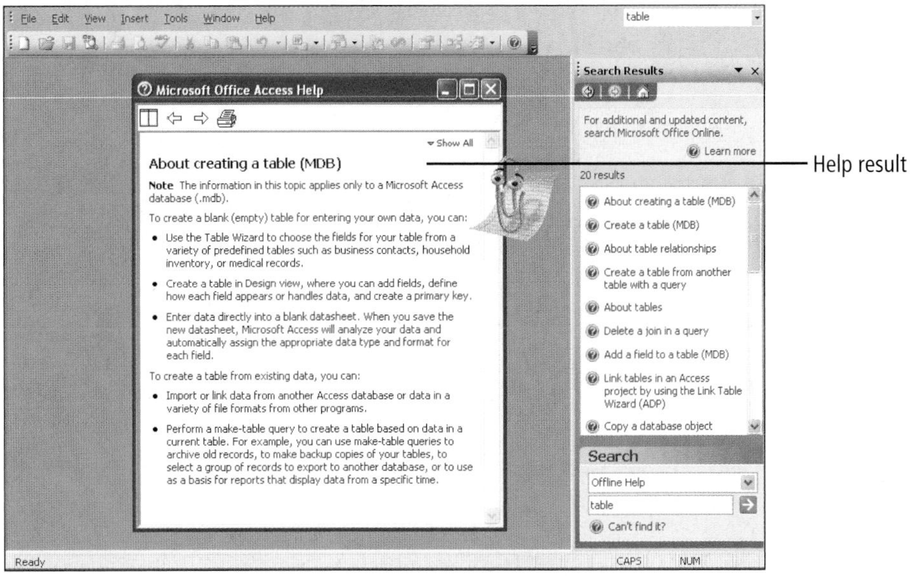

Figure 1.69

10 In the second bullet, click on the words **Design view**. Scroll down if necessary to view this description.

An explanation of Design View displays in green within the paragraph.

11 In the Microsoft Access Help window, on the toolbar, click the **Print** button. See Figure 1.70.

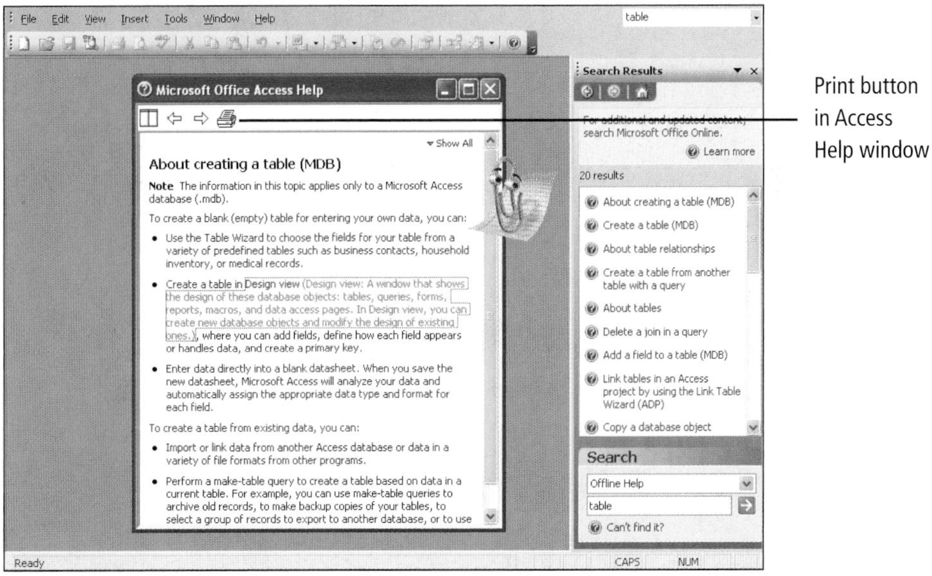

Figure 1.70

12 In the **Print** dialog box, click **Print** (or **OK**).

The Help topic you have displayed is printed. Keep this document for your reference.

13 Close the Microsoft Access Help window.

14 On the title bar of the Access window, click the **Close** button to close Access.

End **You have completed Project 1B**

Summary

Microsoft Access 2003 is a database management system. Databases help you organize information, such as the names and addresses in your address book, a CD collection, or a list of students at a college.

In an existing database, you can either view the information in the database or edit the information. Access contains tools, called objects, which enable you to enter information into a database, and then organize, manipulate, and analyze the information. Information in a database is stored in tables. The data in a table is organized by rows, called records, and columns, called fields. Each record in a table stores information about one database item.

Queries extract information from a table according to the criteria set for the query. Forms are another tool that you can use to either enter or view records—one record at a time. Reports are professional-looking documents that summarize the information in a table.

Information stored in a table can be edited and sorted. Access contains navigation tools to assist you in locating specific records.

In This Chapter You Practiced How To

- Rename a Database
- Start Access, Open an Existing Database, and View Database Objects
- Create a New Database
- Create a New Table
- Create a Primary Key and Add Records to a Table
- Close and Save a Table
- Open a Table
- Modify the Table Design
- Print a Table
- Edit Records in a Table
- Sort Records
- Navigate to Records in a Table
- Close and Save a Database
- Use the Access Help System

Concepts Assessments

Matching

Match each term in the second column with its correct definition in the first column by writing the letter of the term on the blank line in front of the correct definition.

____ **1.** A printing orientation in which the printed page is taller than it is high.

____ **2.** The field that serves as a unique identifier for records in a table.

____ **3.** The Access object that stores the information in a database.

____ **4.** The process of rearranging items in a specific order.

____ **5.** The Access object that displays records one at a time.

____ **6.** A sorting order in which records are sorted alphabetically from A to Z.

____ **7.** The process of pulling out information from a database according to specified criteria.

____ **8.** The Access object that displays selected fields and records in an easy-to-read format.

____ **9.** A printing orientation in which the printed page is wider than it is tall.

____ **10.** A window within a Microsoft Office application that provides commonly used commands.

____ **11.** The Access object that assists you in asking a question about the data.

____ **12.** A sorting order in which records are sorted alphabetically from Z to A.

____ **13.** Data that has been organized in a useful manner.

____ **14.** A collection of data related to a particular topic.

____ **15.** The collection of tools in Access used to enter and manipulate the data in a database.

A Ascending
B Database
C Descending
D Extracting
E Form
F Information
G Landscape
H Objects
I Portrait
J Primary key
K Query
L Report
M Sorting
N Table
O Task pane

Concepts Assessments (continued)

Fill in the Blank

Write the correct answer in the space provided.

1. Tables are the foundation of an Access database, because that is where the data is ____________________.

2. Each table in an Access database stores data about only ____________________ subject.

3. The ____________________ window displays when a database is open.

4. Each horizontal ____________________ of a table stores all the information about one database record.

5. Each vertical ____________________ of a table has a name that describes one category of information contained within each record.

6. The small gray box at the left end of a row in a table is the ____________________.

7. In the ____________________ view of a table, only the names of the fields, and not the records, display.

8. Specifications that determine what records will be displayed as a result of a query are called ____________________.

9. Filling a table with data is referred to as ____________________ the table.

10. A rule that you define for data within a field is referred to as the ____________________.

Skill Assessments

Project 1C — Departments

Objectives: *Rename a Database; Start Access, Open an Existing Database, and View Database Objects; Close and Save a Table; Open a Table; Print a Table; Sort Records; and Close and Save a Database.*

In the following Skill Assessment, you will open an existing database, view the database objects, and add two records to the database table. This database is used by the administration offices at Lake Michigan City College to store information regarding the various departments at the College. Your completed database objects will look like the ones shown in Figures 1.71 and 1.72. You will rename and save the database as *1C_LMccDept_Firstname_Lastname*.

Departments 10/17/2003

Department	Extension	Department Chair	Division
General Manageme	8467	Firstname Lastna	Business
MIS	8619	Bill Derbaugh	Business
Marketing	8922	George Hal	Business
Accounting	8321	Pat Eleanor	Business
Physical Education	3671	Gary Petrie	Education
Music	2763	Jeff Pepper	Fine Arts
Drama	2273	Mikail Schrejiko	Fine Arts
Art	2180	Ann Bebe	Fine Arts
Math	2620	Frank Keller	Humanities
History	5378	Jose Velarde	Humanities
English	5432	Annette Duvaine	Humanities

Page 1

Figure 1.71

LMCC Departments Report

Department	Extension	Department Chair	Division
Accounting	8321	Pat Eleanor	Business
Art	2180	Ann Bebe	Fine Arts
Drama	2273	Mikail Schrejiko	Fine Arts
English	5432	Annette Duvaine	Humanities
History	5378	Jose Velarde	Humanities
Marketing	8922	George Hal	Business
Math	2620	Frank Keller	Humanities
MIS	8619	Bill Derbaugh	Business
Music	2763	Jeff Pepper	Fine Arts
Physical Education	3671	Gary Petrie	Education
General Management	8467	Firstname Lastname	Business
Psychology	5291	Celina Rominov	Humanities

Friday, October 17, 2003 Page 1 of 1

Figure 1.72

(Project 1C–Departments continues on the next page)

Skill Assessments (continued)

(Project 1C–Departments continued)

1. On your Windows desktop, open **My Computer** and navigate to the student files that accompany this textbook. Locate and then click once to select the file **a01C_LMccDept**.
2. Move the mouse pointer over the selected file name and then right-click to display a shortcut menu. On the displayed shortcut menu, click **Copy**. Navigate to the drive and folder where you are storing your projects for this chapter. On the menu bar, click **Edit** and then click **Paste**. The database file is copied to your folder and is selected (highlighted).
3. Move your mouse pointer over the selected file name, right-click to display the shortcut menu, and then on the shortcut menu, click **Rename**. In the **File name** box, clear any existing text. Using your own first and last name, type **1C_LMccDept_Firstname_Lastname** and then press Enter to save the new file name. If the **Confirm File Rename** dialog box displays, click **Yes**. Be sure that the file name is still selected (highlighted) and then right-click to display the shortcut menu.
4. On the displayed shortcut menu, click **Properties**. At the lower part of the displayed dialog box, click to clear the check mark next to **Read-only**, and then click **OK** to close the dialog box. Close **My Computer**.
5. Start Access. On the menu bar, click **File** and then click **Open**. Click the **Look in arrow** and then navigate to the location where you are storing your projects for this chapter. Locate the database file that you renamed and saved with your name in Step 3. Click the database file once to select it, and then, in the lower right corner, click the **Open** button. Alternatively, you can double-click the name of the database, and it will open. If the security warning message displays, click **Yes and/or Open**.
6. In the Database window, on the Objects bar, click **Tables** once to display a list of tables in this database. To the right of the Objects bar, double-click the **Departments** table to open the table in Datasheet view. Notice that the table includes fields for Department, Extension, Department Chair, and Division.
7. In the **Department** column, click in the blank record at the bottom of the table and type **General Management** as the department name for the new record. Press Tab once. In the **Extension** field type **8467** and press Tab once. In the **Department Chair** field and using your own information, type your **Firstname Lastname** and press Tab once. In the **Division** field, type **Business** and then press Enter to complete the record.

(Project 1C–Departments continues on the next page)

(Project 1C–Departments continued)

8. On the Table Datasheet toolbar, click the **View** button to switch to the Design view and notice that the **Department** field is the primary key. Recall that one field in a table is designated as the primary key so that each record has a unique identifier. In this case, each department has a different name—no two departments at the college have the same name.

9. On the Table Design toolbar, click the **View** button to return to the Datasheet view. Click anywhere in the **Division** column, and then, on the Table Datasheet toolbar, click the **Sort Ascending** button. Notice that the records are now sorted in alphabetical order by Division.

10. On the Table Datasheet toolbar, click the **Print** button. In the upper right corner of the table window, click the **Close** button to close the table. A copy of the table is printed, and your name is printed as the Chair of the General Management Department. Save any changes if prompted to do so.

11. On the Objects bar, click **Queries** to display a list of available queries in the database. Double-click the **Business Division** query to open the query. Notice that each entry in the *Business Division* query has *Business* in the **Division** field. Recall that a query locates records from a table that meet specific criteria and then displays the result. In this case, the Business Division query was designed to locate all of the records that have *Business* as the Division. You can see that there are four Departments within the Business Division. In the upper right corner of the table window, click the **Close** button to close the query.

12. On the Objects bar, click **Forms** to display a list of available forms in the database. Recall that forms are another database object, in addition to tables, that allow you to view and enter new records into a table—one record at a time. To the right of the Objects bar, double-click the **Departments Form** to open the form. The Departments Form opens and the first record in the table displays.

13. At the bottom of the Department Form, locate the **New Record** button (the button at the bottom of the form with the *) and click it. With the insertion point blinking in the **Department** box, type **Psychology** and then press Tab once. Use the information below to fill in the remaining information for this record.

Department	Extension	Department Chair	Division
Psychology	5291	Celina Rominov	Humanities

14. In the Form window, click the **Close** button to close the form.

(Project 1C–Departments continues on the next page)

(Project 1C–Departments continued)

15. On the Objects bar, click **Reports** to display a list of available reports that have been created for this database. Recall that a report is a professional-looking document that summarizes information from a table in an easy-to-read format. To the right of the Objects bar, double-click the **LMCC Departments Report** to open the report in Print Preview.
16. In the upper right corner of the report title bar, click the **Maximize** button and then on the Print Preview toolbar, click the **Zoom arrow**. Zoom to **100%**. On the Print Preview toolbar, click the **Print** button to print the report. On the Print Preview toolbar, click the **Close** button to close the report. In the Access window, click the **Close** button to close Access.

End You have completed Project 1C

Project 1D—Office Supplies

Objectives: *Create a New Database, Create a New Table, Create a Primary Key and Add Records to a Table, Close and Save a Table, Modify the Table Design, Print a Table, and Close and Save a Database.*

In the following Skill Assessment, you will create a new database to track office supplies for the Distance Learning Department at Lake Michigan City College. The database table will look like the one shown in Figure 1.73. You will save your database as *1D_Office_Supplies_Firstname_Lastname.*

1. Start Access. From the **File** menu, click **New**. In the **New File** task pane, under **New**, click **Blank database**.
2. In the displayed **File New Database** dialog box, click the **Save in arrow**, and then navigate to the folder in which you are storing your projects for this chapter. In the **File name** box, delete any existing text, type **1D_Office_Supplies_Firstname_Lastname** and then in the lower right corner click **Create**. The Office Supplies database is created and the Database window displays with the new database name indicated in the title bar.
3. In the Database window, double-click the command icon **Create table in Design view**. Because you have not yet named or saved this table, the title bar indicates the default name of *Table1*. The insertion point is blinking in the first **Field Name** box.
4. In the first **Field Name** box, type **Inventory #** and then press Tab to move the insertion point to the **Data Type** column. Recall that Data Type refers to the rules that you can define for data within a field.
5. Press Tab to accept the default Data Type of **Text**. Press Tab again to move to the next **Field Name** box.

(Project 1D–Office Supplies continues on the next page)

Skill Assessments (continued)

(Project 1D–Office Supplies continued)

1D Office Inventory Firstname Lastname 10/17/2003

Inventory #	Inventory Item	Unit Measurement	Cost	Quanitity on Hand
LMCC-101	Black ball point pens	Box/100	$12.00	4
LMCC-102	Blue ball point pens	Box/100	$12.00	2
LMCC-103	Red ball point pens	Box/100	$12.00	2
LMCC-201	Yellow tablets	Box/50	$48.00	1
LMCC-202	White tablets	Box/50	$48.00	3
LMCC-301	Floppy disks	Box/50	$45.00	5
LMCC-401	Large binder clips	Box/50	$8.00	4
LMCC-402	Small binder clips	Box/75	$8.00	4

Page 1

Figure 1.73

6. Use the following information to add the remaining fields to your table. Recall that a description for a field is optional. The descriptions for this table describe the purpose of the corresponding field.

Field Name	Data Type	Description
Inventory Item	Text	
Unit Measurement	Text	Identifies the number of items in a unit
Cost	Currency	Cost per unit
Quantity on Hand	Number	Current number of items available

7. Click in the field name for **Inventory #.** On the toolbar, click the **Primary Key** button to set the **Inventory #** field as the primary key for this table. Within this table, no two items will have the same Inventory number—the Inventory number is a unique identifier. On the Table Design toolbar, click the **View** button to switch to the Datasheet view. When prompted, click **Yes** to save the table.

(Project 1D–Office Supplies continues on the next page)

Skill Assessments (continued)

(Project 1D–Office Supplies continued)

8. In the displayed **Save As** dialog box, in the **Table Name** box, use your own first and last name to type **1D Office Inventory Firstname Lastname** and then click **OK**. The table displays and you can begin to enter records into it.

9. With the table in Datasheet view, be sure your insertion point is in the **Inventory #** column. Type **LMCC-101** and press Tab. Type **Black ball point pens** and press Tab. Type **Box/100** and press Tab. Type **12** in the **Cost** column and press Tab. The dollar sign and the decimal point are inserted for you because a data type of Currency was specified for the Cost field. Type **4** in the Quantity on Hand column and press Enter.

10. Use the following information to add the remaining records to the Inventory table. Press Enter after entering the last record.

Inventory #	Inventory Item	Unit Measurement	Cost	Quantity on Hand
LMCC-102	Blue ball point pens	Box /100	12.00	2
LMCC-103	Red ball point pens	Box/100	12.00	2
LMCC-201	Yellow tablets	Box/50	48.00	1
LMCC-202	White tablets	Box/50	48.00	3
LMCC-301	Floppy disks	Box/50	45.00	5
LMCC-401	Large binder clips	Box/50	8.00	4
LMCC-402	Small binder clips	Box/75	8.00	4

11. Pause the mouse pointer over the gray **Inventory #** column heading, and then click and hold the left mouse button while dragging to the right until all of the columns are selected. With the columns selected, pause your mouse pointer over the vertical line between any of the column headings until the mouse takes the shape of a double-headed arrow, and then double-click. All of the columns are resized to accommodate the widest entry in each column. Recall that you can use this method as a quick way to adjust the widths of several columns at once. Recall also that adjusting the size of columns and rows does not change the data contained in the table's records. It changes only your *view* of the data.

12. Click anywhere in the table to deselect the table. On the Table Datasheet toolbar, click the **Print** button. Because you inserted your name in the table name, it prints in the heading. In the upper right corner of the table window, click the **Close** button to close the table. Click **Yes** to save changes to the layout of the table.

(Project 1D–Office Supplies continues on the next page)

(Project 1D–Office Supplies continued)

13. In the Database window, click the **Close** button to close the Office Supplies database. In the Access window, click the **Close** button to close Access.

End **You have completed Project 1D**

Project 1E — Recipes

Objectives: *Rename a Database; Start Access, Open an Existing Database, and View Database Objects; Open a Table; Print a Table; Edit Records in a Table; Navigate to Records in a Table; and Close and Save a Database.*

In the following Skill Assessment, you will open and edit an existing database that stores information about the recipes that the Computer Club at Lake Michigan City College prepares for social events. Your completed database objects will look like the ones shown in Figure 1.74. You will save the database as *1E_Recipes_Firstname_Lastname* in the folder designated for this chapter.

Recipes 10/17/2003

Recipe #	Recipe Name	Type
1	Artichoke and Mushroom Lasagna	Main Dish
2	Roast Capon with Lemon and Thyme	Main Dish
3	Spring Vegetable Saute	Vegetable
4	Garlic Roasted Potatoes	Vegetable
5	Fizzy Sour Cherry Lemonade	Beverage
6	Shrimp with Orange and Tomato	Salad
7	Grilled Sweet Potatoes	Vegetable
8	Bell Pepper and Onion Crostini	Appetizer
9	Dried Apricots with Goat Cheese and Pistachios	Appetizer
10	Corn Bread Pudding	Dessert
11	Firstname Lastname's Potato Galette	Vegetable
12	Oatmeal Coconut Raspberry Bars	Dessert
13	Blood-Orange and Grapefruit Juice	Beverage
14	Kale and White Bean Soup	Soup
15	Pineapple, Kiwifruit, and Orange in Mint Sauce	Salad

Page 1

Figure 1.74

(Project 1E–Recipes continues on the next page)

(Project 1E–Recipes continued)

1. Open **My Computer** and navigate to the student files that accompany this textbook. Click once to select the file **a01E_recipes**. Move the mouse pointer over the selected file name, right-click, and on the displayed shortcut menu, click **Copy**.
2. Navigate to the drive and folder where you will be storing your projects for this chapter. On the menu bar, click **Edit** and then click **Paste**. The database file is copied to your folder and is selected. Move your mouse pointer over the selected file name, right-click to display the shortcut menu, and then click **Rename**. Using your own first and last name, type **1E_Recipes_Firstname_Lastname**
3. Press Enter to save the new file name. If the Confirm File Rename message displays, click **Yes**. Be sure that the file name is still selected (highlighted), point to the file name, and right-click to display the shortcut menu. On the displayed shortcut menu, click **Properties**.
4. In the lower portion of the displayed dialog box, click to clear the check mark from the **Read-only** check box. Click **OK** to close the dialog box. Close **My Computer** and start Access.
5. On the menu bar, click **File** and then click **Open**. In the displayed dialog box, click the **Look in arrow**, and then navigate to the location where you are storing your projects for this chapter. Locate the database file that you saved and renamed with your name in Step 2. Click the database file once to select it, and then, in the lower right corner, click the **Open** button. Alternatively, you can double-click the name of the database, and it will open.
6. If necessary, in the Database window on the Objects bar, click **Tables** to display a list of tables in this database. To the right of the Objects bar, double-click the **Recipes** table to open the table in Datasheet view.
7. In **record #5**, click in the **Type** field and delete the existing text. Type **Beverage** and then press Enter. In **record #11**, click to place the insertion point in front of *Potato*. Use your own information to type **Firstname Lastname's** and then press Spacebar once.
8. On the Table Datasheet toolbar, click the **Print** button. In the upper right corner of the table window, click the **Close** button to close the table. On the title bar of the Access window, click the **Close** button to close Access.

End You have completed Project 1E

Project 1F—CD Log

Objectives: *Create a New Database, Create a New Table, Create a Primary Key and Add Records to a Table, Close and Save a Table, Sort Records, Print a Table, and Close and Save a Database.*

In the following Performance Assessment, you will create a new database and a new table to store information about the CD collection for the Music Department at Lake Michigan City College. Your completed table will look like the one shown in Figure 1.75. You will save your database as *1F_CDlog_Firstname_Lastname*.

1F CD Table Firstname Lastname 10/17/2003

CD#	Artist	Title	Category
1	Andrea Brightman	18th Century Italian Songs	Opera
6	Anthony String Quartet	Handel Complete Violin Sonatas	Classical
3	Anthony String Quartet	Variations	Classical
4	Butler Symphony	Beethoven Symphonies 3 & 6	Classical
5	Chicago Philharmonic	Mozart: Symphony No. 41 "Jupiter"	Classical
2	Russian Symphony	Berloiz Les Troyens	Opera

Page 1

Figure 1.75

(Project 1F–CD Log continues on the next page)

Performance Assessments (continued)

(Project 1F–CD Log continued)

1. Start Access. Display the **New File** task pane and click **Blank database**. In the **File New Database** dialog box, navigate to the drive and folder where you are storing your projects for this chapter. Name the file **1F_CDlog_Firstname_Lastname**

2. In the Database window, double-click the command icon **Create table in Design view**. Use the following information to create the fields for the table.

Field Name	Data Type	Description
CD#	AutoNumber	
Artist	Text	
Title	Text	
Category	Text	Music Classification

3. Because two CDs could have the same title, you will use the **AutoNumber** field that you created as the primary key. Click in the field name for **CD#** and then click the **Primary Key** button. Click the **View** button to switch to the Datasheet view of the table.

4. When prompted, save the table by typing **1F CD Table Firstname Lastname** in the **Save As** dialog box and then click **OK**.

5. With the table open in the Datasheet view, press Tab to move to the **Artist** field and type the first artist in the following table. As you type in the **Artist** field, Access fills in the AutoNumber to assign a unique number to each CD. You do not need to type the numbers. Use the following information to create the records.

CD#	Artist	Title	Category
1	Andrea Brightman	18th Century Italian Songs	Opera
2	Russian Symphony	Berlioz Les Troyens	Opera
3	Anthony String Quartet	Variations	Classical
4	Butler Symphony	Beethoven Symphonies 3 & 6	Classical
5	Chicago Philharmonic	Mozart: Symphony No. 41 "Jupiter"	Classical
6	Anthony String Quartet	Handel Complete Violin Sonatas	Classical

(Project 1F–CD Log continues on the next page)

Performance Assessments (continued)

(Project 1F–CD Log continued)

6. Select all of the columns in the table. Display the **Format** menu, click **Column Width**, and in the displayed **Column Width** dialog box, click **Best Fit**. All of the columns are resized to accommodate the widest entry in each column.

7. Click anywhere in the table to deselect it. Click the **Artist** column heading to select the column, press and hold Shift, and then click the **Title** column heading. On the toolbar, click the **Sort Ascending** button. The table is sorted by Artist, and within Artist, it is further sorted by title.

8. On the Table Datasheet toolbar, click the **Print** button. Close the table, save any changes, and then close Access.

End You have completed Project 1F

Project 1G—Employees

Objectives: *Rename a Database; Start Access, Open an Existing Database, and View Database Objects; Create a Primary Key and Add Records to a Table; Close and Save a Table; Open a Table; Modify the Table Design; and Print a Table.*

In the following Performance Assessment, you will open an existing database that stores employee information for Lake Michigan City College, add a record, and then work with other objects in the database. The first page of your completed database object will look similar to Figure 1.76. You will rename the database as *1G_Employees_Firstname_Lastname.*

1. Use the Windows My Computer tool to navigate to your student files and then select the file **a01G_Employees**. Copy the file to the drive and folder where you are storing your projects for this chapter. Using your own information, rename the file **1G_Employees_Firstname_Lastname**

2. Remove the Read-only attribute from the renamed file so that you can make changes to the database. Start Access.

3. Open your **1G_Employees** database that you renamed in Step 1. Open the **Employees** table and switch to Design view. Set the primary key for this table to **ID**. This is the employee ID number, which uniquely identifies each employee.

(Project 1G–Employees continues on the next page)

Performance Assessments (continued)

(**Project 1G**–Employees continued)

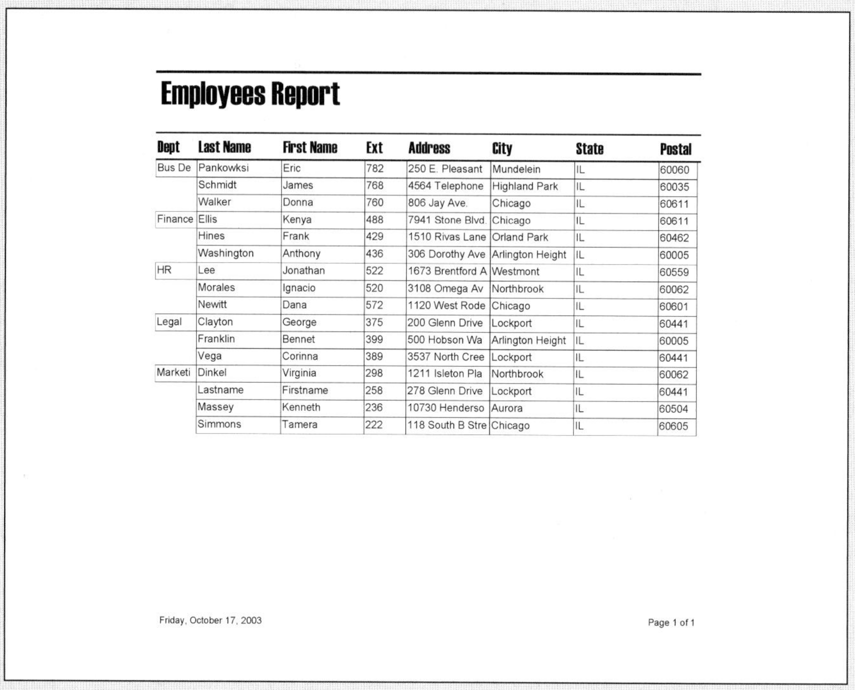

Employees Report

Dept	Last Name	First Name	Ext	Address	City	State	Postal
Bus De	Pankowksi	Eric	782	250 E. Pleasant	Mundelein	IL	60060
	Schmidt	James	768	4564 Telephone	Highland Park	IL	60035
	Walker	Donna	760	806 Jay Ave.	Chicago	IL	60611
Finance	Ellis	Kenya	488	7941 Stone Blvd.	Chicago	IL	60611
	Hines	Frank	429	1510 Rivas Lane	Orland Park	IL	60462
	Washington	Anthony	436	306 Dorothy Ave	Arlington Height	IL	60005
HR	Lee	Jonathan	522	1673 Brentford A	Westmont	IL	60559
	Morales	Ignacio	520	3108 Omega Av	Northbrook	IL	60062
	Newitt	Dana	572	1120 West Rode	Chicago	IL	60601
Legal	Clayton	George	375	200 Glenn Drive	Lockport	IL	60441
	Franklin	Bennet	399	500 Hobson Wa	Arlington Height	IL	60005
	Vega	Corinna	389	3537 North Cree	Lockport	IL	60441
Marketi	Dinkel	Virginia	298	1211 Isleton Pla	Northbrook	IL	60062
	Lastname	Firstname	258	278 Glenn Drive	Lockport	IL	60441
	Massey	Kenneth	236	10730 Henderso	Aurora	IL	60504
	Simmons	Tamera	222	118 South B Stre	Chicago	IL	60605

Friday, October 17, 2003

Page 1 of 1

Figure 1.76

4. Switch to the Datasheet view of the table and save changes to the table when prompted to do so. Add the following record to the table, using your own first and last name.

ID	5588
First Name	Your First Name
Last Name	Your Last Name
Dept	Marketing
Ext	258
Address	278 Glenn Drive
City	Lockport
State	IL
Postal Code	60441
Phone	815-555-0365

5. Use any method to resize all of the columns to accommodate their data and then close the table. On the Objects bar, click **Queries** and open the **Marketing Query**. Because you added your name as a member of the Marketing Department, you should see your record among the other employees in the Marketing Department.

(**Project 1G**–Employees continues on the next page)

(Project 1G–Employees continued)

6. Close the query. On the Objects bar, click the **Reports** button and open the **Employees Report**. Display the **File** menu, and then click **Page Setup**. In the **Page Setup** dialog box, click the **Page tab**, and then click the **Landscape** option button so that the report prints in Landscape orientation. Print the report. Notice that your name will print as one of the employees in the Marketing Department. Close the report and then close the database. Close Access.

End You have completed Project 1G

Project 1H—DL Courses

Objectives: *Create a New Database, Create a New Table, Create a Primary Key and Add Records to a Table, Modify the Table Design, Close and Save a Table, Print a Table, and Close and Save a Database.*

In the following Performance Assessment, you will create a new database and a new table to store information about Distance Learning courses at Lake Michigan City College. Your completed table will look similar to the one shown in Figure 1.77. You will save your database as *1H_DLcourses_Firstname_Lastname*.

1. Start Access and display the **New File** task pane. Click **Blank database**. Navigate to the drive and folder where you are storing your projects for this chapter. In the **File name** box, type **1H_DLcourses_Firstname_Lastname** as the name for your database, and then click **Create**.
2. Use the following information to create a table in Design view and to add fields to the table.

Field Name	Data Type	Description
Course Number	Text	
Course Name	Text	
Credit Hours	Number	Credit hours for this course

3. Switch to the Datasheet view of the table. Using your own first and last name, save the table as **1H DLcourses Firstname Lastname** and then click **OK**. When prompted if you would like to add a primary key now, click **No**.

(Project 1H–DL Courses continues on the next page)

Performance Assessments (continued)

(Project 1H–DL Courses continued)

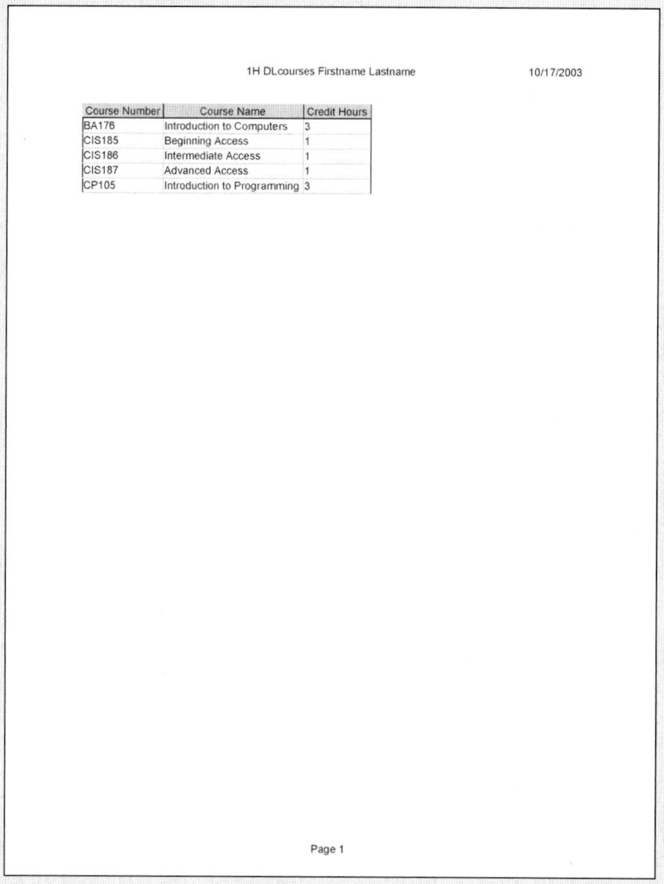
1H DLcourses Firstname Lastname 10/17/2003

Course Number	Course Name	Credit Hours
BA176	Introduction to Computers	3
CIS185	Beginning Access	1
CIS186	Intermediate Access	1
CIS187	Advanced Access	1
CP105	Introduction to Programming	3

Page 1

Figure 1.77

4. Using the following information, fill in the records for the DLcourses table.

Course Number	Course Name	Credit Hours
BA176	Introduction to Computers	3
CP105	Introduction to Programming	3
CIS185	Beginning Access	1
CIS186	Intermediate Access	1
CIS187	Advanced Access	1

5. Switch to the Design view of the table. Set the **Course Number** field as the primary key for this table. Click the **View** button to switch to the Datasheet view of the table. Save the table when prompted. Verify that the records are sorted by the primary key.

6. Use any method to resize the column widths to accommodate their data. Print and then close the table, saving any changes if prompted to do so. Close the database and close Access.

End **You have completed Project 1H**

Mastery Assessments

Project 1I — Suppliers

Objectives: *Create a New Database, Create a New Table, Create a Primary Key and Add Records to a Table, Close and Save a Table, Modify the Table Design, Sort Records, Navigate to Records in a Table, and Close and Save a Database.*

In the following Mastery Assessment, you will create a new database and a new table to store supplier information for Lake Michigan City College. Your completed table will look like the one shown in Figure 1.78. You will save your database as *1I_LMCCsuppliers_Firstname_Lastname.*

1I Suppliers Firstname Lastname 10/17/2003

Supplier Number	Supplier Name	Street Address	City	State	Postal Code	Phone Number	Contact Person
3	Jiffy Cleaning Supplies	3572 Rivas Lane	Orland Park	IL	60462	708-555-9852	Peggy Sharp
1	Plastic Warehouse	11511 Stone Blvd.	Chicago	IL	60611	312-555-0748	Debbie Lucero
2	Wholesale To Go	783 Hobson Way	Arlington Heights	IL	60005	847-555-0123	Bill Franklin

Page 1

Figure 1.78

(**Project 1I**–Suppliers continues on the next page)

Mastery Assessments (continued)

Project 1I–Suppliers continued)

1. Start Access. In your Project folder, create a new database and name it **1I_LMCCsuppliers_Firstname_Lastname**
2. Use the following information to create a new table.

Field Name	Data Type	Description
Supplier Number	AutoNumber	
Supplier Name	Text	
Street Address	Text	
City	Text	
State	Text	
Postal Code	Text	
Phone Number	Text	
Contact Person	Text	Main contact

3. Choose the **Supplier Number** as the primary key for this table. Switch to Datasheet view, and then, using your own information, save the table as **1I Suppliers Firstname Lastname** and then add the following records to the table.

Supplier Number	Supplier Name	Street Address	City	State	Postal Code	Phone Number	Contact Person
1	Plastic Warehouse	11511 Stone Blvd.	Chicago	IL	60611	312-555-0748	Debbie Lucero
2	Wholesale To Go	783 Hobson Way	Arlington Heights	IL	60005	847-555-0123	Bill Franklin
3	Jiffy Cleaning Supplies	3572 Rivas Lane	Orland Park	IL	60462	708-555-9852	Peggy Sharp

4 Resize all of the columns to accommodate their data. Sort the table alphabetically by Supplier Name. Display the **Page Setup** dialog box and change the page orientation to **Landscape**. Print and then close the table. Close the database and then close Access.

End You have completed Project 1I

Project 1J — Expenses

Objectives: *Rename a Database; Start Access, Open an Existing Database, and View Database Objects; Modify the Table Design; Print a Table; Edit Records in a Table; Navigate to Records in a Table; and Close and Save a Database.*

In the following Mastery Assessment, you will open an existing database and modify items in the database that stores information about the expenses of the Computer Club at Lake Michigan City College. Your completed database object will look similar to the one shown in Figure 1.79. You will rename the database as *1J_Expenses_Firstname_Lastname.*

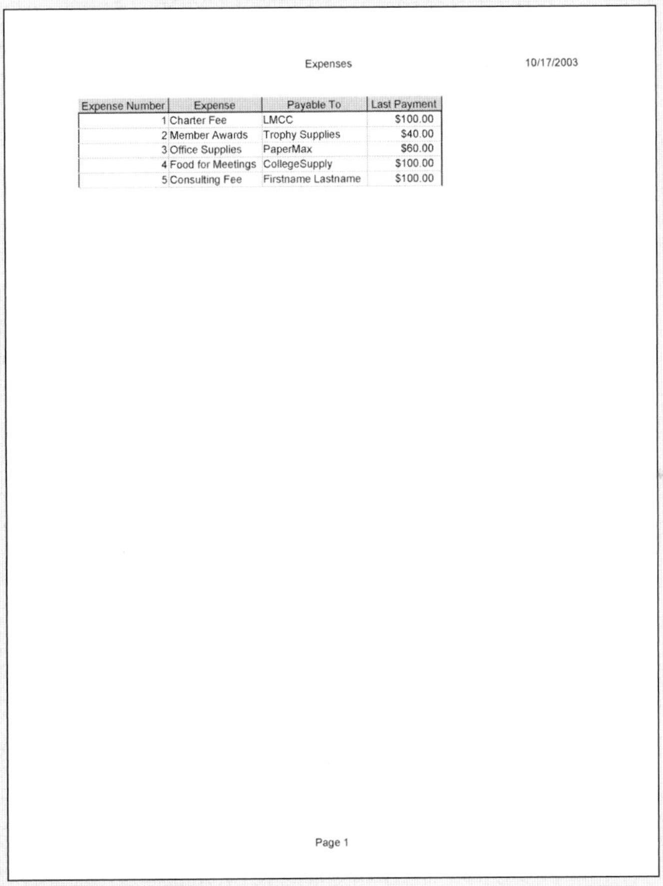
Expenses 10/17/2003

Expense Number	Expense	Payable To	Last Payment
1	Charter Fee	LMCC	$100.00
2	Member Awards	Trophy Supplies	$40.00
3	Office Supplies	PaperMax	$60.00
4	Food for Meetings	CollegeSupply	$100.00
5	Consulting Fee	Firstname Lastname	$100.00

Page 1

Figure 1.79

(Project 1J–Expenses continues on the next page)

Mastery Assessments (continued)

Project 1J–Expenses continued)

1. Copy the student file **a01J_Expenses** to the drive and folder where you are storing your projects for this chapter. Rename the database as **1J_Expenses_Firstname_Lastname** and remove the Read-only attribute.
2. Start Access and open the database you renamed in Step 1. Open the **Expenses** table and make the following changes to the table:

   Change the *Expense ID* field to **Expense Number**

   Change the primary key for the table to **Expense Number**

   For the *Member Awards* expense record, change the information in the Payable To column from *LMCC* to **Trophy Supplies**
3. Add the following record using your own name:

Expense Number	Expense	Payable To	Last Payment
AutoNumber	Consulting Fee	Firstname Lastname	100

4. Resize the fields in the table to accommodate their data. Print and then close the table, saving any changes if prompted to do so. Close the database and close Access.

End You have completed Project 1J

Problem Solving

Project 1K — Video Store

Objectives: *Create a New Database, Create a New Table, Create a Primary Key and Add Records to a Table, Modify the Table Design, Close and Save a Table, Print a Table, and Close and Save a Database.*

Lake Michigan City College has a small video rental shop on campus that rents videos and DVDs to students, staff, and faculty of the college. Create a database that will store information about the movie rentals such as customer names and the names of movies in the inventory. This database should have at least two tables: one for customers and another for the inventory of videos that are available to rent. Create a new database with an appropriate name for the video rental store and add two tables as described above to the database. In each of the tables, add the fields that you think should be included in each of these tables. Designate one field in each table as the primary key. Print your tables.

End You have completed Project 1K

Project 1L — Fix It

Objectives: *Rename a Database; Start Access, Open an Existing Database, and View Database Objects; Create a Primary Key and Add Records to a Table; Open a Table; Modify the Table Design; and Close and Save a Database.*

The Business Division at Lake Michigan City College needs to correct some errors in a student database. Copy the student file a01L_FixIt to your storage location and rename it **1L_FixIt_Firstname_Lastname**. Clear the Read-only property and then open the database. View the FixIt table in this database. Think about the way the data is arranged in the table. Based on the databases you have worked with in this chapter, identify at least four ways this table could be improved. Then make your suggested changes to this database.

End You have completed Project 1L

On the Internet

Databases and Today's Industries

Most of the world's information is stored in some type of database. Databases play a large role in industries today. Their expansive applications have made databases an integral part of business in the current marketplace.

Go online and perform a search to identify the current trends involving databases and the different career paths that include database training as part of their job descriptions.

GO! with Help

Searching Access Help

The Access Help system is extensive and can help you as you work. In this exercise, you will view information about getting help as you work in Access.

1. Start Access. In the **Type a question for help** box, type **Printing a table** and then press Enter.
2. In the displayed **Search Results** task pane, click the result—**Print a record, datasheet, or database object**. Maximize the displayed window, and at the top of the window, click the **Show All** button. Scroll through and read about printing database objects in Access.
3. If you want, print a copy of the information by clicking the printer button at the top of the window.
4. Close the Microsoft Access Help window, then close Access.

Access 2003

chapter two

Forms and Reports

In this chapter you will: complete these projects **and** practice these skills.

Project	Objectives
Project 2A Creating Forms	• View and Navigate to Records with a Form • Create an AutoForm • Save and Close an AutoForm • Use a Form to Add Records to and Delete Records from a Table
Project 2B Creating Forms and Reports	• Create a Form with the Form Wizard • Modify a Form • Create a Report with the Report Wizard • Save a Report • Modify the Design of a Report • Print a Report

Lake Michigan City College

Lake Michigan City College is located along the lakefront of Chicago—one of the nation's most exciting cities. The college serves its large and diverse student body and makes positive contributions to the community through relevant curricula, partnerships with businesses and nonprofit organizations, and learning experiences that allow students to be full participants in the global community. The college offers three associate degrees in 20 academic areas, adult education programs, and continuing education offerings on campus, at satellite locations, and online.

Forms and Reports

You can both enter and view database information in the database table itself. However, for entering and viewing information, it is usually easier to use an Access form.

Think about having to enter the information from hundreds of paper forms into a database. If the form on the screen matches the pattern of information on the paper form, it will be much easier to enter the new information. Additionally, when using a form, only one record is visible at a time, making data entry easier.

When viewing information, it is also easier to view just one record at a time. For example, your college counselor can look at your college transcript in a nicely laid out form on the screen without seeing the records for dozens of other students at the same time.

Reports in Access summarize the data in a database in a professional-looking manner suitable for printing. The design of a report can be modified so that the final report is laid out in a format that is useful for the person reading it.

In this chapter, you will create and modify both forms and reports for Access databases.

Project 2A Computer Club

In Chapter 1, you saw that two database objects can be used to enter data into a database. You can type data directly into a table in Datasheet view. Recall that tables are the place where the data is stored. You can also type data into a form. A ***form*** is an organized view of the fields in one or more database tables or queries laid out in a visually appealing format on the screen. For the purpose of entering new records or viewing existing records, forms are generally easier to use than the table itself.

The Computer Club at Lake Michigan City College maintains a database with two tables—the Members table and the Club Events table. In Activities 2.1 through 2.5 you will use an Access form to view and navigate to the records in the Members table. Then, using AutoForm, you will create and save a new form to view and navigate to the records in the Club Events table. Your completed database objects will look similar to Figure 2.1. In addition, you will use the new form to add and delete records in the Club Events table.

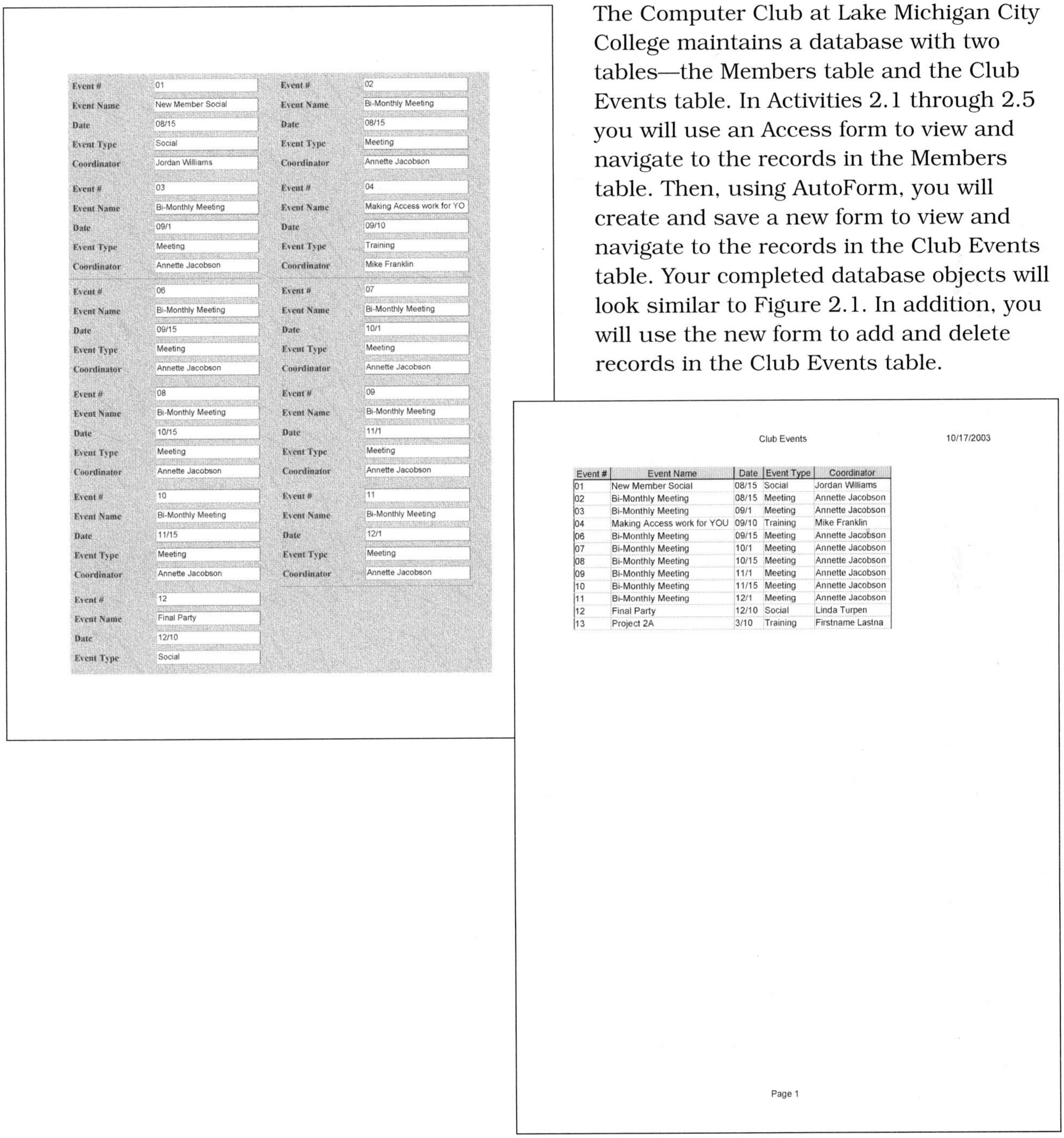

Event #	Event Name	Date	Event Type	Coordinator
01	New Member Social	08/15	Social	Jordan Williams
02	Bi-Monthly Meeting	08/15	Meeting	Annette Jacobson
03	Bi-Monthly Meeting	09/1	Meeting	Annette Jacobson
04	Making Access work for YO	09/10	Training	Mike Franklin
06	Bi-Monthly Meeting	09/15	Meeting	Annette Jacobson
07	Bi-Monthly Meeting	10/1	Meeting	Annette Jacobson
08	Bi-Monthly Meeting	10/15	Meeting	Annette Jacobson
09	Bi-Monthly Meeting	11/1	Meeting	Annette Jacobson
10	Bi-Monthly Meeting	11/15	Meeting	Annette Jacobson
11	Bi-Monthly Meeting	12/1	Meeting	Annette Jacobson
12	Final Party	12/10	Social	

Club Events 10/17/2003

Event #	Event Name	Date	Event Type	Coordinator
01	New Member Social	08/15	Social	Jordan Williams
02	Bi-Monthly Meeting	08/15	Meeting	Annette Jacobson
03	Bi-Monthly Meeting	09/1	Meeting	Annette Jacobson
04	Making Access work for YOU	09/10	Training	Mike Franklin
06	Bi-Monthly Meeting	09/15	Meeting	Annette Jacobson
07	Bi-Monthly Meeting	10/1	Meeting	Annette Jacobson
08	Bi-Monthly Meeting	10/15	Meeting	Annette Jacobson
09	Bi-Monthly Meeting	11/1	Meeting	Annette Jacobson
10	Bi-Monthly Meeting	11/15	Meeting	Annette Jacobson
11	Bi-Monthly Meeting	12/1	Meeting	Annette Jacobson
12	Final Party	12/10	Social	Linda Turpen
13	Project 2A	3/10	Training	Firstname Lastna

Page 1

Figure 2.1
Project 2A—Computer Club

Objective 1
View and Navigate to Records with a Form

Your personal address book would not be useful to you if the addresses or phone numbers in it contained errors. Likewise, a database is useful only if the data in it is accurate. You can see that the process of getting the information into a database is an important one. The individual who performs the ***data entry***—typing in the actual data—has a better chance of entering the data accurately if he or she is provided with a data entry tool that assists in preventing data entry errors. Access forms are an example of such a tool.

Because a form can be set to display only one record in the database at a time, a form is also useful to anyone who has the job of viewing information in a database. For example, when you visit the Records office at your college to obtain a transcript, someone displays your record on a screen. For the viewer, it is much easier to look at one record at a time, using a form, than to look at all the student records in the database table.

Activity 2.1 Viewing and Navigating to Records Using a Form

1. Using the skills you practiced in Chapter 1, and using either My Computer or Windows Explorer, create a new folder named Chapter 2 in the location where you will be storing your projects for this chapter.

2. Locate the file **a02A_ComputerClub** from the student files that accompany this text. Copy and paste the file to the Chapter 2 folder you created in Step 1.

3. Using the technique you practiced in Activity 1.1 of Chapter 1, rename the file as **2A_ComputerClub_Firstname_Lastname** and remove the Read-only property from the file if necessary.

4. Close the Windows accessory you are using, either My Computer or Windows Explorer. Start Access and open your **2A_ComputerClub** database.

5. On the Objects bar, click **Forms**.

   To the right of the Objects bar, two command icons for creating a new form display, followed by the Members form that has been created and saved as part of the Computer Club database.

6. Click to select the **Members** form if necessary, and then on the toolbar above the Objects bar, click the **Open** button. Alternatively, double-click the Members form to open it.

   The Members form, in ***Form view***, displays the first record in the Members table—the record for *Annette Jacobson*. In Form view, you can modify the information in a record or add a new record, one record at a time.

7 At the lower edge of the form, in the navigation area, click the **Last Record** button. See Figure 2.2.

Record 15—*Ceara Thibodeaux*—displays.

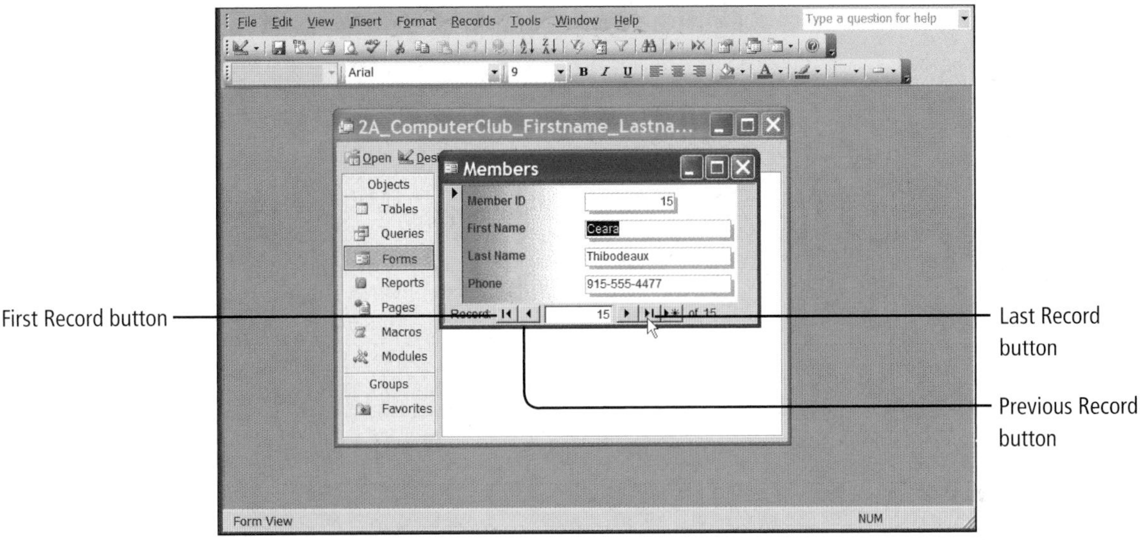

Figure 2.2

8 In the navigation area, click the **Previous Record** button once.

Record 14, the previous record—*Debbie Greggs*—displays.

9 In the navigation area, click the **First Record** button.

Record 1—*Annette Jacobson*—displays.

10 Position your mouse pointer in the navigation area over the number of the current record until the pointer takes the shape of an I-beam. See Figure 2.3.

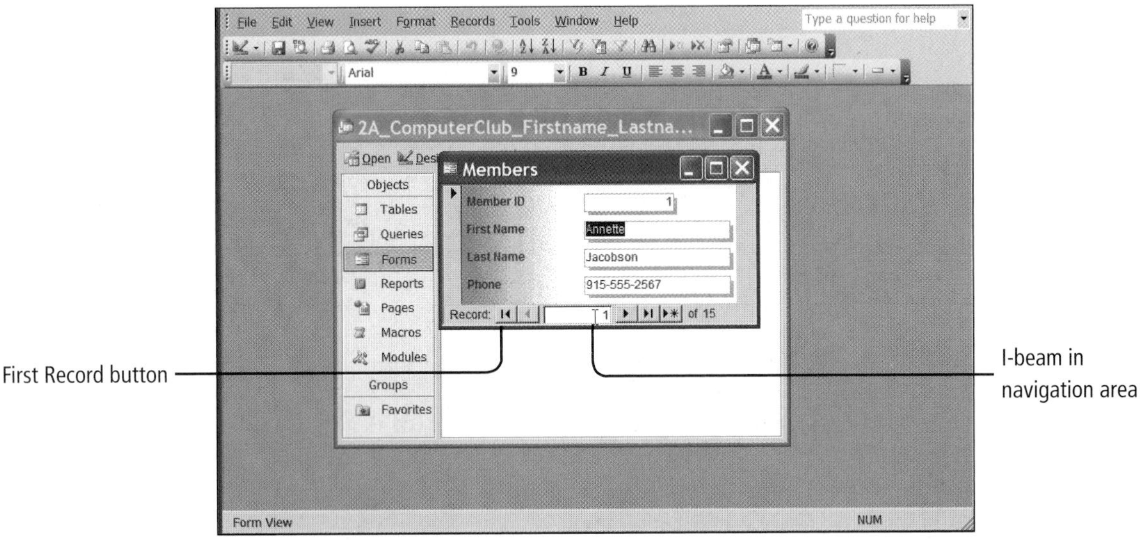

Figure 2.3

11 Drag your mouse over the number **1** to select it. See Figure 2.4.

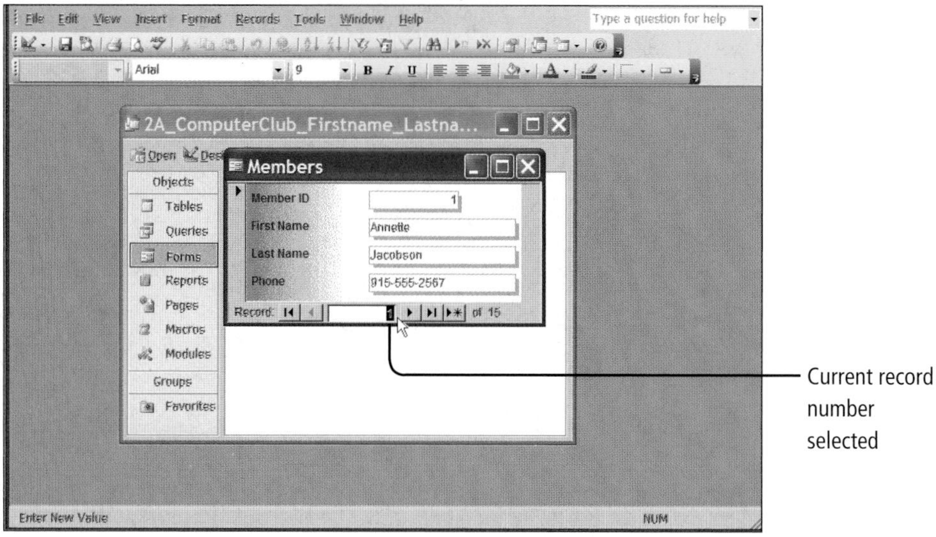

Figure 2.4

12 With the number 1 selected, type **8** and then press Enter.

Record 8 in the Members table—*Kathleen Lightfoot*—displays, as shown in Figure 2.5.

Assuming you know the exact number of the record you want to view, this is a useful method of navigating to a record when there is a large number of records to navigate through.

Use the navigation buttons—Next Record, Last Record, Previous Record, First Record—to jump to specific records in a database table. Use the New Record button to move to the end of the database table for the purpose of entering a new record. You will do this in a later activity.

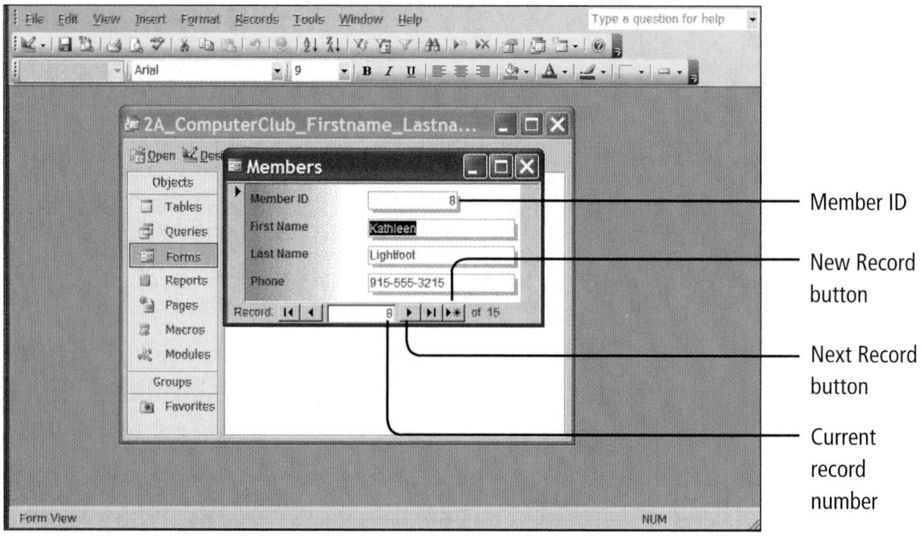

Figure 2.5

13 In the upper right corner of the **Members** form, click the **Close** button to close the form.

Objective 2
Create an AutoForm

AutoForm is a feature that creates a form for an existing database table. AutoForm incorporates all the information, both the field names and the individual records, from an existing table and then creates the form for you.

Activity 2.2 Creating an AutoForm

1. On the Objects bar, verify that **Forms** is selected. Above the Objects bar, locate and then click the **New** button [New].

   The New Form dialog box displays as shown in Figure 2.6. The dialog box lists a variety of form types that can be created with a ***wizard***, an Access feature that walks you step by step through a process by having you answer questions.

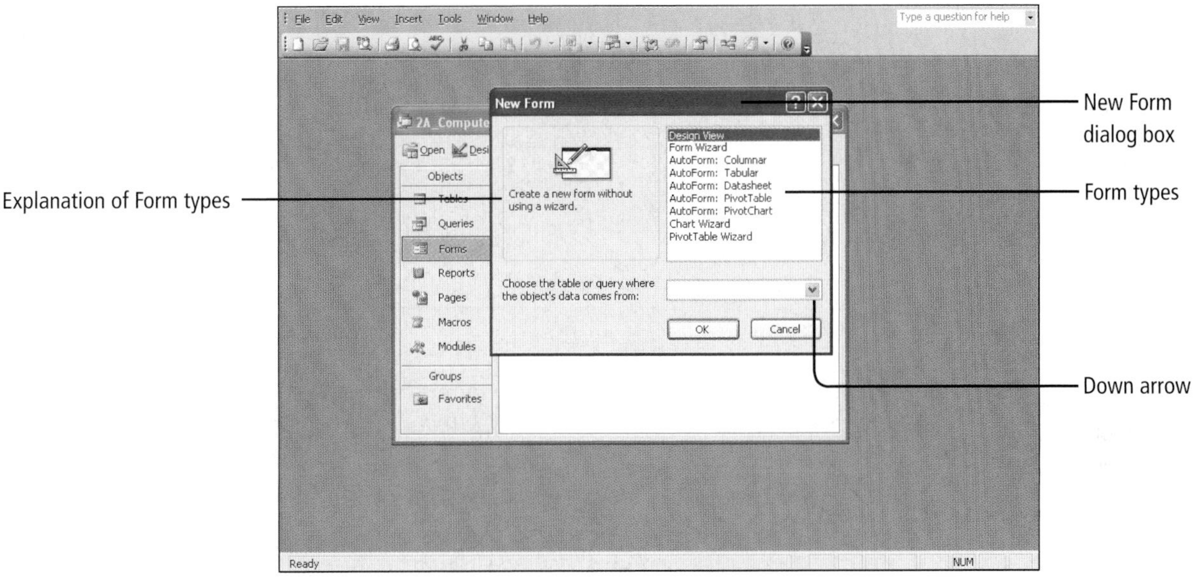

Figure 2.6

2. On the right side of the displayed dialog box, click **AutoForm: Datasheet** and then read the explanation in the box to the left. Then, on the displayed list, click **Chart Wizard** and read the explanation in the box to the left.

   As you progress in your study of Access, you will use many of the New Form wizards, and you can see that Access provides explanations for each one.

3. On the displayed list, click **AutoForm: Columnar** and then read the explanation to the left.

   The Columnar format displays records in a form one at a time in a column format.

4 In the text box to the right of *Choose the table or query where the object's data comes from:* click the **down arrow**.

A list of available tables and queries for this database displays. An AutoForm can be created using the information in either a table or a query. Recall that a query contains only those records that meet specified criteria.

5 From the displayed list, click **Club Events** and then click **OK**. Compare your screen to Figure 2.7.

A new form, based on the fields and records in the Club Events table, is created and displays on your screen. Notice that all five field names in the table are shown and the first record, Event #01, is displayed.

Depending on previous use of the computer at which you are working, your form may have a different background color. The various Form Wizards apply different backgrounds, and Access will apply the most recently used background. The background color will not affect the way the form works.

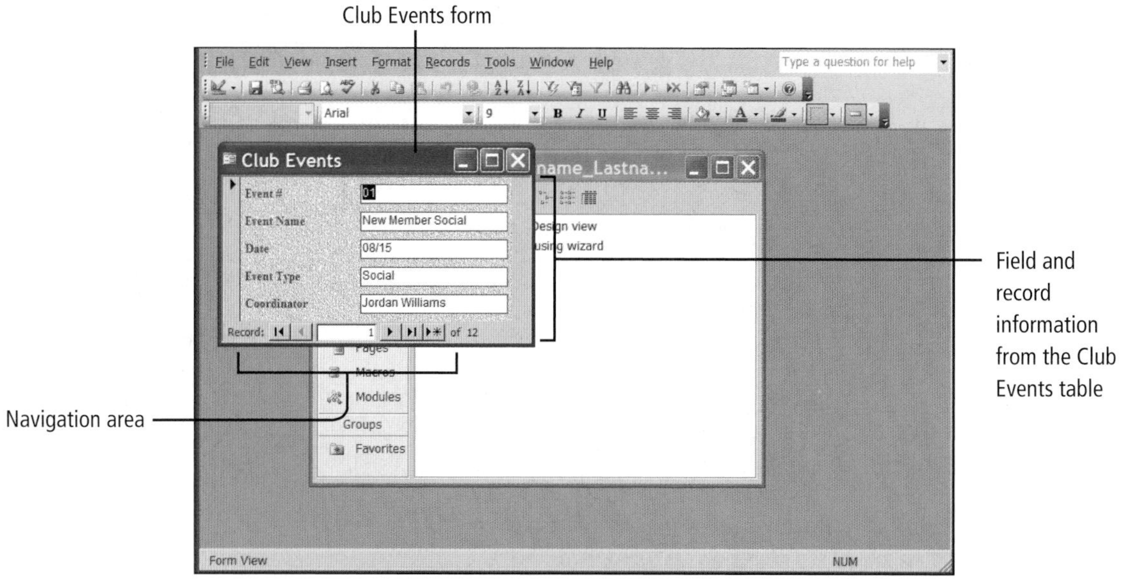

Figure 2.7

6 Click several of the navigation buttons to view the records in the form. All of the records in the Club Events table are available for viewing.

Objective 3
Save and Close an AutoForm

Because this form will be convenient for people who need to enter new data into the Club Events table, and for people who need to look up information about various club events, you will want to save the form for future use. When you close a form, you will be asked to save the changes.

Activity 2.3 Saving and Closing an AutoForm

1. In the upper right corner of the **Club Events** form, click the **Close** button.

   Because you have not previously named or saved this form, a message displays asking you if you want to save the changes to the design of form "Form1."

2. Click **Yes**.

   The Save As dialog box displays.

3. In the **Form Name** box, accept the default form name of *Club Events* by clicking **OK**.

   The form is saved and closed. The new form name, *Club Events*, displays in the Database window. See Figure 2.8. The default name of a form created in this manner is the name of the table upon which the form was based.

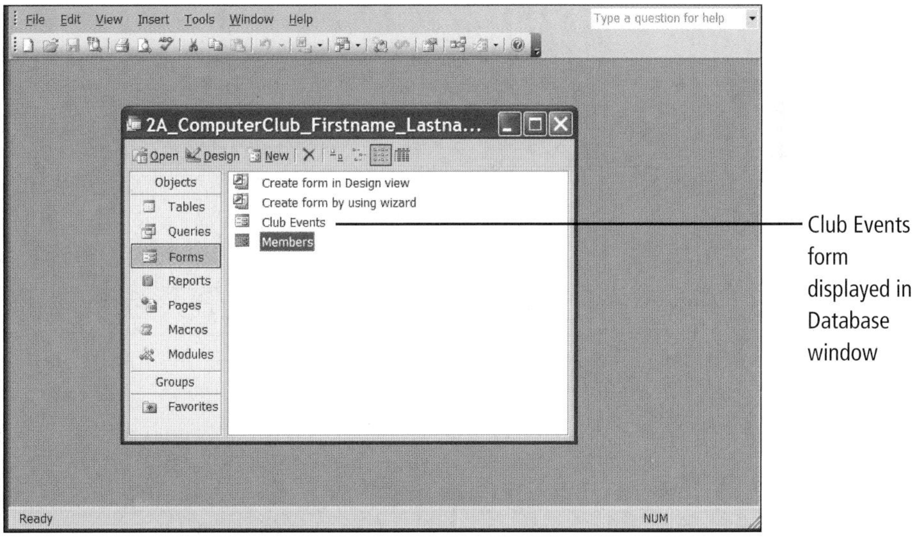

Figure 2.8

Another Way

> ### Using the Database Toolbar to Create an AutoForm
> ***Use the New Object: AutoForm button.***
>
> Access can create an AutoForm directly from the Database toolbar. On the Objects bar, click Tables. Click once on the table that contains the fields and records you would like in your form, then click the New Object: AutoForm button on the Database toolbar.

Objective 4
Use a Form to Add Records to and Delete Records from a Table

Forms and tables are interactive objects in an Access database. That is, when a record is added to a table using a form, the new record is inserted into the corresponding table. The reverse is also true—when a record is added to a table, the new record can be viewed in the corresponding form.

Activity 2.4 Adding Records to a Table Using a Form

1. On the Objects bar, verify that **Forms** is selected and then open the **Club Events** form.

   The Club Events form opens in the Form view.

2. In the navigation area of the form, click the **New Record** button.

   The fields are cleared and ready to accept a new entry. The record number advances to 13, indicating that this will be the 13th record. See Figure 2.9.

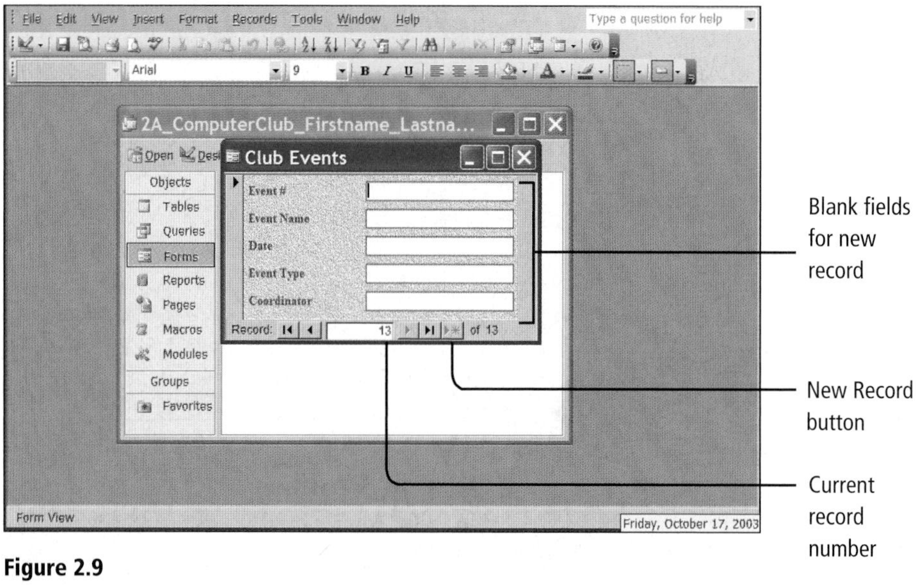

Figure 2.9

3. With the insertion point blinking in the **Event #** box, type **13** and then press Tab. After you start typing, notice that the pencil image displays in the gray bar to the left.
4. In the **Event Name** box, type **Project 2A** and then press Tab.
5. In the **Date** box type **3/10** and then press Tab.
6. In the **Event Type** box, type **Training** and then press Tab.
7. In the **Coordinator** box, using your own information, type **Firstname Lastname**

two

8. On the title bar of the **Club Events** form, click the **Close** button.

   The form closes and the new record is saved and added to the Club Events table.

9. On the Objects bar, click **Tables** and then double-click the **Club Events** table to open it in Datasheet view. Alternatively, select the table name and click the Open button just above the Objects bar.

10. Verify that record 13, the record you just added using the form, displays in the table and that your name is listed as the coordinator.

    Recall that tables and forms are interactive objects—the record you added by using the Club Events *form* displays in the Club Events *table*.

11. On the title bar of the table, click the **Close** button to close the table.

12. On the Objects bar, click **Forms**. Right-click the **Club Events** form and then click **Open**.

13. Using the navigation method of your choice (the **Next Record** button, the **Last Record** button, or by typing the record number in the Record box), navigate to record **13**.

    Record 13 displays and your name displays in the Coordinator field.

Activity 2.5 Deleting Records from a Table Using a Form

Using a form, you can also delete records from a database table. You should delete records when they are no longer needed in your database. In this activity, you will delete a record in the Club Events table—the record for the Introduction to Outlook event.

1. With the **Club Events** form displayed, navigate to **Event #5**, *Introduction to Outlook*. Then, on the left side of the form, locate the gray bar that contains a right-pointing arrow, as shown in Figure 2.10.

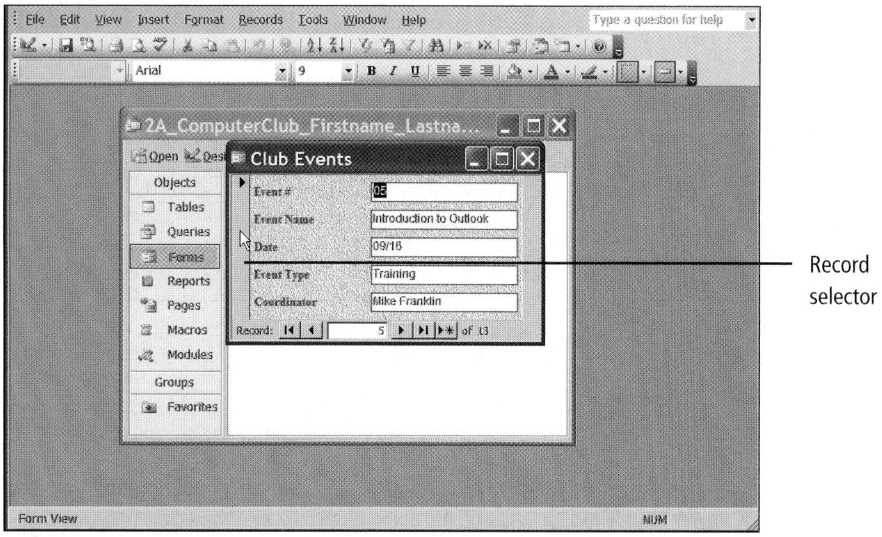

Figure 2.10

2 Click anywhere in the gray bar area.

The gray bar is selected; this area is known as the ***record selector***. The record selector in the form is similar to the record selector in a table. The record selector selects an entire record in a form, just as the record selector in a table allows you to select the entire row (record) in the table. When the record selector is highlighted in black—selected—all the fields in the displayed record are selected.

3 On the Form View toolbar, click the **Delete Record** button. Alternatively, press Delete on the keyboard.

A message displays alerting you that you are about to delete a record. If you click Yes and delete the record, you cannot use the Undo button to reverse the action. If you delete a record by mistake, you will have to re-create the record.

4 Click **Yes** to delete the record.

The record is deleted from the Club Events table, reducing the number of records in the table to 12.

5 On the title bar of the **Club Events** form, click the **Close** button to close the form.

6 Be sure the **Club Events** form is selected in the Database window. Display the **File** menu, click **Page Setup**, and in the displayed **Page Setup** dialog box, click the **Columns tab**. See Figure 2.11.

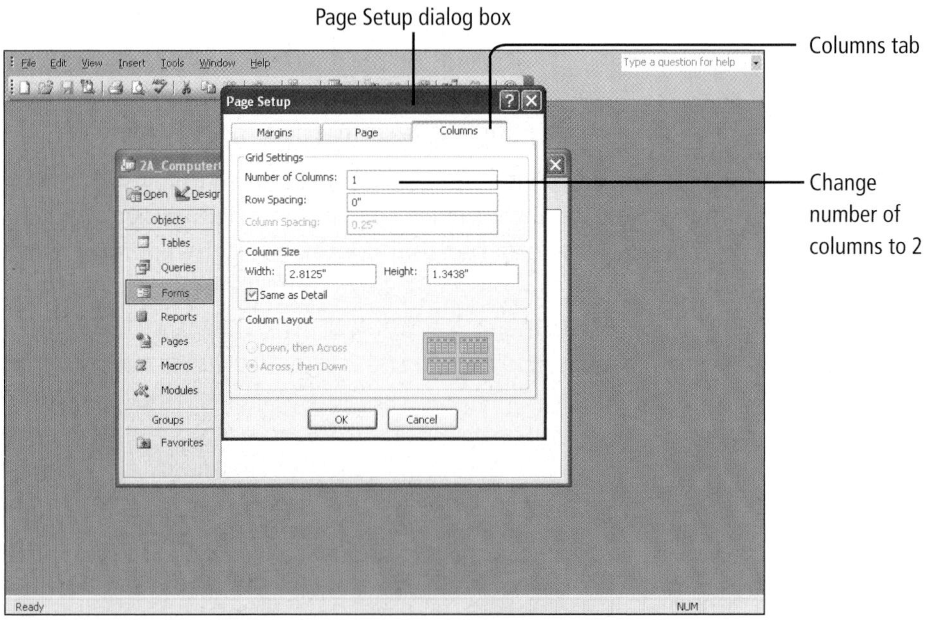

Figure 2.11

7 Under **Grid Settings**, change the **Number of Columns** to **2** and then click **OK**. On the Database toolbar, click the **Print** button.

Each record in the table will print in a newspaper column format. By selecting 2 columns, all the records will print on a single sheet. Recall that record 13 contains your name and that record 5 was deleted. Depending upon previous usage of your computer, your printed format may vary slightly from the one shown in Figure 2.1.

8 On the Objects bar, click **Tables** and then click the **Club Events** table. On the Database toolbar, click the **Print** button. Compare this printout to your forms printout.

You can see that all of the records are contained within both printouts. In the printed table, each record occupies a single row. In the Forms view, each record displays in its own individual form. The current date will print on the table printout.

9 On the title bar of the Database window, click the **Close** button to close the database. On the title bar of the Access window, click the **Close** button to close Access.

End You have completed Project 2A

Project 2B School

In Project 2A, you used AutoForm to create a form that incorporated all the fields from the table on which it was based. AutoForm creates a form in a simple top-to-bottom layout, with all the fields lined up in a single column. For the individual who is typing in the records, this layout is efficient and easy to use. Whereas AutoForm creates a form using all the fields in the table, and lays them out in a simple column, the ***Form Wizard*** creates a form in a manner that gives you much more flexibility in the design, layout, and number of fields included.

In Activities 2.6 through 2.15, you will use the Form Wizard to create a form for the Students database at Lake Michigan City College. Then you will modify the form and add a Page Footer to the form. You will also create a report for the Students database. See Figure 2.12.

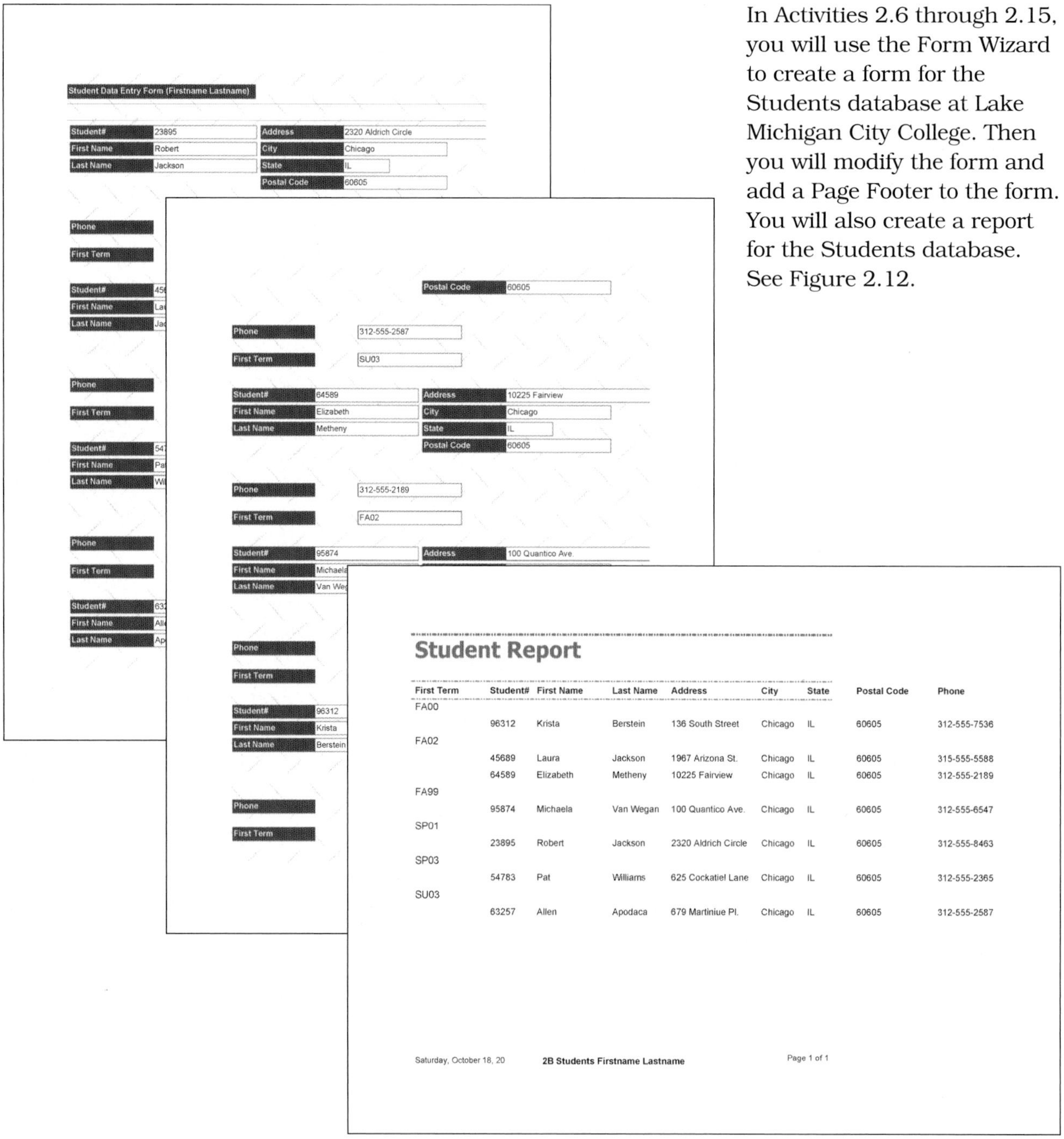

Figure 2.12
Project 2B—School

Objective 5
Create a Form with the Form Wizard

Different form layouts are useful for individuals who both view database information with a form and enter information into a database using a form. For example, when the admissions representative at your college displays your information to answer a question for you, it is easier to view the information spread out in a logical pattern across the screen rather than in one long column.

Activity 2.6 Creating a Form Using the Form Wizard

Recall that a wizard is an Access feature that walks you step by step through a process by asking you questions.

1. Using either **My Computer** or **Windows Explorer**, locate the file **a02B_School** from your student files. Copy the file and then paste it into your Chapter 2 folder. Rename the file as **2B_School_Firstname_Lastname** and remove the Read-only attribute. Close the Windows accessory you are using.

2. Start Access and open your **2B_School** database. On the Objects bar, click **Forms**.

3. To the right of the Objects bar, double-click the command icon **Create form by using wizard**. Alternatively, right-click the command icon and click Open on the displayed shortcut menu.

   The Form Wizard dialog box displays, as shown in Figure 2.13. The first step is to indicate the table for which you want the wizard to design a form, and then indicate what fields from the table that you want to include in the form.

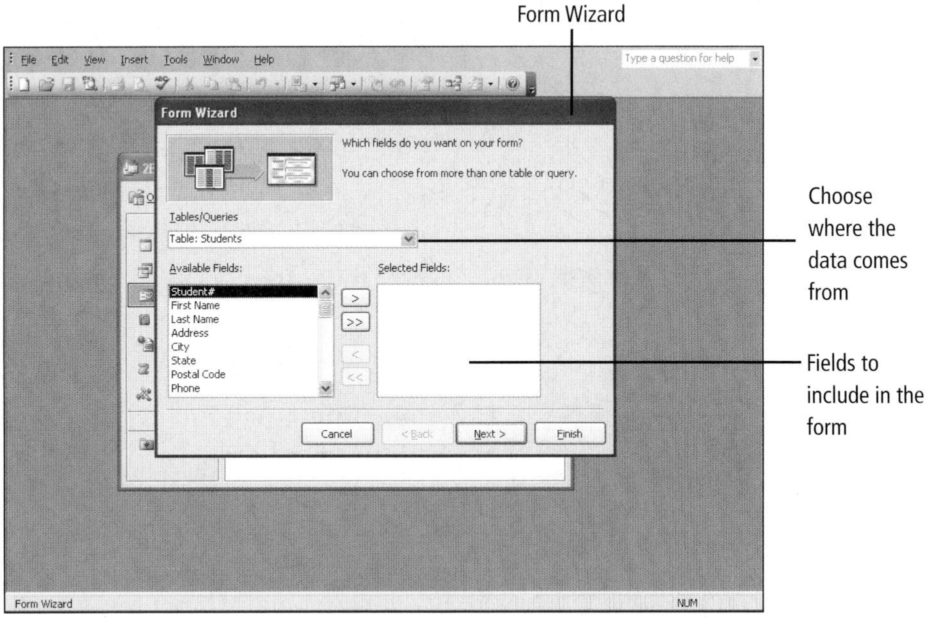

Figure 2.13

4 Under **Tables/Queries**, click the **down arrow**.

A list of tables and queries available for this database displays. Currently, only one object, the Students table, has been created in this database.

5 Click **Table: Students**.

Under Available Fields, a list of the fields in the Students table displays.

6 To the right of the **Available Fields** list, click the **All Fields** button to select all of the fields from the Students table and move them into the Selected Fields column. See Figure 2.14.

This action will place *all* of the fields from the table into the new form. It is also possible to use the **One Field** button to select fields one at a time so that you can select only those fields you want to include in the form.

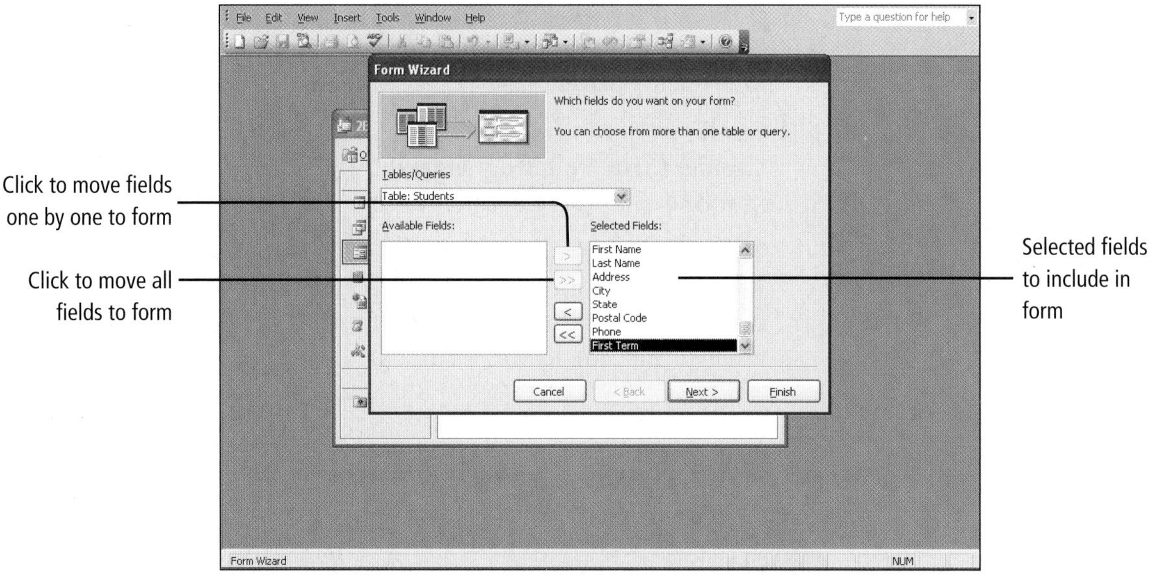

Figure 2.14

7 In the lower right corner of the dialog box, click the **Next** button.

The next step in the Form Wizard displays requesting information about the desired layout of your form.

8 Make sure the **Columnar** option button is selected and then click the **Next** button.

The next step in the Form Wizard displays requesting information about the desired style of your form, similar to Figure 2.15. Depending on previous use of your computer, a different style might be highlighted. Styles are combinations of attractive colors and graphics that are applied to the form to make it more visually appealing.

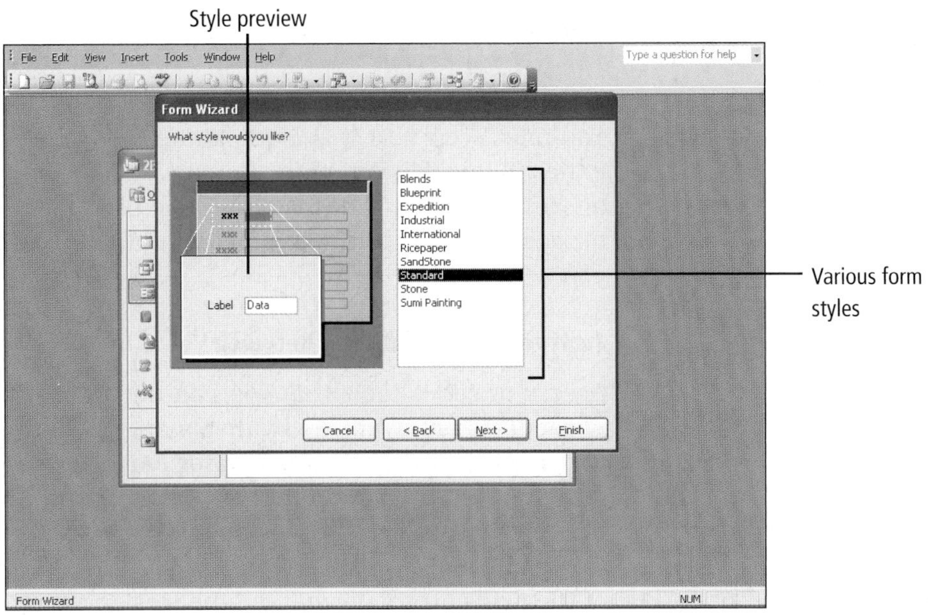

Figure 2.15

9 Click the **Industrial** style, notice the small preview of the style on the left, and then click the **Next** button.

The final step in the Form Wizard displays, and the default name for the form—*Students*—displays and is highlighted. Access always uses the table name as the default name for the form.

10 With the default name highlighted, press Delete and then, using your own first and last name, type **Students Firstname Lastname**

11 Click the **Finish** button.

Access creates the form using the responses you provided in the Wizard. The completed form displays in Form view. See Figure 2.16. Leave the form open for the next activity.

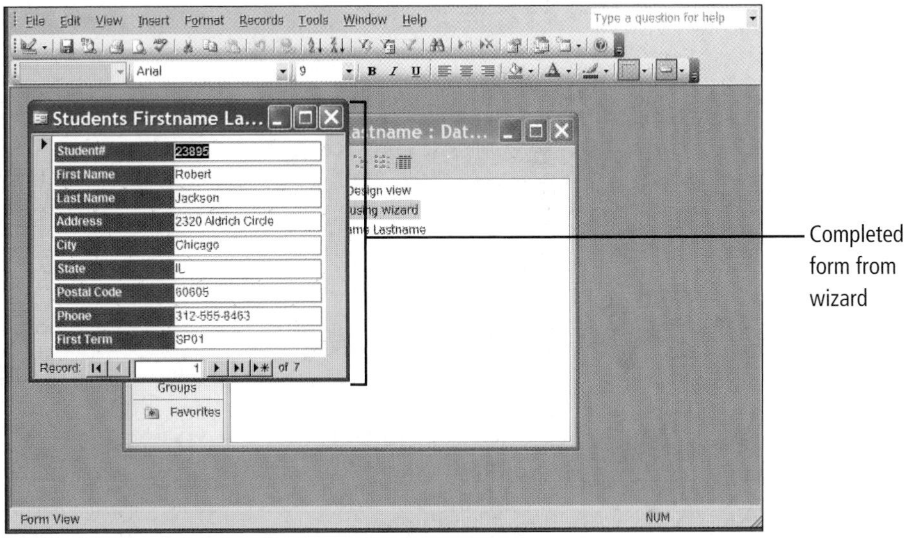

Figure 2.16

Objective 6
Modify a Form

You have seen that it is a quick and easy process to create a form using either the AutoForm method or the Form Wizard. After you have created a form, you may want to change the placement of the fields on the form for easier viewing or more efficient data entry. In the following activities, you will modify a form.

Activity 2.7 Switching Between Views in a Form and Adding a Form Header

Access provides tools that you can use to modify the layout of a form. These tools are available by displaying the form in its Design view. You can open a form in Design view or Form view, depending on what action you want to perform on the form. For example, if you want to view, add, delete, or modify records using a form, use the Form view. If you want to view, add, delete, or modify the field information (such as the placement of the fields on the form), use the Design view.

1 With your **Students** form displayed, on the Form View toolbar, click the **View** button. See Figure 2.17. In a manner similar to viewing tables, the View button will change depending on the current view to allow you to switch back and forth between *Design view* and *Form view*.

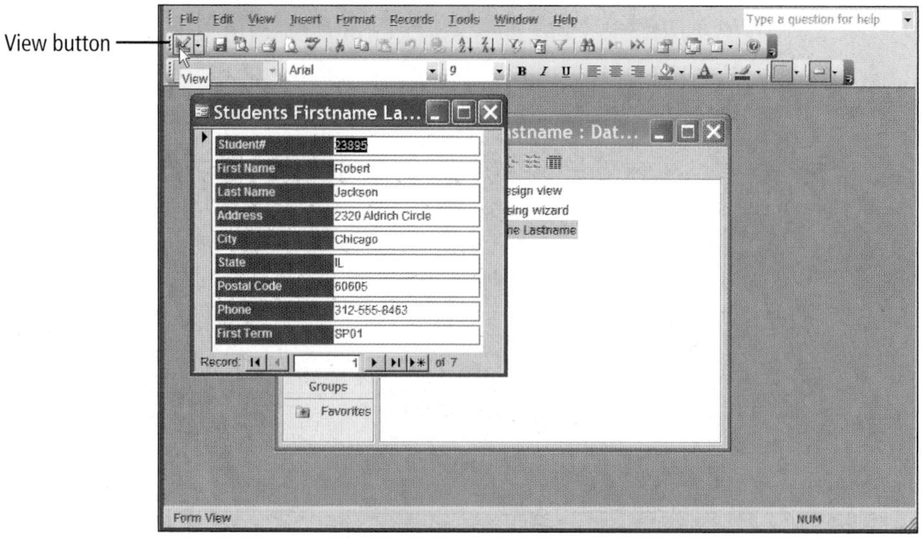

Figure 2.17

The form displays in Design view and the Toolbox toolbar displays, floating on your screen.

Notice that in Design view, you do not see the names of the students—or other information contained in the records. You see only the names of the fields. In this view, you can change the design of the form, such as the location of the fields on the form.

2 If necessary, drag the Toolbox by its title bar into the gray area of your screen. On the form's title bar, click the **Maximize** button.

The Design view of the form is maximized on your screen. This larger view is helpful to view the various sections of the form. See Figure 2.18.

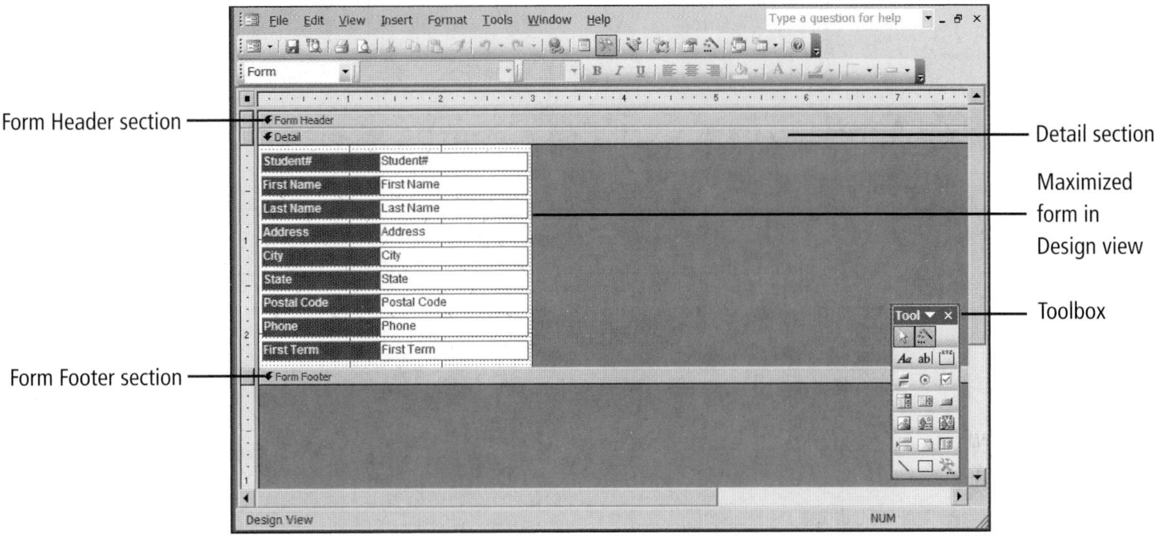

Figure 2.18

3 On your screen, locate the following three sections of the form, as shown in Figure 2.18: the Form Header section, the Detail section, and the Form Footer section.

Information typed into the ***Form Header*** or ***Form Footer*** sections displays at the top (header) or bottom (footer) of the form when it is viewed in Form view or when the form is printed. For example, on a form that displays transcript information for students, the form header could indicate *Official Transcript* and the form footer could indicate the name of the college. The ***Detail*** section contains the fields and records that display in the form. The small dots behind the Detail section create a grid to guide your eye in rearranging the layout of the form if you decide to do so.

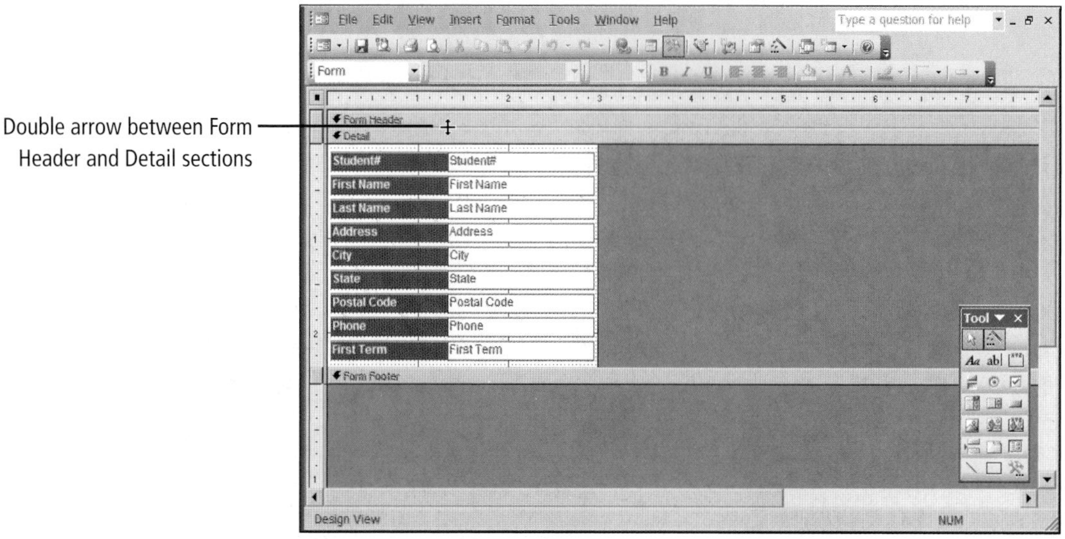

Figure 2.19

4 Position your pointer on the horizontal line between the **Form Header** section and the **Detail** section until the pointer changes to a large double arrow, as shown in Figure 2.19.

5 Drag downward approximately 0.5 inch. Use your eye or the vertical ruler to determine this distance; it need not be exact. Release the mouse button.

The Form Header section expands and a grid pattern of dots displays.

6 On the Toolbox toolbar floating on your screen, click the **Label** button, as shown in Figure 2.20.

The ***Toolbox*** toolbar has various ***controls*** that can be added to forms in Access. Controls are the objects in a form, such as the brown labels and white text boxes currently displayed on your screen, with which you view or manipulate information stored in tables or queries.

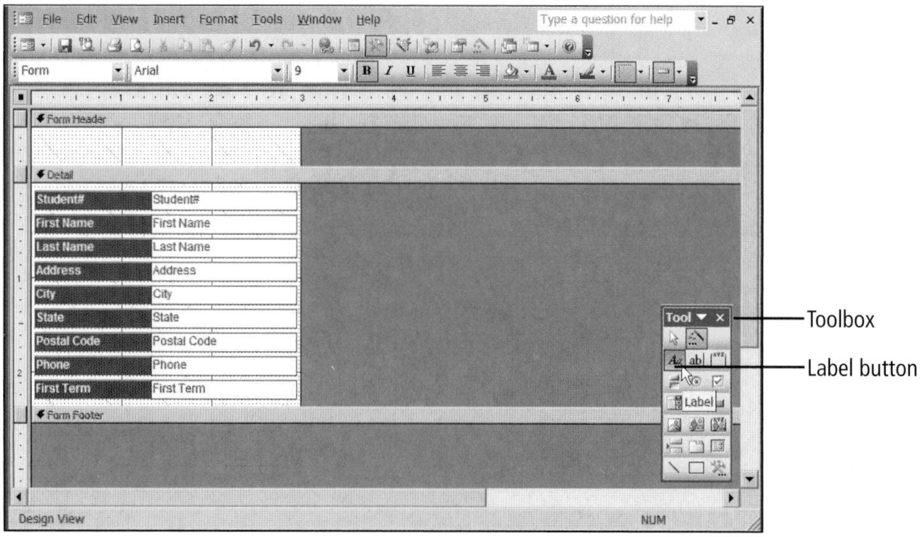

Figure 2.20

Alert!

Is your Toolbox missing?

If the toolbox is not displayed, click the Toolbox button on the Form Design toolbar. Alternatively, from the View menu, click Toolbox.

7 Move your pointer into the **Form Header section** and notice that the pointer shape is a plus sign and the letter A. See Figure 2.21.

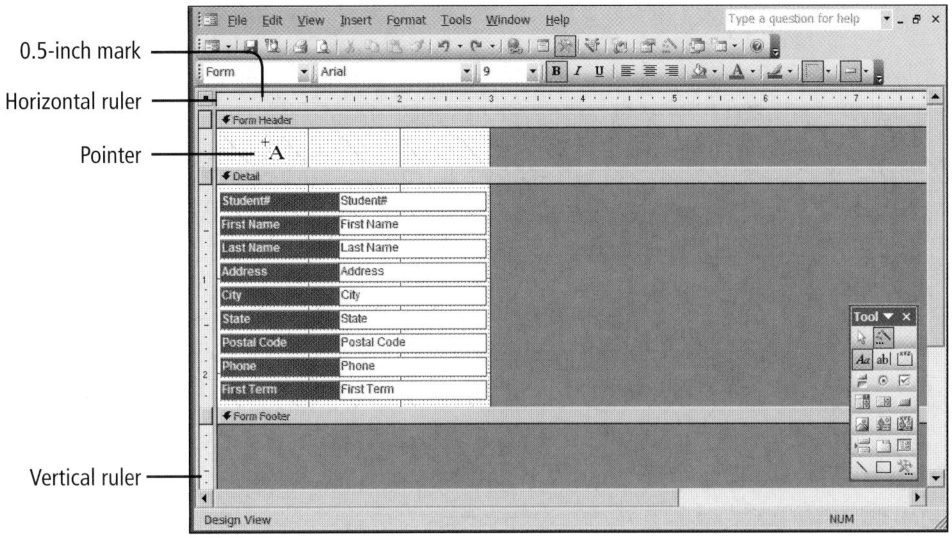

Figure 2.21

8 On your screen, locate the horizontal and vertical rulers as shown in Figure 2.21 and then locate the 0.5-inch mark on the horizontal ruler.

Note — Displaying Rulers in Form Design View

Click Ruler on the View menu.

If the rulers are not displayed in the Design view of your form, display the View menu and then click Ruler.

9 With the plus sign of your mouse pointer positioned at the left edge of the **Form Header section**, drag down about 0.25 of an inch and to the right to **2.5 inches on the horizontal ruler**. Release the mouse button and compare your result to Figure 2.22.

If you are not satisfied with your result, click the Undo button and begin again. A new label control is created in the Form Header section and the insertion point is blinking in the control.

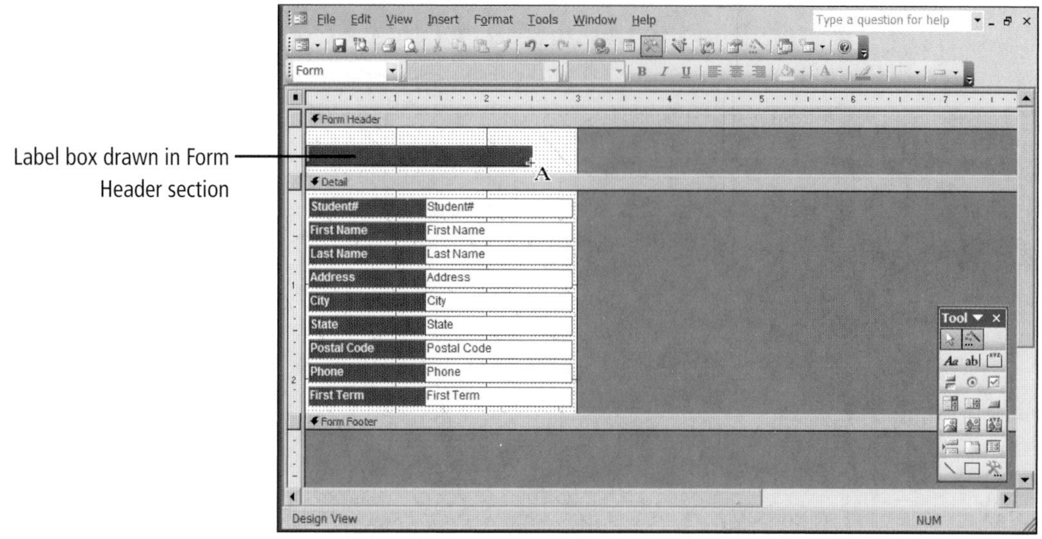

Figure 2.22

10 In the label control that you just created, using your own first and last name, type **Student Data Entry Form (Firstname Lastname)**

The label expands to accommodate your typing.

11 Press Enter and then notice that the label is surrounded by small squares.

The small squares surrounding the label are ***sizing handles*** that indicate that the label control is selected.

12 On the Form View toolbar, click the **View** button to switch to the Form view.

The form header displays with the information you inserted. See Figure 2.23. By placing a form header on the form, you have created information that will display at the top of the form when it is viewed, and also print at the top of the form when it is printed.

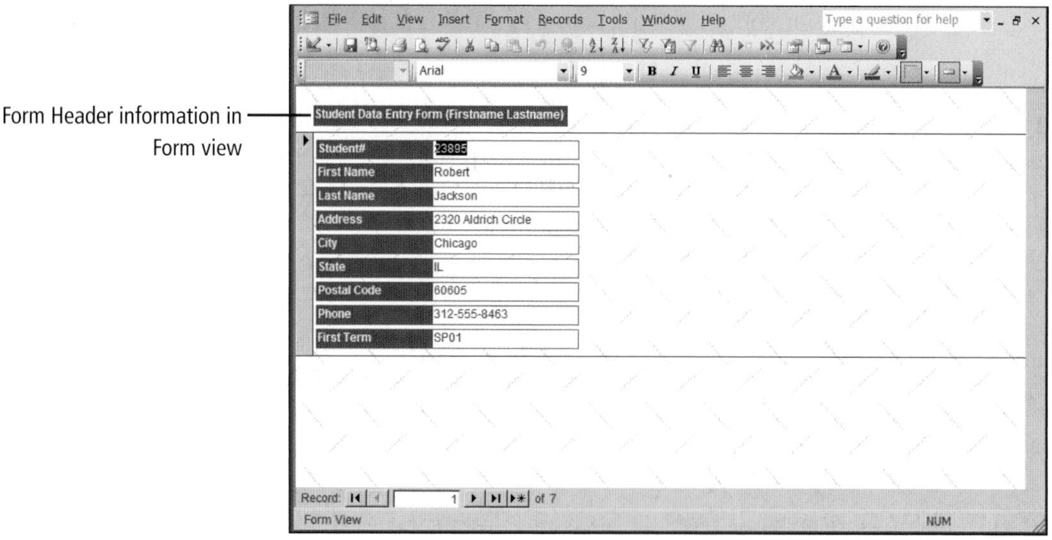

Figure 2.23

13 Click the **View** button again to return to the Design view of the form for the next activity.

Activity 2.8 Moving and Resizing Fields in a Form

The Design view of any database object is the view that is used to change the layout—the design—of the object. The reason for changing the layout of a form is usually to make it easier for the people using it to view and enter data. Sometimes forms are modified to match an existing paper form already in use by an organization. For example, the Student Registration Department at your college may have an existing paper form that you fill out when registering for courses. Transferring or entering this information from the paper form is easier if the Access form on the screen matches the pattern on the paper form.

1 With your form displayed in Design view, locate the horizontal and vertical rulers on your screen. Notice that the form is 3 inches wide.

2 As shown in Figure 2.24, position your mouse pointer on the right edge of the form until your pointer changes to a large, double arrow. Then, drag the right edge of the form to **6.5 inches on the horizontal ruler**.

By increasing the width of the form area, you have more space in which to rearrange the various form controls.

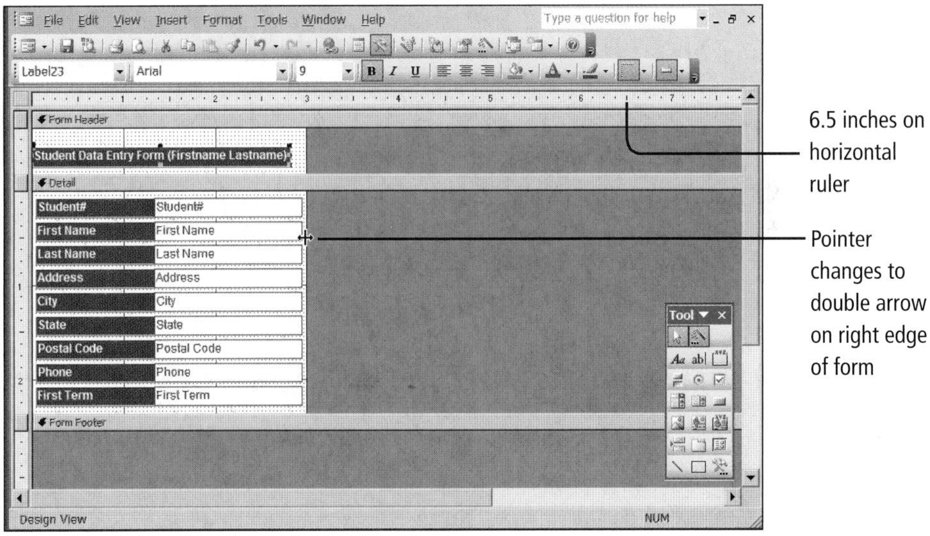

Figure 2.24

3 Click once in the white **Address text box control**. See Figure 2.25.

The Address ***text box control*** is selected and handles surround the selected object. A text box control on a form is where data from the corresponding table is displayed when the form is viewed.

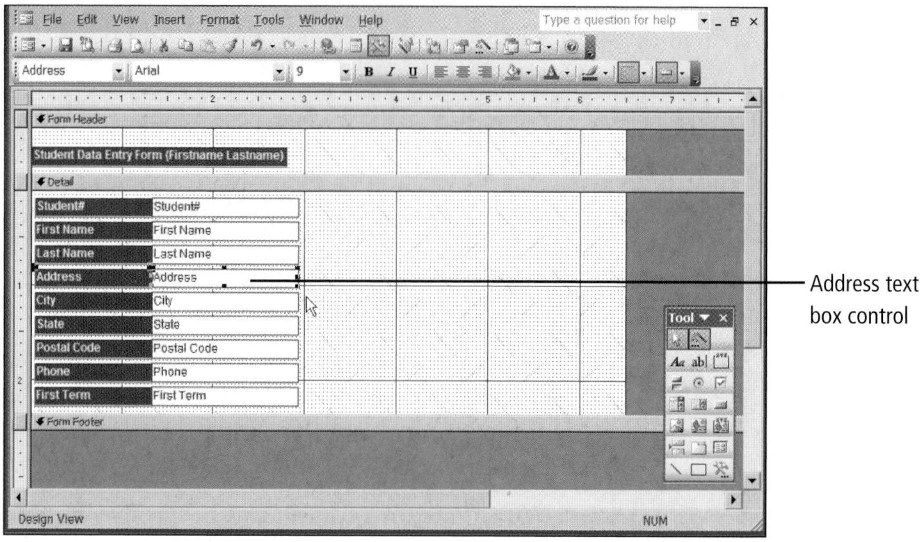

Figure 2.25

4 Position your mouse pointer over any border of the selected text box control until the **hand** pointer displays. See Figure 2.26. The hand pointer displays when the mouse pointer is positioned on the border of a control.

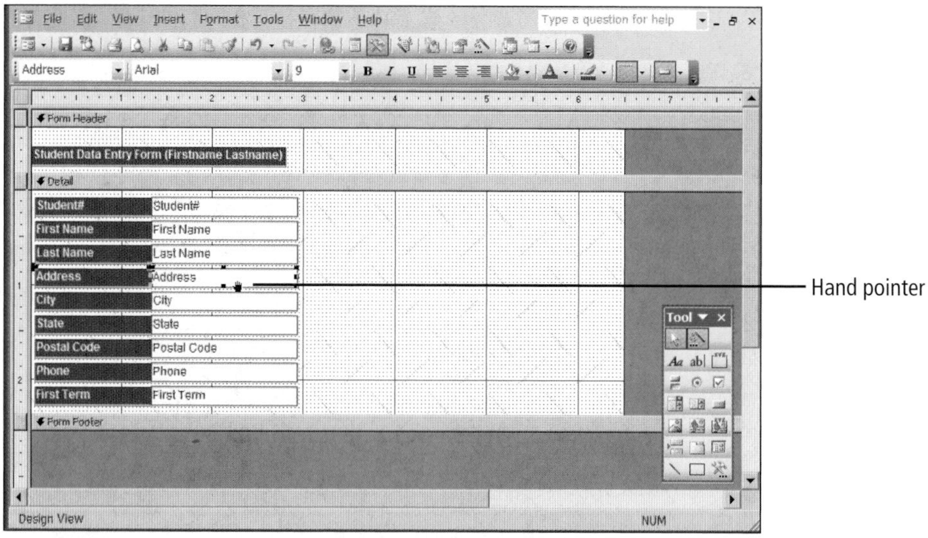

Figure 2.26

5 With the **hand** pointer displayed, drag the text box up and to the right of the Student# field as shown in Figure 2.27. Make sure that the left edge is positioned at approximately **3 inches on the horizontal ruler**.

Notice that both the *label* control—the brown box that, when viewed in Form view, contains the field name—and the *text box* control—the white box that, when viewed in Form view, contains the actual data—move together to the new location. Dragging with the hand pointer on the border of a control allows you to reposition both the label control and the text box control as one unit.

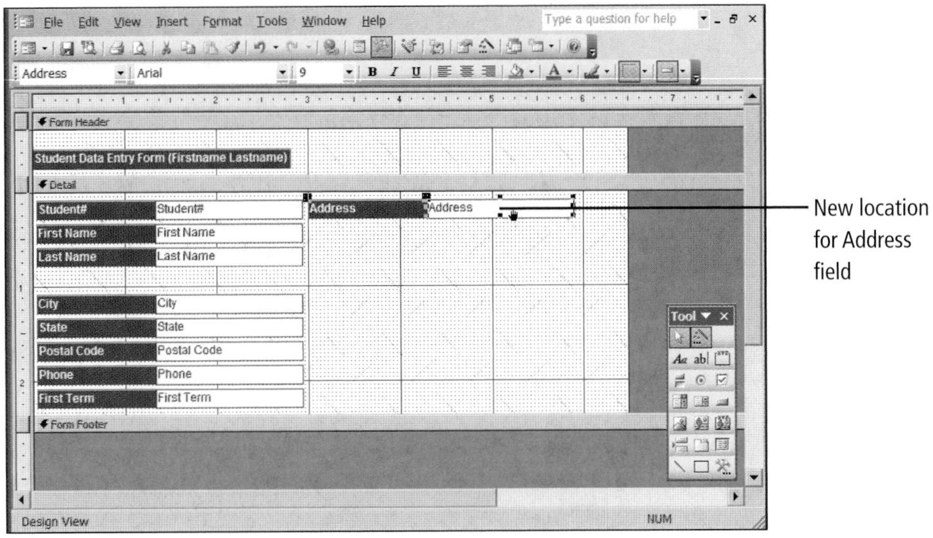

Figure 2.27

6 Click once in the white **City text box control** to select it, then position your pointer over any border of the text box to display the **hand pointer** .

7 Drag to position the **City controls** directly under the **Address controls**, to the right of the First Name controls, as shown in Figure 2.28.

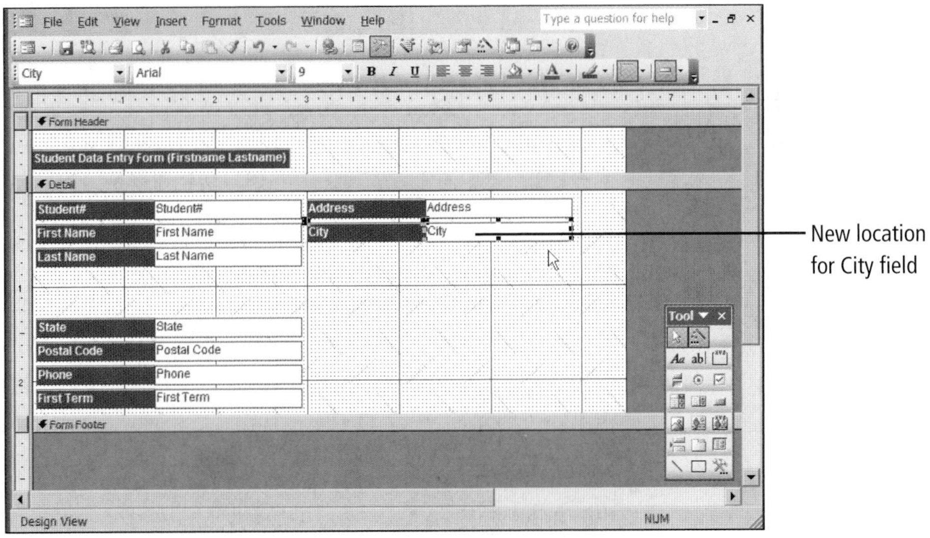

Figure 2.28

8 Using the technique you just practiced, move the **State controls** and the **Postal Code controls**, as shown in Figure 2.29.

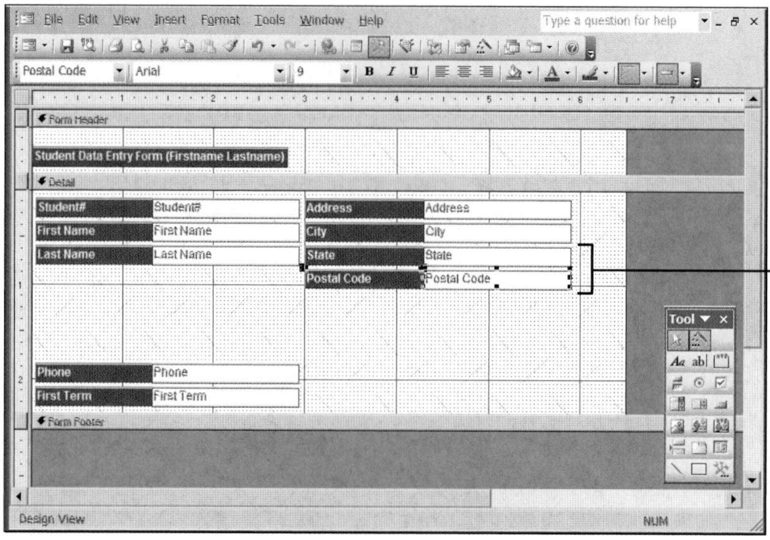

Figure 2.29

9 Click once in the **Phone text box control** to select it. Position your pointer over the large black handle that is between the Phone label control and the Phone text box control until the **pointing hand** pointer  displays. See Figure 2.30.

The pointing hand displays when your mouse pointer is positioned on the larger, upper left handle. With this pointer shape, you can move the text box control separately from the label control.

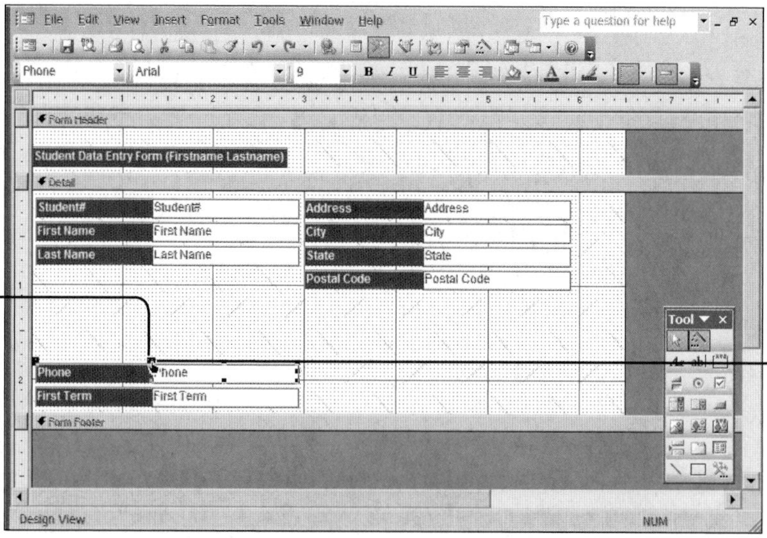

Figure 2.30

10 With the **pointing hand** pointer displayed, drag the white **Phone text box control** to the position shown in Figure 2.31—positioning its left edge at **2 inches on the horizontal ruler** and its top edge at **1.5 inches on the vertical ruler**.

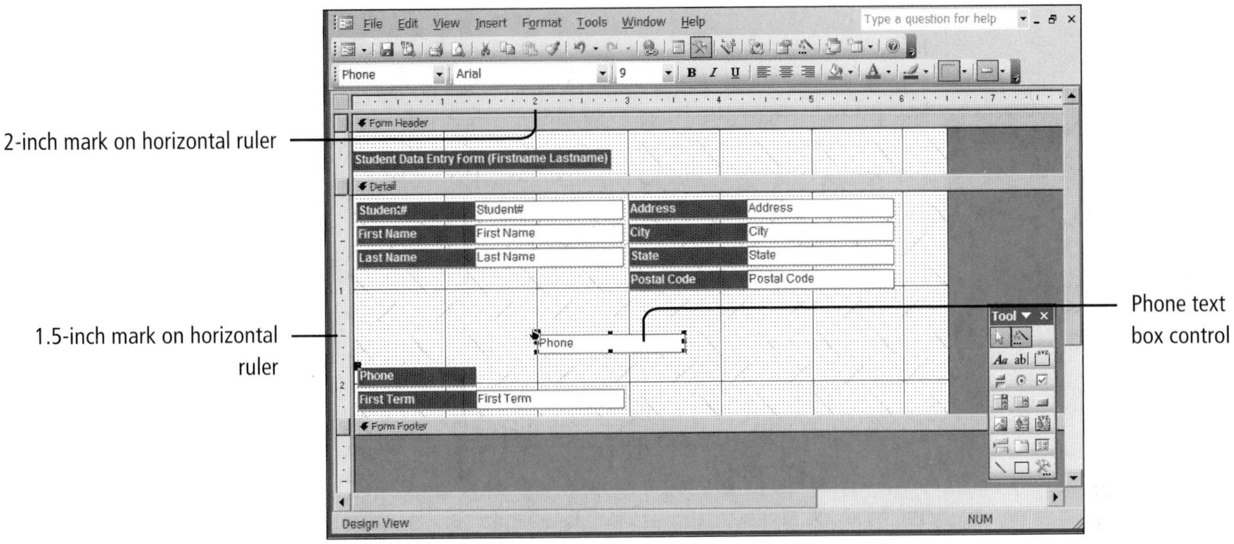

Figure 2.31

11 Select the brown **Phone label control**, point to the large black handle at the upper left corner to display the **pointing hand** pointer, and then drag to position it as shown in Figure 2.32.

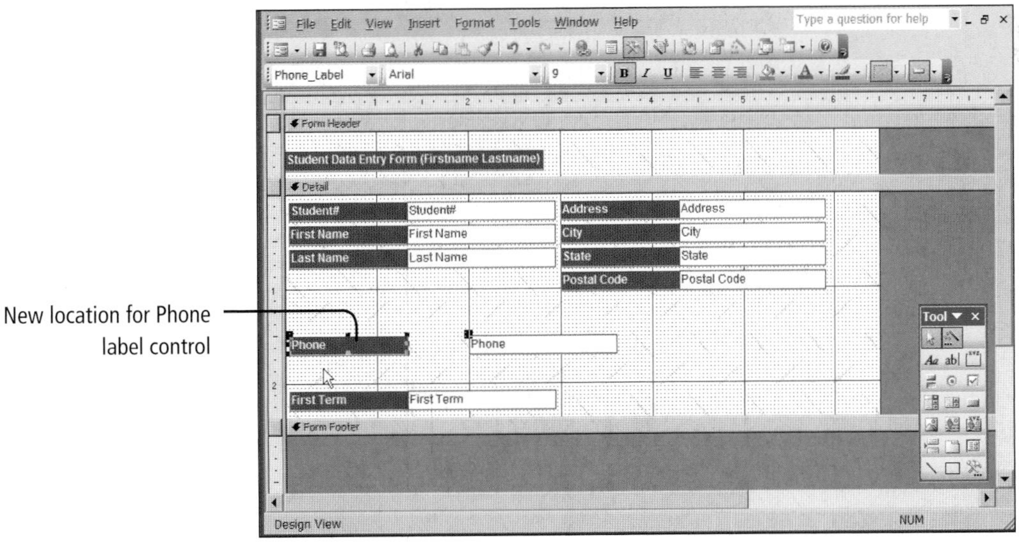

Figure 2.32

12 Move the white **First Term text box control** directly under the Phone text box control aligning its left edge at **2 inches on the horizontal ruler** and its top edge **at 1⅞ inches on the vertical ruler**, as shown in Figure 2.33.

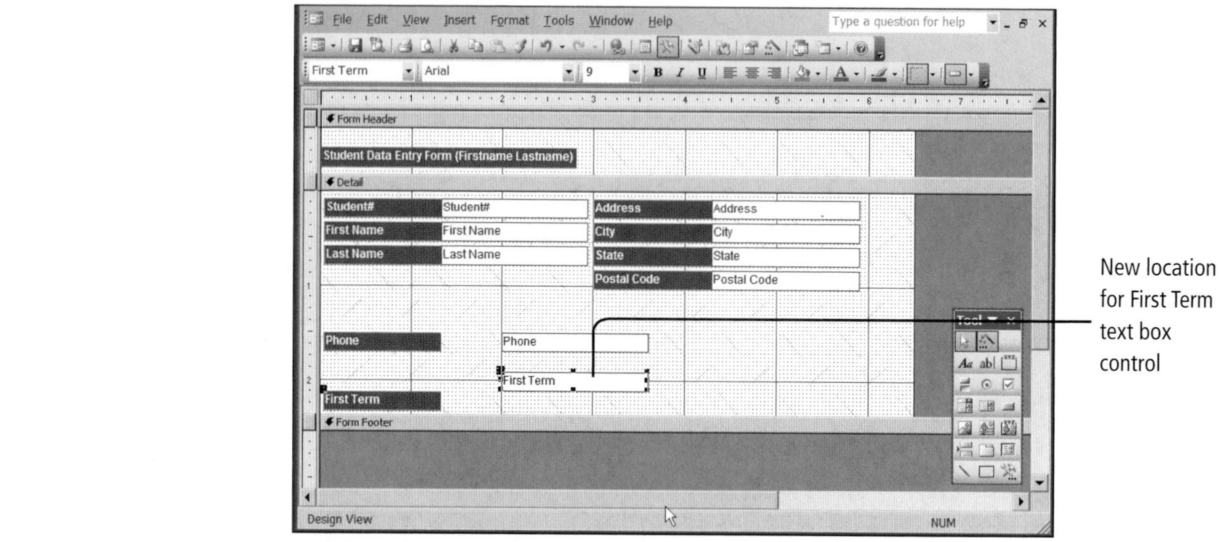

Figure 2.33

13 Move the brown **First Term label control** as shown in Figure 2.34.

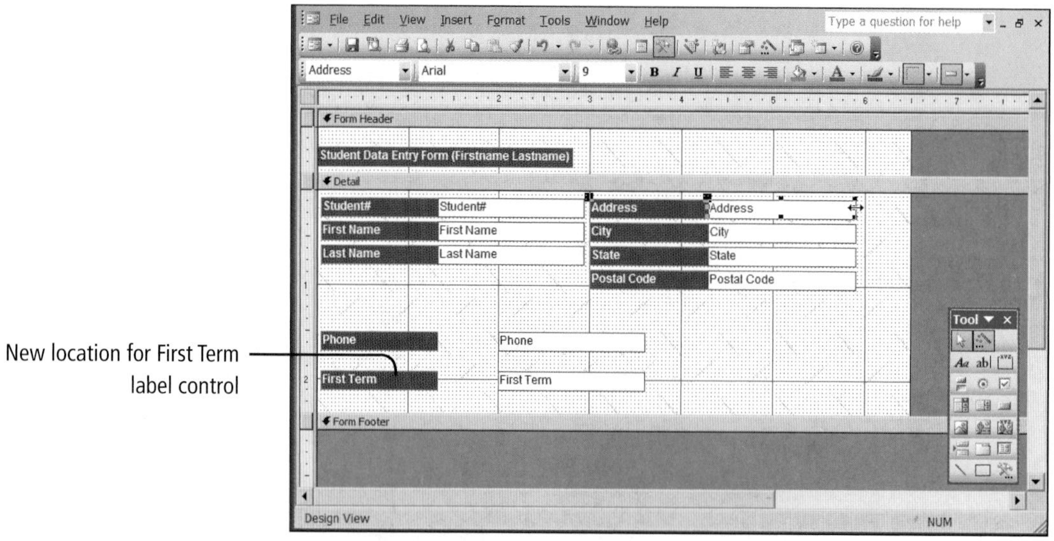

Figure 2.34

14 Click to select the white **Address text box control**, then position your pointer over the right center handle until the pointer changes to a horizontal double arrow, as shown in Figure 2.35.

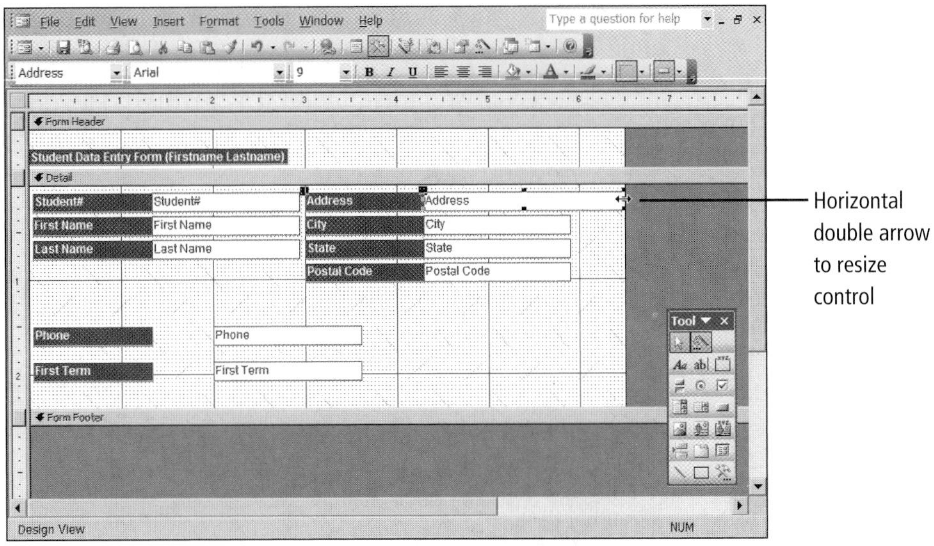

Figure 2.35

15 Drag the center right handle to **6.5 inches on the horizontal ruler**.

The width of the Address text box control is increased. This is a good idea because addresses are typically longer than the data in a City or State field.

16 Use the technique you just practiced to *decrease* the width of the **State text box control**, as shown in Figure 2.36.

You can see how the grid pattern provides a visual guide in placing the controls exactly where you want them.

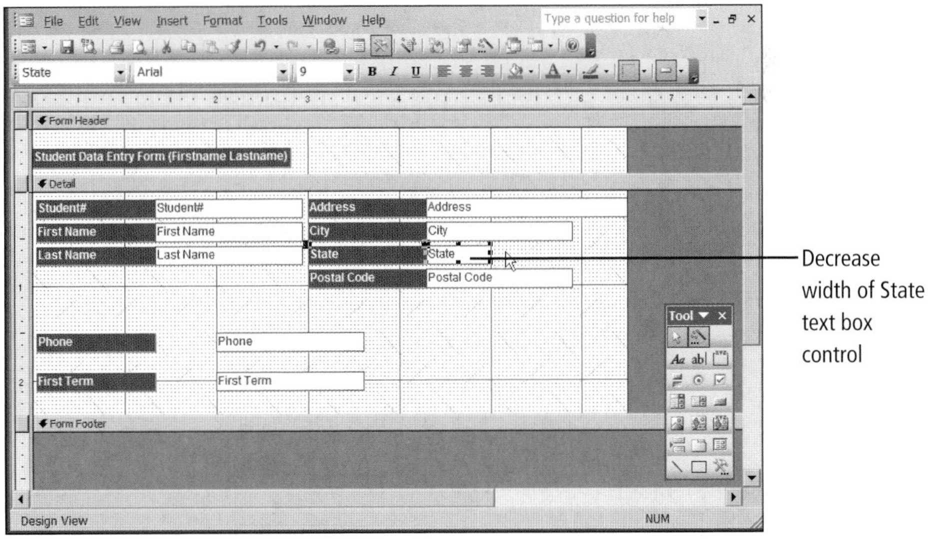

Figure 2.36

17 On the Form Design toolbar, click the **View** button to switch to the Form view and notice the changes you have made to the layout of the form.

18 Click the **View** button again to return to the Design view of the form for the next activity.

Activity 2.9 Adding a Page Footer to a Form

A ***Page Header*** or ***Page Footer*** contains information that displays on every page of a form when it is printed. Header information displays at the top of a printed page and footer information displays at the bottom of a printed page.

1. On the menu bar, click **View** and then click **Page Header/Footer**.

   Page Header and Page Footer sections are added to your form, as shown in Figure 2.37.

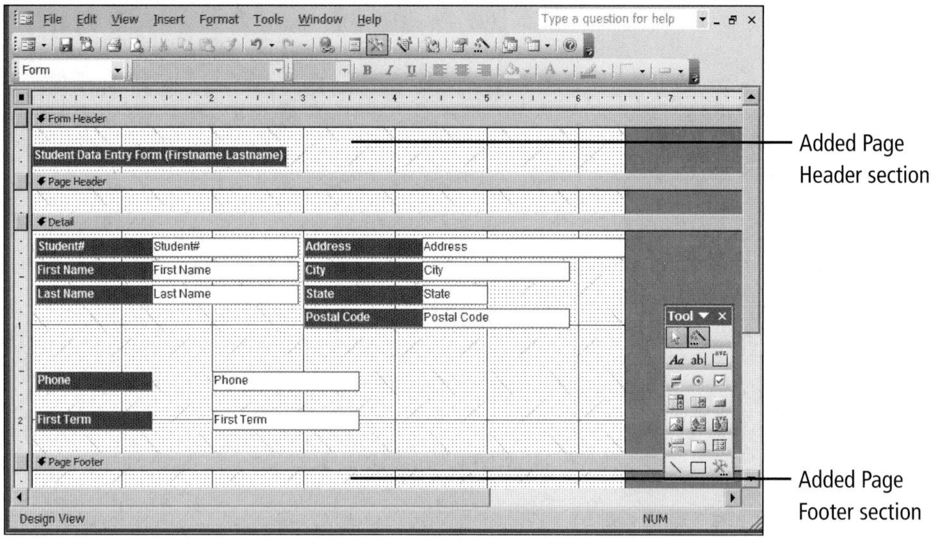

Figure 2.37

2. Locate the Toolbox toolbar floating on your screen. If it is not visible, display the View menu and click **Toolbox**. On the Toolbox, click the **Label** button .

3. Position the plus sign of your pointer just below the Page Footer separator at **2 inches on the horizontal ruler**, and then drag down to the lower separator and to the right to **4.5 inches on the horizontal ruler**, as shown in Figure 2.38.

   If you are not satisfied with your result, recall that you can click the Undo button and begin again. An insertion point is blinking at the left edge of the control.

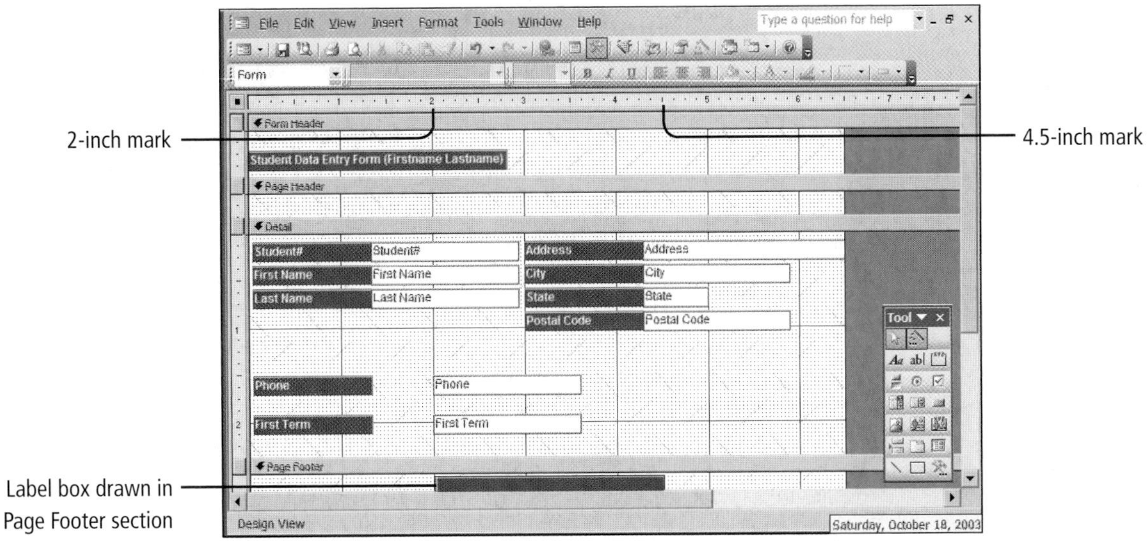

Figure 2.38

4. In the label control you just created, using your own first and last name, type **2B Students Firstname Lastname** and then press Enter.

   Label controls, when placed in headers or footers, function as descriptors to either clarify the contents of a text box control, or to add additional information—such as a title or your name—to a form.

5. Click the **View** button to switch to the Form view.

   Notice that the Page footer you created does *not* display in the Form view of the form. Page Headers and Footers only display when the form is printed.

6. On the Form View toolbar, click the **Print Preview** button. Locate your name in the Page footer at the lower edge of the page in Print Preview.

7. On the Print Preview toolbar, click the **Print** button to print the form.

   Three pages will print; the last page will contain only the page footer.

8. To the right of *Type a question for help*, click the small **Close Window** button ✕.

9. Click **Yes** when prompted to save changes to the design of the form.

   The Database window, maximized, displays.

Objective 7
Create a Report with the Report Wizard

Recall that a report is a database object that displays the fields and records from a table in an easy-to-read format suitable for printing. Reports are created to summarize information in a database in a professional-looking manner.

The ***Report Wizard*** assists you in creating a professionally designed report. The Report Wizard asks you a series of questions and then creates a report based on your answers.

Activity 2.10 Creating a Report Using the Report Wizard

1. If desired, to the right of the *Type a question for help box*, click the small **Restore Window** button. On the Objects bar, click **Reports**.

2. To the right of the Objects bar, double-click the command icon **Create report by using wizard**.

   The Report Wizard displays with its first question. See Figure 2.39. Here you will select the table from which you want to get information, and then select the fields that you want to include in the report.

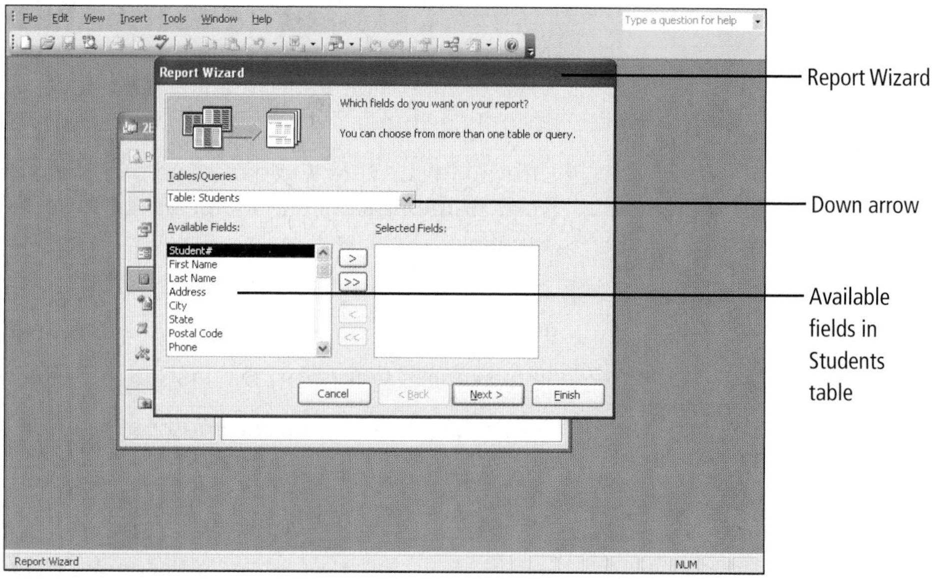

Figure 2.39

3. Under **Tables/Queries**, click the **down arrow**.

   A list of tables and queries available for this database displays. Currently, only one object, the Students table, has been created in this database.

4. Click **Table: Students**.

   Under Available Fields, a list of the fields in the Students table displays.

5 To the right of the list of available fields, click the **All Fields** button [>>] to move all of the fields from the Students table to the Selected Fields column on the far right.

This action will cause all of the fields to be included in the report.

6 Click the **Next** button.

7 Under **Do you want to add any grouping levels?** click **State** and then to the right, click the **One Field** button [>].

The preview on the right displays the State field as the field by which to group the records in the report. Grouping data helps you organize and summarize the data in your report. Grouping data in a report places all of the records within the same group field together.

8 In the center column, click the **One Field Back** button [<].

The State field is removed as the field by which to group the data. Because each of the records in the Students table has the same State information, it would not be useful to group the records by State.

9 Click **First Term** and then click the **One Field** button [>].

This action will cause the data in the report to be grouped by the First Term field.

10 Click the **Next** button.

11 In the **1** box on the right, click the **down arrow** to select a sort order for the records in the report. See Figure 2.40.

A list of fields in the report displays.

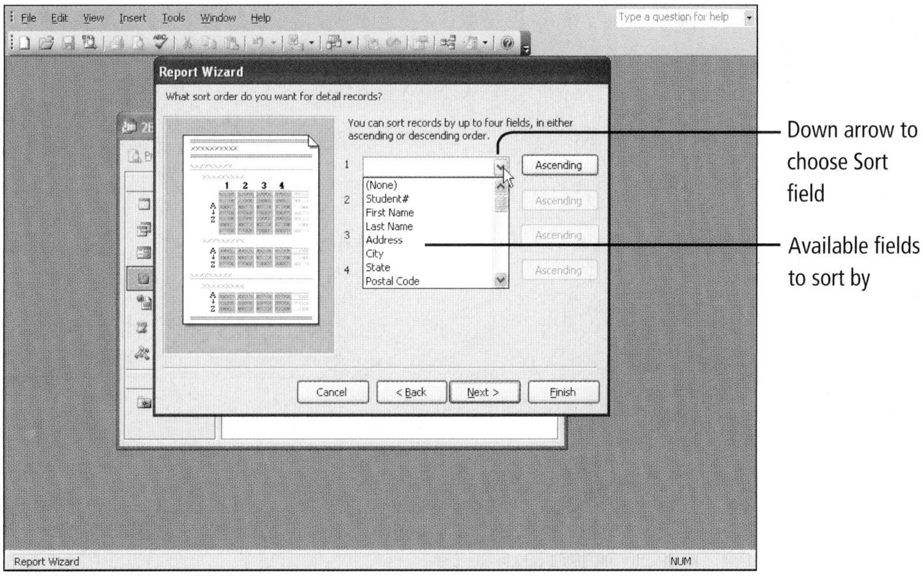

Figure 2.40

12 Click **Student#** and leave the default order as **Ascending**.

This action will cause the records in the report to be sorted numerically by each Student's Student# *within* the grouping option specified, which was First Term. Sorting records in a report presents a more organized report.

13 Click the **Next** button.

14 Under **Layout**, click the **Block** option button and notice the preview on the left. Click the **Outline 1** option button and notice the preview on the left.

15 Click the remaining **Layout** option buttons and view the preview.

The layout you choose for a report determines the arrangement of the data on the printed pages of your report.

16 After you are finished viewing the layout options, click the **Stepped** option button to select it as the layout option for the report.

17 On the right side of the dialog box, under **Orientation**, be sure that **Portrait** is selected, and keep the check mark next to *Adjust the field width so all fields fit on a page.*

18 Click the **Next** button. In the displayed list of styles, click **Soft Gray**.

19 Notice the preview to the left and then click **Compact** to view its preview. Click to view each of the remaining styles and then click **Casual**.

20 Click the **Next** button. In the **What title do you want for your report?** box type **Student Report** and then click the **Finish** button.

The report displays in Print Preview.

21 Maximize the window if necessary. On the toolbar, click the **Zoom arrow** and then click **75%**.

22 If necessary, use the vertical scroll bar to examine the data in the report. Notice that each of the specifications you defined for the report in the Report Wizard is reflected in the Print Preview of the report. Students are grouped by First Term. See Figure 2.41.

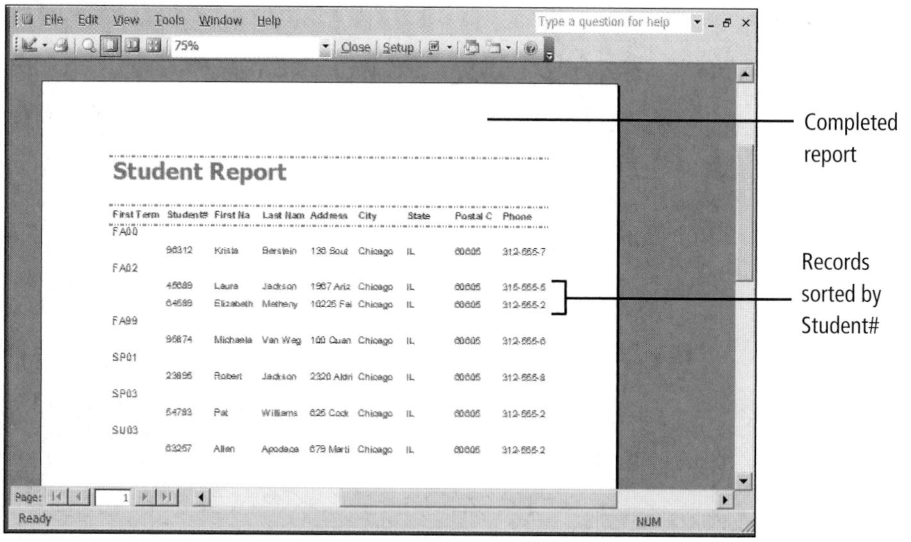

Figure 2.41

Objective 8
Save a Report

You do not need to create a new report each time data in the corresponding table is modified. Once you have created a report and laid it out in a format that is useful to you, you can save the report for future use. Each time the report is opened, any changes made to the table will be automatically reflected in the report.

Activity 2.11 Saving a Report

1. Click the **Close Window** button [X] to close the report.

   The report name, *Student Report*, displays in the Database window. Reports created with the Report Wizard are named in the final step of the wizard. When the report is closed, it is automatically saved.

2. Double-click the **Student Report**.

   The report opens in Print Preview.

3. Adjust the zoom to **75%** so you can view the records in the report, and if necessary, maximize the window.

   In the displayed report, notice that some of the field names are not completely displayed; they are cut off. For example, the *First Name*, *Last Name*, and *Postal Code* field names are not fully displayed.

4. Leave the report displayed in Print Preview for the next activity.

Objective 9
Modify the Design of a Report

After a report is created, you can still make modifications to its design by opening the report in Design view.

Activity 2.12 Switching Between Report View and Design View

1. On the Print Preview toolbar, click the **View** button to switch to the Design view of the report.

2. In the Design view of the report, examine the sections of the report, and notice that the report contains a Page Header and a Page Footer section. See Figure 2.42.

   Design view for a report is similar to the Design view of a form. You can make modifications, and the dotted grid pattern assists you with alignment. Reports created with the Report Wizard contain a Page Header and Page Footer. You do not need to manually add these as you did with the form created with the Form Wizard.

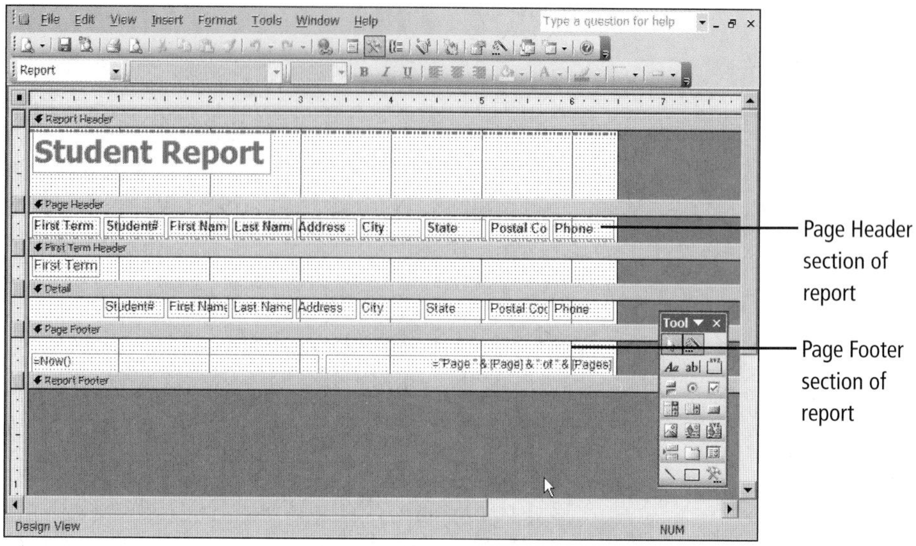

Figure 2.42

3 On the Report Design toolbar, click the **View** button.

The report displays in Print Preview..

4 On the Print Preview toolbar, click the **Setup** button. Alternatively, click File, Page Setup.

5 In the displayed **Page Setup** dialog box, click the **Page tab**. See Figure 2.43.

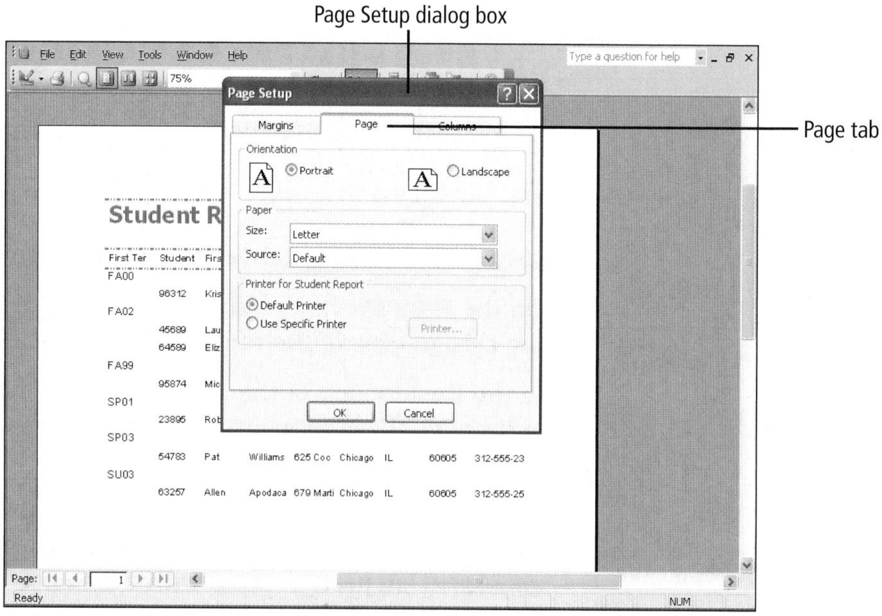

Figure 2.43

6 Under **Orientation**, click the **Landscape** option button and then click **OK**.

The report displays in landscape orientation. Changing the report to landscape orientation will allow more information to print across the page.

7 On the Print Preview toolbar, click the **View** button to switch to Design view, and leave the report open in Design view for the next activity.

Now that you have adjusted the page orientation, you can move to Design view to make additional modifications to the report.

Activity 2.13 Moving and Resizing Fields in a Report

Moving and resizing fields in the Design view of a report is accomplished with the same techniques you practiced when you moved and resized controls in a form in Design view.

1 If necessary, use the horizontal scroll bar to scroll the report to the right so that you can see the 9-inch mark on the horizontal ruler.

2 Position your pointer on the right edge of the report until your pointer changes to a large double arrow, and then drag the right edge of the report to the right to **9 inches on the horizontal ruler**. See Figure 2.44.

The width of the report is increased. By increasing the width of a report, you create more working space to move and reposition fields on the report.

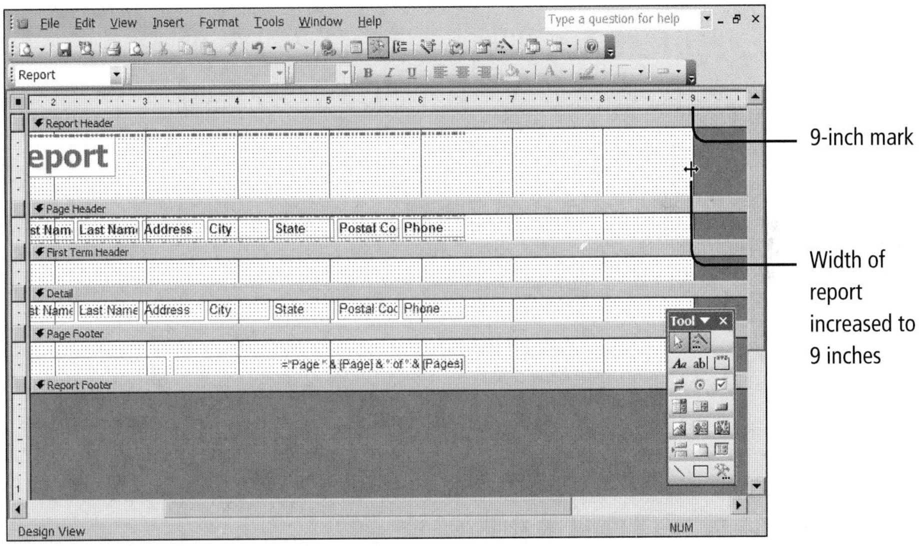

Figure 2.44

3 In the **Detail section**, click to select the **Phone text box control**. See Figure 2.45.

The Phone text box control is selected and handles surround the selected object.

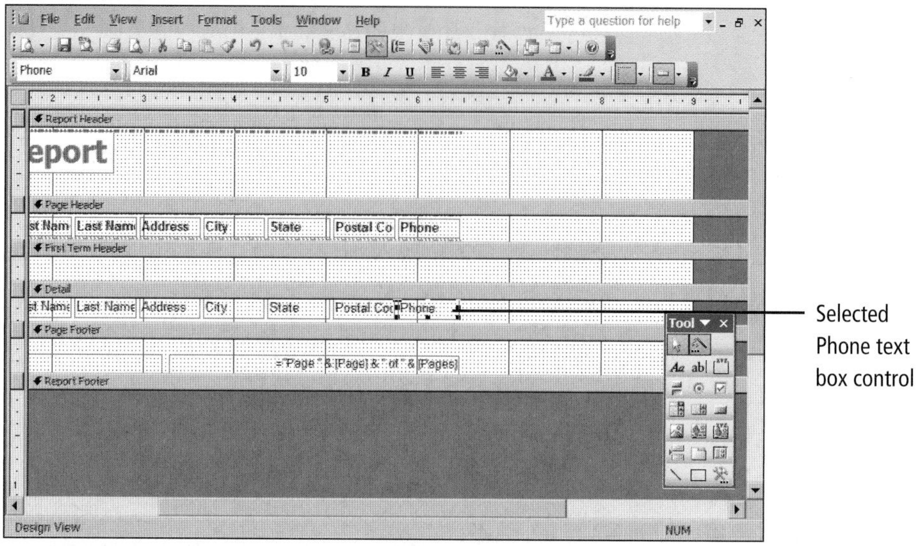

Figure 2.45

4 Press and hold down Shift. In the **Page Header section**, click the **Phone label control**. Then release the Shift key.

Both the Phone text box control and the Phone label control are selected, as shown in Figure 2.46.

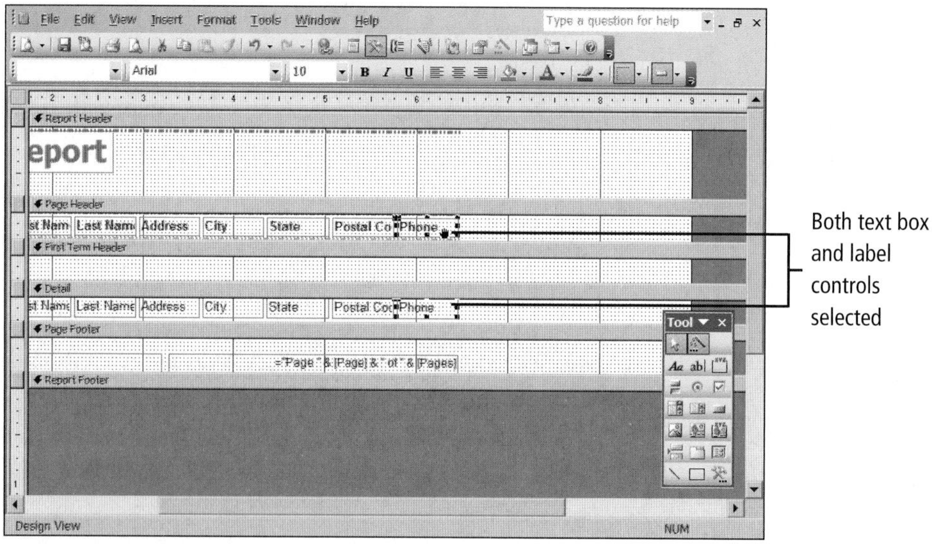

Figure 2.46

5 In the **Page Header section**, position your pointer in the **Phone label control** until the **hand** pointer displays, and then drag to position the right edge of the two objects, which will move together, at **8.75 inches on the horizontal ruler**.

Both controls are repositioned. Because the text box control and corresponding label control are in different sections of the report, you must use Shift to select both of the controls and then move them together.

6 With both controls still selected, resize the controls by dragging the center right handle of either control so that the right edge of the controls is stretched to **9 inches on the horizontal ruler**. See Figure 2.47.

The width of both controls is increased.

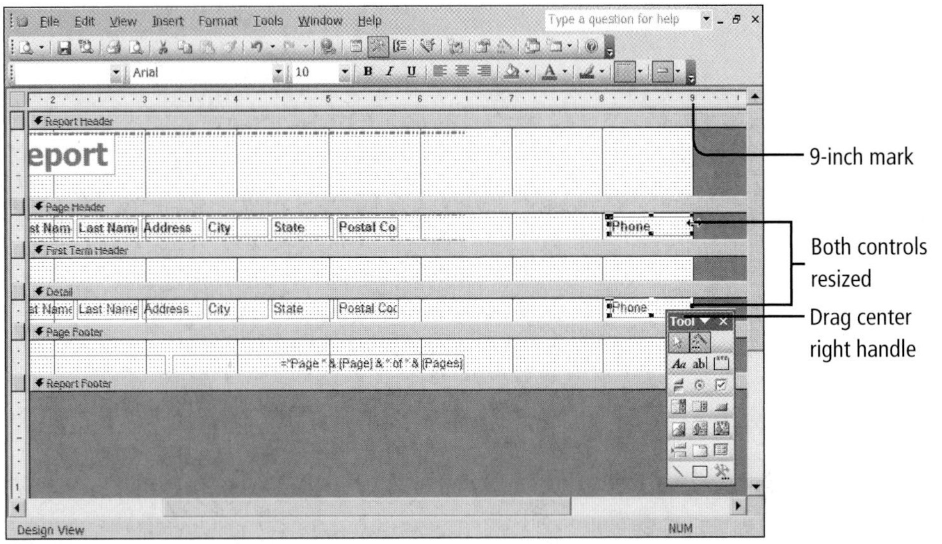

Figure 2.47

7 In the **Detail section**, click the **Postal Code text box control** to select it. Hold down Shift, and then in the **Page Header section**, click the **Postal Code label control**. Release Shift and then point to one of the controls to display the **hand** pointer. Drag to reposition the right edge of the two controls at **7.5 inches on the horizontal ruler**.

8 In the **Detail section**, resize the controls by dragging the center right handle of the **Postal Code text box control** so that the right edge of the control is stretched to **7.75 inches on the horizontal ruler**. See Figure 2.48.

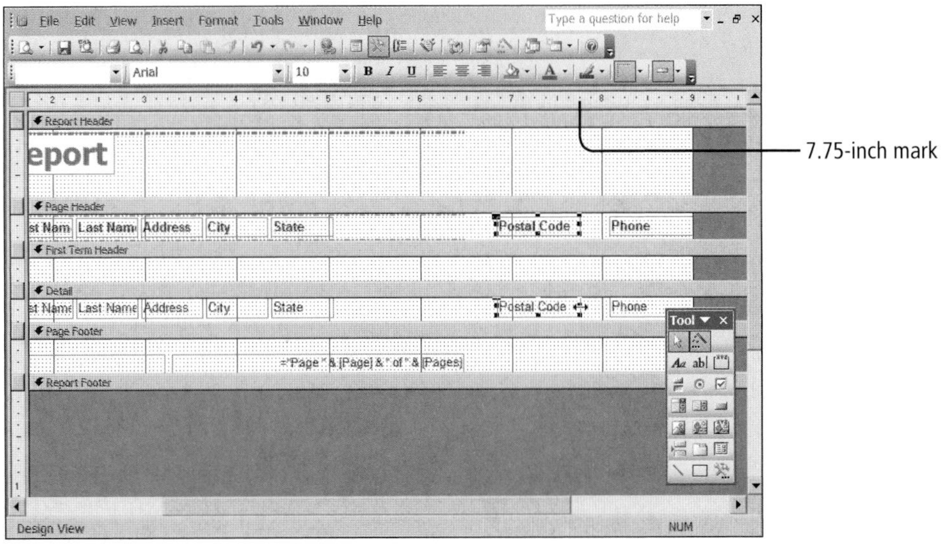

Figure 2.48

9 In the **Detail section**, click the **City text box control**, hold down Shift, and then click the **State text box control**. Continue to hold down Shift, and in the **Page Header section**, click the **City label control** and the **State label control**. Release Shift.

Four controls are selected—the City and State label controls in the Page Header section and the City and State text box controls in the Detail section, as shown in Figure 2.49.

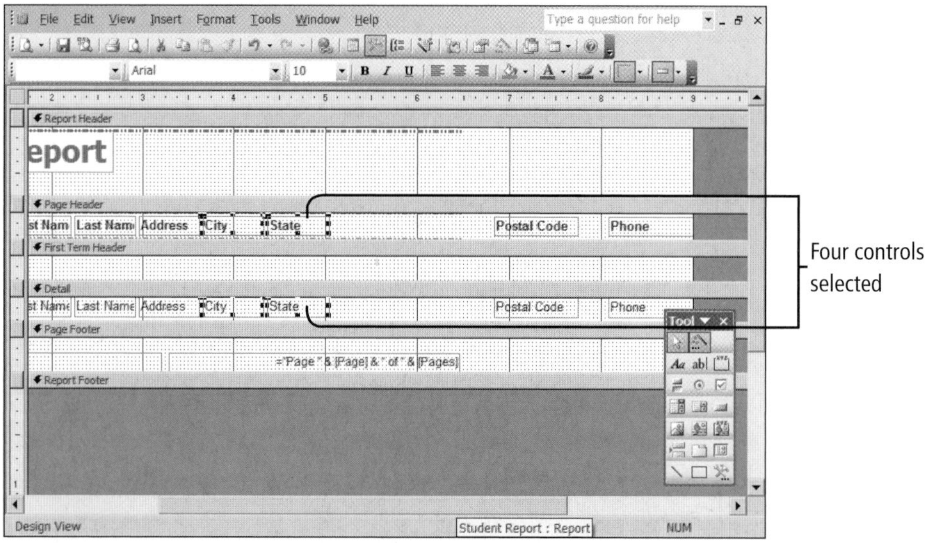

Figure 2.49

10 Position your pointer over any of the selected controls until the **hand** pointer displays. Move the grouped controls to the right until the right edge of the State controls are positioned at **6.75 inches on the horizontal ruler**. See Figure 2.50.

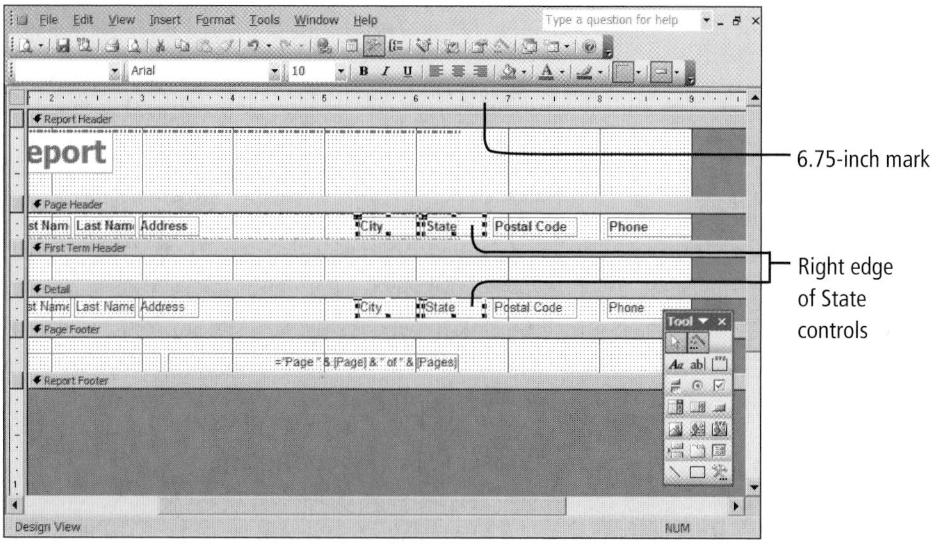

Figure 2.50

11 In the **Detail section**, click the **Address text box control**. Hold down Shift, and in the Page Header section, click the **Address label control**.

12 Position your pointer over the center right handle of the **Address label control** until the pointer changes to a double horizontal arrow, and then resize the controls by stretching the right edge to **4.25 inches on the horizontal ruler**. See Figure 2.51.

The width of the two controls is increased.

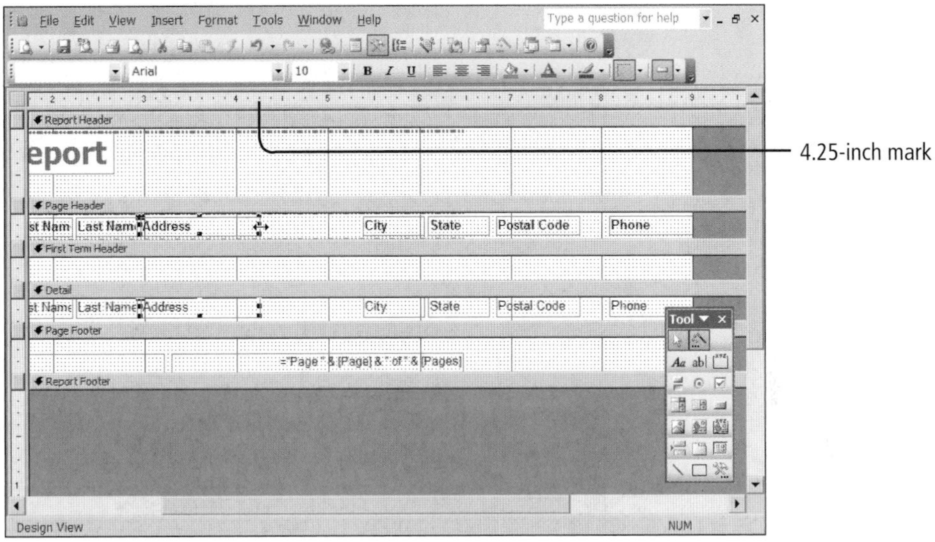

Figure 2.51

13 With the two objects still selected, position the pointer over one of the objects until the **hand** pointer displays, then move the two controls until their right edges are at **5.25 inches on the horizontal ruler**.

The two controls are moved one inch to the right.

14 With the two controls still selected, hold down Ctrl and press →.

The two objects are ***nudged***—moved slightly—to the right. Nudging is a useful technique to move controls with precision.

15 Using the Ctrl + → technique, nudge the selected controls to the right two more times.

16 Using the techniques you have just practiced, select, as a group, the **Last Name text box control** and the **Last Name label control**. Then move the selected objects to the right so that their right edge is at **3.75 inches on the horizontal ruler**. See Figure 2.52.

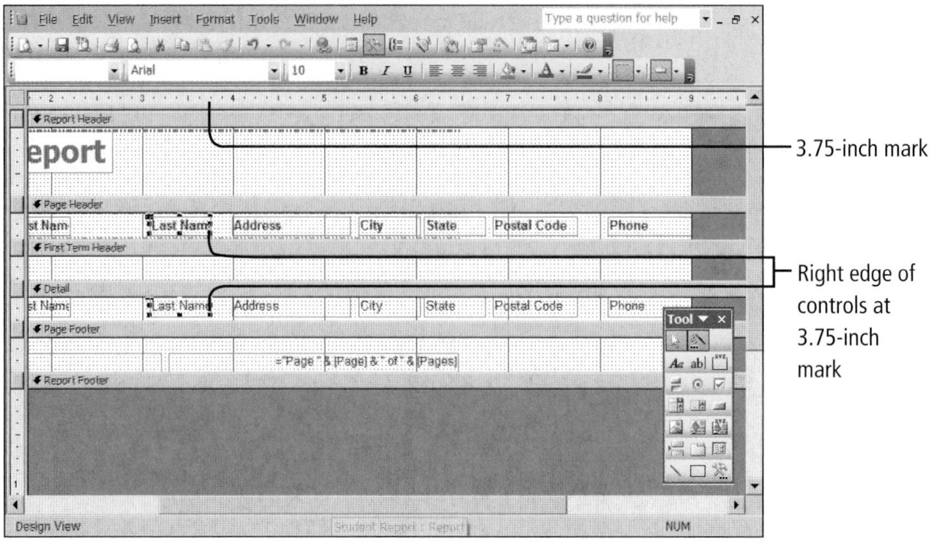

Figure 2.52

17 With the objects still selected, lengthen the controls by dragging their right edge to match Figure 2.53.

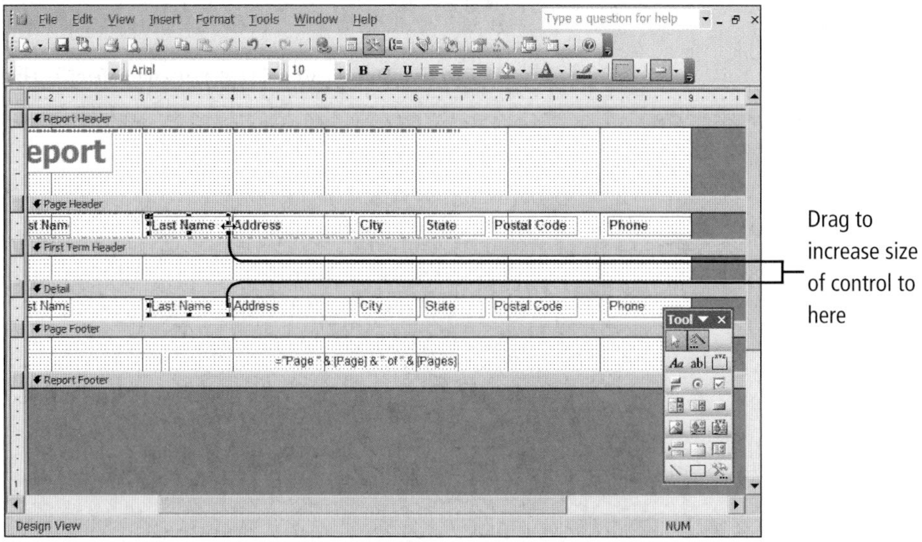

Figure 2.53

18 If necessary, use the horizontal scroll bar to scroll the report so you can see the remainder of the fields to the left. Using the techniques you have practiced to resize the controls, select, then resize the **First Name controls** so their right edge is at **2⅜ inches on the horizontal ruler,** as shown in Figure 2.54.

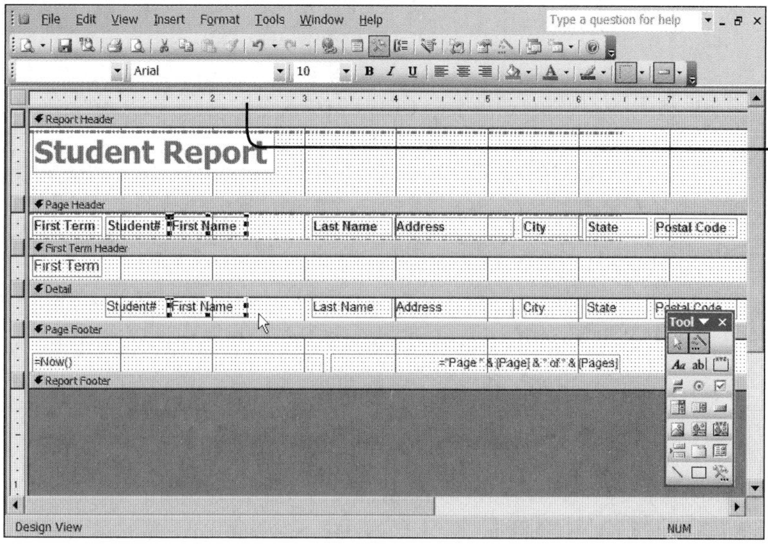

Figure 2.54

19 With the First Name controls still selected, hold Shift and select the **Student# text box contro**l and the **Student # label control**. Move the fields as a group until the right edge of the First Name field is positioned at **2.75 inches on the horizontal ruler**.

20 On the Report Design toolbar, click the **View** button to switch to the Print Preview of the report. Verify that the changes you made to the report are reflected in the Print Preview of the report, and then compare your screen to Figure 2.55.

Note — Using Graphic Elements on Reports

Graphic lines can be lengthened.

The aqua graphic line on the report does not continue across the length of the report. As you progress in your study of Access, you will learn about graphic elements on reports.

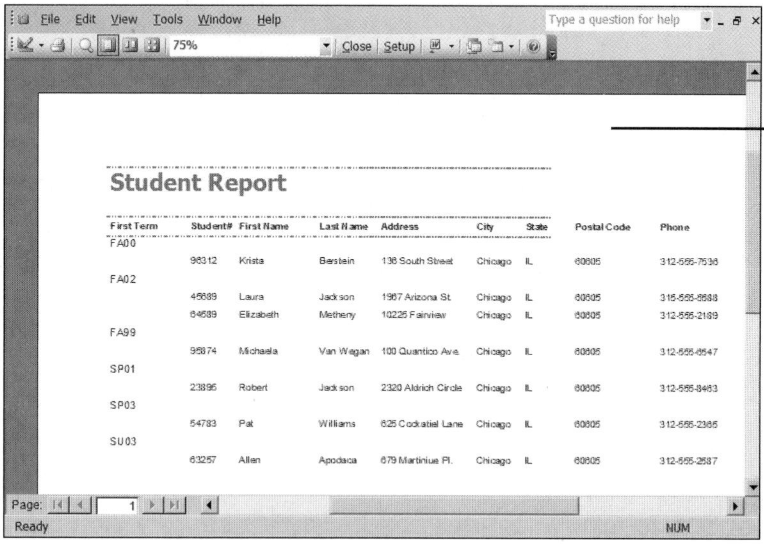

Figure 2.55

21 On the Print Preview toolbar, click the **View** button to switch to the Design view of the report. Leave the report open in Design view for the next activity.

Activity 2.14 Adding a Page Footer and a Report Footer to a Report

1 Locate the **Page Footer** section of the report. Notice that there are two controls in this section. See Figure 2.56.

The control on the left, identified as *=Now( ),* will insert the current date each time the report is opened. The control on the right, identified as *="Page " & [Page] & " of " & [Pages],* will insert the page numbers of the pages in the report when the report is displayed in Print Preview or when the report is printed.

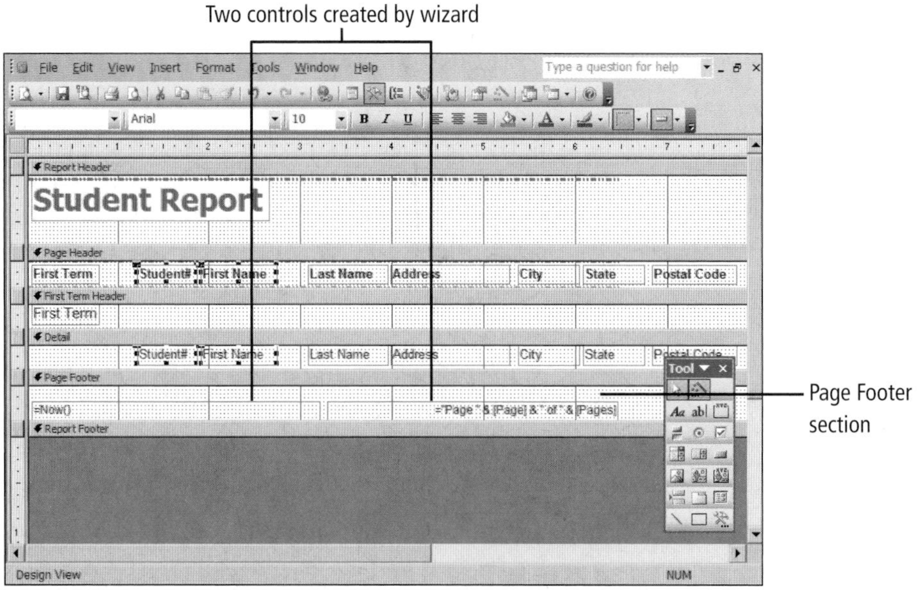

Figure 2.56

2 Click once in the control on the left, the control containing *=Now ( ),* to select it. Shorten this control by dragging its right center handle to the left to **1.5 inches on the horizontal ruler**.

3 Select the control on the right, the control that contains the *="Page " & [Page] & " of " & [Pages]*. Shorten this control by dragging the left center handle of that control to **4.5 inches on the horizontal ruler**.

4 In the Toolbox, click the **Label** button .

5 Beginning at **2 inches on the horizontal ruler** and aligned with the top of the other two controls, drag down and to the right to **4.25 inches on the horizontal ruler** to draw a new label control, as shown in Figure 2.57.

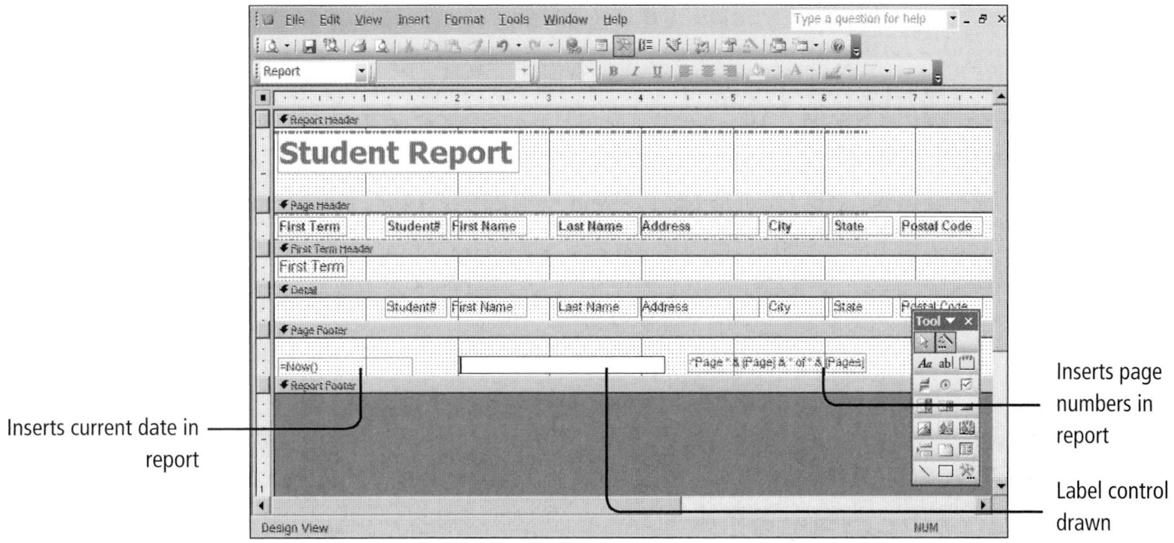

Figure 2.57

6 In the label box you just created, and using your own information, type **2B Students Firstname Lastname** and then press Enter.

An Alert button may display, which when pointed to, indicates *This is a new label and is not associated with a control.*

7 Switch to the Print Preview of the report and verify that your name displays at the lower edge of the report. If you are not satisfied with the positioning of the label control containing your name, return to Design view and use the Nudge feature (Ctrl + any arrow key) to nudge the control into a precise position.

Objective 10
Print a Report

An attractively formatted report printed on paper is much easier to view than looking at the database table on the screen or viewing one record at a time in a form on the screen. Reports are routinely printed for management, staff, or customers who need to look at information. For example, when you visit the Records Office of your college, you probably request a printed copy of your transcript. This is easier than viewing your records on the screen.

Activity 2.15 Printing a Report

1. On the Print Preview toolbar, click the **Print** button.

   The report prints on one page.

2. To the right of *Type a question for help*, click the small **Close Window** button to close the report. Click **Yes** to save your changes.

3. Close the database and then click the **Close** button to close Access.

End **You have completed Project 2B**

Summary

A form is a tool for either entering or viewing information in a database. Although you can both enter and view database information in the database table itself, the use of a form is usually preferable for two reasons.

First, for entering data, a form is convenient and time saving, because the person entering the data using a form is not distracted by seeing the entire database table on the screen. He or she sees only the record being entered. Additionally, the fields on the form can be laid out in a manner that is easy for the person entering information to navigate.

Second, for viewing data, a form is easier to view than an entire table of information, because only the record needed is displayed. This is much easier for the person whose job it is to look up information in a database. For example, your college counselor can look at your college transcript in a nicely laid out form on the screen without seeing the records for hundreds of other students at the same time.

Two methods for creating forms in Access are through an AutoForm or through the Form Wizard. Once created, a form can be opened in Design View and further modified to make data entry or viewing even easier. Page headers and footers can be added that will display on each page of the form.

Reports in Access summarize the data in a database in a professional-looking manner suitable for printing. The design of a report can be modified so that the final report is laid out in a format that is useful for the person reading it.

In This Chapter You Practiced How To

- View and Navigate to Records with a Form
- Create an AutoForm
- Save and Close an AutoForm
- Use a Form to Add Records to and Delete Records from a Table
- Create a Form with the Form Wizard
- Modify a Form
- Create a Report with the Report Wizard
- Save a Report
- Modify the Design of a Report
- Print a Report

Concepts Assessments

Matching

Match each term in the second column with its correct definition in the first column by writing the letter of the term on the blank line in front of the correct definition.

____ **1.** Information that displays at the top of the form when the form is viewed in Form view or is printed.

____ **2.** A bar that is used to select an entire record in a form or a table.

____ **3.** An object such as a label or text box in a form or report that allows you to view or manipulate information stored in tables or queries.

____ **4.** Information that displays at the lower edge of each page of a form or report.

____ **5.** An Access feature that guides you step by step to create a form.

____ **6.** A toolbar from which you can add various types of controls to forms and reports in Access.

____ **7.** A feature in Access that quickly creates a form using the information from one table.

____ **8.** A control on a form or report where data from the corresponding table is displayed

____ **9.** A feature in Access used to create a professionally designed report.

____ **10.** Using a form, the view in which you can enter and modify the information in a record.

____ **11.** In the Design view of a form or report, the section that contains the fields and records that display in the form or report.

____ **12.** The small squares that surround a selected object.

____ **13.** The database object that provides an organized view of the fields in one or more tables or queries.

____ **14.** The database object that displays the fields and records from a table in a format suitable for printing.

____ **15.** A useful technique to move controls in Design view with precision.

A AutoForm

B Control

C Detail

D Form

E Form header

F Form view

G Form Wizard

H Nudge

I Page footer

J Record selector

K Report

L Report Wizard

M Sizing handles

N Text box

O Toolbox

Concepts Assessments (continued)

Fill in the Blank

Write the correct answer in the space provided.

1. Using a form simplifies the data entry process because forms display only ____________________ record at a time.
2. The navigation buttons on a form include methods to go directly to the next record, last record, first record, and the ____________________ record in a table, as well as a button to create a new record.
3. Forms and tables are ____________________ database objects, meaning information entered into one will be automatically entered in the other.
4. A bar in Access used to select an entire record in a form or a table is the ____________________.
5. Creating a form using the Form Wizard offers more flexibility in the design of the form than creating a form using a(n) ____________________.
6. To change the layout and arrangement of fields on a form or report you must use the ____________________ view of the form or report.
7. Two visual aids that guide your placement of controls on a report or form in Design view are the dotted grid pattern and the ____________________ at the top and left of the screen.
8. Access reports are printed so individuals can view the information in the report without ____________________ the database itself.
9. To select more than one field simultaneously in the Design view of a form or report, you must hold down the ____________________ key on the keyboard.
10. The layout that you choose for a report in the Report Wizard determines the ____________________ of the data in the report.

Skill Assessments

Project 2C—LMccDepts

Objectives: *View and Navigate to Records with a Form, Create an AutoForm, Save and Close an AutoForm, and Use a Form to Add Records to and Delete Records from a Table.*

In the following Skill Assessment, you will create an AutoForm for use with the database of Department names at Lake Michigan City College. You will use the new form to add records to and delete records from the database. Your completed form will look like the one shown in Figure 2.58. You will rename the database as *2C_LMccDepts_Firstname_Lastname* in the folder you have created for this chapter.

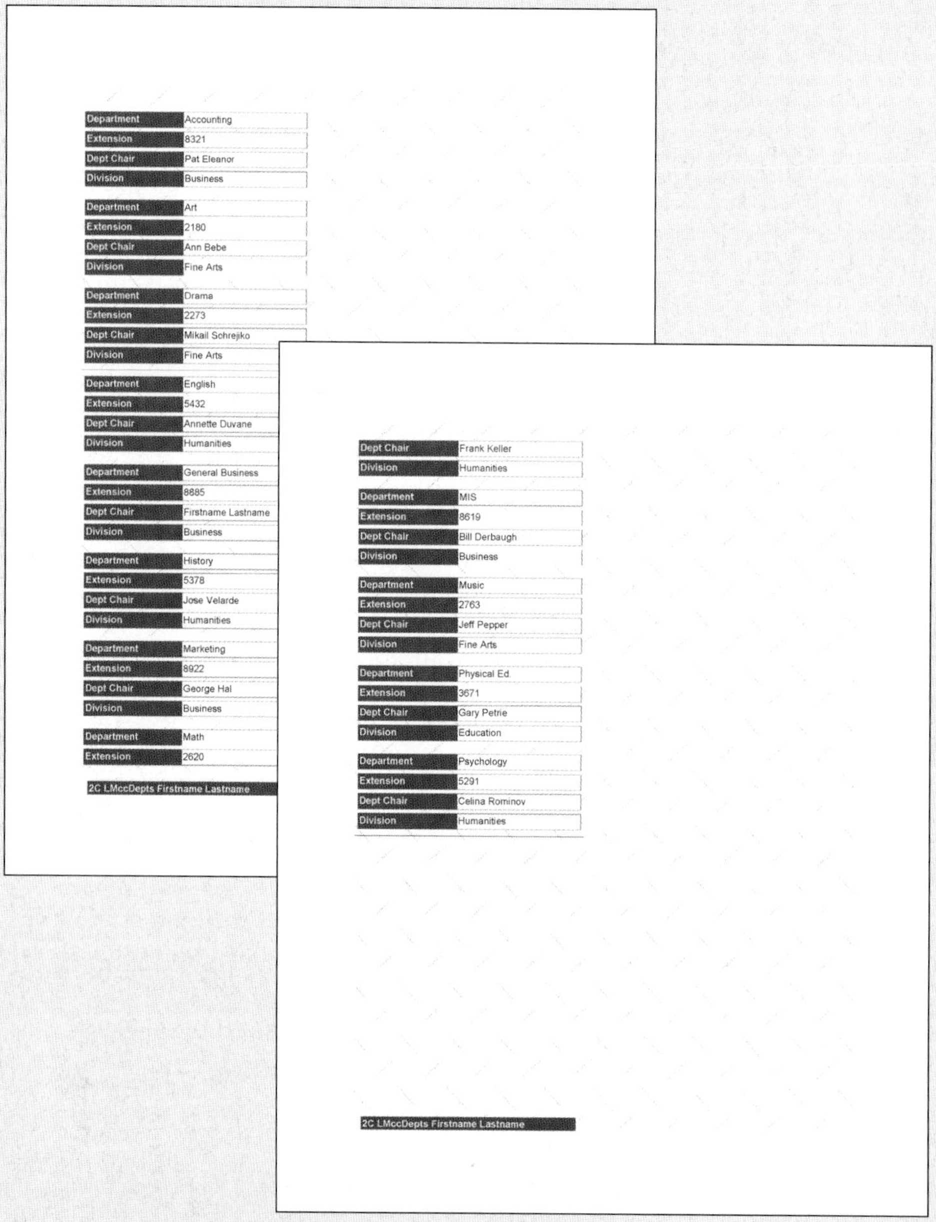

Department	Accounting
Extension	8321
Dept Chair	Pat Eleanor
Division	Business
Department	Art
Extension	2180
Dept Chair	Ann Bebe
Division	Fine Arts
Department	Drama
Extension	2273
Dept Chair	Mikail Schrejiko
Division	Fine Arts
Department	English
Extension	5432
Dept Chair	Annette Duvane
Division	Humanities
Department	General Business
Extension	8885
Dept Chair	Firstname Lastname
Division	Business
Department	History
Extension	5378
Dept Chair	Jose Velarde
Division	Humanities
Department	Marketing
Extension	8922
Dept Chair	George Hal
Division	Business
Department	Math
Extension	2620

2C LMccDepts Firstname Lastname

Dept Chair	Frank Keller
Division	Humanities
Department	MIS
Extension	8619
Dept Chair	Bill Derbaugh
Division	Business
Department	Music
Extension	2763
Dept Chair	Jeff Pepper
Division	Fine Arts
Department	Physical Ed
Extension	3671
Dept Chair	Gary Petrie
Division	Education
Department	Psychology
Extension	5291
Dept Chair	Celina Rominov
Division	Humanities

2C LMccDepts Firstname Lastname

Figure 2.58

(Project 2C–LMccDepts continues on the next page)

Skill Assessments (continued)

(Project 2C–LMccDepts continued)

1. Open **My Computer** or **Windows Explorer** and navigate to the location where the student files that accompany this textbook are located. Click once to select the file **a02C_LMccDepts**.
2. Copy and paste the **a02C_LMccDepts** file to the folder where you are storing your projects for this chapter.
3. Rename the file **2C_LMccDepts_Firstname_Lastname**
4. Right-click the file you just renamed and click **Properties**. On the displayed **Properties** dialog box, remove the Read-only property from the file and then click **OK**.
5. Close the Windows accessory you are using—either My Computer or Windows Explorer.
6. Start Access and open your **2C_LMccDepts** database. On the Objects bar, click **Forms**.
7. Above the Objects bar, locate and then click the **New** button. On the displayed **New Form** dialog box, click **AutoForm: Columnar**.
8. In the text box to the right of *Choose the table or query where the object's data comes from:*, click the **downward pointing arrow**. There is only one table for this database. Click **Departments** and then click **OK**. A new form based on the information in the Departments table is created and displays on your screen.

   Recall that AutoForm places all of the table's fields into the form. Access will apply the most recently used form formatting; thus, the format displayed on your screen will depend on previous use of the computer at which you are working.
9. At the lower edge of the form, in the navigation area, click the **Last Record** button. The last record in the table, for the Psychology Department, displays.
10. In the navigation area, click the **Previous Record** button once. The previous record, for the Physical Ed. Department, displays. In the navigation area, click the **First Record** button. The first record, for the Accounting Department, displays.
11. Position your mouse pointer in the navigation area over the number of the current record until the pointer turns into an I-beam. Then, drag to select the number. Type **9** and then press Enter. The record for the MIS Department displays.

    Recall that if you know the exact number of the record you want to view, this method of navigating to a record in a form is quicker than moving through the records one by one with the navigation buttons.

(Project 2C–LMccDepts continues on the next page)

(Project 2C–LMccDepts continued)

12. On the title bar of the **Departments** form, click the **Close** button. Because you have not previously named or saved this form, a message displays asking you if you want to save the changes to the design of form "*Form1*." Click **Yes**.

13. In the displayed **Save As** dialog box, in the **Form Name** box, accept the default form name of *Departments* by clicking **OK**. For this database, you now have a convenient form with which you can view or enter records, rather than viewing or entering records in the database table itself. Notice that the name of the form displays in the Database window.

14. Click to select the **Departments** form, and then above the Objects bar, click **Design**. The **Departments** form that you created opens in Design view. On the form's title bar, click the **Maximize** button. Maximizing a form in Design view allows you to view the different sections of the form and provides space to make changes to the layout of the form.

15. From the **View** menu, click **Page Header/Footer**. Page Header and Page Footer sections are added to your form.

16. Locate the Toolbox floating on your screen. If necessary, open the Toolbox by displaying the View menu and clicking Toolbox. Recall that the Toolbox is a toolbar that is used to add various types of controls to forms and reports in Access. On the Toolbox, click the **Label** button.

17. Move your pointer into the **Page Footer** section and create a label control approximately **2.75 inches wide**, centered vertically and horizontally in the available space. If you are not satisfied with your result, click the Undo button and begin again. Recall that you can use the Nudge feature (Ctrl + any arrow key) to position the object precisely. In the label, using your own information, type **2C LMccDepts Firstname Lastname** and then press Enter.

18. Switch to Form view. In the navigation area of the form, click the **New Record** button. The fields are cleared and ready to accept a new entry. The record number advances by one to 13.

19. In the blank **Department** field, where the insertion point is blinking, type **General Business** and then press Tab.

20. In **Extension** field, type **8885** and then press Tab. In the **Dept Chair** field, using your own information, type **Firstname Lastname** and then press Tab.

21. In the **Division** field, type **Business**

22. Navigate to record 5, the Department of General Mgt. On the left side of the form, locate the record selector bar that contains a right-pointing arrow. Click once in the record selector. The entire record is selected.

(Project 2C–LMccDepts continues on the next page)

(Project 2C–LMccDepts continued)

23. On the Form View toolbar, click the **Delete Record** button, or press Delete. In the displayed alert, click **Yes**. The record is deleted from the Departments table.

24. To the right of *Type a question for help*, click the **Close Window** button. Click **Yes** if prompted to save your changes. The form closes and your changes are saved.

25. On the Objects bar, click **Tables**, and then double-click the **Departments** table to open it in Datasheet view. Examine the table and notice that the changes you made using the form are updated in the corresponding table. The Department of General Business has been added, and the Department of General Mgt. has been deleted. Notice that the records in the table have been sorted by the primary key.

26. To the right of *Type a question for help*, click the **Close Window** button to close the table. On the Objects bar, click **Forms**, and then, if necessary, click the **Departments** form once to select it.

27. On the Database toolbar, click the **Print** button to print the form. Two pages will print, and your name will print in the page footer on each page. Recall that depending on previous use of your computer, the format applied to your form may differ from the one shown in Figure 2.58. To the right of *Type a question for help*, click the **Close Window** button to close the database and then close Access.

End You have completed Project 2C

Project 2D—Office Supplies

Objectives: *Create a Form with the Form Wizard and Modify a Form.*

In the following Skill Assessment, you will use the Form Wizard to create a form for the Office Supplies database at Lake Michigan City College, and then make modifications to the layout of the form. Your completed database objects will look similar to Figure 2.59. You will rename and save your database as *2D_Office_Supplies_Firstname_Lastname.*

1. Open **My Computer** or **Windows Explorer** and navigate to the location where the student files that accompany this textbook are located. Click once to select the file **a02D_Office_Supplies**.

2. Copy and paste the **a02D_Office_Supplies** file to the folder where you are storing your projects for this chapter. Rename the file **2D_Office_Supplies_Firstname_Lastname**

3. Right-click the file you just renamed and click **Properties**. From the displayed **Properties** dialog box, remove the Read-only property from the file, and then click **OK**.

(Project 2D–Office Supplies continues on the next page)

(Project 2D–Office Supplies continued)

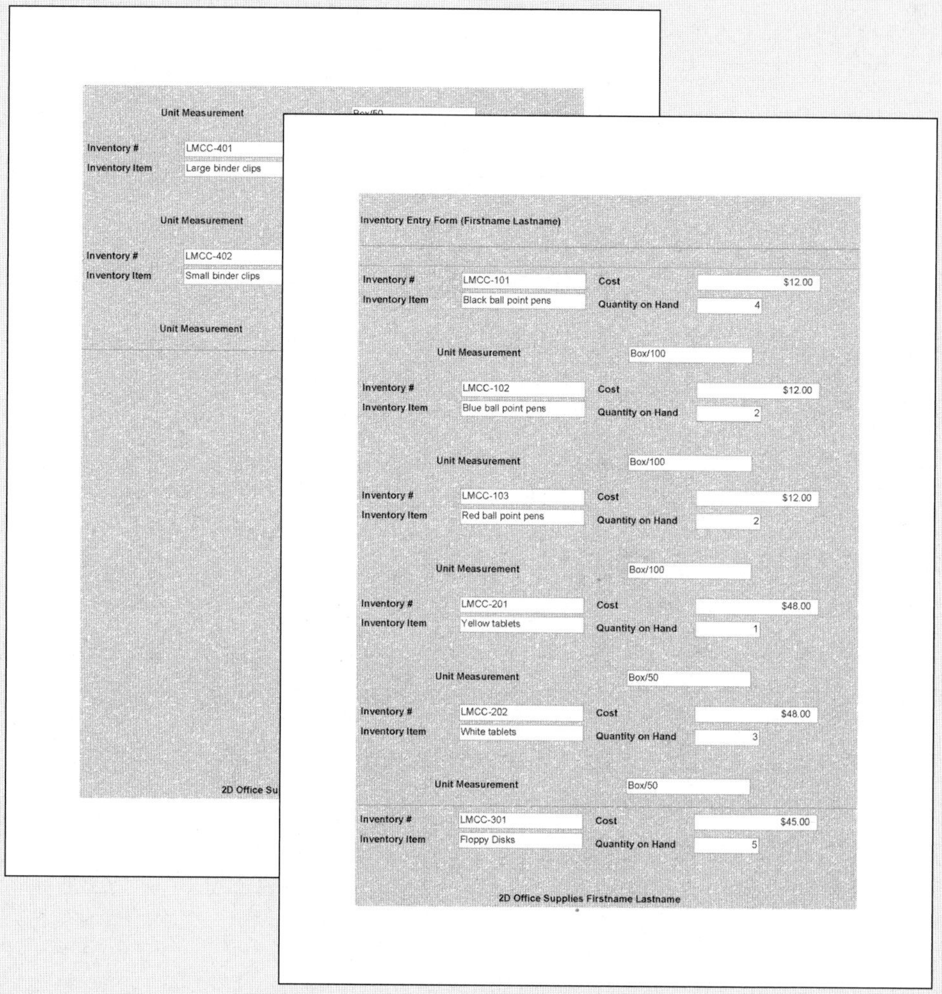

Figure 2.59

4. Close the Windows accessory you are using—either My Computer or Windows Explorer. Start Access and open your **2D_Office_Supplies** database. On the Objects bar, click **Forms**.

5. To the right of the Objects bar, double-click the command icon ***Create form by using wizard***. The Form Wizard opens requesting information about the table (or query) upon which the form will be based, and the fields from the table to include on the form.

6. Under **Tables/Queries**, click the **down arrow**. A list of tables and queries available for this database displays. Currently only one object, the **Office Inventory** table, has been created in this database. Click **Table: Office Inventory**.

7. To the right of the list of available fields, click the **All Fields** button to move all of the fields from the **Office Inventory** table to the **Selected Fields** column on the right.

(Project 2D–Office Supplies continues on the next page)

Skill Assessments (continued)

(Project 2D–Office Supplies continued)

8. Click the **Next** button. For the layout of the form, make sure the **Columnar** option button is selected, and then click the **Next** button. For the style of the form, click **SandStone**. A preview of the SandStone style displays on the left. Click the **Next** button.

9. With *Office Inventory* highlighted, press Delete to delete the default text. Then, using your own information type **Inventory Firstname Lastname**

10. Click the **Finish** button. Access creates the form using the information you specified in the Wizard screens. The completed form displays in Form view. On the Form View toolbar, click the **View** button to switch to Design view, and then on the form's title bar, click the **Maximize** button.

11. Position your pointer on the horizontal line between the **Form Header section** and the **Detail section** until the pointer changes to a large double arrow. Drag down approximately 0.5 inch. Use your eye and the vertical ruler to determine this distance. The **Form Header** section expands and grid dots display in this area.

12. Locate the **Toolbox** on your screen. (If necessary, display the View menu and click Toolbox.) On the Toolbox, click the **Label** button.

13. Move your pointer into the **Form Header section**, and position the pointer's plus sign at the **left edge of the Form Header area** and centered vertically (use your eye to approximate this distance) in the **Form Header section**. Drag down **about 0.25 inch and to the right to 3.0 inches on the horizontal ruler**. If you are not satisfied with your result, click the Undo button and begin again. In the label box you just created, use your own information to type **Inventory Entry Form (Firstname Lastname)** and then press Enter.

14. On the Form Design toolbar, click the **View** button to switch to the Form view, and notice the Form Header information you added with your name. On the Form View toolbar, click the **View** button to return to Design view. By placing a Form Header on the form, you have created an informative title that will print at the beginning of the form. Someone who reads the printed form will have an indication as to the contents of the form.

15. Position your pointer on the right edge of the form until your pointer changes to a large double arrow. Drag the right edge of the form to the right to **6.5 inches on the horizontal ruler**. The width of the form is expanded. By increasing the dimensions of a form, you create more working space to move and reposition the controls on the form.

16. Click once in the white text box control **Cost**. The Cost text box control is selected and handles surround the selected object. Recall that a text box control on a form is where data from the corresponding table is displayed, or where new data for the table is entered.

(Project 2D–Office Supplies continues on the next page)

Skill Assessments (continued)

(Project 2D–Office Supplies continued)

17. Position your pointer over any border of the text box until the **hand** pointer displays. Using the grid dots and the horizontal ruler as a guide, drag the **Cost controls** up and to the right of the Inventory# controls—until the right edge of the Cost controls are positioned at approximately **6.0 inches on the horizontal ruler** and aligned with the Inventory# controls, as shown in Figure 2.59.

18. Click once on the white **Quantity on Hand** text box control to select it. Position your pointer over any border of the text box until the **hand** pointer displays. Drag the **Quantity on Hand** controls up and position them directly under the Cost controls—and to the right of the Inventory Item controls. See Figure 2.59.

19. Click once in the white **Unit Measurement** text box control to select it. Position your pointer over the large black handle that is between the **Unit Measurement text box control** and the **Unit Measurement label control** until the **pointing hand** pointer displays. Recall that with this pointer, you can move the text box control independently of the label control. Drag only the **Unit Measurement text box control** to the right, so that its left edge is positioned at **3.5 inches on the horizontal ruler** and its top edge is positioned at **1.0 inch on the vertical ruler**. See Figure 2.59.

20. Position your pointer over the large black handle in the **Unit Measurement label control** until the **pointing hand** pointer displays. Drag the label control until it left edge is positioned at **1.0 inch on the horizontal ruler** and its top edge is positioned at **1.0 inch on the vertical ruler**.

21. Display the **View** menu and click **Page Header/Footer**. On the Toolbox, click the **Label** button. Move your pointer into the **Page Footer** section and create a label control approximately 3 inches wide, centered vertically and horizontally in the available space. Recall that you can use the Nudge feature (Ctrl + any arrow key) to position the object precisely. In the label, using your own information, type **2D Office Supplies Firstname Lastname** and then press Enter.

22. On the Form Design toolbar, click the **View** button to switch to the Form view and then view the changes to your form. The Form Header displays; recall that Page Footers display only when printed or in Print Preview. Then, on the Form View toolbar, click the **Print** button to print the form. Two pages will print.

23. To the right of *Type a question for help*, click the **Restore Window** button. The form is restored to its original size. On the title bar of the form, click the **Close** button. Click **Yes** to save your changes. Close the database and then close Access.

End You have completed Project 2D

Skill Assessments (continued)

Project 2E—Inventory

Objectives: *Create a Report with the Report Wizard, Save a Report, Modify the Design of a Report, and Print a Report.*

The Computer Club at Lake Michigan City College has an inventory of hardware, software, and other equipment that it uses for training and various club events. The club maintains a database of this inventory. In the following Skill Assessment, you will use the Report Wizard to create a report listing the information from a table in the Inventory database. After creating the report, you will modify its design. Your completed report will look like the one shown in Figure 2.60. You will rename and save your database as *2E_Inventory_Firstname_Lastname*.

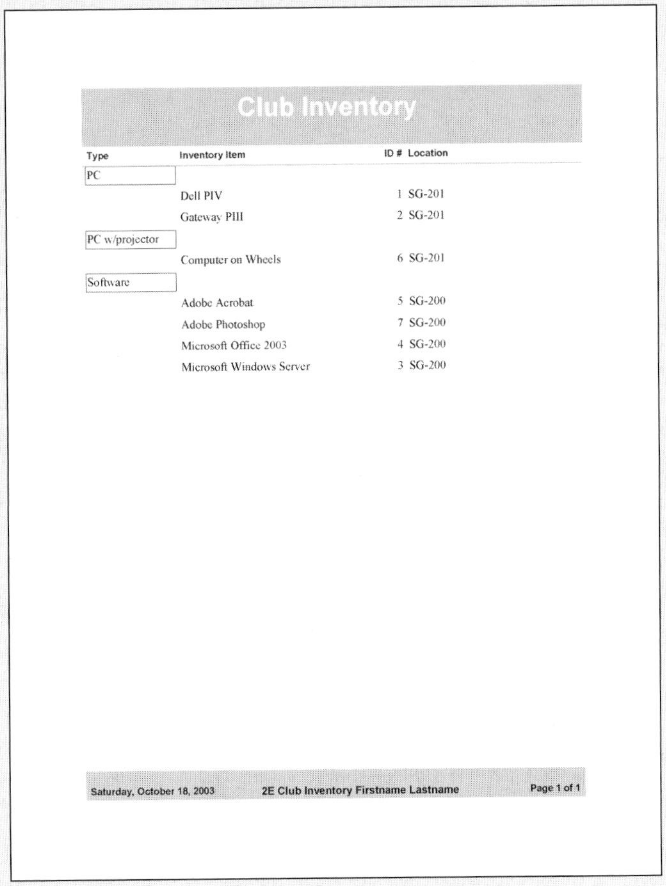
Club Inventory

Type	Inventory Item	ID #	Location
PC			
	Dell PIV	1	SG-201
	Gateway PIII	2	SG-201
PC w/projector			
	Computer on Wheels	6	SG-201
Software			
	Adobe Acrobat	5	SG-200
	Adobe Photoshop	7	SG-200
	Microsoft Office 2003	4	SG-200
	Microsoft Windows Server	3	SG-200

Saturday, October 18, 2003 2E Club Inventory Firstname Lastname Page 1 of 1

Figure 2.60

1. Open **My Computer** or **Windows Explorer** and navigate to the location where the student files that accompany this textbook are located. Click once to select the file **a02E_Inventory**.
2. Copy and paste the **a02E_Inventory** file to the folder where you are storing your projects for this chapter. Rename the file **2E_Inventory_Firstname_Lastname**

(Project 2E–Inventory continues on the next page)

Skill Assessments (continued)

(Project 2E–Inventory continued)

3. Right-click the file you just renamed and click **Properties**. From the displayed **Properties** dialog box, remove the Read-only property from the file and then click **OK**.
4. Close the Windows accessory you are using—either My Computer or Windows Explorer. Start Access and open your **2E_Inventory** database. On the Objects bar, click **Reports**.
5. To the right of the Objects bar, double-click ***Create report by using wizard***. The Report Wizard opens. The first step in the Report Wizard is to determine from which table (or query) information for the report will be taken, and also what fields from the table to include in the report. Under **Tables/Queries**, click the **down arrow**. A list of tables and queries available for this database displays. Currently only one object, the Inventory table, has been created in this database.
6. Click **Table: Inventory**. A list of the fields in the Inventory table displays in the Available Fields column on the left. To the right of the list of available fields, click the **All Fields** button to move all of the fields from the Inventory table to the Selected Fields column on the far right. All of the fields that were listed under Available Fields display in the Selected Fields list. Click the **Next** button.
7. Recall that it is often useful to group information on a printed report by one or more of the fields in the table. In the displayed list of field names, click **Type**, and then click the **One Field** button. The preview on the right displays the **Type** field, indicating that on the finished report, records will be grouped by type. Click the **Next** button.
8. In this step of the Report Wizard, you can designate an order by which records in the table will be sorted. To the right of the **1** text box, **click** the **down arrow**. In the list of available fields, click **Inventory Item**. Leave the default order as **Ascending**. Click the **Next** button.
9. Under **Layout**, make sure the **Stepped** option button is selected. Under **Orientation**, make sure the **Portrait** option button is selected. Click the **Next** button.
10. From the list of styles that can be applied to the report, click **Soft Gray** and then click the **Next** button. With *Inventory* highlighted, press Delete. Type **Club Inventory** and then click the **Finish** button. The report displays in Print Preview.
11. If necessary, on the Club Inventory title bar, click the **Maximize** button. On the Print Preview toolbar, click the **Zoom arrow** and then click **75%**. Notice that the specifications you defined for the report in the Report Wizard are reflected in the Print Preview of the report. For example, the inventory items are grouped by Type—PC, PC w/projector, and Software. Within each type, the equipment is alphabetized by Inventory Item name.

(Project 2E–Inventory continues on the next page)

Skill Assessments (continued)

(Project 2E–Inventory continued)

12. To the right of *Type a question for help*, click the **Close Window** button. The report closes and the report name displays in the Database window. Reports created with the Report Wizard are named in the final step of the wizard. When the report is closed, it is automatically saved.

13. Double-click the **Club Inventory** report to open the report in Print Preview. On the Print Preview toolbar, click the **View** button to switch to the Design view of the report. If necessary, on the title bar of the report, click the **Maximize** button. The Design view of the report fills the working area.

14. In the **Report Header section**, click the label **Club Inventory**. The label is selected and handles surround the selected object. Position your pointer over a border of the selected object to display the **hand pointer**. Drag the label to the right, until the left edge is positioned at **2.0 inches on the horizontal ruler**, maintaining its vertical placement.

15. In the **Page Footer section** of the report, notice the two controls. The control on the left causes the current date to display in this section each time the report is opened. The control on the right causes the page numbers, as well as the total number of pages, to display in the report.

16. Click to select the **date** control on the left. Drag the center right handle to the left to **2 inches on the horizontal ruler**. Select the page number control on the right. Drag the center left handle to the right to **5.25 inches on the horizontal ruler**.

17. Locate the **Toolbox** floating on your screen. (If necessary, display the View menu and click Toolbox to display it.) Click the **Label** button. In the **Page Footer section**, position the pointer's plus sign near the upper edge of the existing controls at **2.25 inches on the horizontal ruler**. Drag down about **0.25 inch** and to the right to **5.0 inches on the horizontal ruler**.

18. In this label, using your own information, type **2E Club Inventory Firstname Lastname** and then press Enter.

19. On the Report Design toolbar, click the **Print Preview** button to verify that your information displays at the lower edge of the report. If you are not satisfied with the placement of your information, return to Design view, select the label, and use the Nudge feature (Ctrl + any arrow key) to reposition the label.

20. If necessary, return to **Print Preview**. On the Print Preview toolbar, click the **Print** button. One page will print. To the right of *Type a question for help*, click the **Close Window** button. Click **Yes** to save your changes. Close the database and close Access.

End **You have completed Project 2E**

Performance Assessments

Project 2F—Music Dept

Objectives: *Create an AutoForm, Save and Close an AutoForm, and Create a Form with the Form Wizard.*

In the following Performance Assessment, you will create two new forms for the Music Department at Lake Michigan City College: one by using the Form Wizard and another by creating an AutoForm. Your completed forms will look similar to Figure 2.61. You will rename and save your database as *2F_Music_Dept_Firstname_Lastname*.

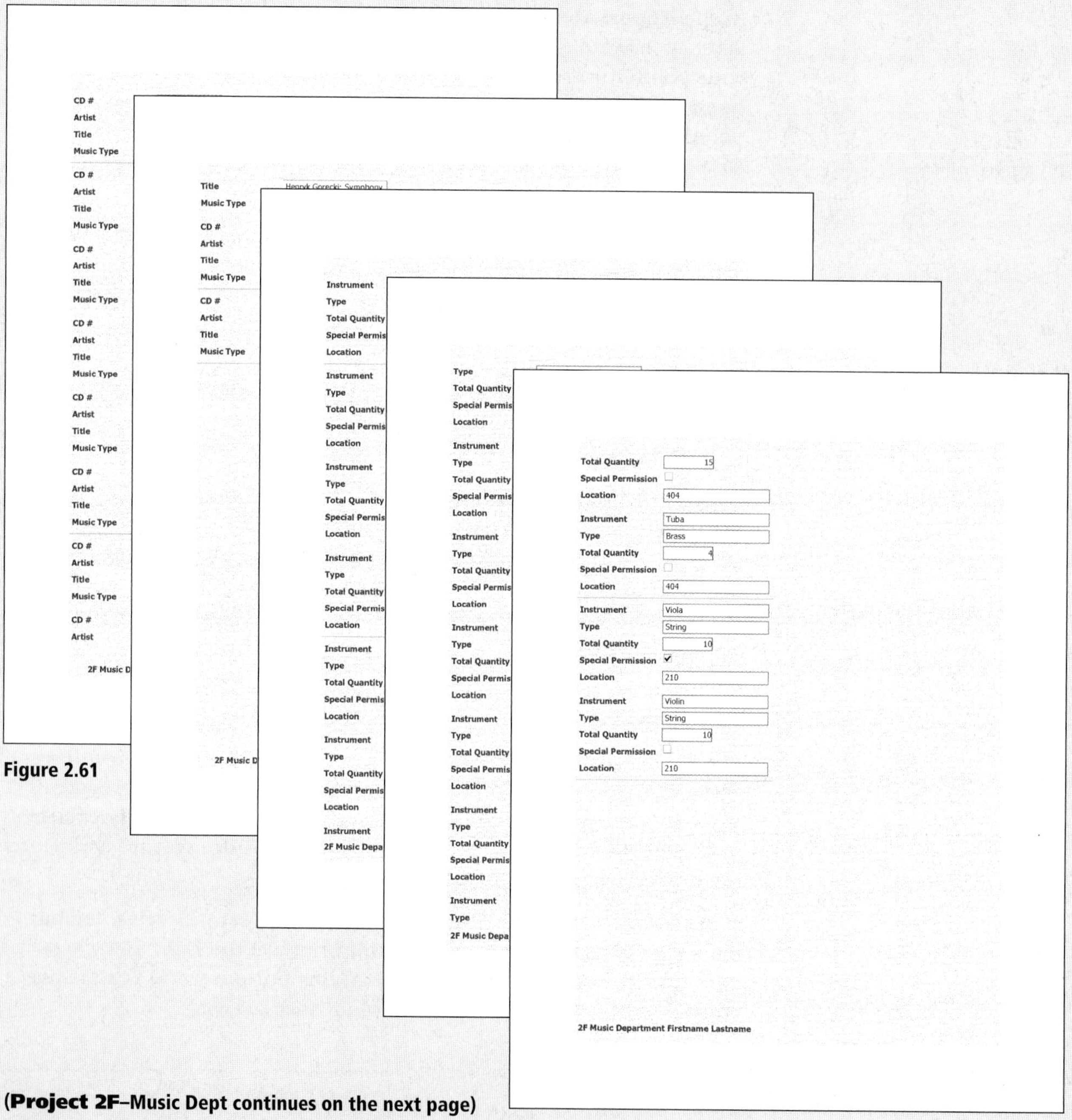

Figure 2.61

(**Project 2F**–Music Dept continues on the next page)

Performance Assessments (continued)

(Project 2F–Music Dept continued)

1. Open **My Computer** or **Windows Explorer** and navigate to the student files for this textbook. Copy and paste the file **a02F_Music_Dept** to the folder where you are storing your projects for this chapter. Rename the file, using your own information, **2F_Music_Dept_Firstname_Lastname** and remove the Read-only property. Close My Computer or Windows Explorer.

2. Start Access and open your **2F_Music_Dept** database. On the Objects bar, click **Forms** and then start the Form Wizard. Under **Tables/Queries**, click the **down arrow**, and then click **Table: CD Collection**. Include all of the fields from the table in the form. Click the **Next** button.

3. Select the **Columnar** layout, click **Next**, and then click the **Sumi Painting** style for the form. Click **Next**. As the title for the form, type **CD Collection Firstname Lastname** and then click **Finish**.

4. Maximize the form and switch to the Design view of the form. Display the **View** menu and then click **Page Header/Footer**.

5. On the Toolbox, click the **Label** button and then move the pointer into the **Page Footer section**. Position the pointer plus sign just below the Page Footer separator at **0.25 inch on the horizontal ruler**. Drag down to the lower edge and to the right to **3 inches on the horizontal ruler**. In the label, and using your own information, type **2F Music Dept Firstname Lastname** and then press Enter.

6. Switch to the Form view and print the form. Two pages will print. Click the **Close Window** button and save your changes.

7. Make sure **Forms** is selected on the Objects bar and then click the **New** button. In the displayed **New Form** dialog box, click **AutoForm: Columnar**. To the right of *Choose the table or query where the object's data comes from*, click the **down arrow**, and then from the displayed list, click **Rental Instruments**. Click **OK**. Click the **Close Window** button and save the form using the default name of *Rental Instruments*.

8. Open the **Rental Instruments** form, switch to the Design View, display the **View** menu, and then click **Page Header/Footer**. In the Toolbox, click the **Label** button. In the **Page Footer** section, just below the Page Footer separator, create a label within the space beginning at the **left edge of the form** and ending at **3.0 inches on the horizontal ruler**. In the label box, use your own information and type **2F Music Dept Firstname Lastname** and then press Enter.

9. Switch to Form view and print the form. Three pages will print. Click the **Close Window** button, save your changes, close the database, and then close Access.

End You have completed Project 2F

Performance Assessments (continued)

Project 2G — Music

Objectives: *Create a Report with the Report Wizard and Save a Report.*

In the following Performance Assessment, you will use the Report Wizard to create a report for the Music Department at Lake Michigan City College. Your completed report will look similar to Figure 2.62. You will save your database as *2G_Music_Firstname_Lastname.*

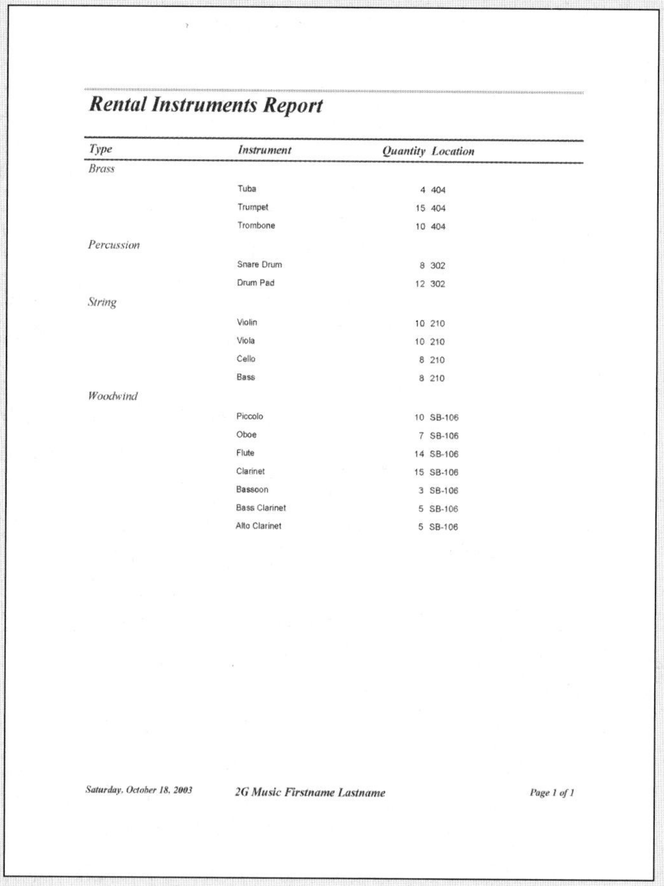

Rental Instruments Report

Type	*Instrument*	*Quantity*	*Location*
Brass			
	Tuba	4	404
	Trumpet	15	404
	Trombone	10	404
Percussion			
	Snare Drum	8	302
	Drum Pad	12	302
String			
	Violin	10	210
	Viola	10	210
	Cello	8	210
	Bass	8	210
Woodwind			
	Piccolo	10	SB-106
	Oboe	7	SB-106
	Flute	14	SB-106
	Clarinet	15	SB-106
	Bassoon	3	SB-106
	Bass Clarinet	5	SB-106
	Alto Clarinet	5	SB-106

Saturday, October 18, 2003 *2G Music Firstname Lastname* *Page 1 of 1*

Figure 2.62

1. Open **My Computer** or **Windows Explorer** and navigate to the student files for this textbook. Copy and paste the file **a02G_Music** to the folder where you are storing your projects for this chapter. Rename the file, using your own information, **2G_Music_Firstname_Lastname** and remove the Read-only property. Close My Computer or Windows Explorer.

2. Start Access and open your **2G_Music** database. On the Objects bar, click **Reports** and then start the Report Wizard. Under **Tables/Queries**, click the **down arrow** and then click **Table: Rental Instruments**. Include all of the fields from the **Rental Instruments** table in the report. Click the **Next** button.

(Project 2G–Music continues on the next page)

(Project 2G–Music continued)

3. Group the records by **Type** and click **OneField** button to display Type in the Preview. Click the **Next** button. Sort the records by **Instrument** in **Ascending** order. Click the **Next** button. Select the **Stepped** layout and the **Portrait** orientation. Click the **Next** button. As the style for the report, click **Corporate** and then click the **Next** button. For the name of the report, type **Rental Instruments Report** and then click the **Finish** button.
4. If necessary, maximize the displayed **Print Preview** and then zoom to **75%**. After examining the report, click the **View** button to switch to Design view.
5. In the **Page Footer** section of the report, click the **date control** on the left to select it and then drag the center right handle to the left until the right edge of the control is positioned at **2.0 inches on the horizontal ruler**. Select the **page number control** on the right, and drag its left center handle to **5.25 inches on the horizontal ruler**.
6. In the Toolbox, click the **Label** button. In the **Page Footer** section, starting at approximately the **2.0-inch mark on the horizontal ruler** and vertically aligned with the other controls, drag down and to the right to **5.25 inches on the horizontal ruler**. In the **Label** box, using your own information, type **2G Music Firstname Lastname** and press Enter.
7. Switch to the **Print Preview** of the report and verify that your information displays in the footer. **Print** the report. Click the **Close Window** button and save your changes. Close the database and then close Access.

End You have completed Project 2G

Project 2H—DL Courses

Objectives: *View and Navigate to Records with a Form, Use a Form to Add Records to and Delete Records from a Table, Modify the Design of a Report, and Print a Report.*

In the following Performance Assessment, you will open an existing form for the Distance Learning Courses database at Lake Michigan City College. You will add and delete records using the form. Additionally, you will open an existing report and make changes to the design of the report. Your completed database objects will look similar to Figure 2.63. You will rename and save your database as *2H_DL_Courses_Firstname_ Lastname*.

(Project 2H–DL Courses continues on the next page)

Performance Assessments (continued)

(Project 2H–DL Courses continued)

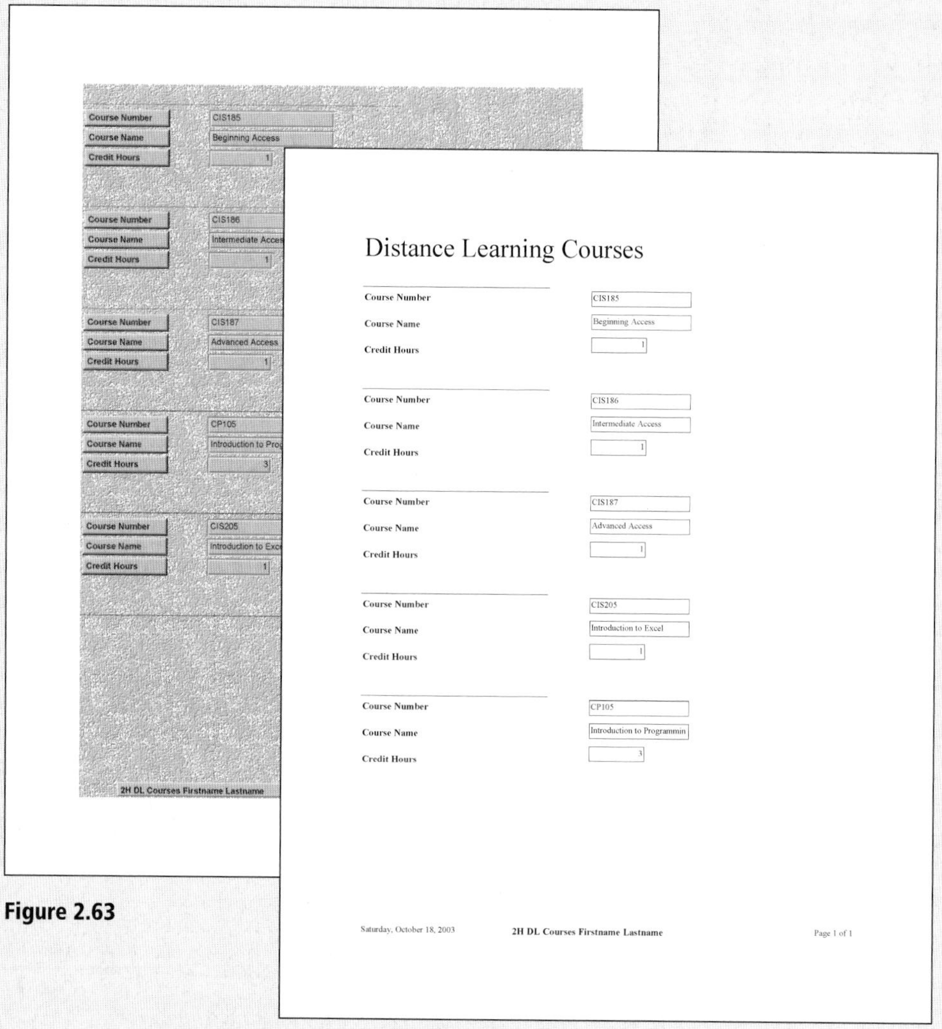

Figure 2.63

1. Open **My Computer** or **Windows Explorer** and navigate to the student files for this textbook. Copy and paste the file a02H_DL_Courses to the folder where you are storing your projects for this chapter. Rename the file, using your own information, **2H_DL_Courses_Firstname_Lastname** and remove the Read-only property. Close My Computer or Windows Explorer.
2. Start Access and open your **2H_DL_Courses** database. On the Objects bar, click **Forms** and then open the **Distance Learning Courses** form. Click the **New Record** button. In the **Course Number** field, type **CIS205** and press Tab. In the **Course Name** field type **Introduction to Excel** and in the **Credit Hours** field type **1**
3. Navigate to record 1, which has the course name *Introduction to Computers*. Use the record selector bar to select the entire record and then delete the record.

(Project 2H–DL Courses continues on the next page)

(Project 2H–DL Courses continued)

4. Switch to Design view and maximize the form window. Display the **View** menu and then click **Page Header/Footer**. On the Toolbox, click the **Label** button. In the **Page Footer section**, just below the Page Footer separator at **0.5 inch on the horizontal ruler**, drag down to the lower separator and to the right to **3 inches on the horizontal ruler**. In the label box, using your own information, type **2H DL Courses Firstname Lastname** and press Enter.
5. Switch to Form view and print the form. Close the form and save your changes.
6. On the Objects bar, click **Reports** and then open the **Distance Learning Courses** report in Print Preview. If necessary, maximize the window and then zoom to 100%. View the report and notice that the labels and their corresponding text boxes are formatted in a manner that is difficult to read. Switch to Design view. Using the techniques you practiced in this chapter, arrange the label and text box controls to match Figure 2.64.

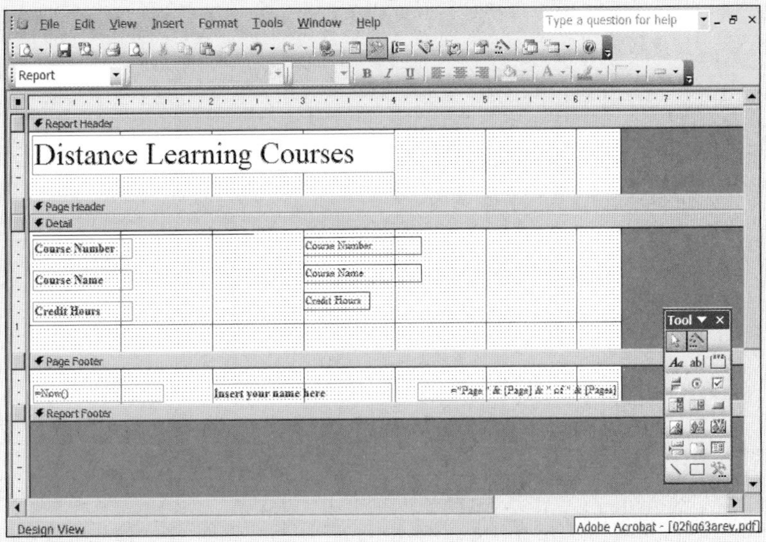

Figure 2.64

7. In the **Page Footer section** of the report, in the control *Insert your name here*, click the control once to select it, and then delete the text in the control. Using your own information, type **2H DL Courses Firstname Lastname** and then press Enter.
8. Switch to the **Print Preview** of the report. Verify that your information is at the lower edge of the report and then print the report. Close the report, save your changes, close the database, and then close Access.

End You have completed Project 2H

Mastery Assessments

Project 2I—Employees

Objectives: *Create an AutoForm, Save and Close an AutoForm, Create a Report with the Report Wizard, Save a Report, and Print a Report.*

In the following Mastery Assessment, you will create an AutoForm and a report that corresponds to the Employees table for Lake Michigan City College. Your completed database objects will look similar to Figure 2.65. You will save your database as *2I_Employees_Firstname_Lastname.*

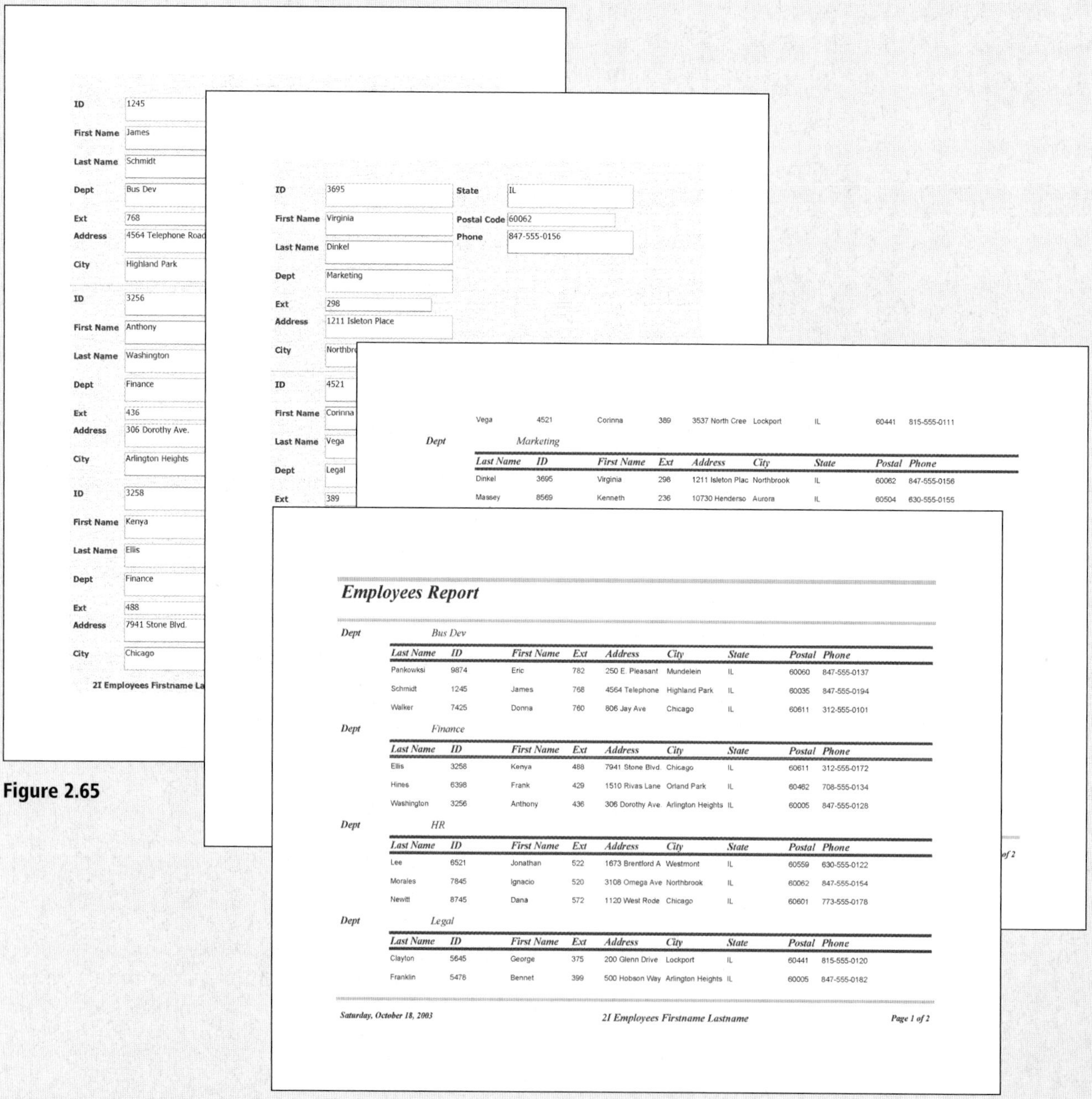

Figure 2.65

(Project 2I–Employees continues on the next page)

(Project 2I–Employees continued)

1. From the student files that accompany this textbook, copy the file **a02I_Employees** and then paste the file to the folder where you are storing your projects for this chapter. Using your own information, rename this file to **2I_Employees_Firstname_Lastname** and remove the Read-only attribute.
2. Start Access and then open your **2I_Employees** database.
3. Create an AutoForm based on the **Employees** table. Use the **Columnar** format for the form. Add a Page Footer to the form and in it type **2I Employees Firstname Lastname** and then save the AutoForm as **Employees Form** Print the form. Five pages will print.
4. Use the Report wizard to create a report based on the **Employees** table. As you proceed through the wizard, use the following specifications for your report:

   Include all of the fields from the Employees table
   Group the records by Dept
   Sort the records alphabetically by Last Name
   Use the Outline 1 layout for the report in Landscape orientation
   Use the Corporate style for the report
   Save the report as **Employees Report**
5. In the **Page Footer** section, decrease the width of the control on the right by dragging its left edge to **7.5 inches on the horizontal ruler**. Create a label in the **Page Footer** section, and in it type **2I Employees Firstname Lastname**
6. Print the report. Two pages will print. Close any open database objects, the database, and then close Access.

End You have completed Project 2I

Project 2J — Suppliers

Objectives: *Use a Form to Add Records to and Delete Records from a Table, Create a Form with the Form Wizard, and Modify a Form.*

In the following Mastery Assessment, you will use the Form Wizard to create a new form for the Suppliers database at Lake Michigan City College. Your completed form will look similar to Figure 2.66. You will save your database as *2J_Suppliers_Firstname_Lastname.*

1. From the student files that accompany this textbook, copy the file a02J_Suppliers and then paste the file to the folder where you are storing your projects for this chapter. Using your own information, rename this file as **2J_Suppliers_Firstname_Lastname** and remove the Read-only attribute.

(Project 2J–Suppliers continues on the next page)

Mastery Assessments (continued)

(Project 2J–Suppliers continued)

Figure 2.66

2. Start Access and then open your **2J_Suppliers** database.
3. Create a form using the Form Wizard based on the **Suppliers** table. Use the following specifications in your form:

   Include all of the fields from the Suppliers table
   Apply the Columnar layout to the form
   Apply the Expedition style to the form
   Accept the default name for the form

(Project 2J–Suppliers continues on the next page)

Mastery Assessments (continued)

(Project 2J–Suppliers continued)

4. Add a **Page Footer** to the form and in it type **2J Suppliers Firstname Lastname**
5. Delete the record for **Jiffy Cleaning Supplies**. Edit the record for **Plastic Warehouse** by changing the name of the contact person from **Debbie Lucero** to **Beau Gellard**.
6. Modify the design of the form by widening it to **6 inches on the horizontal ruler**. Then, instead of one column of eight fields, create two columns of four fields. Begin the second column with the **State** controls, aligning them at **3 inches on the horizontal ruler**. Refer to Figure 2.67. Print and close the form. Two pages will print. Close the database and then close Access.

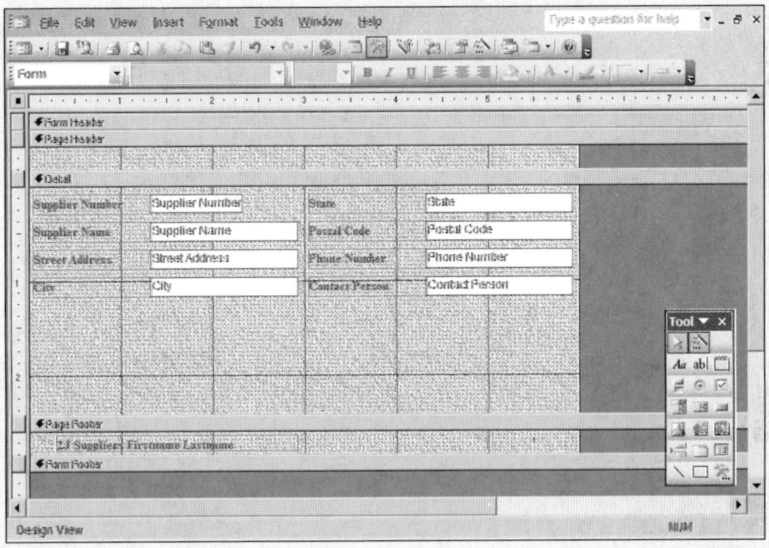

Figure 2.67

End You have completed Project 2J

Problem Solving

Project 2K — Employees

Objectives: *Create an AutoForm* or *Create a Form with the Form Wizard and Modify a Form.*

In this Problem Solving assessment, you will create a form for entering data into the Employees database at Lake Michigan City College.

1. From the student files that accompany this textbook, copy the file *a02K_Employees* and then paste the file to the folder where you are storing your projects for this chapter. Using your own information, rename this file as **2K_Employees_Firstname_Lastname** and remove the Read-only attribute.
2. New employees fill out a paper form similar to the one shown in Figure 2.68. Then, the data entry clerk uses the paper forms to enter the new employees into the database. Create a form, using any method you choose, and then modify the layout of the form so that it closely resembles the layout of the paper form. This will make it much easier and faster to enter new employees into the database.

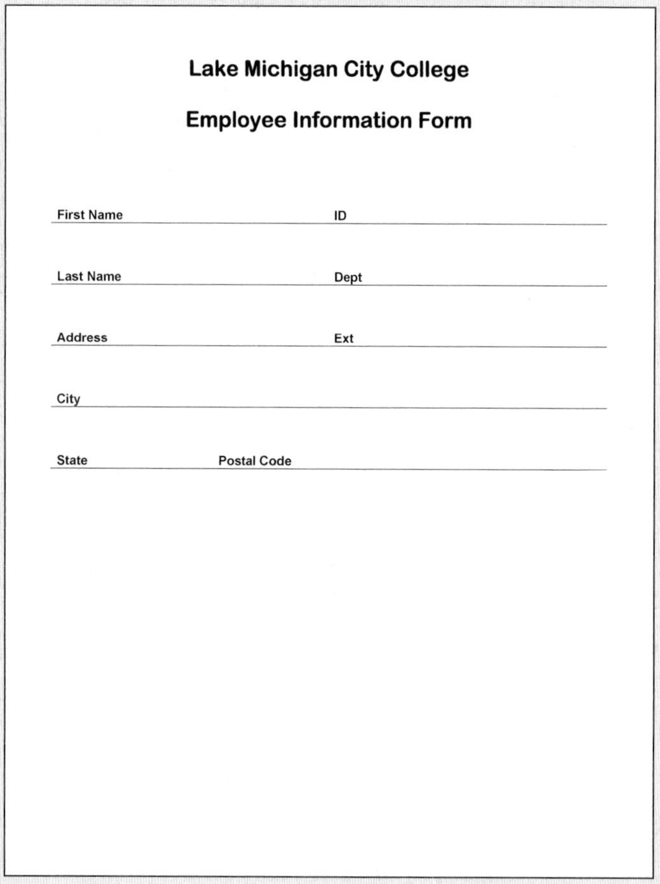

Lake Michigan City College

Employee Information Form

First Name ______ ID ______

Last Name ______ Dept ______

Address ______ Ext ______

City ______

State ______ Postal Code ______

Figure 2.68

3. Add your name and the project name in a Page Footer on the form and print the form.

End You have completed Project 2K

Problem Solving (continued)

Project 2L — Depts

Objectives: *Create a Report with the Report Wizard, Save a Report, Modify the Design of a Report, and Print a Report.*

In this Problem Solving assessment, you will create a report that faculty and staff members at Lake Michigan City College can consult to obtain information about the departments at the college.

1. From the student files that accompany this textbook, copy the file *a02L_Depts* and then paste the file to the folder where you are storing your projects for this chapter. Using your own information, rename this file as **2L_Depts_Firstname_Lastname** and remove the Read-only attribute.
2. Use the Report Wizard to create a report that includes all the fields in alphabetical order by department name. Arrange the fields on the report in an attractive, easy-to-ready layout. In Design view, create a label in the footer area with the project name and your name. Print the report.

End You have completed Project 2L

On the Internet

Discovering What's New in Access

Working with current database software is an important part of your database training.

Go to **www.microsoft.com** and perform a search to identify the changes from Access 2002 Access 2003.

GO! with Help

Creating a Form in Design View

Besides using the Form Wizard to create a form, you can also create a form from the Design view. Use the Access Help system to find out how to create a form using Design view.

1. Start Access. if necessary, from the **View** menu, click **Task Pane** to display the **Getting Started** task pane. On the task pane, to the right of *Getting Started*, click the **down arrow**. From the displayed list of available task panes, click **Help**.
2. Click in the **Search for** box and type **Create a form**
3. Press Enter, scroll the displayed list as necessary, and then click **Create a form**.
4. At the lower part of the pane, locate the text *On your own in Design view*, and under this result, click **How?**
5. If you would like to keep a copy of this information, click the **Print** button. One page will print.
6. Click the **Close** button in the top right corner of the Help window to close the Help window and then close Access.

3 chapterthree

Queries

In this chapter, you will: complete these projects **and** practice these skills.

Project	Objectives
Project 3A Creating Queries	• Create a New Select Query • Run, Save, and Close a Query • Open and Edit an Existing Query • Specify Text Criteria in a Query
Project 3B Defining Queries	• Use Wildcards in a Query • Specify Numeric Criteria in a Query • Use Compound Criteria • Sort Data in a Query
Project 3C Using Calculated Fields and Calculating Statistics in a Query	• Use Calculated Fields in a Query • Group Data and Calculate Statistics in a Query

Lake Michigan City College

Lake Michigan City College is located along the lakefront of Chicago—one of the nation's most exciting cities. The college serves its large and diverse student body and makes positive contributions to the community through relevant curricula, partnerships with businesses and nonprofit organizations, and learning experiences that allow students to be full participants in the global community. The college offers three associate degrees in 20 academic areas, adult education programs, and continuing education offerings on campus, at satellite locations, and online.

Queries

Access queries allow you to isolate specific data in a database by asking questions and setting conditions that Access can interpret. The conditions, known as criteria, can be either text or numeric in nature. Wildcard characters can be used when a portion of what you are looking for is unknown.

Access provides comparison operators that, combined with numeric criteria, can further refine the query search. Logical operators such as AND and OR, as well as statistical functions, can be used in queries. In this chapter, you will create and modify queries for an Access database.

3A Project 3A School

Just like tables, forms, and reports, queries are also database objects. Queries can be used to locate information in an Access database based on certain ***criteria*** that you specify as part of the query. Criteria are conditions that identify the specific records you are looking for. Queries can also be created to view only certain fields from a table.

Lake Michigan City College uses queries to locate information about the data in their databases that meet certain criteria. In Activities 3.1 through 3.6 you will use queries to locate information about the records in the Students table. Your query result will look similar to Figure 3.1.

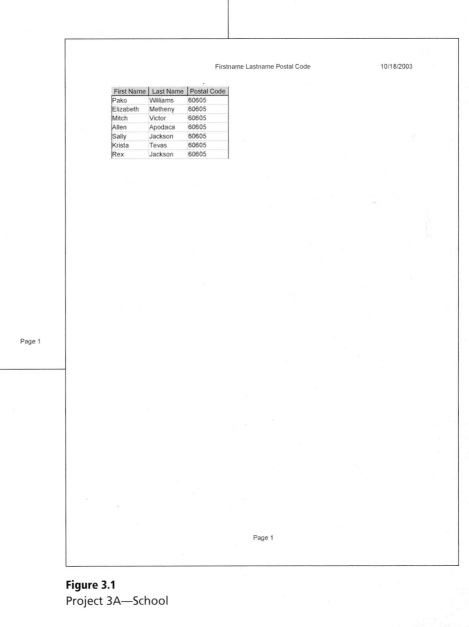

Firstname Lastname Business Major 10/18/2003

Student#	First Name	Last Name	Major
64589	Elizabeth	Metheny	Business
27232	Angela	Meyers	Business
41671	Tina	Hurst	Business
74527	Tiffany	Blume	Business

Page 1

Firstname Lastname Postal Code 10/18/2003

First Name	Last Name	Postal Code
Pako	Williams	60605
Elizabeth	Metheny	60605
Mitch	Victor	60605
Allen	Apodaca	60605
Sally	Jackson	60605
Krista	Tevas	60605
Rex	Jackson	60605

Page 1

Figure 3.1
Project 3A—School

Objective 1
Create a New Select Query

A ***query*** is a question formed in a manner that Access can interpret. The question that is asked may be simple or complex. For example, you might want to ask, "Which students are Business Majors?" Unless a query has already been set up to ask this question, you must create a new one. A query that retrieves data from one or more tables and then displays the results is called a ***select query***. In the following activity, you will create a simple select query with no criteria specified.

Activity 3.1 Creating a New Query, Using the Select Query Window, and Adding Fields to the Design Grid

1. Using the skills you practiced in Chapter 1, and using either My Computer or Windows Explorer, create a new folder named *Chapter 3* in the location where you will be storing your projects for this chapter.

2. Locate the file **a03A_School** from the student files that accompany this text. Copy and paste the file to the Chapter 3 folder you created in Step 1.

3. Using the technique you practiced in Activity 1.1 of Chapter 1, remove the Read-only property from the file and rename the file as **3A_School_Firstname_Lastname**

4. Close the Windows accessory you are using—either My Computer or Windows Explorer. Start Access and open your **3A_School** database.

5. On the Objects bar, click **Queries**.

   To the right of the Objects bar, two command icons for creating a new query display.

6. Double-click **Create query in Design view**.

   A new Select Query window opens and the **Show Table** dialog box displays. See Figure 3.2. The **Show Table** dialog box lists all of the tables in the database.

> **Note — Creating Queries in Design View**
>
> *Queries in Design view.*
>
> In this chapter, you will create queries only in Design view. Creating queries using the wizard will be addressed as you progress in your study of Access.

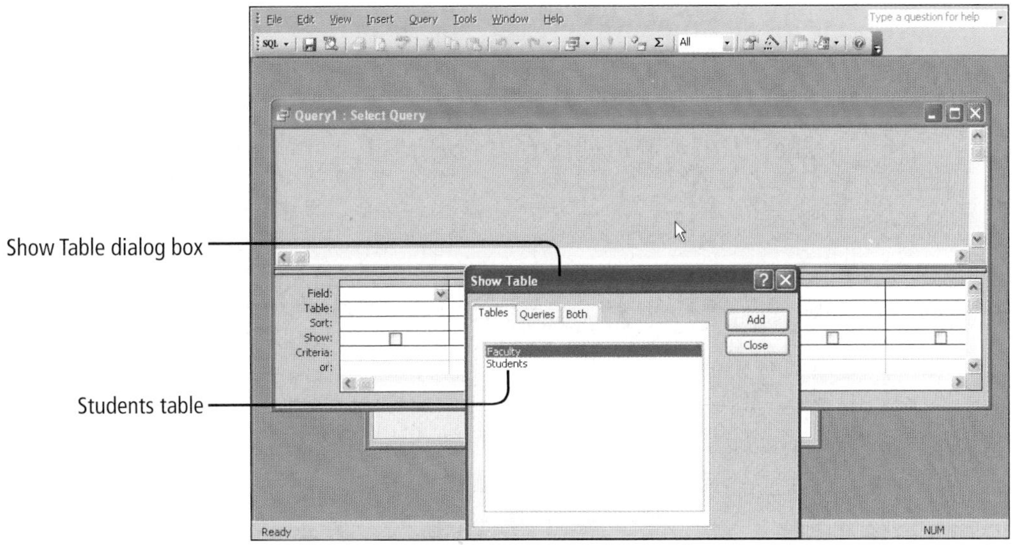

Figure 3.2

7 In the **Show Table** dialog box, click **Students**, click the **Add** button, and then click the **Close** button. See Figure 3.3. Alternatively, you can double-click Students and then click Close.

A list of the fields in the Students table displays in the upper pane of the Select Query window. The **Student#** field is bold, unlike the other fields in the list, because the **Student#** field is the primary key in the Students table.

The Select Query window has two parts: the ***table area*** (upper pane) and the ***design grid*** (lower pane). After a table has been selected from the **Show Table** dialog box, it displays in the table area, as shown in Figure 3.4.

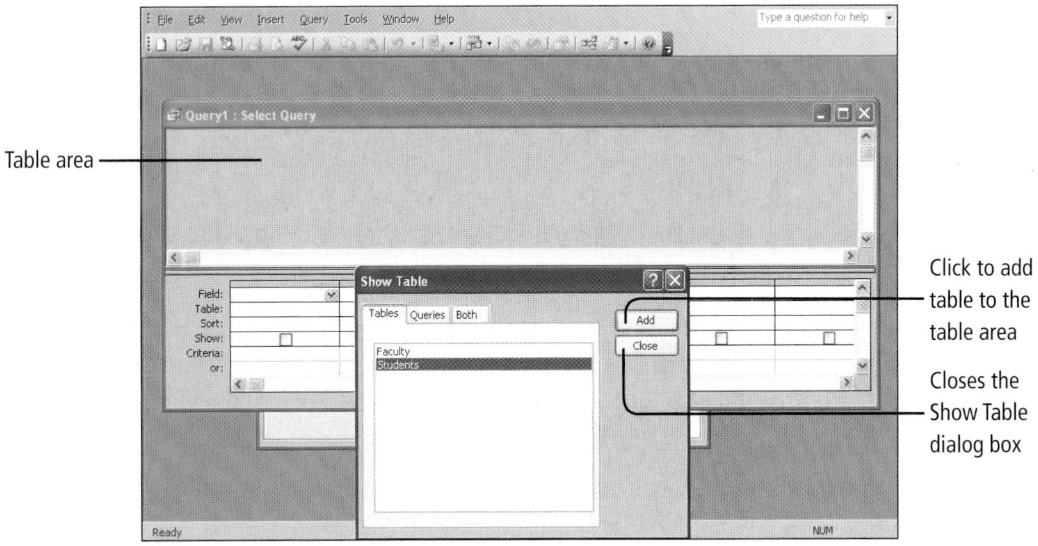

Figure 3.3

8 In the **Students** field list, double-click **Student#**.

The **Student#** field displays in the design grid. See Figure 3.4. The design grid of the Select Query window is where you specify the fields and other criteria to be used in the query.

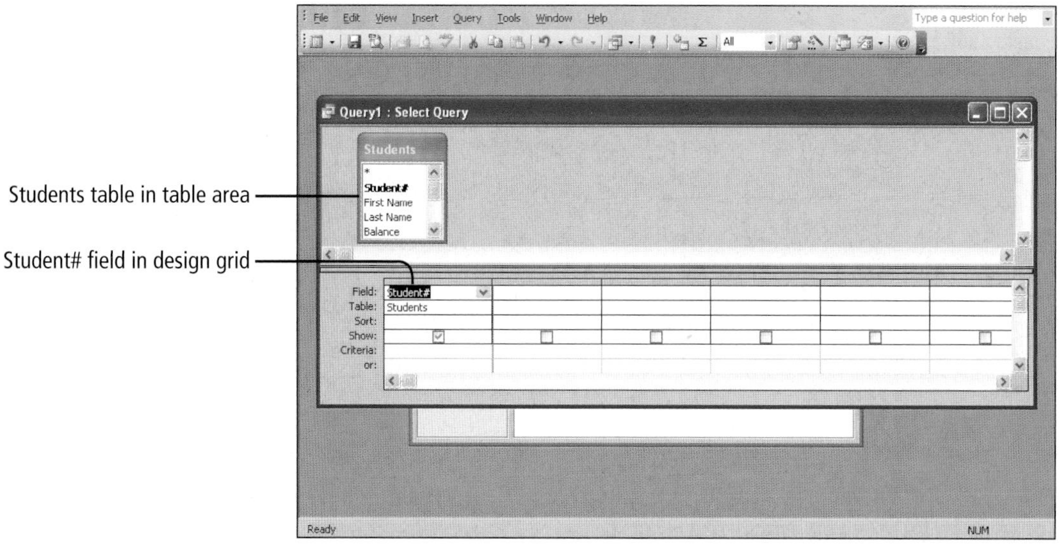

Figure 3.4

9 In the **Students** field list, double-click **First Name**. Repeat this action for all the remaining fields in the field list. Use the vertical scroll bar in the field list window to view the fields toward the end of the list.

As you double-click each field, notice the fields display one by one to the right of the previous field in the design grid. See Figure 3.5.

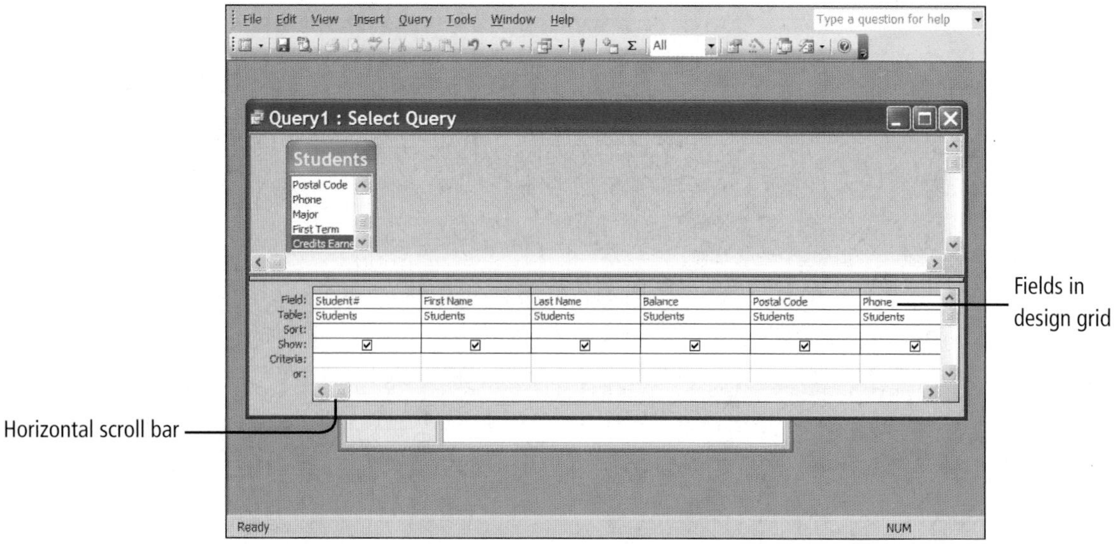

Figure 3.5

10 Use the horizontal scroll bar to scroll to the right to view all the fields in the design grid. Verify that all of the fields from the field list are displayed in the design grid.

Another Way

Adding All Fields to a Query

Double-click the *.

You can add all the fields to a query by double-clicking the * at the top of the field list. The field row will display the name of the table followed by .* indicating that all of the fields in the table have been added to the design grid. You will see each field displayed in the datasheet when you run the query.

11 Maximize the Select Query window.

The Select Query window is maximized. The Select Query window can be manipulated like any other window.

12 Position your mouse pointer over the thin gray line in between the table area and the design grid until the pointer changes to a vertical double arrow. See Figure 3.6. Drag the line separating the table area and the design grid down about one inch. See Figure 3.7.

The table area size is increased.

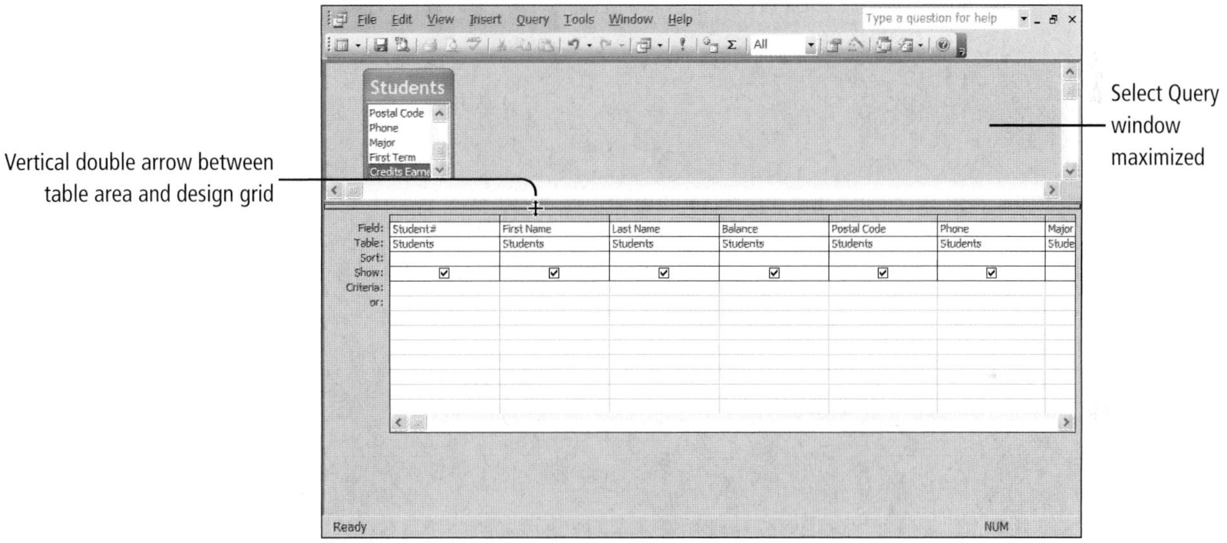

Figure 3.6

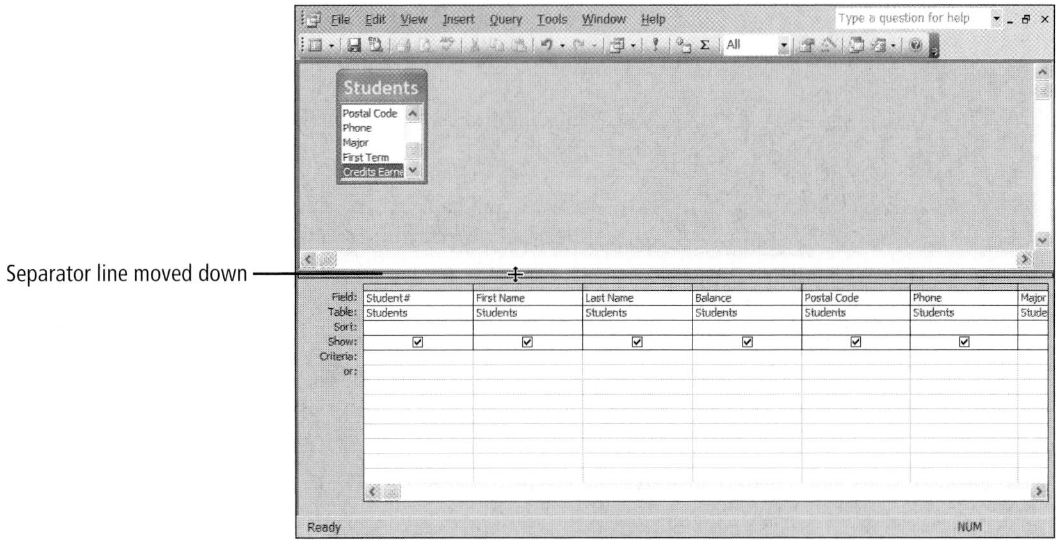

Figure 3.7

chapter three

13 In the table area, position your mouse pointer on the lower edge of the field list until it displays as a black double arrow, as shown in Figure 3.8. Drag the lower edge of the field list down until all of the fields in the Students table are visible. See Figure 3.9.

The field list displays all of the fields in the table. Use the techniques you just practiced whenever you need to enlarge the upper or lower panes of the Select Query window to gain a better working view.

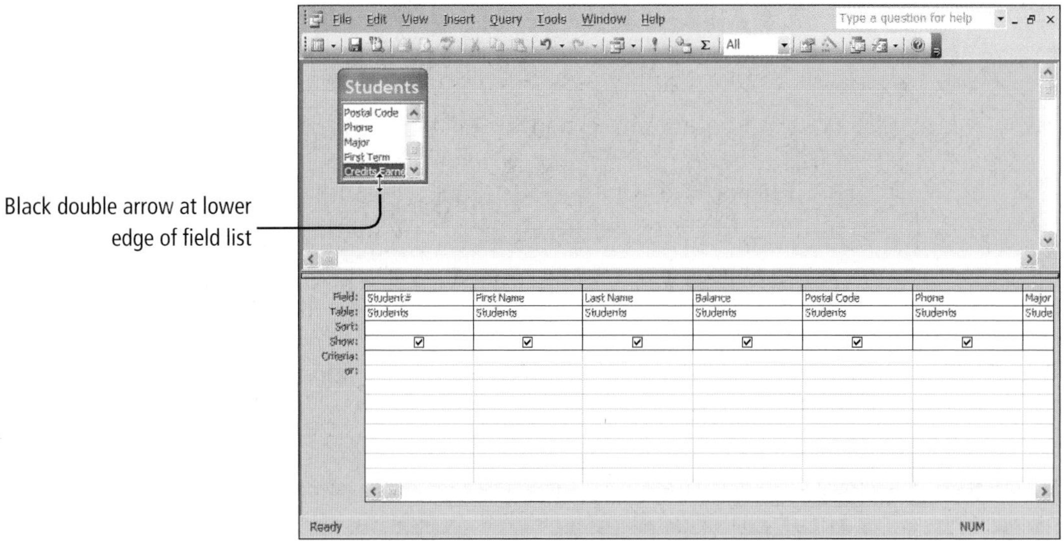

Figure 3.8

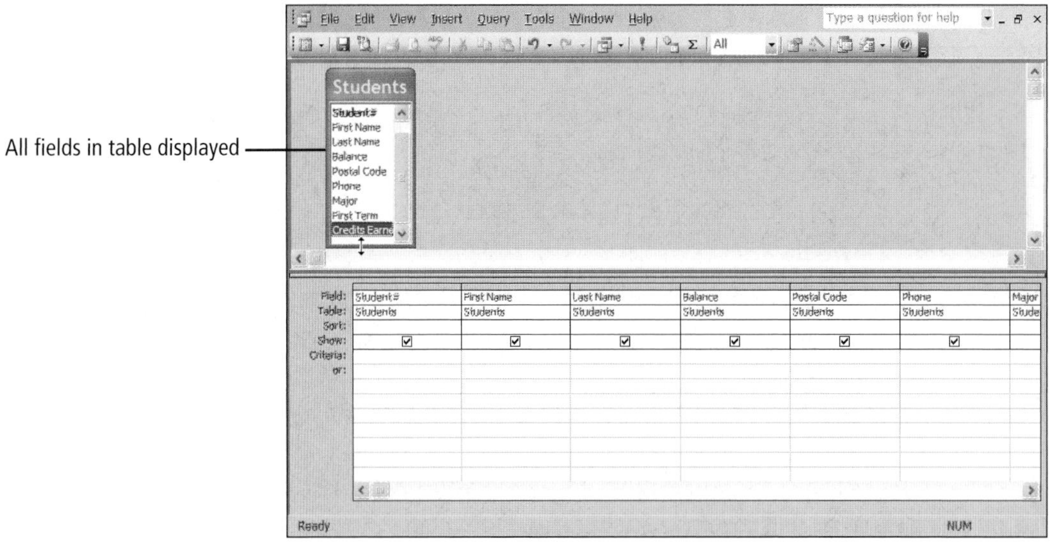

Figure 3.9

14 If desired, resize the elements that you adjusted in Steps 11 through 13 and restore the Select Query window. The following figures show the Select Query window resized to the previous sizes. Leave the query window open for the next activity.

Objective 2
Run, Save, and Close a Query

When you run a query, Access looks at the records in the table (or tables) you have defined, finds the records that match the specified criteria (if any), and displays those records in a table.

Activity 3.2 Running, Saving, and Closing a Query

1 On the Query Design toolbar, click the **Run** button. See Figure 3.10.

The results of the query display in a table in Datasheet view. The fields display in columns, the records display in rows, and a Navigation area displays at the lower edge, in the same manner as in a table. See Figure 3.11. Because no criteria were specified in the design grid of the query, the query results are the same as the data in the Students table.

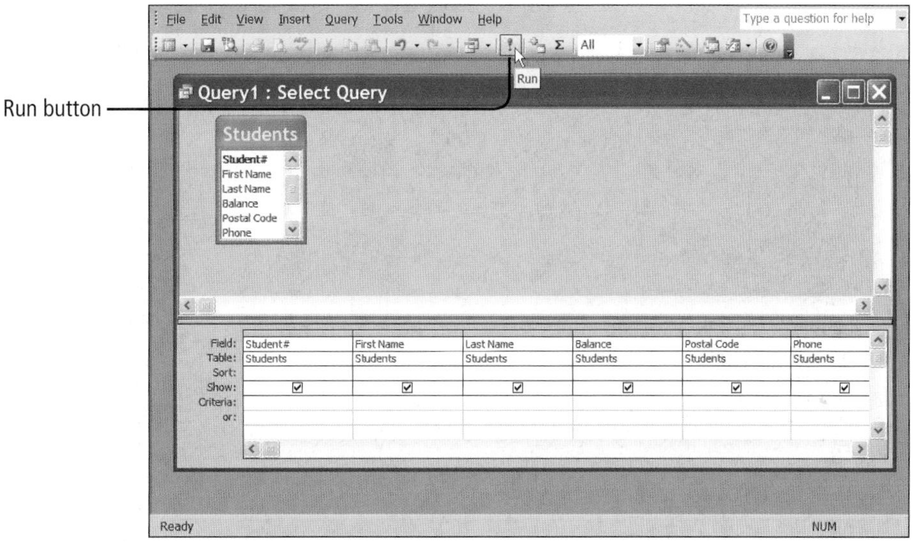

Figure 3.10

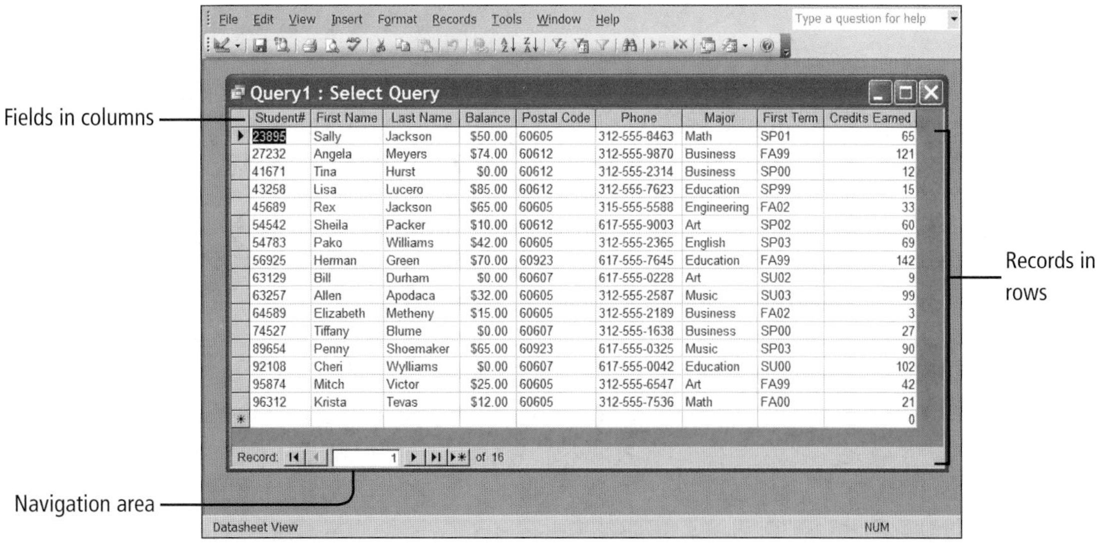

Student#	First Name	Last Name	Balance	Postal Code	Phone	Major	First Term	Credits Earned
23895	Sally	Jackson	$50.00	60605	312-555-8463	Math	SP01	65
27232	Angela	Meyers	$74.00	60612	312-555-9870	Business	FA99	121
41671	Tina	Hurst	$0.00	60612	312-555-2314	Business	SP00	12
43258	Lisa	Lucero	$85.00	60612	312-555-7623	Education	SP99	15
45689	Rex	Jackson	$65.00	60605	315-555-5588	Engineering	FA02	33
54542	Sheila	Packer	$10.00	60612	617-555-9003	Art	SP02	60
54783	Pako	Williams	$42.00	60605	312-555-2365	English	SP03	69
56925	Herman	Green	$70.00	60923	617-555-7645	Education	FA99	142
63129	Bill	Durham	$0.00	60607	617-555-0228	Art	SU02	9
63257	Allen	Apodaca	$32.00	60605	312-555-2587	Music	SU03	99
64589	Elizabeth	Metheny	$15.00	60605	312-555-2189	Business	FA02	3
74527	Tiffany	Blume	$0.00	60607	312-555-1638	Business	SP00	27
89654	Penny	Shoemaker	$65.00	60923	617-555-0325	Music	SP03	90
92108	Cheri	Wylliams	$0.00	60607	617-555-0042	Education	SU00	102
95874	Mitch	Victor	$25.00	60605	312-555-6547	Art	FA99	42
96312	Krista	Tevas	$12.00	60605	312-555-7536	Math	FA00	21
								0

Figure 3.11

2 In the title bar of the query result, click the **Close** button ☒.

Because you have not previously named or saved this query, a message displays asking you if you want to save the changes to the design of query "Query1." The default name of a query created in this manner is "Query" followed by a number, such as "Query1."

3 Click **Yes**.

The Save As dialog box displays. Once created, a query can be run multiple times; thus, queries are frequently saved for future use.

4 In the **Save As** dialog box, in the **Query Name** box, delete the highlighted text. Then using your own information, type **Firstname Lastname Query1** and click **OK**.

The query is saved and closed. The new query name displays in the Database window. See Figure 3.12.

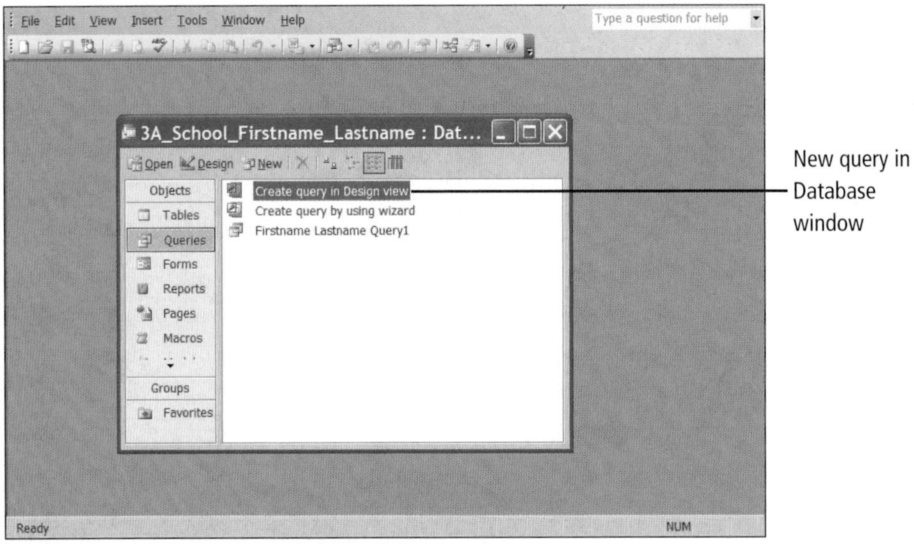

Figure 3.12

Objective 3
Open and Edit an Existing Query

After you have created and saved a query, you can open the query. Opening an existing query will cause the query to run and the results display in Datasheet view. You do not need to create a new query each time data in the corresponding table is modified. Each time the query is run, any changes made to the table will be automatically reflected in the query results.

Activity 3.3 Opening an Existing Query and Switching Between Views

1 In the Database window, be sure **Queries** is selected on the Objects bar and then double-click your **Query1** saved in Activity 3.2.

The query opens in the Datasheet view. If you want to view the records in a query result, use Datasheet view.

2 On the Query Datasheet toolbar, click the **View** button.

The query displays in Design view.

3 On the title bar of the Query window, click the **Close** button to close the query.

The query closes.

4 With your **Query1** selected in the Database window, above the Objects bar, click the **Design** button, as shown in Figure 3.13.

Your Query1 query opens directly in Design view. This is another way to display the query in Design view. From the Design view of a query you can make changes to the structure of the query. You can open a query in Design view or Datasheet view, depending on what you want to do with the query. If you want to modify the design of the query, such as the fields included in the query, use Design view.

Leave your query open in Design view for the next activity.

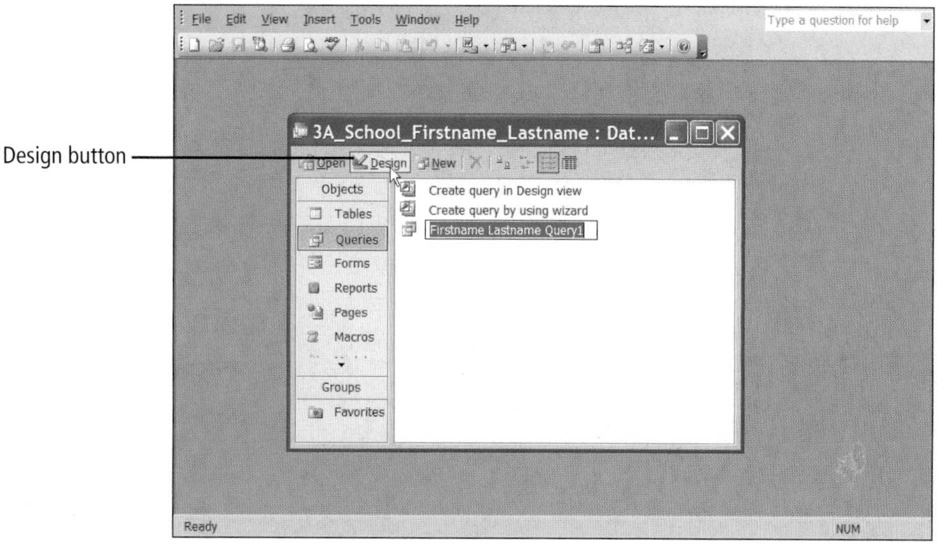

Figure 3.13

Activity 3.4 Editing a Query

A query does not have to contain all the fields from the table.

1 If necessary, open your **Query1** in Design view. In the design grid, move your pointer above the **Balance** field until it displays as a black downward-pointing arrow and click. See Figure 3.14.

The Balance column is selected (highlighted), as shown in Figure 3.15.

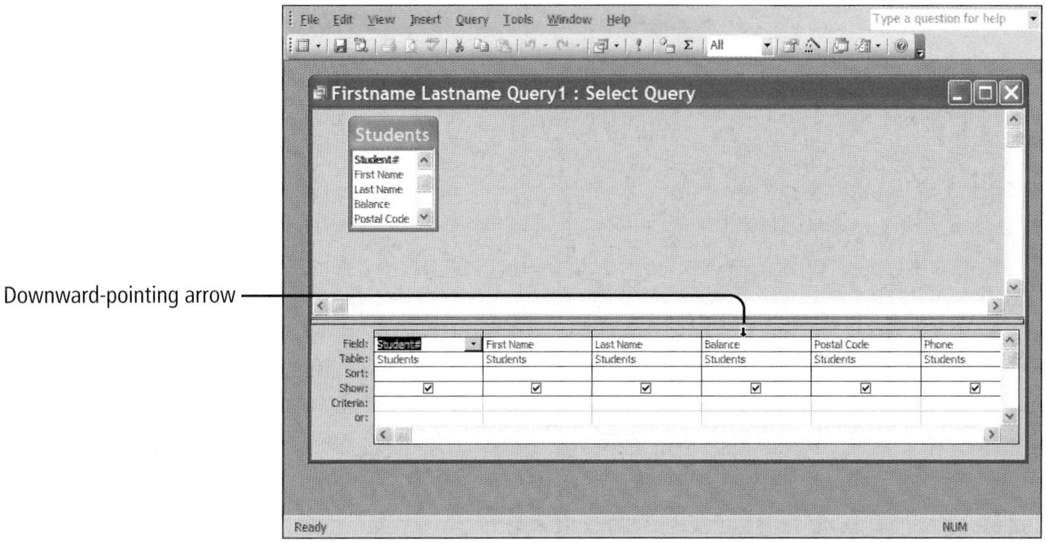

Figure 3.14

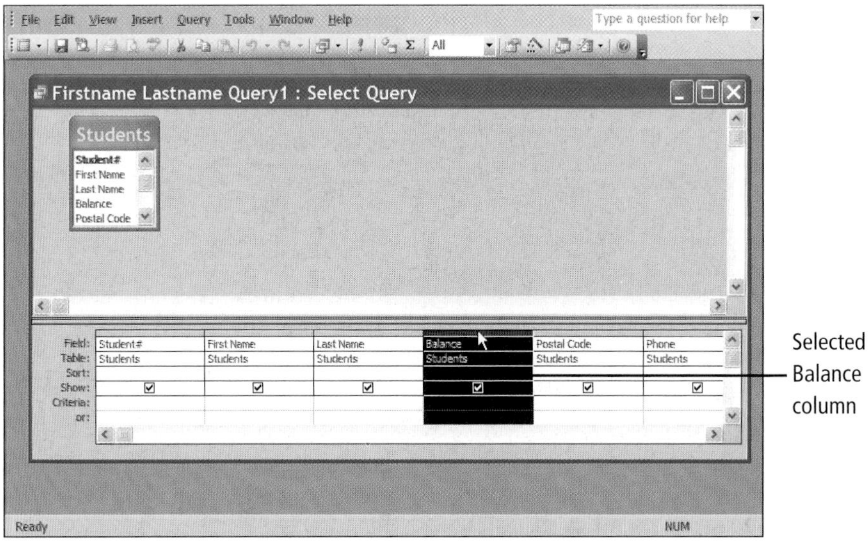

Figure 3.15

2 Press Delete.

The Balance field is removed from the design grid, and the remaining fields shift to the left. Removing a field from the design grid of a query does *not* affect the field in its corresponding table.

3 In the design grid, move your pointer above the **Postal Code** field until it displays as a black downward-pointing arrow and click to select the **Postal Code** field.

The Postal Code field is selected (highlighted). See Figure 3.16.

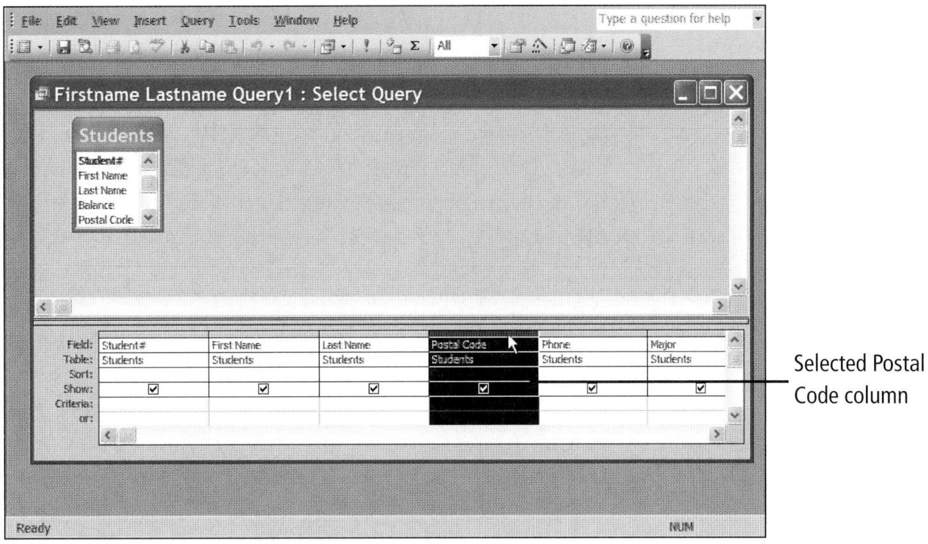

Figure 3.16

4. Press Delete to remove the **Postal Code** field from the design grid.

5. Repeat the technique you have just practiced to remove the **Phone**, **First Term**, and **Credits Earned** fields from the design grid.

   The Student#, First Name, Last Name, and Major fields remain in the design grid. See Figure 3.17.

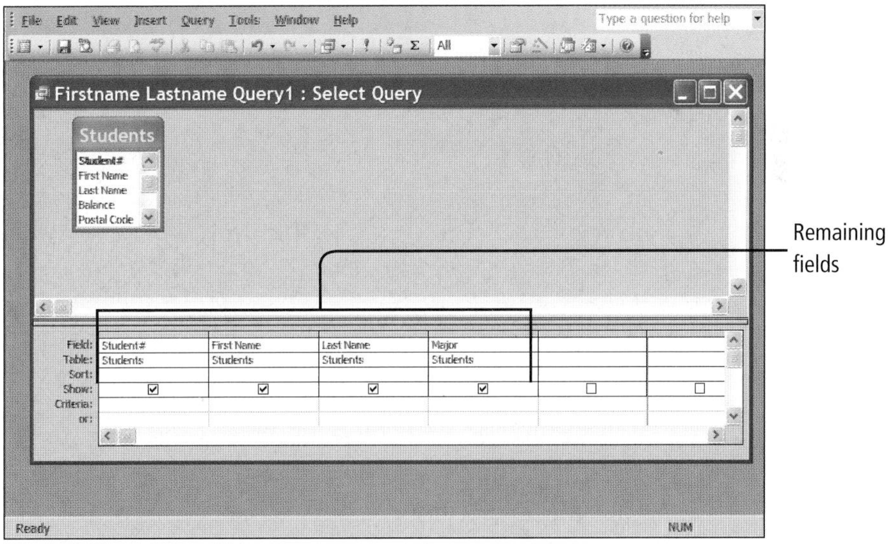

Figure 3.17

6. On the Query Design toolbar, click the **Run** button.

   The results of the query display in a table with only the four specified fields displayed. This is a convenient method to use when you want to see only some of the fields from the table.

7. On the Query Datasheet toolbar, click the **View** button to return to Design view. Leave your query open in Design view for the next activity.

Objective 4
Specify Text Criteria in a Query

Specifying criteria in a query will limit the records that display in the query result. Up to this point, the query you created and ran did not limit the number of records displayed by specifying specific criteria; thus all of the records from the corresponding table displayed in the result.

Recall that to query is to ask a question. When criteria is specified in a query, you are asking a more specific question, and therefore you will get a more specific result. For example, suppose you want to find out which students live in a particular area. You could specify a specific Postal Code in the query criteria and only records that match the specified Postal Code will display. Keep in mind that queries do not have to contain all of the fields from a table in order to locate the requested information.

Activity 3.5 Specifying Text Criteria in a Query

In this activity, you will specify the criteria in the query so that only records in the Students table that have *Business* in the Major field display. Records that indicate a major other than Business will not display. You will save the query with a new name.

1. If necessary, open your **Query1** query in Design view. In the design grid, locate the **Criteria** row as indicated in Figure 3.18.

   The Criteria row is where you will specify the criteria that will limit the results of the query to your exact specifications.

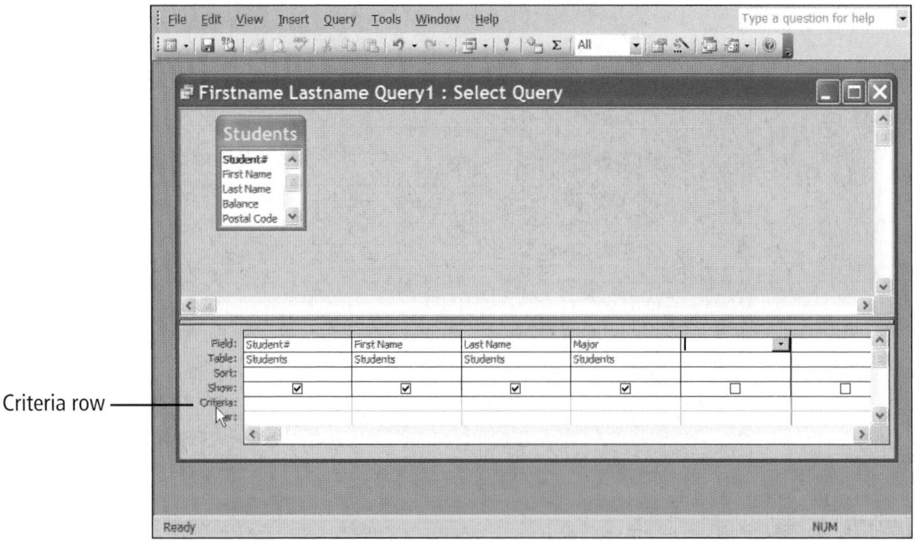

Figure 3.18

2. In the **Criteria** row, under the **Major** field, click and then type **Business** See Figure 3.19.

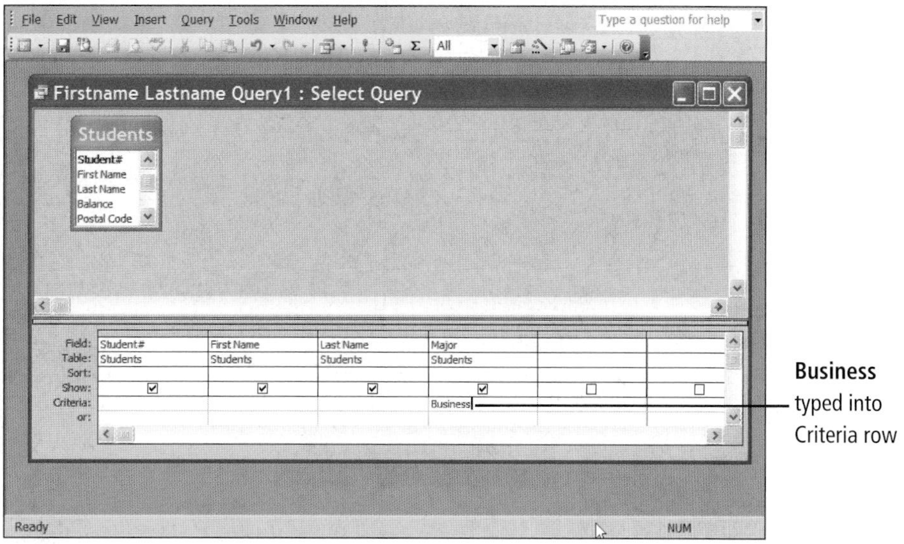

Figure 3.19

3 On the Query Design toolbar, click the **Run** button.

The query runs and the query results display in a table in Datasheet view. See Figure 3.20. Clicking the Run button causes Access to look at all the records in the Students table and locate those records that meet the specified criteria—records that have *Business* in the Major field.

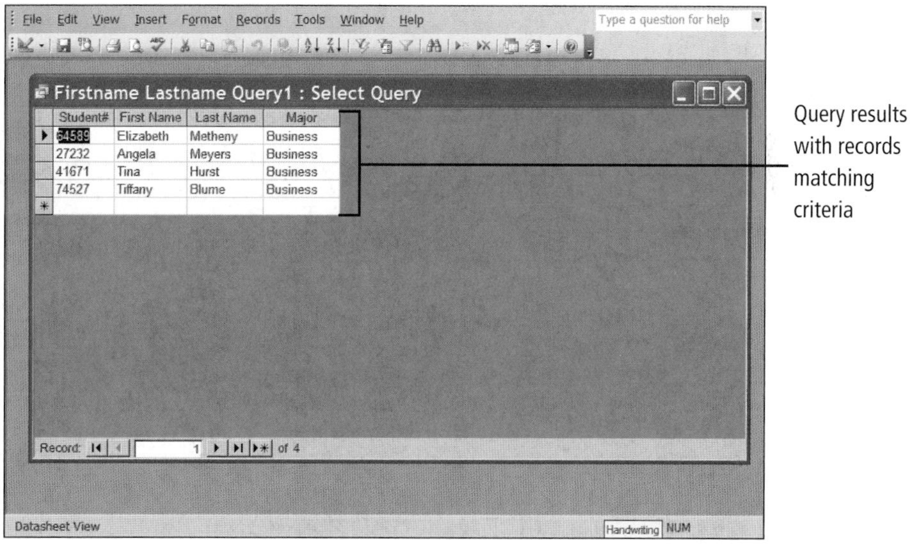

Figure 3.20

4 Examine the records in the query result and verify that the records that display have been limited to those students that have Business as their major.

5 On the **File** menu, click **Save As**.

The Save As dialog box displays. Here you can give this query a different name from the first query and thus have both as saved queries.

6 Under **Save Query 'Firstname Lastname Query1' To:**, and using your own information, type **FirstName LastName Business Major** and click **OK**.

The query with the criteria you specified is saved with the new name and the new name displays in the title bar of the query window. See Figure 3.21.

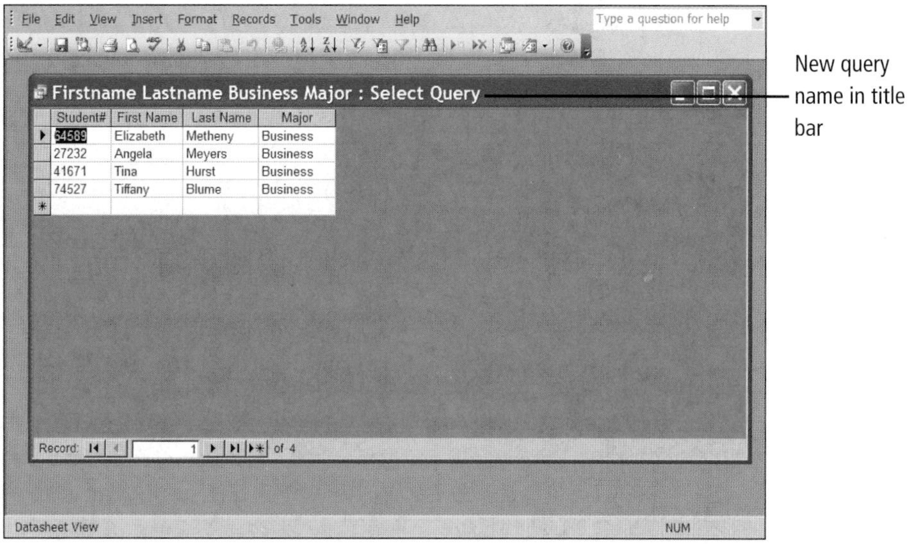

Figure 3.21

7 On the title bar of the query window, click the **Close** button ☒ to close the query.

The name of your new query displays in the Database window.

8 If necessary, click **Queries** on the Objects bar and then double-click **Create query in Design view**.

A new query window displays and the Show Table dialog box lists the tables in the database.

9 In the **Show Table** dialog box, click the **Queries tab** shown in Figure 3.22.

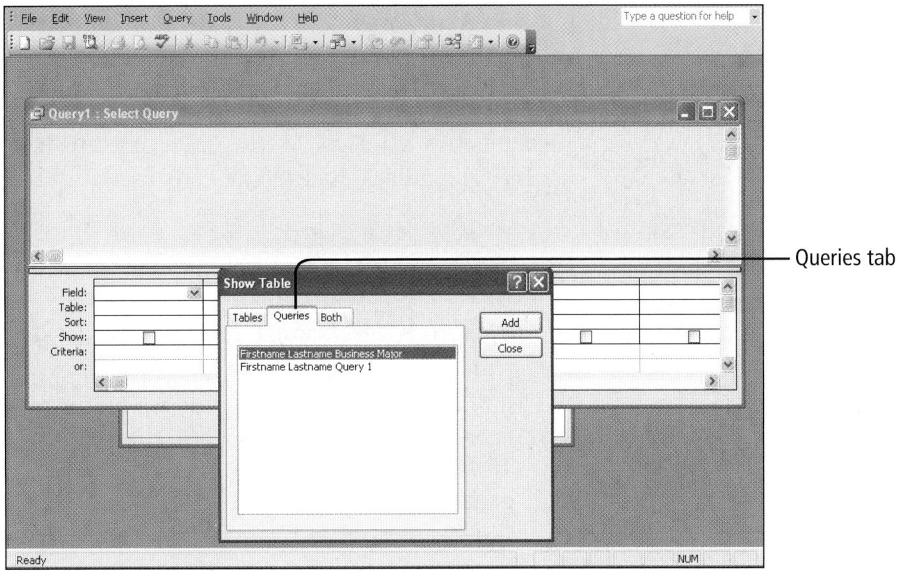

Figure 3.22

10 On the **Queries tab**, notice that the names of the two queries you have created thus far display. Click the **Both tab** and notice that the names of the two tables in the database as well as the names of the two queries you created display. See Figure 3.23.

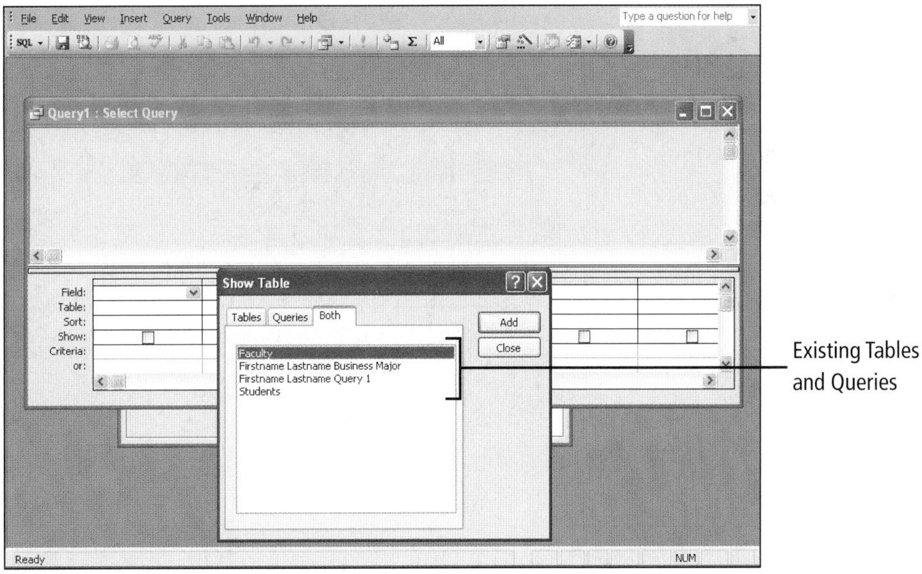

Figure 3.23

11 Click the **Tables tab**, double-click the **Students** table, and then click **Close**.

The field list for the Students table is added to the table area of the query and the Show Table dialog box closes. Next, you will add criteria to the query that will find the records that have a particular Postal Code.

12 In the **Students** field list, double-click the **First Name**, **Last Name**, and **Postal Code** fields to add them to the design grid. If necessary, use the vertical scroll bar to view the **Postal Code** field.

Recall that queries do not have to contain all of the fields from a table in order to locate the requested information.

Another Way

Adding Fields to the Design Grid

Drag fields from the field list or click in the Field row.

You can also add fields to the design grid by dragging the field from the field list and dropping it into the desired location in the design grid.
Or, you can click in the field row and then choose the field from the drop-down list.

13 In the **Criteria** row, under **Postal Code**, type **60605** See Figure 3.24.

Although fields such as Postal Code contain numbers, they are considered text because mathematical calculations are not performed on them.

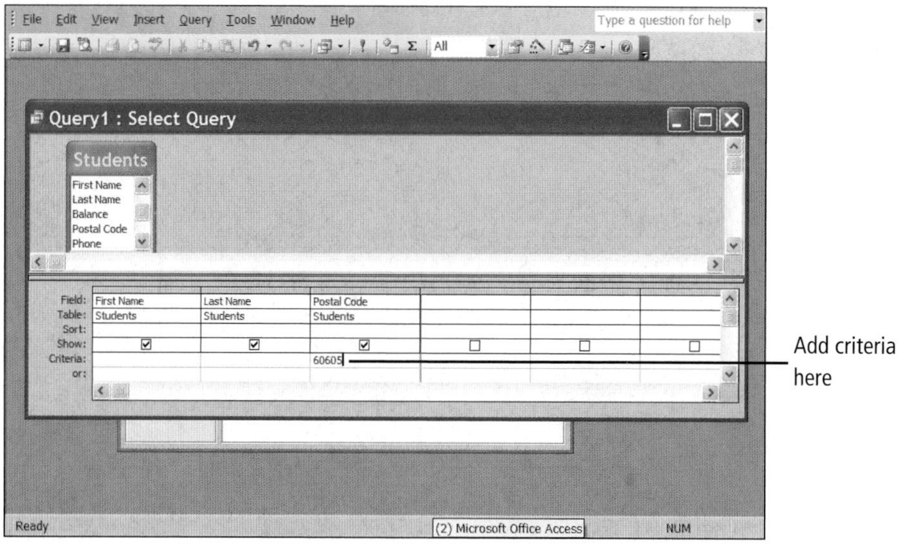

Figure 3.24

14 On the Query Design toolbar, click the **Run** button.

The query results display only the First Name, Last Name, and Postal Code fields for those records in the Students table that have a Postal Code of 60605. See Figure 3.25.

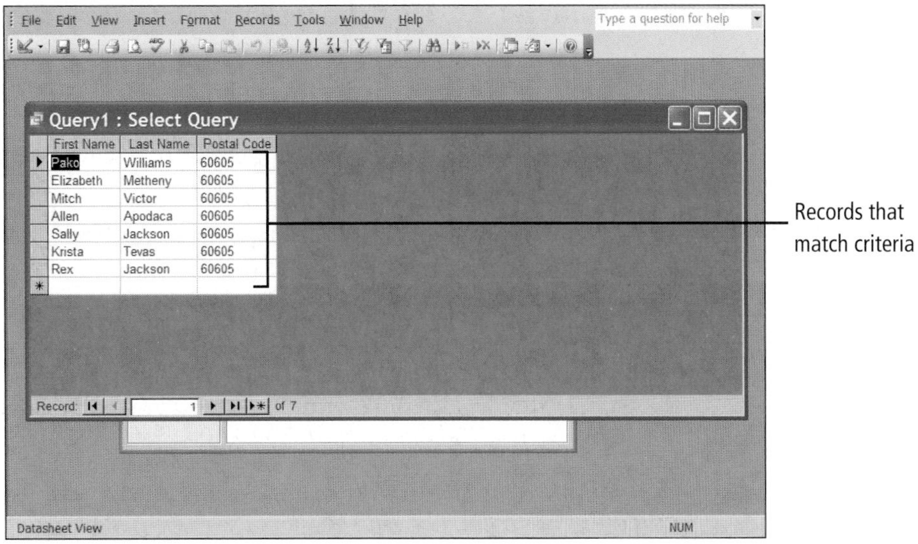

Figure 3.25

15 On the title bar of the query window, click the **Close** button.

16 When prompted to save the changes to the design of query "Query1", click **Yes**. For the query name, using your own information, type **Firstname_Lastname Postal Code** and click **OK**.

The name of the Postal Code query you created displays in the Database window as shown in Figure 3.26.

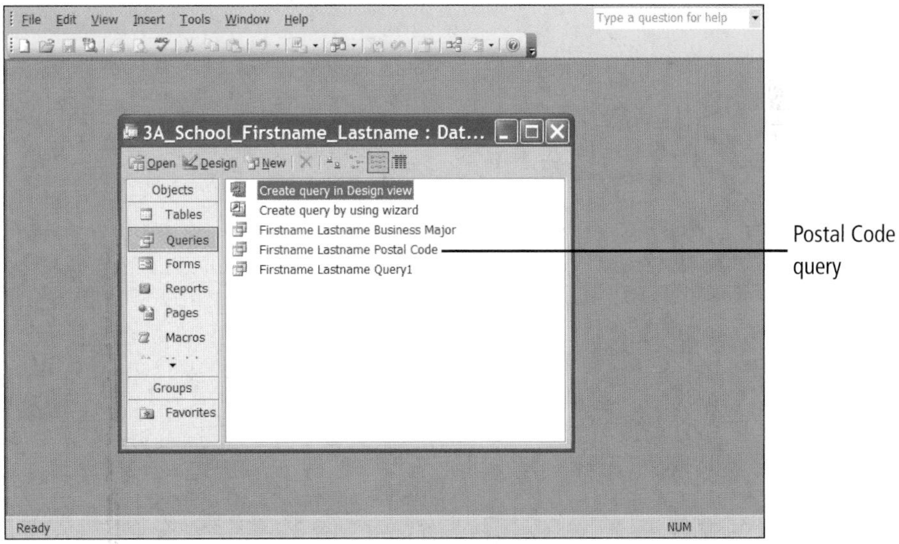

Figure 3.26

Activity 3.6 Printing a Query

Query results in Datasheet view can be printed similar to other database objects.

1. If necessary, on the Objects bar, click **Queries** and then click your **Business Major** query to select it.

2. On the Database toolbar, click the **Print** button. Alternatively, you could display the File menu and click Print.

   The query results print with *your* name in the query name at the top of the page.

3. In the Database window, click your **Postal Code** query once to select it.

4. On the Database toolbar, click the **Print** button.

   The query results of the Postal Code query print with your name at the top of the page in the query name.

5. Close your **School** database and then close Access.

End **You have completed Project 3A**

Project 3B **Students**

In this project you will explore new ways to refine queries with more specific information.

In Activities 3.7 through 3.15 you will continue to create new queries and specify criteria in more detail. Your queries will look similar to Figure 3.27.

Figure 3.27
Project 3B—Students

Objective 5
Use Wildcards in a Query

Wildcard characters in a query serve as a placeholder for an unknown character or characters in your criteria. When you are unsure of the particular character or set of characters to include in your criteria, you can use wildcard characters in place of the characters in the criteria of the query.

Activity 3.7 Using the * Wildcard in a Query

The asterisk, *, is used to represent any group of characters. For example, if you use the * wildcard in the criteria *Fo**, the results would return *Foster*, *Forrester*, *Forrest*, *Fossil*, and so forth. In this activity, you will use the * wildcard and specify the criteria in the query so that only records that have a postal code beginning with 606 will display.

1. Locate the file **a03B _School** from the student files that accompany this text. Copy and paste the file to the Chapter 3 folder you created in Project 3A.
2. Using the technique you practiced in Activity 1.1 of Chapter 1, remove the Read-only property from the file and rename the file as **3B_School_Firstname_Lastname**
3. Close the Windows accessory you are using—either My Computer or Windows Explorer. Start Access and open your **3B_School** database.
4. Click **Queries** on the Objects bar and then double-click **Create query in Design view**.

   A new query window displays and the Show Table dialog box lists the tables in the database.
5. In the **Show Table** dialog box, double-click **Students** and then click **Close**.
6. Add the following fields to the design grid by double-clicking the fields in the **Students** field list: **Student#**, **First Name**, **Last Name**, **Postal Code**.

   Four fields are added to the design grid, as shown in Figure 3.28.

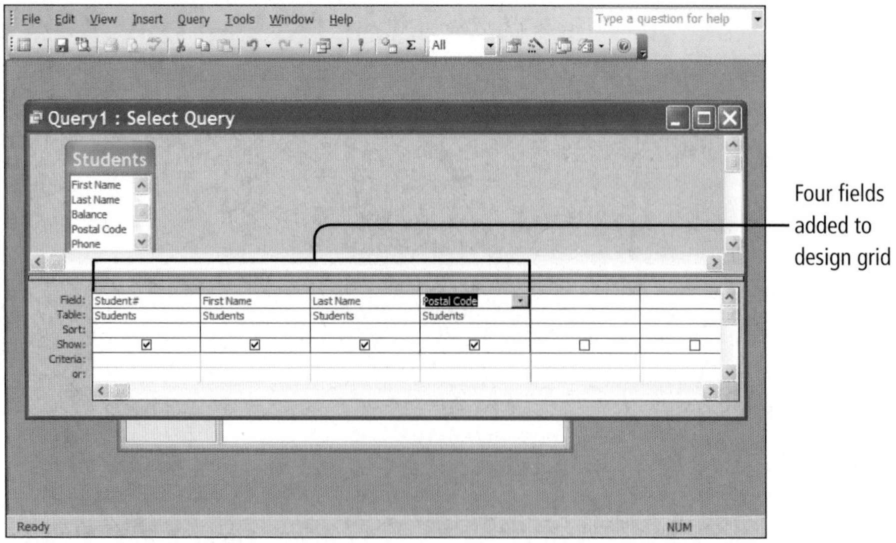

Figure 3.28

7 In the **Criteria** row, under **Postal Code**, type **606*** as shown in Figure 3.29 and then click the **Run** button.

The query results display 14 records.

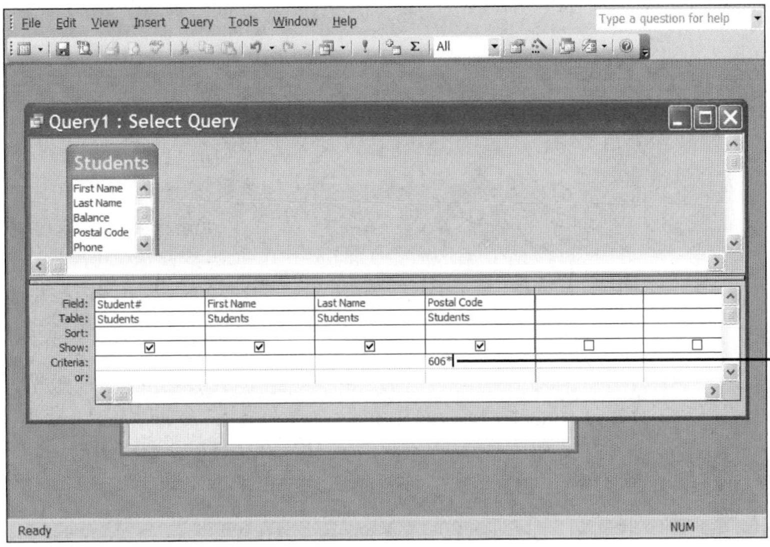

Figure 3.29

8 Examine the entries in the **Postal Code** field and notice that each entry begins with *606* but that the last digits vary, as illustrated in Figure 3.30.

The wildcard character, *, is used as a placeholder to match any number of characters.

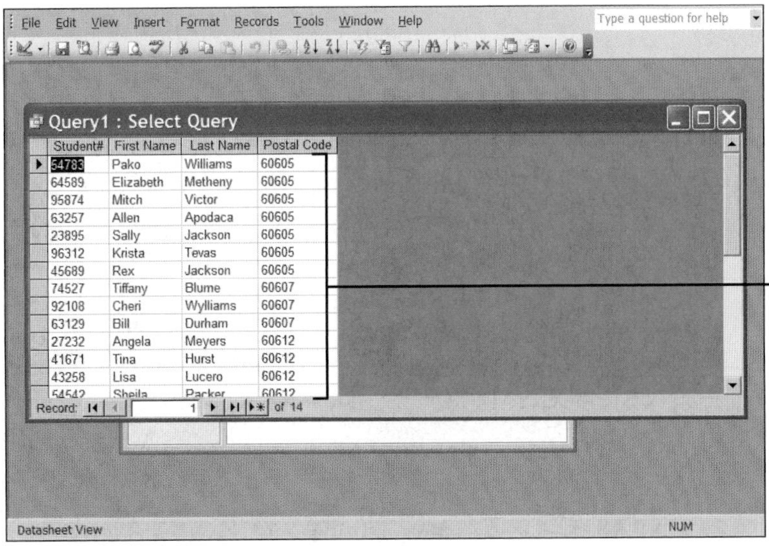

Figure 3.30

9 On the Query Datasheet toolbar, click the **View** button to return to Design view.

Notice that Access has inserted the criteria *Like "606*"* in the Criteria row under Postal Code. *Like* is used by Access to compare a sequence of characters and test whether or not the text matches a pattern. Access will automatically insert expressions similar to this when creating queries.

More Knowledge — Structured Query Language

SQL: Structured Query Language.

SQL (Structured Query Language) is a language used in querying, updating, and managing relational databases. The term *Like* is used in SQL to compare string expressions. In Access, the term *expression* is the same thing as a formula. A *string expression* looks at a sequence of characters and compares them to the criteria in a query. You will learn more about SQL as you advance in your studies of Access.

10 In the **Criteria** row under **Postal Code**, select and then delete the existing text *Like "606*"*.

11 In the **Criteria** row under **Last Name**, type **m*** as shown in Figure 3.31 and then click the **Run** button.

The query results display two records, both with Last Names that begin with M. This search was not case sensitive; that is, lowercase *m** will find text beginning with either *m* or *M*.

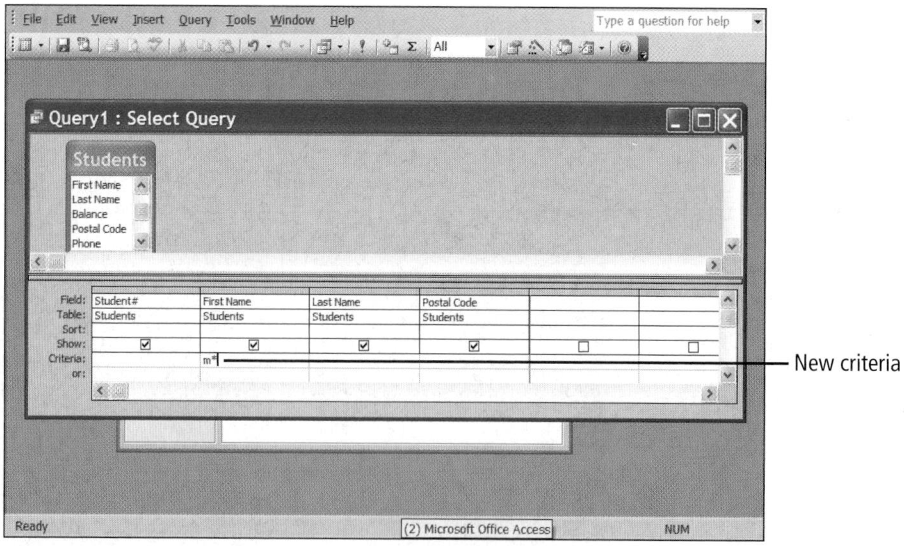

Figure 3.31

12 Notice that *Metheny* and *Meyers* have a different number of characters; *Metheny* contains seven characters and *Meyers* contains six.

The * wildcard can be used to find entries that have a any number of characters.

13 On the Query Datasheet toolbar, click the **View** button to return to Design view. In the **Criteria** row under **Last Name**, select and then delete the existing text *Like "m*"*.

14 In the **Criteria** row under **Student#**, type ***5** as shown in Figure 3.32 and then click the **Run** button.

Two records display, both with Student# entries ending in 5. See Figure 3.33. Wildcard characters can be used either at the beginning or at the end of the criteria.

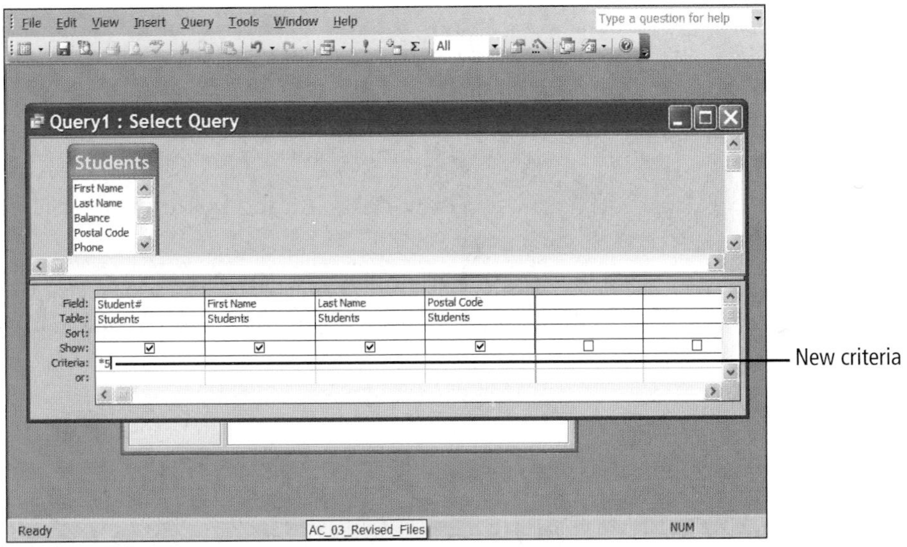

Figure 3.32

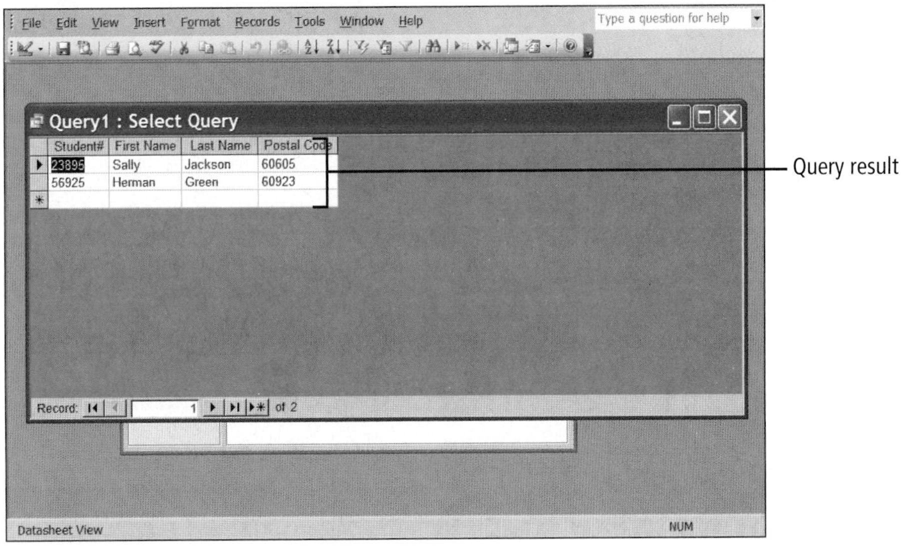

Figure 3.33

15 In the title bar of the query window, click the **Close** button. Click **Yes** to save changes to the query, and then in the **Save As** dialog box and using your own information, type **Firstname Lastname Wildcard 1** as the query name. Click **OK**.

16 In the Database window, select your **Wildcard 1** query and then on the Database toolbar, click the **Print** button.

The query results print.

Activity 3.8 Using the ? Wildcard in a Query

The ? wildcard is a placeholder for only one character in a query. For example, if you use the ? wildcard in the criteria *"l?ne"*, the results could be *lane*, *line*, or *lone*. In this activity, you will use the ? wildcard and specify the criteria in the query so that only those records with either spelling of the last name of *Williams* or *Wylliams* will display.

1 Be sure **Queries** is selected on the Objects bar, then double-click **Create query in Design view**.

A new query window displays and the Show Table dialog box lists the tables in the database.

2 In the **Show Table** dialog box, double-click **Students** and then click **Close**.

3 Add the following fields to the design grid by double-clicking the fields in the **Students** field list: **Student#**, **First Name**, **Last Name**.

Three fields are added to the design grid, as shown in Figure 3.34.

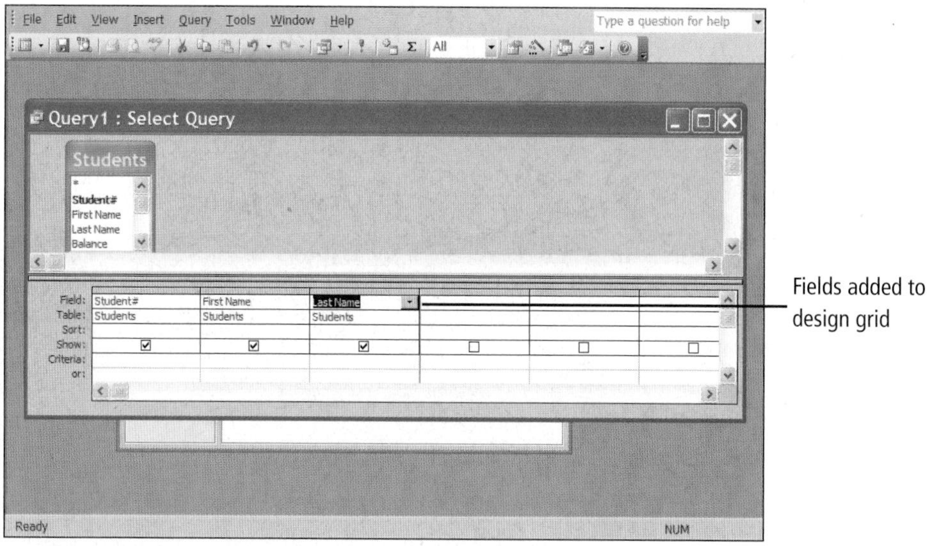

Figure 3.34

4 In the **Criteria** row under **Last Name**, type **w?lliams** as shown in Figure 3.35 and then click the **Run** button.

Two results display with the Last Names of *Williams* and *Wylliams*. See Figure 3.36.

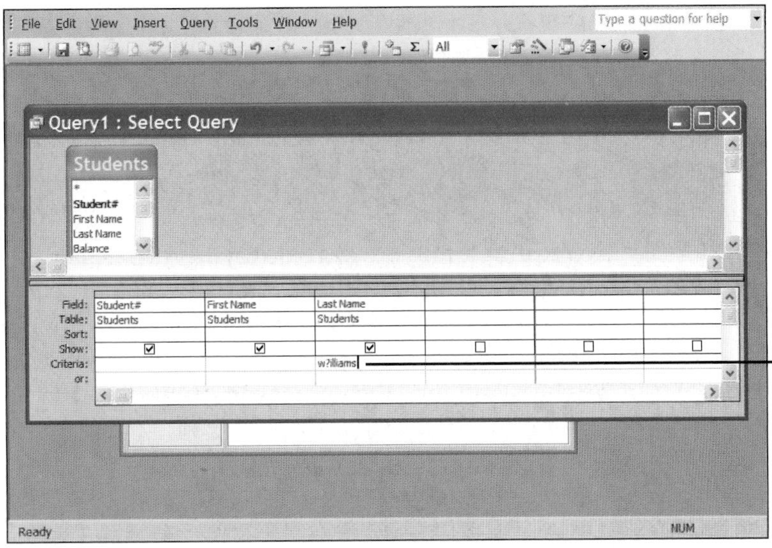

Criteria with ? wildcard

Figure 3.35

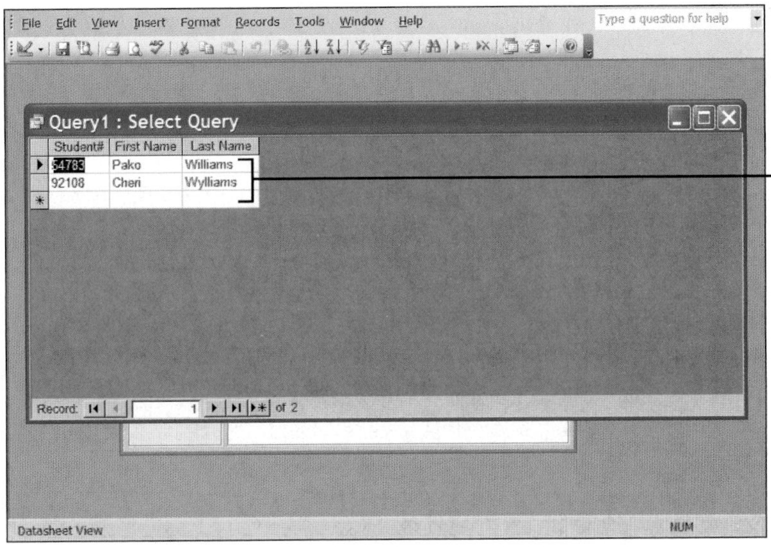

Results of ? wildcard query

Figure 3.36

5 In the title bar of the query window, click the **Close** button. Click **Yes** to save changes to the query and in the **Save As** dialog box, using your own information, type **Firstname Lastname Wildcard 2** as the query name. Click **OK**.

The Database window displays.

6 Be sure your **Wildcard 2** query is selected and then on the Database toolbar, click the **Print** button.

The query results print.

Activity 3.9 Specifying Criteria Using a Field Not Displayed in the Query Result

In the queries you have created thus far, all of the fields that you included in the query design have also been included in the query result. It is not required, however, that every field in the query also display in the result, and there will be times when you will not want all the fields to display in the result.

For example, if you were querying your CD Collection database to find out what records in the CD table were performed by a particular artist, you would need the CD Artist field in the query design, but you would not need the field to display in the query result because the artist would be the same for all the records. Including the field would be redundant and not particularly useful.

1. Be sure **Queries** is selected on the Objects bar, then double-click **Create query in Design view**.

   A new query window displays and the Show Table dialog box lists the tables in the database.

2. In the **Show Table** dialog box, double-click **Students** and then click **Close**.

3. Add the following fields to the design grid by double-clicking the fields in the **Students** field list: **Student#**, **First Name**, **Last Name**, and **Major**.

   Four fields are added to the design grid, as shown in Figure 3.37.

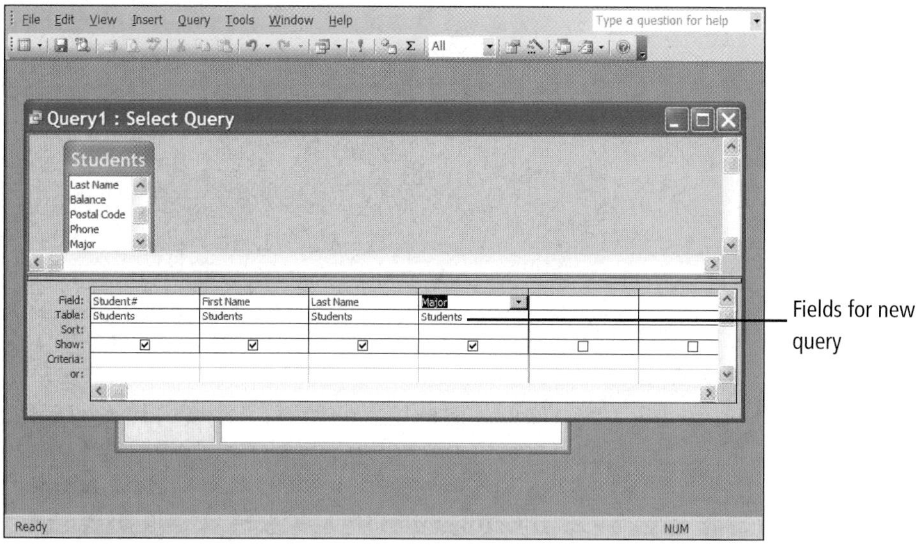

Figure 3.37

4. In the **Criteria** row under **Major**, type **Music** as shown in Figure 3.38 and then click the **Run** button.

   The query results display the two records in the Students table that have Music as entries in the Major field.

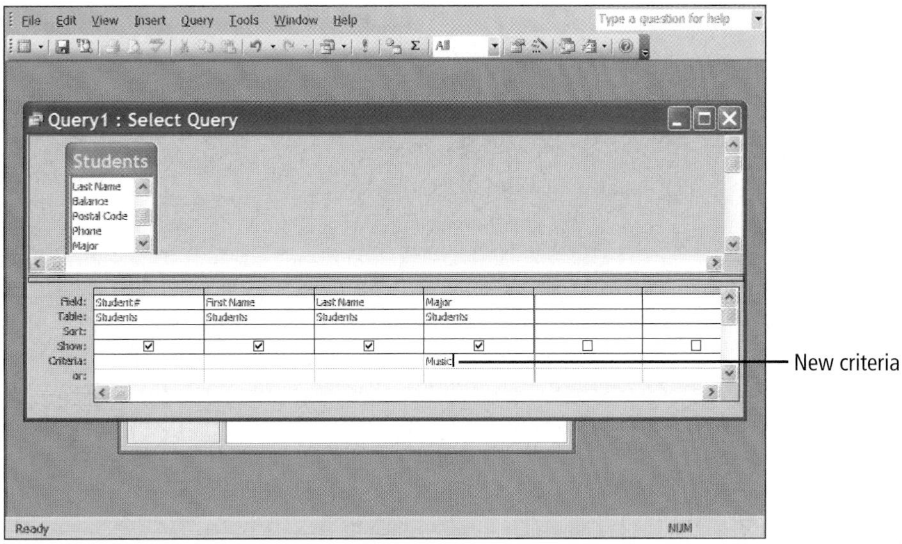

Figure 3.38

5 On the Query Datasheet toolbar, click the **View** button to return to Design view.

6 Directly above the **Criteria** row, in the **Show** row, under **Major**, notice the **Show** check box with a check mark in it. See Figure 3.39.

Fields where the Show check box is checked in the design grid display in the query results.

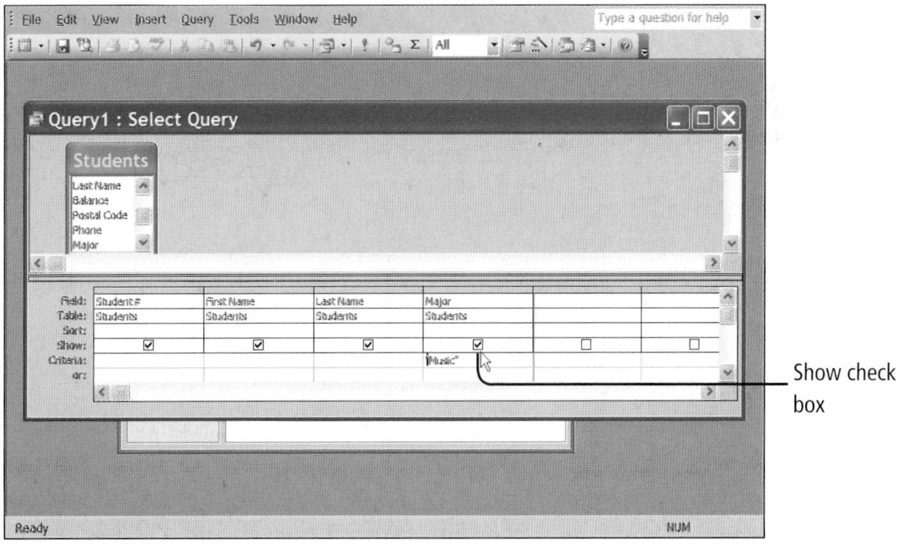

Figure 3.39

7 In the **Show** check box under **Major**, click to clear the **check mark**, as shown in Figure 3.40.

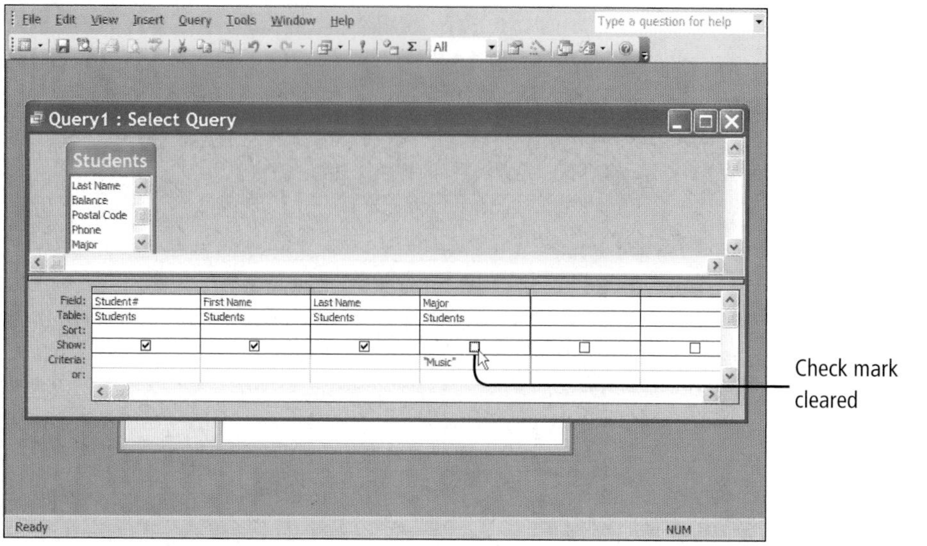

Figure 3.40

8 On the Query Design toolbar, click the **Run** button.

The query results display the same two records but the Major field does not display. See Figure 3.41. Although the Major field was still included in the query criteria for the purpose of identifying specific records, it is not necessary to display the field in the result.

Clear the Show check box when necessary to avoid cluttering the query results with redundant data.

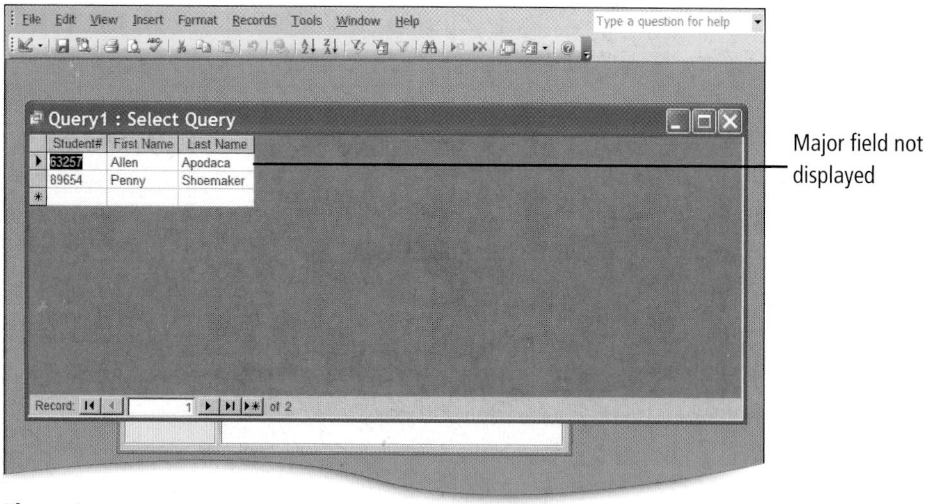

Figure 3.41

9 On the Query Datasheet toolbar, click the **View** button to return to Design view.

10 On the Menu bar, click **Edit**, **Clear Grid**.

The fields are cleared in the design grid. Use this method to quickly clear the design grid to begin a new query. Leave the query open in Design view for the next activity.

Objective 6
Specify Numeric Criteria in a Query

Criteria can be set for fields that contain numeric data as well as text data. Numeric data types are set for fields that will contain numbers on which mathematical calculations will be performed. Because the data is numeric, you can use mathematical symbols to further specify the criteria and locate the desired records.

Activity 3.10 Specifying Numeric Criteria in a Query

In this activity, you will specify the criteria in the query so that only records in the Students table that have a balance of zero will display.

1 With your cleared query window from the previous activity open in Design view, add the following fields to the design grid by double-clicking the fields in the **Students** field list: **Student#**, **First Name**, **Last Name**, and **Balance**.

Four fields are added to the design grid.

2 In the **Criteria** row under **Balance**, type **0** as shown in Figure 3.42 and then click the **Run** button.

Four records display in the query results; each has a balance of $0.00.

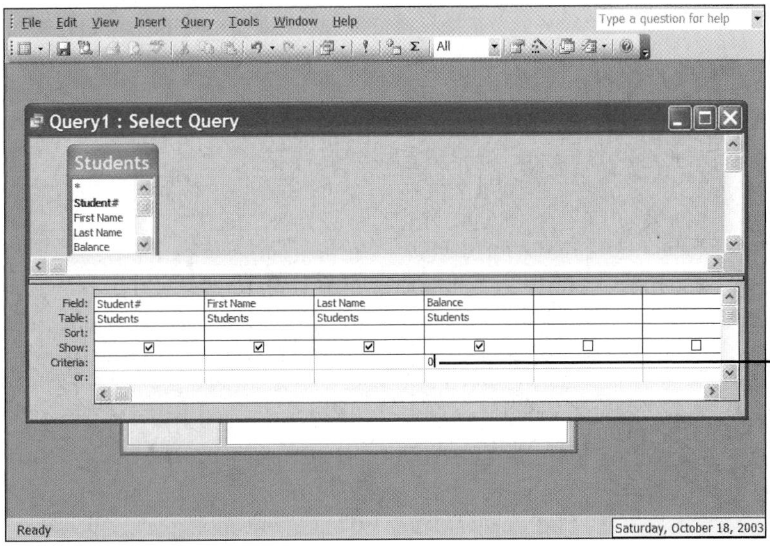

Figure 3.42

3 On the Query Datasheet toolbar, click the **View** button. Leave the query open in Design view for the next activity.

Activity 3.11 Using Comparison Operators

In Activity 3.10, you created a query to display those records where the student's balance was equal to zero. The equal sign, =, is a comparison operator that, when used in query criteria, causes Access to display those records that have entries equal to the number specified (zero in the previous activity). Other comparison operators can be used in query criteria to cause Access to display a different set of records based on the numeric criteria specified. The most common comparison operators include the < (less than), > (greater than), and the = (equal) signs. In this activity, you will specify the criteria in the query so that the records in the Students table that have a balance that is greater than $50.00 will display.

1. Be sure your query from the last activity is displayed in Design view.
2. In the **Criteria** row, under **Balance**, select the existing text, *0*, type **>50** as illustrated in Figure 3.43, and then click the **Run** button.

   Five records display and each of these has a Balance greater than (but not equal to) $50.00. See Figure 3.44.

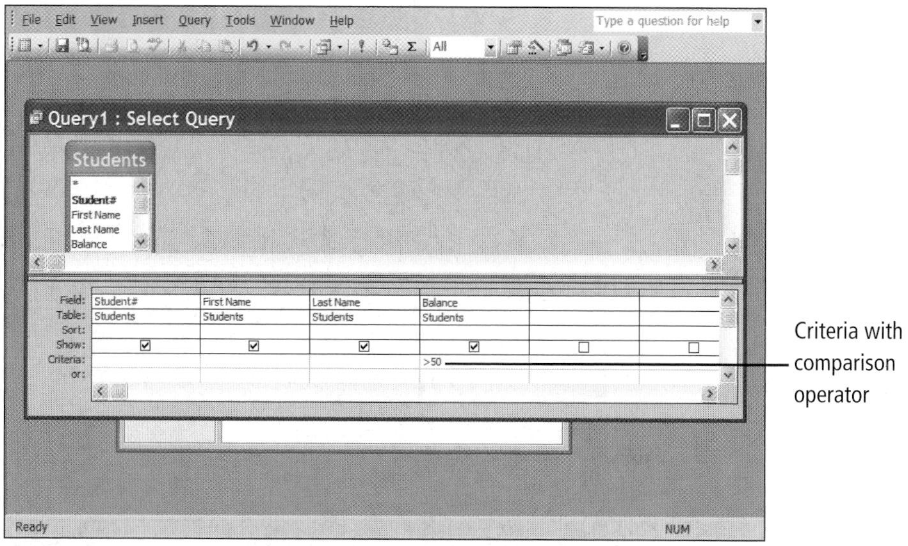

Figure 3.43

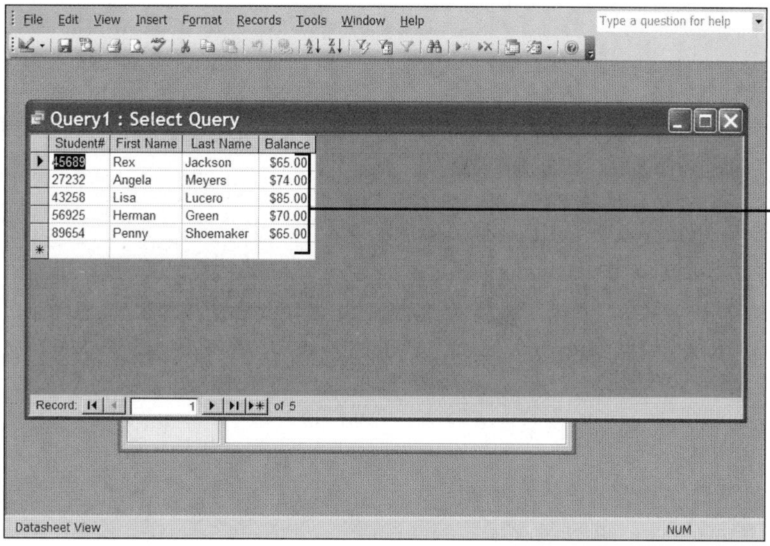

Figure 3.44

3 On the Query Datasheet toolbar, click the **View** button.

4 In the **Criteria** row, under **Balance**, change the greater than sign (>) to the less than sign (<) and then click the **Run** button.

Ten records display and each has a balance less than $50.00. Notice that the results show those records for which the Balance is less than $50.00, but not equal to $50.00. See Figure 3.45.

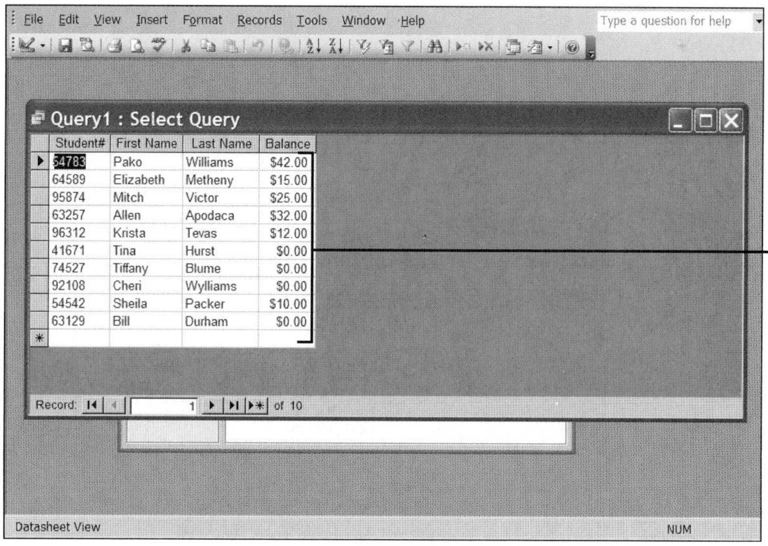

Figure 3.45

5 On the Query Datasheet toolbar, click the **View** button.

6 In the **Criteria** row, under **Balance** and to the right of the less than sign <, type the equal sign, = but do not replace the less than, < sign. See Figure 3.46.

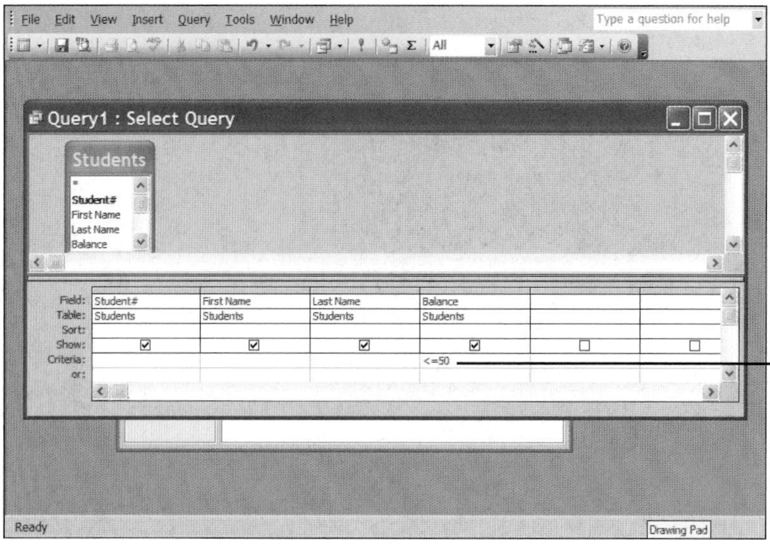

Figure 3.46

7 On the Query Design toolbar, click the **Run** button.

Eleven records display, including the record for Sally Jackson, who has a balance of exactly $50.00. See Figure 3.47. Comparison operators can be combined to form operators, such as the less than or equal to <= symbol.

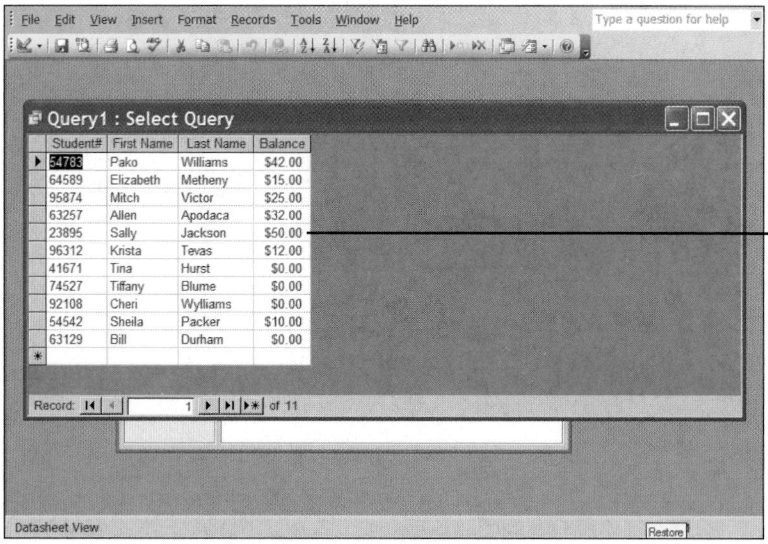

Figure 3.47

8 In the title bar of the query window, click the **Close** button. Click **Yes** to save changes to the query. Then in the **Save As** dialog box and using your own information, type **Firstname Lastname Balance Query** as the query name. Click **OK**.

The Database window displays.

9 Be sure your **Balance Query** is selected and then on the Database toolbar, click the **Print** button.

The query results print.

Objective 7
Use Compound Criteria

You may find that you need to specify more than one condition—criteria—in a query. Two or more criteria are called ***compound criteria***. Compound criteria are used to create more specific criteria and thus further limit the query results. Two types of compound criteria used in queries are AND and OR. Both of these are ***logical operators***. Logical operators allow you to enter criteria for the same field or different fields. For example, suppose you wanted to find those students who have a balance greater than $100.00 *and* who have earned more than 120 credits. You could specify both of those conditions in the same query using AND. Compound criteria that create an AND condition will return those records in the query result that meet *both* parts of the specified criteria.

Activity 3.12 Using AND in a Query

In this activity, you will specify the criteria in the query so that the records in the Students table that have a postal code of 60612 *and* a Business major will display.

1 With **Queries** selected on the Objects bar, double-click **Create query in Design view**.

A new query window displays and the Show Table dialog box lists the tables in the database.

2 In the **Show Table** dialog box, double-click **Students** and then click **Close**.

3 Add the following fields to the design grid by double-clicking the fields in the **Students** field list: **First Name**, **Last Name**, **Postal Code**, and **Major**.

Four fields are added to the design grid.

4 In the **Criteria** row under **Postal Code**, type **60612**

5 In the **Criteria** row under **Major**, type **Business** as shown in Figure 3.48 and then click the **Run** button.

The query results show two records, Angela Meyers and Tina Hurst. These records have *both* the specified Postal Code (60612) *and* the specified Major (Business). The criteria in the above query has two parts: the Postal Code part and the Major part. Criteria specifying an AND condition is always on the same line in the Criteria row.

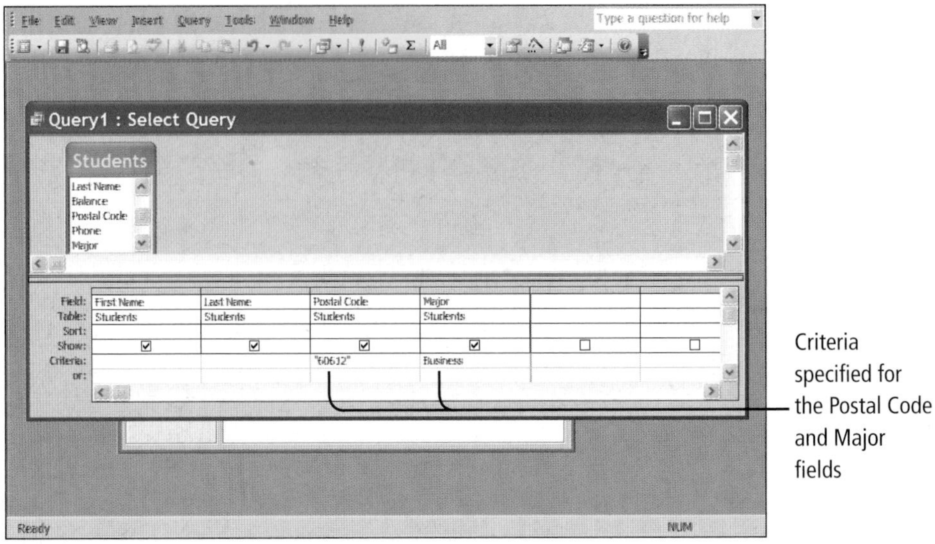

Figure 3.48

6 In the title bar of the query window, click the **Close** button. Click **Yes** to save changes to the query and in the **Save As** dialog box and using your own information, type **Firstname Lastname AND Query** as the query name. Click **OK**.

The Database window displays.

7 Be sure your **AND Query** is selected and then, on the Database toolbar, click the **Print** button.

Activity 3.13 Using OR in a Query

1 With **Queries** selected on the Objects bar, double-click **Create query in Design view**. In the **Show Table** dialog box, double-click **Students** and then click **Close**.

2 Add the following fields to the design grid by double-clicking the fields in the **Students** field list: **First Name**, **Last Name**, and **Major**.

Three fields are added to the design grid.

3 In the **Criteria** row under **Major**, type **Music**

4 Under **Major**, below the **Criteria** row, in the **or** row, type **Art** See Figure 3.49.

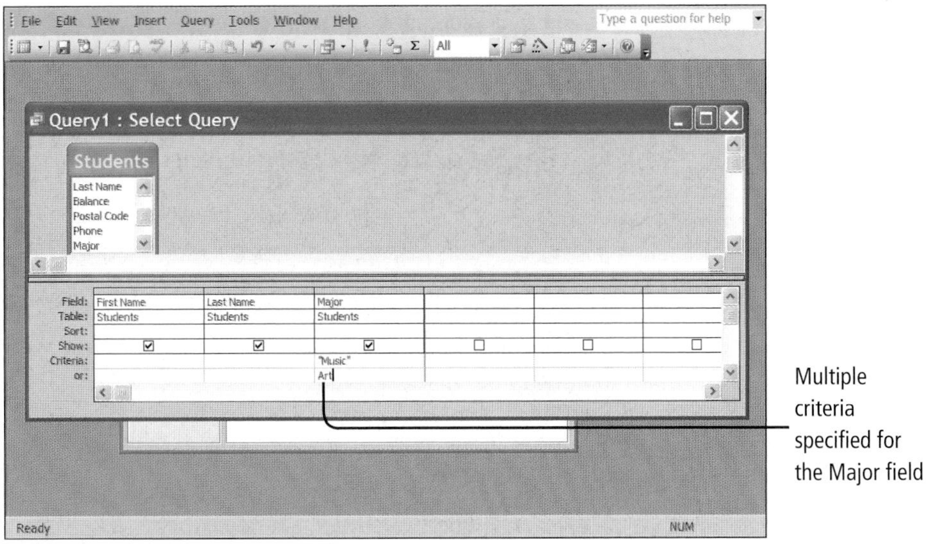

Figure 3.49

5 On the Query Design toolbar, click the **Run** button.

The query results display those records whose Major has an entry that is either Music *or* Art. Use the OR condition to specify multiple criteria for a single field.

6 In the title bar of the query window, click the **Close** button. Click **Yes** to save changes to the query and in the **Save As** dialog box and using your own information, type **Firstname Lastname OR Query** as the query name. Click **OK**.

The Database window displays.

7 Be sure your **OR Query** is selected and then, on the Database toolbar, click the **Print** button. Leave the database open for the next activity.

Objective 8
Sort Data in a Query

To better organize your data, you will find it useful to sort query results. Sorting results in a query is similar to sorting in a table. Records can be sorted in either ascending or descending order. Data in a query can be sorted either from the Datasheet view or from the Design view.

Activity 3.14 Sorting Data in a Query

In this activity, you will sort the results of the Balance Query you created in an earlier activity.

1 With **Queries** selected on the Objects bar, right-click the **Balance Query** that you created in an earlier activity, and then from the displayed shortcut menu, click **Open**.

The query opens in Datasheet view.

2 Click anywhere in the **Last Name column** and then on the Query Datasheet toolbar click the **Sort Ascending** button.

The records are sorted alphabetically by Last Name.

3 Click anywhere in the **Balance column** and then on the Query Datasheet toolbar, click the **Sort Descending** button.

The records are sorted by the entries in the Balance column from the largest to the smallest balance. See Figure 3.50.

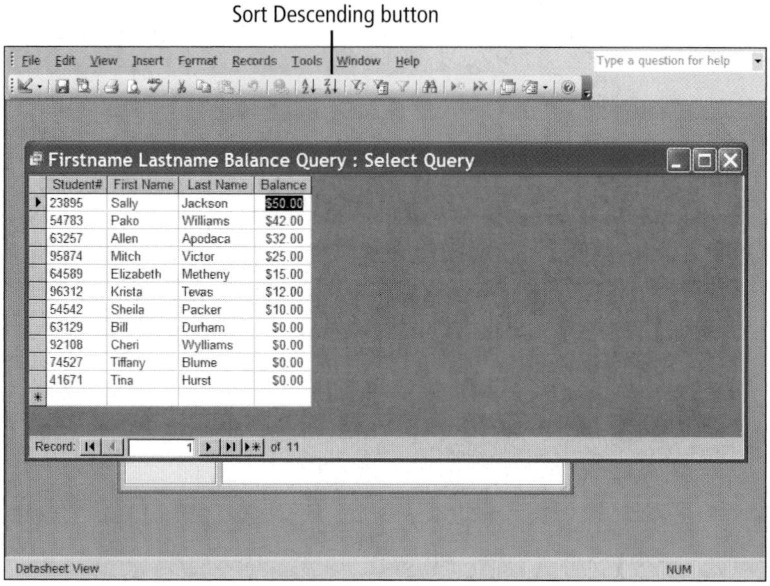

Figure 3.50

4 Switch to the Design view of the query for the next activity.

Activity 3.15 Modifying the Query Design and Sorting Data Using Multiple Fields in a Query

Sorting data in a query using more than one field allows you to further organize your query results. In this activity, you will sort the records in your Balance Query first by balance and then by last name.

1 In the design grid, move your pointer just above the **Balance** column until the pointer displays as a black downward-pointing arrow. See Figure 3.51.

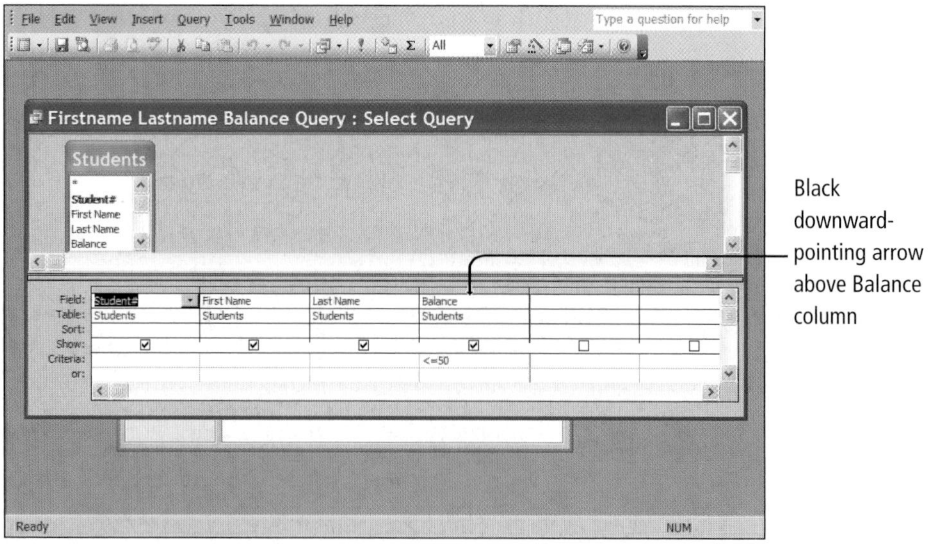

Figure 3.51

2 With the black downward-pointing arrow displayed, click once to select the **Balance** column.

The Balance column in the design grid is selected.

3 With the **Balance** column selected and your mouse pointer displayed as an arrow and positioned in the black bar above the **Balance** column, click and hold the left mouse button and then drag the **Balance** column to the left until you see a black vertical line between the **Student#** column and the **First Name** column. See Figure 3.52. Release the mouse button.

The Balance column is repositioned in between the Student# field and the First Name field. Recall from Chapter 1 that the field that is to be sorted first (Balance) must be to the left of the field that is sorted next (Last Name).

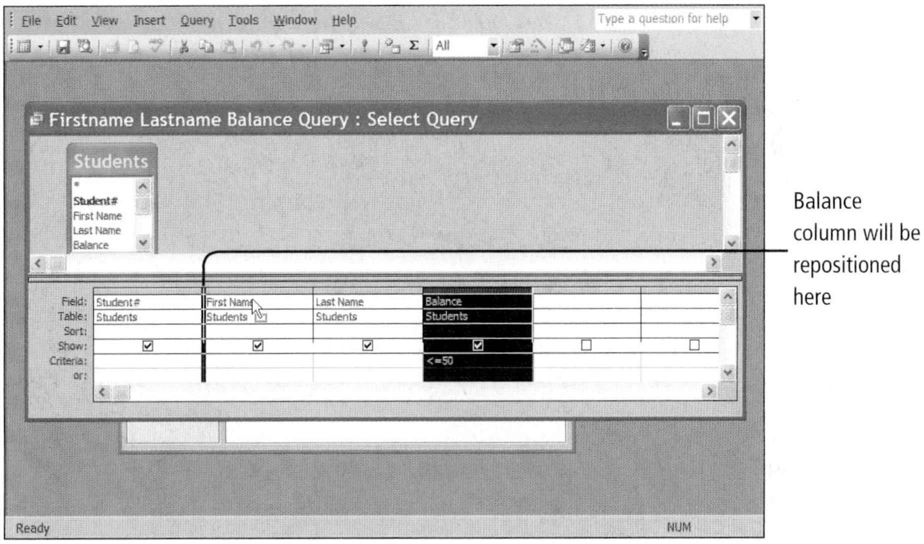

Figure 3.52

4 Repeat this action for the **Last Name** field by moving your pointer just above the **Last Name** column until the pointer displays as a black downward-pointing arrow.

5 With the black downward-pointing arrow displayed, click once to select the **Last Name** column.

The Last Name column in the design grid is selected.

6 With the **Last Name** column selected, click and hold the left mouse button and then drag the **Last Name** column to the left until you see a black vertical line between the **Balance** column and the **First Name** column. Release the mouse button.

The Last Name column is repositioned between the Balance field and the First Name field. See Figure 3.53.

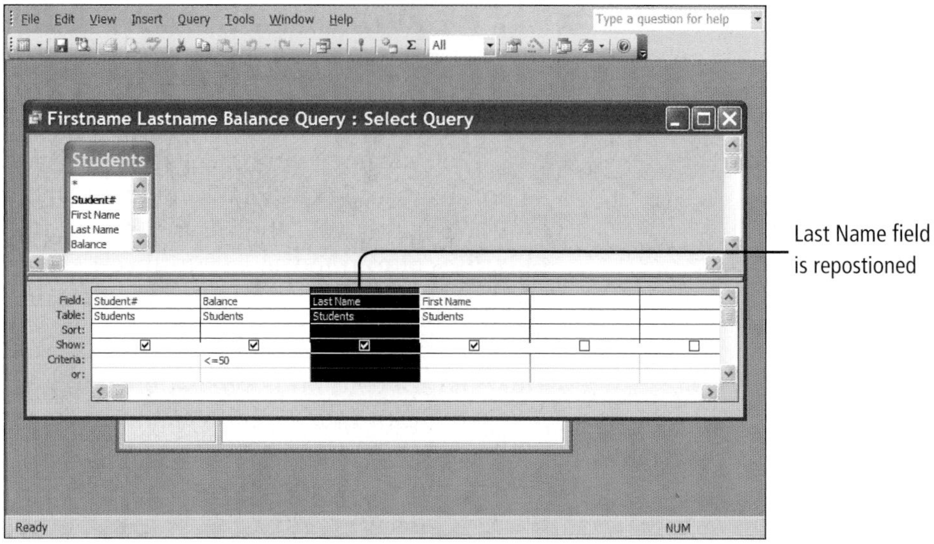

Figure 3.53

7 In the design grid, in the **Sort** row, under **Balance**, click once. See Figure 3.54.

The insertion point is blinking in the Sort row in the Balance field and a downward-pointing arrow displays.

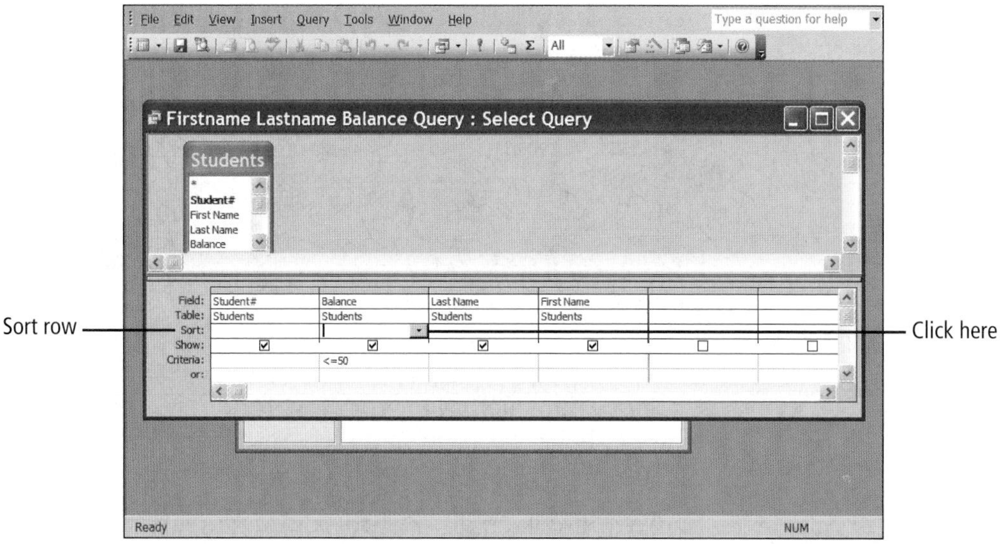

Figure 3.54

8 Click the **downward-pointing arrow** and then from the displayed list, click **Descending**. See Figure 3.55.

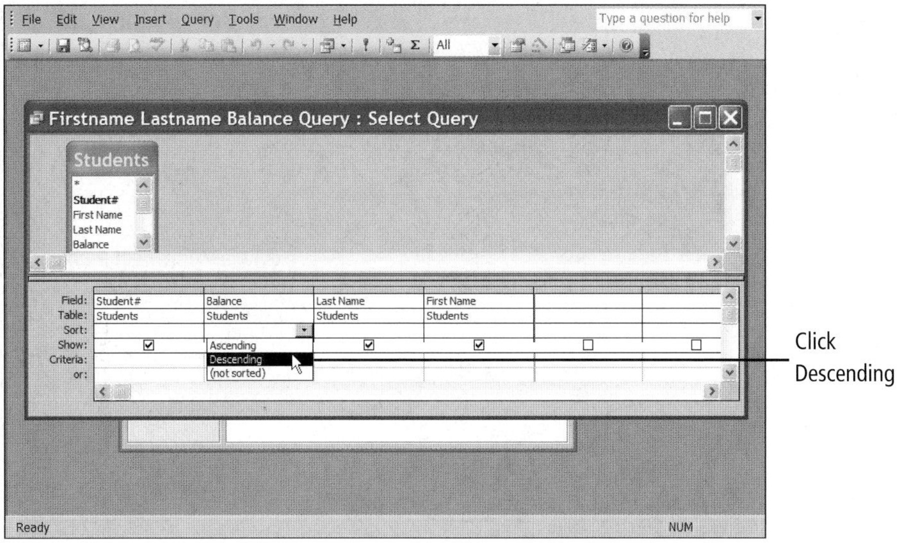

Figure 3.55

9 In the **Sort** row, under **Last Name**, click once.

The insertion point is blinking in the Sort row in the Last Name field and a downward-pointing arrow displays.

10 Click the **downward-pointing arrow** and then click **Ascending**. See Figure 3.56.

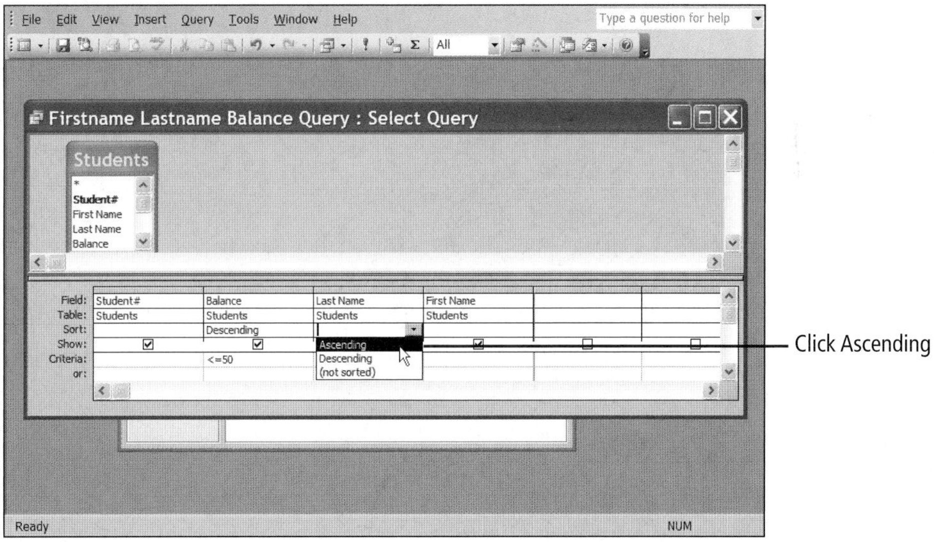

Figure 3.56

11 On the Query Design toolbar, click the **Run** button.

The query results display with the records sorted first by the Balance field in descending order and then, for those records who have the same balances, the records are further sorted alphabetically by Last Name. See Figure 3.57.

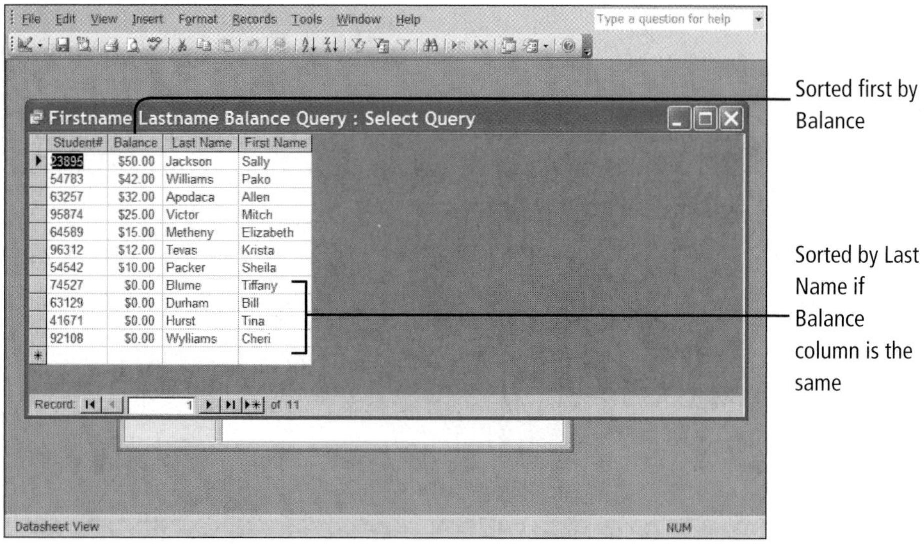

Figure 3.57

12 From the **File** menu, click **Save As**. In the **Save As** dialog box and using your own information, type **Firstname Lastname Sorted Balance Query** and then click **OK**.

The query displays in Datasheet view. The original sorted query remains and now there is a new sorted query.

13 On the Database toolbar, click the **Print** button.

The query results print.

14 Close the query. Close the database and then close Access.

End **You have completed Project 3B**

3C Project 3C Faculty

Using calculated fields, statistics, and group data in queries allows you to calculate additional information beyond what is contained in the fields.

In Activities 3.16 through 3.18 you will create queries using calculated fields and statistical functions. Your queries will look like Figure 3.58.

Firstname Lastname Faculty Raise 10/19/2003

First Name	Last Name	Salary	Raise Amount	New Salary
Pat	Eleanor	$75,000.00	$6,000.00	$81,000.00
Ann	Bebe	$62,000.00	$4,960.00	$66,960.00
Mikail	Schrejiko	$86,000.00	$6,880.00	$92,880.00
Annette	Duvane	$72,000.00	$5,760.00	$77,760.00
Stephan	Rosenbaum	$72,000.00	$5,760.00	$77,760.00
Jose	Velarde	$72,500.00	$5,800.00	$78,300.00
George	Hal	$68,000.00	$5,440.00	$73,440.00
Frank	Keller	$68,000.00	$5,440.00	$73,440.00
Bill	Derbaugh	$87,000.00	$6,960.00	$93,960.00
Jeff	Pepper	$75,000.00	$6,000.00	$81,000.00
Gary	Petrie	$75,000.00	$6,000.00	$81,000.00
Celina	Rominov	$75,000.00	$6,000.00	$81,000.00

Page 1

Firstname Lastname Max Salary 10/19/2003

Division	MaxOfSalary
Business	$87,000.00
Education	$75,000.00
Fine Arts	$86,000.00
Humanities	$75,000.00

Page 1

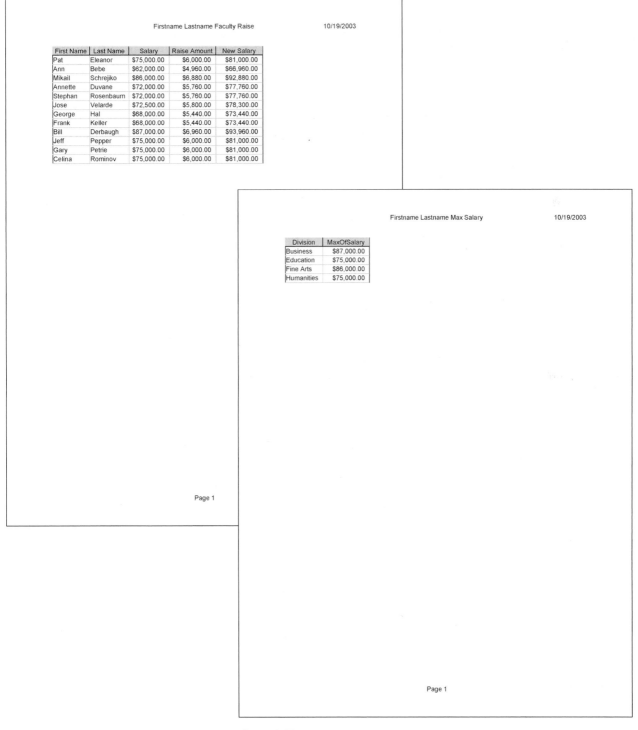

Figure 3.58
Project 3C—Faculty

Objective 9
Use Calculated Fields in a Query

As an example of using calculated fields in queries, you could multiply two fields together, such as Inventory Quantity and Cost per Item and get a Total Cost amount for each Inventory item. Or, as illustrated in the following activity, you could calculate a raise amount for Faculty Salaries by multiplying the salary amount by the raise percentage.

There are two steps to produce a calculated field in a query. First, you must provide a new name for the field that will store the calculated values. Second, you must specify the expression that will perform the calculation. Any field names used in the calculation must be enclosed within square brackets, [ ].

Activity 3.16 Using Calculated Fields in a Query

1. Locate the file **a03C_School** from the student files that accompany this text. Copy and paste the file to the Chapter 3 folder you created in Project 3A of this chapter.
2. Using the technique you practiced in Activity 1.1 of Chapter 1, remove the Read-only property from the file and rename the file as **3C_School_Firstname_Lastname**
3. Close the Windows accessory you are using—either My Computer or Windows Explorer. Start Access and open your **3C_School** database.
4. On the Objects bar, select **Queries** and then double-click **Create query in Design view**. In the **Show Table** dialog box, double-click **Faculty** and then click **Close**.
5. Add the following fields to the design grid by double-clicking the fields in the **Faculty** field list: **First Name**, **Last Name**, and **Salary**.

   Three fields are added to the design grid.
6. In the design grid, in the **Field** row, click in the first empty column on the right, right-click to display a shortcut menu, and then click **Zoom**.
7. In the **Zoom** dialog box, type **Raise Amount: [Salary]*.08** as shown in Figure 3.59.

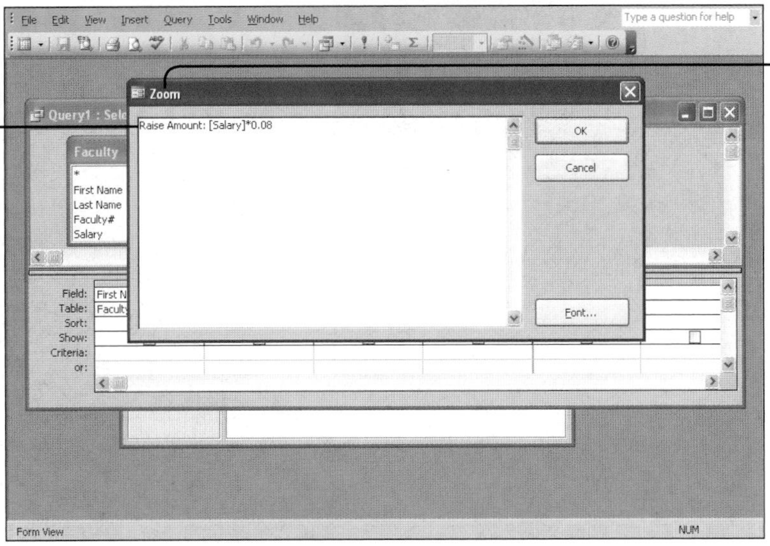

Figure 3.59

8 Look at the expression you have just typed.

The first element, *Raise Amount*, is the name of the new field where the calculated amounts will display. Following that is a colon (:). A colon in a calculated field separates the new field name from the expression. *Salary* is in square brackets because it is an existing field name from the Faculty table. It contains the information on which the calculation will be performed. Following the square brackets is an asterisk (*), which in math calculations signifies multiplication. Finally, the percentage (8% or .08) is indicated.

Alert!

Does Your Screen Differ?

If your calculations in a query do not work, carefully check the expression you typed. Spelling or syntax errors will prevent calculated fields from working properly.

9 In the **Zoom** dialog box, click **OK**, and then click the **Run** button.

The query results display the three fields from the Faculty table plus a fourth field—*Raise Amount*—in which a calculated amount displays. Each calculated amount equals the amount in Salary field multiplied by .08. See Figure 3.60.

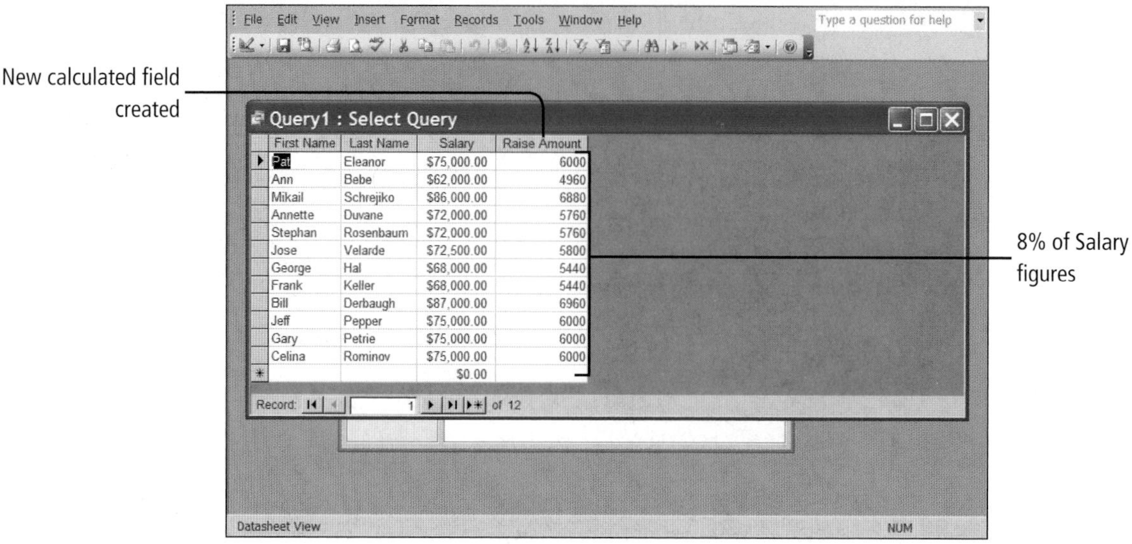

Figure 3.60

10 Notice the formatting of the **Raise Amount** field. There are no dollar signs, commas, or decimal places. You will change this formatting in a later step. Switch to **Design view**. In the **Field** row, in the first empty column, right-click and then click **Zoom**.

The Zoom dialog box displays. Although you can type directly into the Field box in the column, it is easier to use the Zoom dialog box for a better view of the calculations you want to type.

11 In the **Zoom** dialog box, type **New Salary: [Salary]+[Raise Amount]** and then click **OK**.

12 Click the **Run** button [!] to run the query.

Access has calculated the New Salary amount by adding together the Salary field and the Raise Amount field. The New Salary column includes dollar signs, commas, and decimal points because the Salary field, on which the calculation was based, uses a format that includes them.

13 Switch to **Design view**. In the **Raise Amount** column, right-click and then click **Properties**. See Figure 3.61.

The Field Properties dialog box displays. In the Field Properties dialog box, you can customize fields in a query, for example, the format of numbers in the field. As you progress in your study of Access, you will learn more about the Field Properties dialog box.

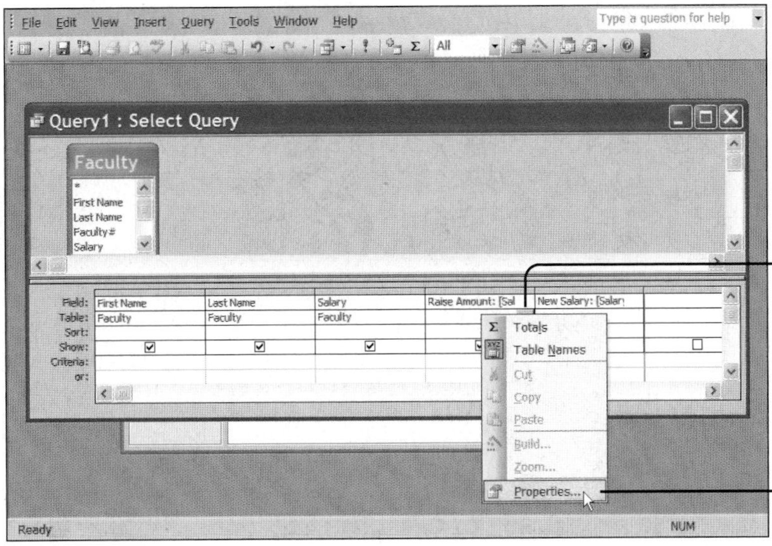

Figure 3.61

14 In the **Field Properties** dialog box, to the right of **Format**, click in the white box and then click the **downward-pointing arrow** that displays. See Figure 3.62.

A list of possible formatting options for this field displays.

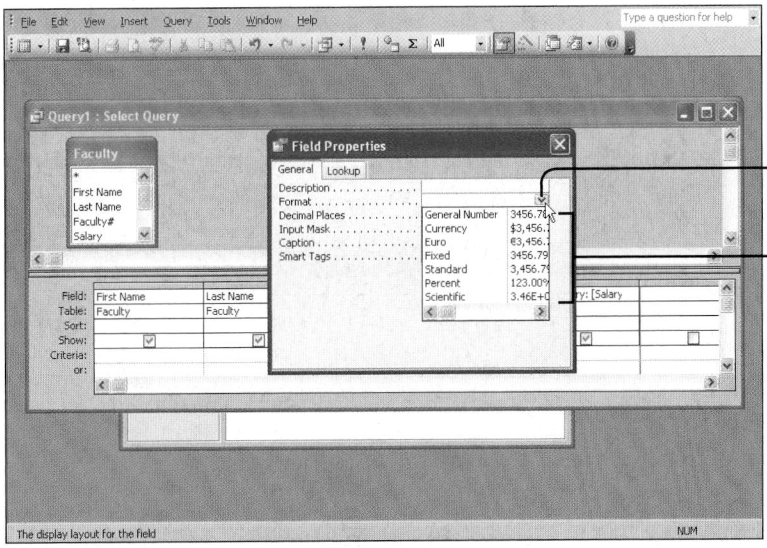

Figure 3.62

15 In the list of formatting options, click **Currency**. Then on the title bar of the **Field Properties** dialog box, click the **Close** button. See Figure 3.63.

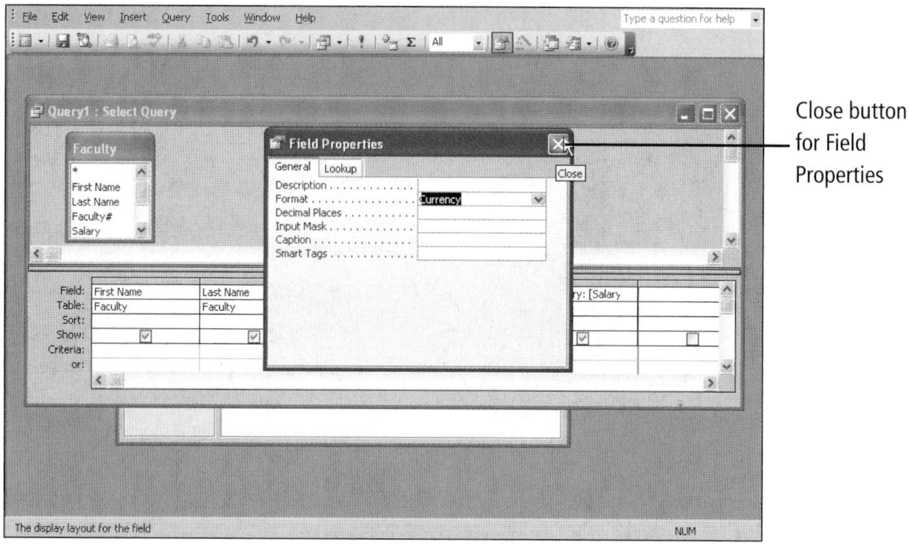

Figure 3.63

16 Click the **Run** button to run the query.

The Raise Amount column displays with Currency formatting—a dollar sign, thousands comma separators, and two decimal places. See Figure 3.64.

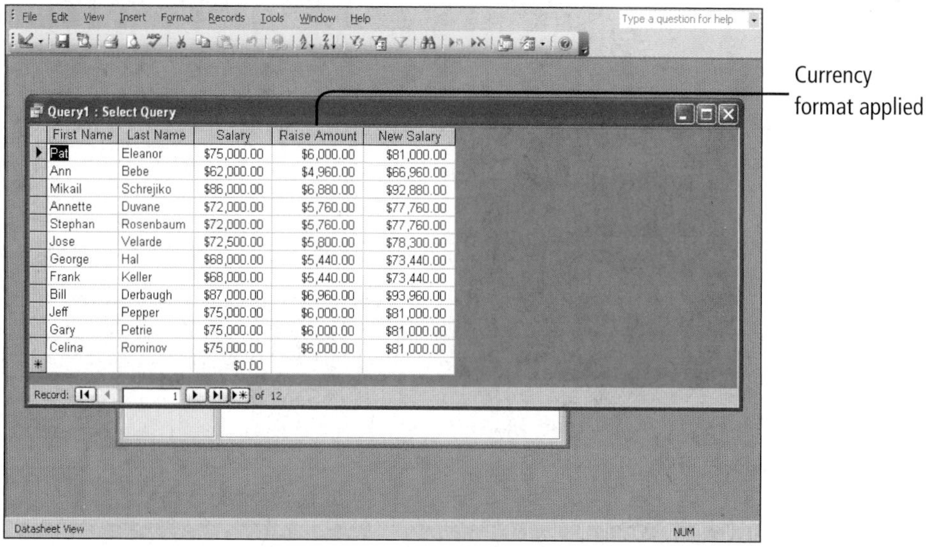

Figure 3.64

17 In the title bar of the query window, click the **Close** button. Click **Yes** to save changes to the query and in the **Save As** dialog box and using your own information, type **Firstname Lastname Faculty Raise** as the query name. Click **OK**.

The Database window displays.

18 Be sure your **Faculty Raise** query is selected and on the Database toolbar, click the **Print** button. Leave the database open for the next activity.

Objective 10
Group Data and Calculate Statistics in a Query

In Access queries, you can perform statistical calculations on a group of records. Statistics that are performed on a group of records are called ***aggregate functions***. Access supports the aggregate functions summarized in the table shown in Figure 3.65.

Aggregate Functions

Function Name	What It Does
SUM	Totals the values in a field
AVG	Averages the values in a field
MAX	Locates the largest value in a field
MIN	Locates the smallest value in a field
STDEV	Calculates the Standard Deviation on the values in a field
VAR	Calculates the Variance on the values in a field
FIRST	Displays the First value in a field
LAST	Displays the Last value in a field

Figure 3.65

In the activities that follow, you will use the first four functions in Figure 3.65: SUM, AVG, MAX, and MIN. As you progress in your study of Access, you will use the remaining functions.

Activity 3.17 Grouping Data in a Query

When you want to group records in a query by a specific field, include only that field in the query. For example, if you wanted to group (summarize) the CDs in your CD Collection database by the type of music, you would include only the Type field in your query. To group data in a query, you must insert a Total row in the query design. The Total row does not appear by default. In this activity, you will create a query and group the records by Division.

1 Be sure **Queries** is selected on the Objects bar and then double-click **Create query in Design view**. In the **Show Table** dialog box, double-click **Faculty** and then click **Close**.

2 From the list of fields for the Faculty table, double-click the **Division** field to add it to the design grid.

3 On the Query Design toolbar, click the **Totals** button [Σ]. See Figure 3.66.

A Total row is inserted as the third row of the design grid. See Figure 3.66.

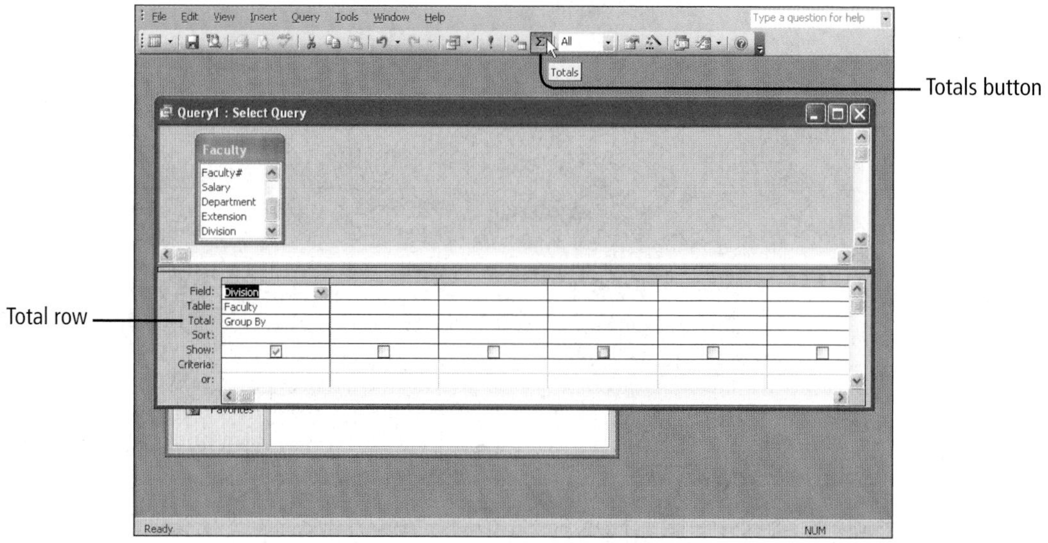

Figure 3.66

4 In the **Total** row, under **Division**, click and then click the arrow that displays to the right of *Group By*.

The list of aggregate functions displays.

5 Click **Group By** and then click the **Run** button [!] to run the query.

The query results display summarized by the entries in the Division field: Business, Education, Fine Arts, and Humanities. See Figure 3.67.

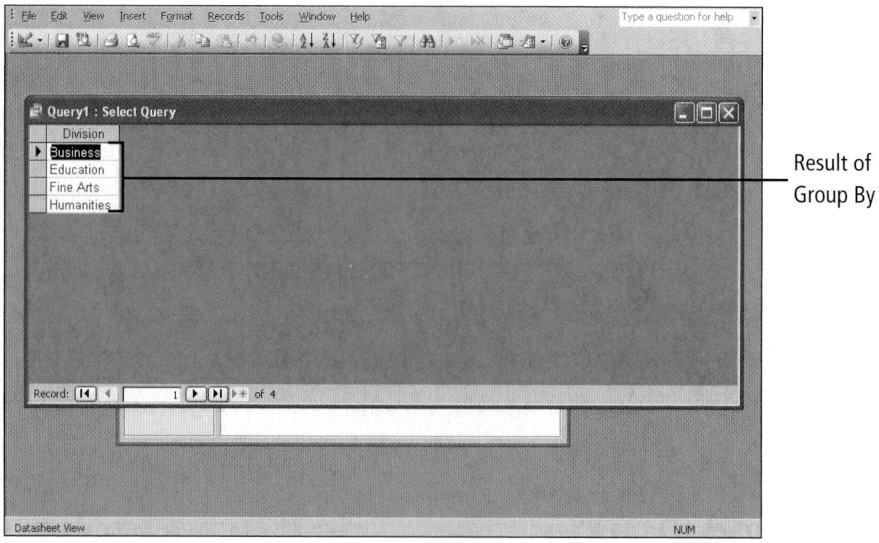

Figure 3.67

Activity 3.18 Using the AVG, SUM, MAX, and MIN Functions in a Query

In this activity, you will create a query that will display the Faculty salary amounts grouped by Division.

1 Switch to **Design view** and then add the **Salary** field to the design grid.

2 Click the **Run** button to run the query.

The query results contain the individual salary amounts, grouped together by division, as shown in Figure 3.68.

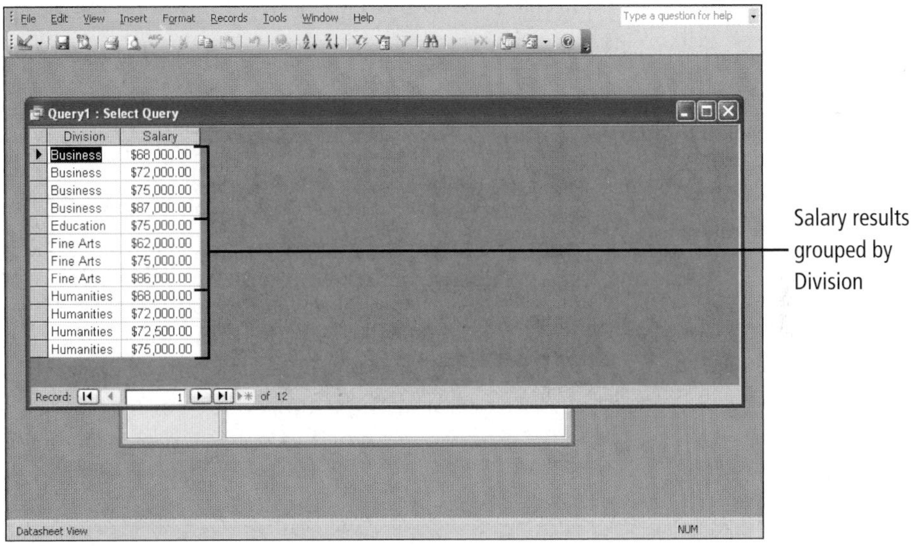

Figure 3.68

3 Switch to **Design view**. In the **Total** row, under **Salary**, click and then click the arrow that displays.

4 From the list of functions, click **Avg** as shown in Figure 3.69 and then click the **Run** button.

Access calculates an average salary for each of the four divisions. Notice the field name, *AvgOfSalary*, for the calculation. This query answers the question, "What is the average faculty salary within each division?"

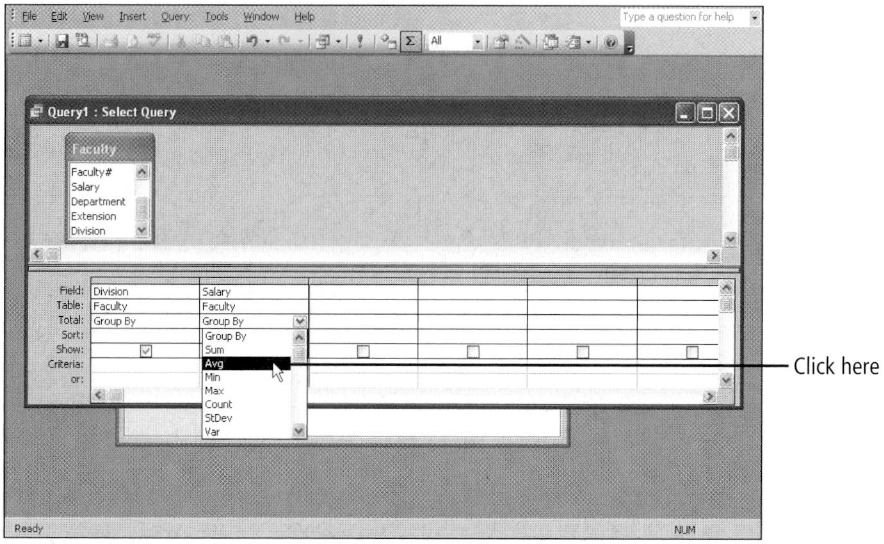

Figure 3.69

5 Switch to **Design view**. In the **Total** row under **Salary**, click and then click the arrow that displays. From the list of functions, click **Sum**.

6 Run the query.

Access sums the Salaries for each of the four Divisions. Notice the field name, *SumOfSalary*, for the calculation. Thus, the total annual salary amount for all of the faculty members in the Business Division is $302,000.00.

7 Switch to **Design view**. In the **Total** row, under **Salary**, click and then click the arrow that displays. From the list of functions, click **Min**.

8 Run the query.

Access locates the smallest value in each of the Divisions and displays the results. Thus, the lowest paid faculty member in the Fine Arts Division earns an annual salary of $62,000.00.

9 Switch to **Design view**. In the **Total** row, under **Salary**, click and then click the arrow that displays. From the list of functions, click **Max**.

10 Run the query.

Access locates the largest value in each of the Divisions and displays the results. See Figure 3.70. Thus, the highest paid faculty member in the Humanities Division earns $75,000.00.

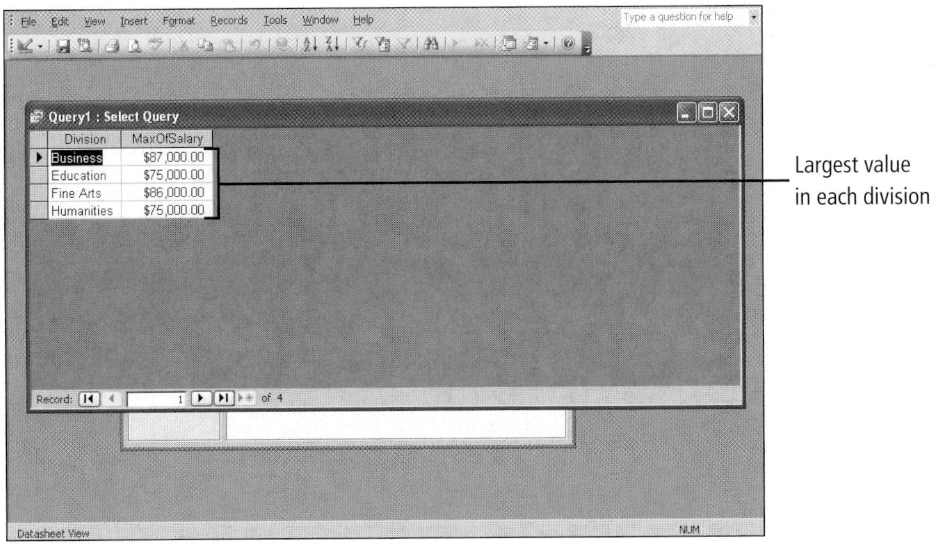

Figure 3.70

11 In the title bar of the query window, click the **Close** button. Click **Yes** to save changes to the query and in the **Save As** dialog box and using your own information, type **Firstname Lastname Max Salary** as the query name. Click **OK**.

The Database window displays.

12 Print your **Max Salary** query.

13 Close your **School** database and then close Access.

End **You have completed Project 3C**

Summary

Queries allow you to ask questions about the data in a database in a manner that Access can interpret. Queries are useful for locating data that matches the criteria, or conditions, that you specify.

Text is one type of criteria that can be specified. Wildcard characters such as the *, which serves as a placeholder for a group of characters, are included as part of the criteria when a portion of what you are looking for is unknown. The wildcard character ? serves as a placeholder for a single character in textual criteria.

Numeric criteria can also be specified in a query. Specifying numeric criteria allows you to use comparison operators, such as less than (<), greater than (>), and equal to (=).

Queries can also have more than one criteria, known as compound criteria, to assist you in locating specific data. There are two types of compound criteria, AND and OR.

Calculations can be performed in a query. Statistical calculations such as SUM, AVG, MAX, and MIN can be used on grouped data in a query.

In This Chapter You Practiced How To

- Create a New Select Query
- Run, Save, and Close a Query
- Open and Edit an Existing Query
- Specify Text Criteria in a Query
- Use Wildcards in a Query
- Specify Numeric Criteria in a Query
- Use Compound Criteria
- Sort Data in a Query
- Use Calculated Fields in a Query
- Group Data and Calculate Statistics in a Query

Concepts Assessments

Matching

Match each term in the second column with its correct definition in the first column by writing the letter of the term on the blank line in front of the correct definition.

____ **1.** The symbols < (less than) > (greater than) and = (equal).

____ **2.** The upper portion of the query design grid where selected tables used in the query display.

____ **3.** The category that includes AND and OR operators.

____ **4.** Statistics performed on a group of records.

____ **5.** Two or more conditions in a query.

____ **6.** A question formed in a manner that Access can interpret.

____ **7.** The conditions that identify the specific records you are looking for.

____ **8.** The lower pane of the query window where the fields are added to the query.

____ **9.** Characters that serve as a placeholder for an unknown character or characters in a query.

____ **10.** Displays the tables available for use in a query.

____ **11.** Language used in querying, updating, and managing relational databases.

____ **12.** Term used to compare expressions.

____ **13.** Examines a sequence of characters and compares them to the criteria in a query.

____ **14.** Wildcard character used as a placeholder to match any number of characters.

____ **15.** Wildcard character used as a placeholder to match one character.

A Aggregate functions
B Asterisk (*)
C Comparison operators
D Compound criteria
E Criteria
F Design grid
G "Like"
H Logical operators
I Query
J Question mark (?)
K Show Table dialog box
L SQL
M String expression
N Table area
O Wildcard characters

Concepts Assessments (continued)

Fill in the Blank

Write the correct answer in the space provided.

1. When a query is run, the results display in a(n) ____________________.
2. To include, but not display, a field in query results, clear the ____________________ box in the design grid.
3. In an ____________________ condition, both parts of the query must be met.
4. In an ____________________ condition, either part of the query may be met.
5. If sorting records by multiple fields, the field that is to be sorted first must be positioned to the ____________________ of the field that is sorted next.
6. Use the ____________________ to better view the calculations entered into a calculated field in a query.
7. To locate the largest value in a group of records, use the ____________________ function.
8. To display the row in the design grid where you can specify statistical functions, such as Sum or Avg, click the ____________________ button.
9. To locate the smallest value in a group of records, use the ____________________ function.
10. To save an existing query with a new name, use the ____________________ command.

Skill Assessments

Project 3D—Rental Instruments

Objectives: *Create a New Select Query; Run, Save, and Close a Query; and Specify Text Criteria in a Query.*

In the following Skill Assessment, you will create a query that will locate specific information for rental instruments at the Lake Michigan City College Music Department. Your completed query will look similar to the one shown in Figure 3.71. You will rename the database as *3D_Rental_Instruments_Firstname_Lastname* in the folder you have created for this chapter.

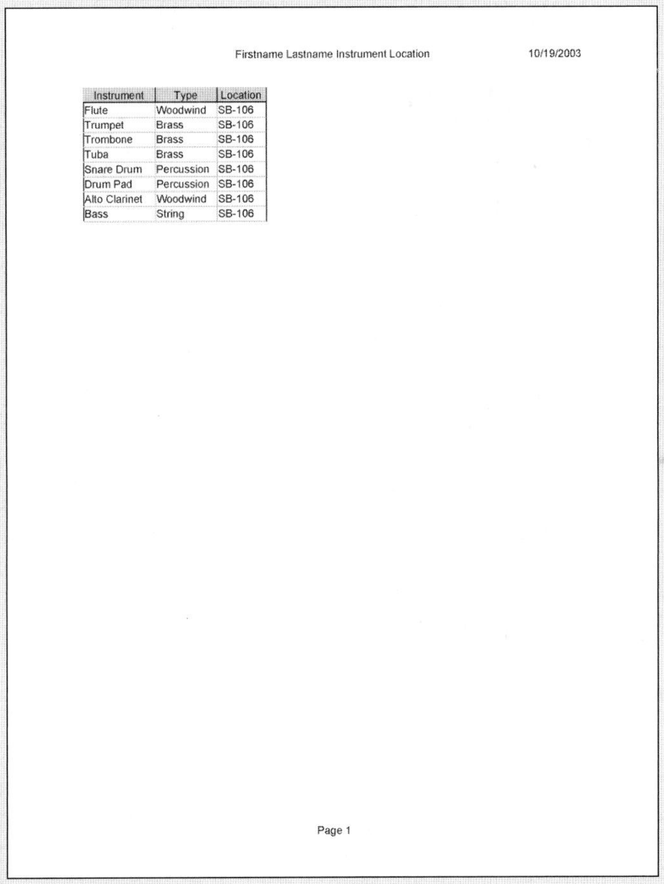

Firstname Lastname Instrument Location 10/19/2003

Instrument	Type	Location
Flute	Woodwind	SB-106
Trumpet	Brass	SB-106
Trombone	Brass	SB-106
Tuba	Brass	SB-106
Snare Drum	Percussion	SB-106
Drum Pad	Percussion	SB-106
Alto Clarinet	Woodwind	SB-106
Bass	String	SB-106

Page 1

Figure 3.71

1. Locate the file **a03D_Rental_Instruments** from the student files that accompany this text. Copy and paste the file to the Chapter 3 folder you created earlier in this chapter.
2. Using the technique you practiced in Activity 1.1 of Chapter 1, remove the Read-only property from the file and rename the file as **3D_Rental_Instruments_Firstname_Lastname**

(Project 3D–Rental Instruments continues on the next page)

(Project 3D–Rental Instruments continued)

3. Close the Windows accessory you are using—either My Computer or Windows Explorer. Start Access and open your **3D_Rental_Instruments** database.
4. On the Objects bar, click **Queries**.
5. Double-click **Create query in Design view**. A new Select Query window opens and the **Show Table** dialog box displays. The Show Table dialog box lists all of the tables in the database.
6. In the **Show Table** dialog box, click **Rental Instruments**, click the **Add** button, and then click the **Close** button. Alternatively, you can double-click Rental Instruments and then click Close.
7. In the **Rental Instruments** field list, double-click **Instrument**. The **Instrument** field displays in the design grid.
8. In the **Rental Instruments** field list, double-click **Type**. Repeat this action for the **Location** field. As you double-click each field, notice the fields display one by one in the design grid.
9. In the **Criteria** row, under the **Location** field, type **SB-106**
10. On the Query Design toolbar, click the **Run** button. The query runs and the query results display in a table in Datasheet view. Clicking the Run button causes Access to look at all the records in the Rental Instruments table and locate only the records that meet the specified criteria, which, in this case, are the records that have SB-106 in the Location field.
11. In the title bar of the query window, click the **Close** button. Click **Yes** to save changes to the query and, in the **Save As** dialog box using your own information, type **Firstname Lastname Instrument Location** as the query name. Click **OK**.
12. Be sure your **Instrument Location** query is selected. Then on the Database toolbar, click the **Print** button.
13. Close the database and then close Access.

End You have completed Project 3D

Project 3E—Inventory

Objectives: *Create a New Select Query; Run, Save, and Close a Query; Specify Numeric Criteria in a Query; and Use Compound Criteria.*

In the following Skill Assessment, you will create a new query to locate information about the inventory at LMCC. Your completed query will look similar to Figure 3.72. You will rename and save your database as *3E_Inventory_Firstname_Lastname.*

(Project 3E–Inventory continues on the next page)

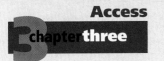

Skill Assessments (continued)

(Project 3E–Inventory continued)

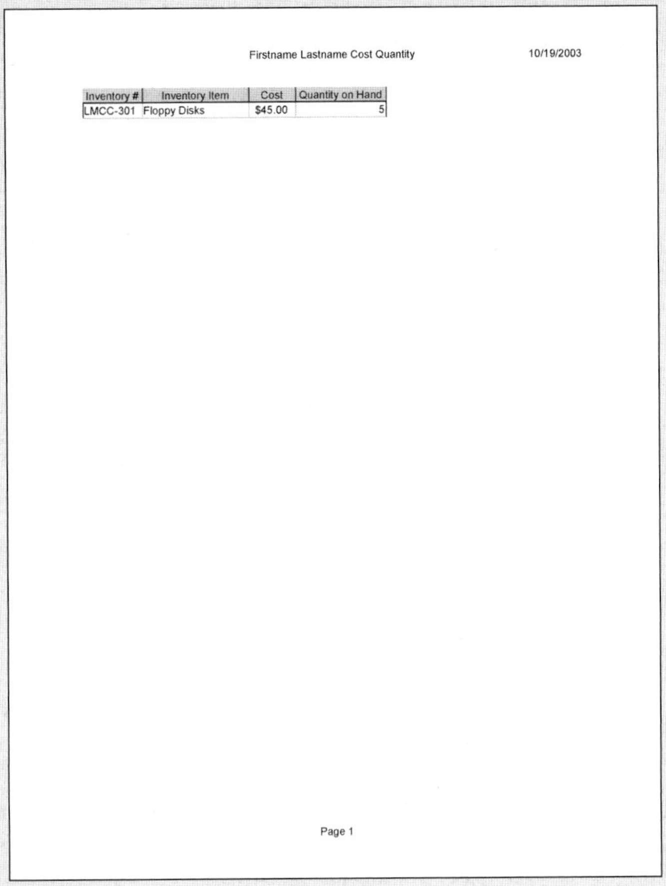
Firstname Lastname Cost Quantity 10/19/2003

Inventory #	Inventory Item	Cost	Quantity on Hand
LMCC-301	Floppy Disks	$45.00	5

Page 1

Figure 3.72

1. Locate the file **a03E_Inventory** from the student files that accompany this text. Copy and paste the file to the Chapter 3 folder you created earlier in this chapter.
2. Using the technique you practiced in Activity 1.1 of Chapter 1, remove the Read-only property from the file and rename the file as **3E_Inventory_Firstname_Lastname**
3. Close the Windows accessory you are using—either My Computer or Window Explorer. Start Access and open your **3E_Inventory** database.
4. On the Objects bar, click **Queries**. To the right of the Objects bar, two command icons for creating a new query display.
5. Double-click **Create query in Design view**. A new **Select Query** window opens and the **Show Table** dialog box displays. The Show Table dialog box lists all of the tables in the database.

(Project 3E–Inventory continues on the next page)

(Project 3E–Inventory continued)

6. In the **Show Table** dialog box, double-click **Office Inventory** and then click the **Close** button. A list of the fields in the Office Inventory table displays in the upper pane of the Select Query window. The **Inventory #** field is bold, unlike the other fields in the list, because the Inventory # field is the primary key in the Office Inventory table.
7. In the **Office Inventory** field list, double-click **Inventory #**. The Inventory # field displays in the design grid. The design grid of the Select Query window is where you specify the fields and other criteria to be used in the query.
8. In the **Office Inventory** field list, double-click **Inventory Item**. Repeat this action for the **Cost** and **Quantity on Hand** fields in the field list. Use the vertical scroll bar in the field list window to view the fields toward the end of the list. As you double-click each field, notice the fields display one by one in the design grid.
9. In the **Criteria** row, under **Cost**, type **>40** and then click the **Run** button. Three records display in the query results; each has a Cost greater than $40.00. On the Query Datasheet toolbar, click the **View** button to switch to Design view.
10. In the **Criteria** row, under **Quantity on Hand**, type **>=5** and then click the **Run** button. One record displays for Floppy Disks. This record meets the criteria of a Cost that is greater than $40.00 AND a Quantity on Hand that is greater than or equal to 5.
11. In the title bar of the query window, click the **Close** button. Click **Yes** to save changes to the query and in the **Save As** dialog box using your own information, type **Firstname Lastname Cost Quantity** as the query name. Click **OK**.
12. Be sure your **Cost Quantity** query is selected, then on the Database toolbar, click the **Print** button.
13. Close the database and then close Access.

End You have completed Project 3E

Project 3F—Computer Inventory

Objectives: *Create a New Select Query; Run, Save, and Close a Query; Use Calculated Fields in a Query; and Group Data and Calculate Statistics in a Query.*

In the following Skill Assessment you will create two queries for the Computer Inventory database at LMCC. Your completed queries will look similar to Figure 3.73. You will rename and save your database as *3F_Computer_Inventory_Firstname_Lastname.*

(Project 3F–Computer Inventory continues on the next page)

(Project 3F–Computer Inventory continued)

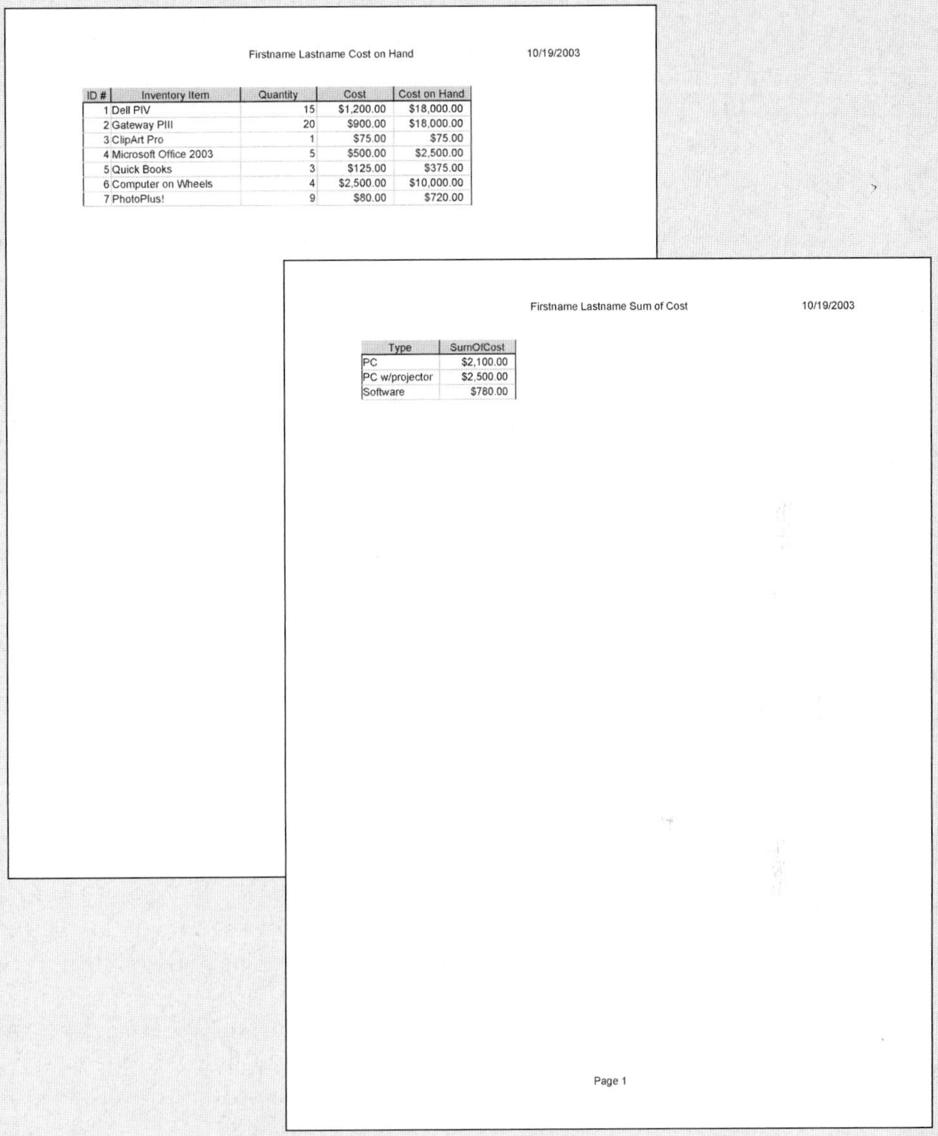

Firstname Lastname Cost on Hand 10/19/2003

ID #	Inventory Item	Quantity	Cost	Cost on Hand
1	Dell PIV	15	$1,200.00	$18,000.00
2	Gateway PIII	20	$900.00	$18,000.00
3	ClipArt Pro	1	$75.00	$75.00
4	Microsoft Office 2003	5	$500.00	$2,500.00
5	Quick Books	3	$125.00	$375.00
6	Computer on Wheels	4	$2,500.00	$10,000.00
7	PhotoPlus!	9	$80.00	$720.00

Firstname Lastname Sum of Cost 10/19/2003

Type	SumOfCost
PC	$2,100.00
PC w/projector	$2,500.00
Software	$780.00

Page 1

Figure 3.73

1. Locate the file **a03F_Computer_Inventory** from the student files that accompany this text. Copy and paste the file to the Chapter 3 folder you created earlier in this chapter.
2. Using the technique you practiced in Activity 1.1 of Chapter 1, remove the Read-only property from the file and rename the file as **3F_ComputerInventory_Firstname_Lastname**
3. Close the Windows accessory you are using—either My Computer or Windows Explorer. Start Access and open your **3F_ComputerInventory** database.

(Project 3F–Computer Inventory continues on the next page)

Skill Assessments (continued)

(Project 3F–Computer Inventory continued)

4. On the Objects bar, click **Queries**. To the right of the Objects bar, two command icons for creating a new query display.
5. Double-click **Create query in Design view**. A new Select Query window opens and the **Show Table** dialog box displays. The **Show Table** dialog box lists all of the tables in the database.
6. In the **Show Table** dialog box, double-click **Inventory** and then click the **Close** button. A list of the fields in the Inventory table displays in the upper pane of the Select Query window. The ID # field is bold, unlike the other fields in the list, because the ID # field is the primary key in the Inventory table.
7. In the **Inventory** field list, double-click **ID #**. The ID # field displays in the design grid. The design grid of the Select Query window is where you specify the fields and other criteria to be used in the query.
8. In the **Inventory** field list, double-click **Inventory Item**. Repeat this action for the **Quantity** and **Cost** fields in the field list. Use the vertical scroll bar in the field list window to view the fields toward the end of the list. As you double-click each field, notice the fields display one by one in the design grid.
9. In the design grid, in the **Field** row, click in the first empty column on the right, right-click to display the shortcut menu, and then click **Zoom**.
10. In the Zoom dialog box, type **Cost on Hand:[Quantity]*[Cost]**
11. Look at the expression you have just typed. The first element, *Cost on Hand*, is the name of the new field where the calculated amounts will display. Following that is a colon (:). A colon in a calculated field separates the new field name from the equation. *Quantity* and *Cost* are in square brackets because they are existing fields from the Inventory table. In between the fields is an asterisk (*), which in mathematical calculations signifies multiplication.
12. In the **Zoom** dialog box, click **OK** and then click the **Run** button. The query results display the four specified fields from the Inventory table plus a fifth field, *Cost on Hand*, that, for each record, displays a calculated amount that results from multiplying the figure in the *Quantity* field by the figure in the *Cost* field.
13. In the title bar of the query window, click the **Close** button. Click **Yes** to save changes to the query and in the **Save As** dialog box and using your own information, type **Firstname Lastname Cost on Hand** as the query name. Click **OK**. The Database window displays.
14. In the Database window, be sure your **Cost on Hand** query is selected and then on the Database toolbar, click the **Print** button.

(Project 3F–Computer Inventory continues on the next page)

Skill Assessments (continued)

(Project 3F–Computer Inventory continued)

15. If necessary, on the Objects bar, click **Queries**, then double-click **Create query in Design view**.
16. In the **Show Table** dialog box, double-click **Inventory** and then click the **Close** button.
17. In the **Inventory** field list, double-click **Type** and **Cost** to add these fields to the design grid.
18. On the Query Design toolbar, click the **Totals** button. The **Total** row displays in the design grid.
19. In the **Total** row, under **Cost**, click and then click the **arrow** that displays to the right of *Group By*. The list of aggregate functions displays.
20. From the list of functions, click **Sum** and then click the **Run** button to run the query. Access calculates a total cost amount for each type of inventory.
21. In the title bar of the query window, click the **Close** button. Click **Yes** to save changes to the query and in the **Save As** dialog box using your own information, type **Firstname Lastname Sum of Cost** as the query name. Click **OK**. The Database window displays.
22. Be sure your **Sum of Cost** query is selected and on the Database toolbar, click the **Print** button.
23. Close the database. Close Access.

End **You have completed Project 3F**

Performance Assessments

Project 3G—Distance Learning

Objectives: *Create a New Select Query; Run, Save, and Close a Query; and Use Wildcards in a Query.*

In the following Performance Assessment, you will create queries to locate information about Distance Learning courses at Lake Michigan City College. Your completed query will look similar to Figure 3.74. You will rename and save your database as *3G_Distance_Learning_Firstname Lastname.*

Firstname Lastname Extra Capacity Query 10/19/2003

Lecture#	Lecture Name	Room#	Capacity	Attendance	Extra Capacity
0410	Introduction to Sales at Home	MH-105	400	75	325
0405	Introduction to Real Estate	MH-105	400	115	285
0404	Ancient Pottery of North America	MH-110	500	250	250
0403	Ghost Stories of the Southwest	MH-110	500	257	243

Page 1

Figure 3.74

1. From the student files that accompany this textbook copy the file **a03G_Distance_Learning** and then paste the file to the folder where you are storing your projects for this chapter. Remove the Read-only attribute and using your own information, rename this file as **3G_Distance_Learning_Firstname_Lastname**
2. Start Access and then open your **3G_Distance_Learning** database.
3. On the Objects bar, click **Queries**, then double-click **Create query in Design view**.

(Project 3G–Distance Learning continues on the next page)

(Project 3G–Distance Learning continued)

4. In the **Show Table** dialog box, double-click **Distance Learning Courses** and then click the **Close** button.
5. In the **Distance Learning Courses** field list, double-click the following fields to add them to the design grid: **Course Number**, **Course Name**, and **Credit Hours**.
6. Enter the criteria to search for the records whose Course Name contains either Access or Excel by performing the following: In the **Criteria** row, under the **Course Name** field, type ***Access** and in the **or** row, under the **Course Name** field, type ***Excel** and then click the **Run** button.
7. In the title bar of the query window, click the **Close** button. Click **Yes** to save the changes to the query and in the **Save As** dialog box using your own information, type **Firstname Lastname Access Excel Query** as the query name. Click **OK**.
8. Print your Access Excel query.
9. Close the database and then close Access.

End You have completed Project 3G

Project 3H — Lecture Series

Objectives: *Open and Edit an Existing Query, Specify Numeric Criteria in a Query, Sort Data in a Query, and Use Calculated Fields in a Query.*

In the following Performance Assessment, you will create a query to locate information about the lectures in the college's new Lecture Series. Your completed query will look similar to Figure 3.75. You will rename and save your database as *3H_Lecture_Series_Firstname_Lastname.*

1. From the student files that accompany this textbook copy the file **a03H_Lecture_Series** and then paste the file to the folder where you are storing your projects for this chapter. Remove the Read-only attribute and using your own information, rename this file as **3H_Lecture_Series_Firstname_Lastname**
2. Start Access and then open your **3H_Lecture_Series** database.
3. Open the **Extra Capacity Query** in Design view.
4. Create a calculated field, called *Extra Capacity*, that will subtract the figures in the **Attendance** field from the figures in the **Capacity** field. (Hint: Capacity—Attendance.) Run the query.
5. Switch to the **Design view**. Add criteria to the query that will limit the query results to those records that have an Extra Capacity that is greater than 200. Sort the records by the **Extra Capacity** field in **Descending** order. Run the query.

(Project 3H–Lecture Series continues on the next page)

Performance Assessments (continued)

(Project 3H–Lecture Series continued)

Firstname Lastname Extra Capacity Query 10/19/2003

Lecture#	Lecture Name	Room#	Capacity	Attendance	Extra Capacity
0410	Introduction to Sales at Home	MH-105	400	75	325
0405	Introduction to Real Estate	MH-105	400	115	285
0404	Ancient Pottery of North America	MH-110	500	250	250
0403	Ghost Stories of the Southwest	MH-110	500	257	243

Page 1

Figure 3.75

6. Using **File**, **Save As**, save the query as **Firstname Lastname Extra Capacity Query**
7. Print your Extra Capacity Query query. Close the database and then close Access.

End **You have completed Project 3H**

Project 3I—Lecture Hall

Objectives: *Create a New Select Query; Run, Save, and Close a Query; and Group Data and Calculate Statistics in a Query.*

In the following Performance Assessment, you will create a query to locate information about the lectures in LMCC's new Lecture Series. Your completed query will look similar to Figure 3.76. You will rename and save your database as *3I_Lecture_Hall_Firstname_Lastname.*

(Project 3I–Lecture Hall continues on the next page)

(Project 3I–Lecture Hall continued)

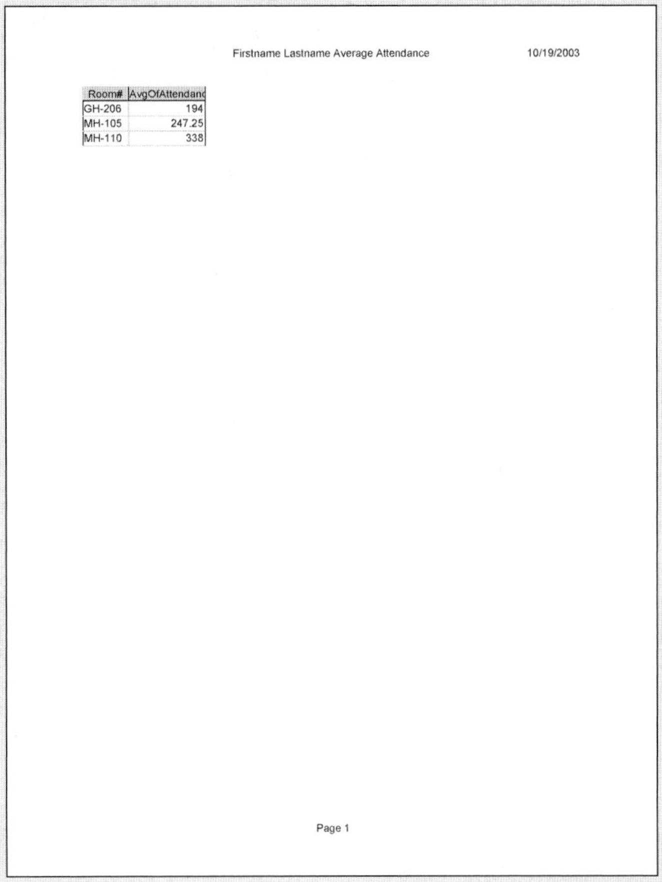
Firstname Lastname Average Attendance 10/19/2003

Room#	AvgOfAttendanc
GH-206	194
MH-105	247.25
MH-110	338

Page 1

Figure 3.76

1. From the student files that accompany this textbook copy the file **a03I_Lecture_Hall** and then paste the file to the folder where you are storing your projects for this chapter. Remove the Read-only attribute and using your own information, rename this file as **3I_Lecture_Hall_Firstname_Lastname**
2. Start Access and then open your **3I Lecture_Hall** database.
3. Open the **Average Attendance** query in Design view. Click the **Totals** button to display the **Total** row. In the **Total** row, under **Attendance**, click the **arrow** that displays and then click **Avg.** Group the query results by Room#.
4. Run the query. Using **File**, **Save As**, save the query using your own information, as **Firstname Lastname Average Attendance**
5. Print the query you created. Close the database and then close Access.

End **You have completed Project 3I**

Mastery Assessments

Project 3J — Employees

Objectives: *Create a New Select Query, Run, Save, and Close a Query, Open and Edit an Existing Query, Specify Numeric Criteria in a Query, and Use Calculated Fields in a Query.*

In the following Mastery Assessment, you will create a new query for the Employees database at LMCC. Your completed query will look like Figure 3.77. You will rename and save your database as *3J_Employees_Firstname_Lastname.*

Firstname Lastname Training Query 10/19/2003

First Name	Last Name	Trainings Attempted	Trainings Completed
Kenya	Ellis	11	8
Anthony	Washington	12	8

Firstname Lastname Training Query2 10/19/2003

First Name	Last Name	Trainings Attempted	Trainings Completed	Left to Complete
George	Clayton	9	7	2
Virginia	Dinkel	12	8	4
Kenya	Ellis	11	8	3
Bennet	Franklin	10	9	1
Frank	Hines	6	5	1
Jonathan	Lee	2	2	0
Kenneth	Massey	9	8	1
Ignacio	Morales	9	9	0
Dana	Newitt	12	11	1
Eric	Pankowksi	11	11	0
James	Schmidt	10	7	3
Tamera	Simmons	8	8	0
Corinna	Vega	12	8	4
Donna	Walker	10	9	1
Anthony	Washington	12	8	4

Page 1

Figure 3.77

1. From the student files that accompany this textbook copy the file **a03J_Employees** and then paste the file to the folder where you are storing your projects for this chapter. Remove the Read-only attribute and using your own information, rename this file as **3J_Employees_Firstname_Lastname** Open your **3J_Employees** database.

(Project 3J–Employees continues on the next page)

(Project 3J–Employees continued)

2. Create a query based on the **Employees** table that will locate the records of the employees in the Finance Department that have completed seven or more trainings. Include the **Trainings Attempted** field in the design grid. (Hint: Trainings Completed is greater than or equal to 7.)
3. Clear the **Show** box for the **Dept** field so it will not display in the query result. Sort the Query alphabetically by the employee's last name. Run the query.
4. Using your own information, save the query as **Firstname Lastname Training Query**
5. Open the **Training** query you just created in Design view. Delete the existing criteria and then remove the **Dept** field from the design grid. Using **File**, **Save As**, save the query with the name **Firstname Lastname Training Query2**
6. Create a calculated field, called *Left to Complete*, which will subtract the figures in the **Trainings Completed** field from the figures in the **Trainings Attempted** field. Run the query. Close the query and save changes.
7. Print both queries. Close the database and then close Access.

End You have completed Project 3J

Project 3K—Employee Training

Objectives: *Open and Edit an Existing Query; Group Data and Calculate Statistics in a Query.*

In the following Mastery Assessment, you will modify an existing query for the Employee Training database at LMCC. Your completed query will look similar to Figure 3.78. You will rename and save your database as *3K_Employee_Training_Firstname_Lastname.*

1. From the student files that accompany this textbook copy the file **a03K_Employee_Training** and then paste the file to the folder where you are storing your projects for this chapter. Remove the Read-only attribute and using your own information, rename this file as **3K_Employee_Training_Firstname_Lastname** Open your **3K Employee Training** database.
2. Open the **Average Trainings** query in Design view. Add a Totals row and calculate an average number of **Trainings Completed** and group them by **Dept**. (Hint: Delete all the fields except Dept and Trainings Completed.)
3. Run the query. Use **File**, **Save As** to save the query with the name (using your own information) **Firstname Lastname Average Trainings** and then close the query.

(Project 3K–Employee Training continues on the next page)

Mastery Assessments (continued)

(Project 3K–Employee Training continued)

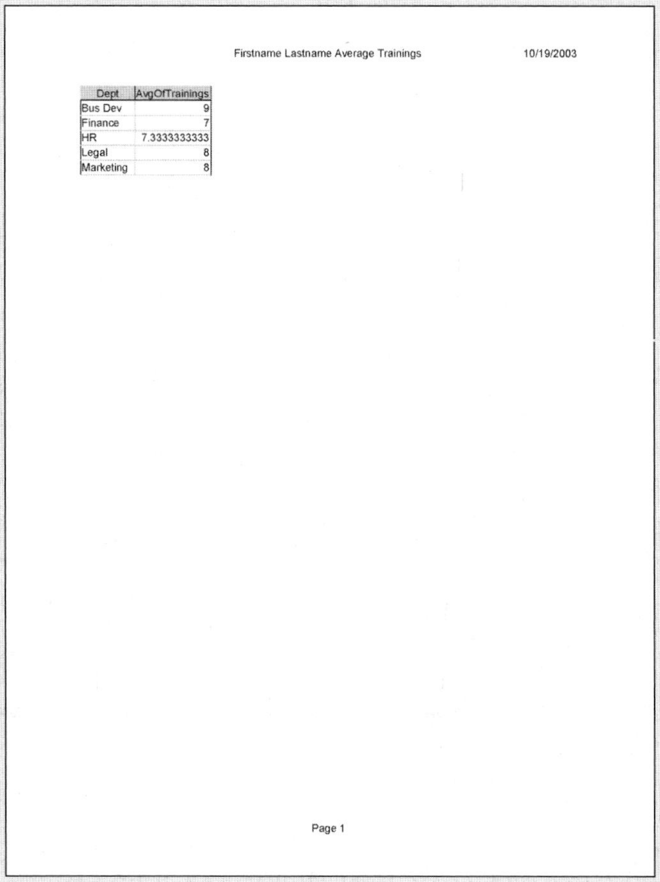
Firstname Lastname Average Trainings 10/19/2003

Dept	AvgOfTrainings
Bus Dev	9
Finance	7
HR	7.3333333333
Legal	8
Marketing	8

Page 1

Figure 3.78

4. Print your **Average Trainings** query. Close the database and then close Access.

End You have completed Project 3K

Problem Solving

Project 3L — Bookstore

Objectives: *Open and Edit an Existing Query, Use Calculated Fields in a Query, and Group Data and Calculate Statistics in a Query.*

In the following Problem Solving exercise, you will modify an existing query for the Bookstore database at LMCC.

1. From the student files that accompany this textbook copy the file **a03L_Bookstore** and then paste the file to the folder where you are storing your projects for this chapter. Remove the Read-only attribute and using your own information, rename this file as **3L_Bookstore_FirstName_LastName** Open your **3L Bookstore** database.
2. Modify the **Bookstore Balance** query so that a total sum of all student balances displays in the query result. Run and then save your query as **Firstname Lastname Bookstore Balance** Print the query.
3. Modify the **New Balance Query** using the following information: The manager of the bookstore has decided to give all students a 15% reduction in their bookstore balances. Create the calculated fields in the manner you choose to determine, first, the 15% discount and then to calculate what the students' new balances will be. Run and then save your query as **Firstname Lastname New Balance Query** Print the query.

End You have completed Project 3L

Project 3M — LMCC

Objectives: *Create a New Select Query; Run, Save, and Close a Query; and Specify Text Criteria in a Query.*

In the following Problem Solving exercise, you will modify an existing query for the Bookstore database at LMCC.

1. From the student files that accompany this textbook copy the file **a03M_LMCC** and then paste the file to the folder where you are storing your projects for this chapter. Remove the Read-only attribute and using your own information, rename this file as **3M_LMCC_Firstname_Lastname** Open your **3M_LMCC** database.
2. Create a query that will locate those students who began attending Lake Michigan City College in the FA02 term. Save your query as **Firstname_Lastname_First Term** Print the query.

End You have completed Project 3M

On the Internet

Microsoft Certification Exam

As you progress with your study of Access, you will learn skills necessary to complete the Microsoft certification test for Access 2003. Go to the Microsoft Web site at **www.microsoft.com** and then search the site to locate information regarding the certification exam. Print the core objectives for the Microsoft Access user certification and any additional information about taking the test.

GO! with Help

Getting Help Using Wildcards

There are many types of wildcards that you can use in your queries. Use the Access Help system to find out more about wildcards in Access.

1. Start Access. If necessary, from the **View** menu, click **Task Pane** to display the **Getting Started** task pane. On the task pane, to the right of *Getting Started*, click the **downward-pointing arrow**. From the displayed list of available task panes, click **Help**.
2. Click in the **Search For** box, then type **wildcards**
3. Press Enter, scroll the displayed list as necessary, and then click **About using wildcard characters**.
4. If you would like to keep a copy of this information, click the **Print** button.
5. Click the **Close** button in the top right corner of the Help window to close the Help window and then close Access.

Access 2003 Task Guide

Each book in the *GO! Series* is designed to be kept beside your computer as a handy reference, even after you have completed all the activities. Any time you need to recall the sequence of steps or a shortcut needed to achieve a result, look up the general category in the alphabetized listing that follows and then find your task. To review how to perform a task, turn to the page number listed in the second column to locate the step-by-step exercise or other detailed description. Additional entries without page numbers describe tasks that are closely related to those presented in the chapters.

Access Task	Page	Mouse	Menu Bar	Shortcut Menu	Shortcut Keys
AutoForm, close	89	in form window	File | Close		Ctrl + F4 or Ctrl + W
AutoForm, create	87	On Objects bar, click Forms, and then click and select an AutoForm Select a table, and then click on Database toolbar	Insert | Form, and then select an AutoForm		
Close, database	54	in the Database window	File | Close		Ctrl + F4 or Ctrl + W
Close, Database window	23	in Database window	File | Close		Ctrl + F4 or Ctrl + W
Close, query	20, 161	in query window	File | Close		Ctrl + F4 or Ctrl + W
Close, table	18	in table window	File | Close		Ctrl + F4 or Ctrl + W
Create, new blank database	28	then click Blank data-base in New File task pane	File | New		Ctrl + N
Create, table in Design view	29	On Objects bar, click Tables; double-click *Create table in Design view* or click , and then click Design View	Insert | Table, Design View	Right-click Create table in Design view command, and then click Open	
Data type, select	29	In Table Design view, click a field's Data Type column, and then select from drop-down list			
Database window, close	23	in Database window			

Access Task	Page	Mouse	Menu Bar	Shortcut Menu	Shortcut Keys
Database window, restore	23				
Database, clear Read-only property	4		File | Properties (in My Computer); clear Read-only	In My Computer, right-click database file name, and then click Properties; clear Read-only	
Database, close	54	in the Database window	File | Close		
Database, copy	4		Edit | Copy, and then Edit | Paste in same or other folder (in My Computer)	In My Computer, right-click database file name, and then click Copy; right-click in file name area of destination folder, and then click Paste	Ctrl + C and Ctrl + V
Database, create new (blank)	28	and then click Blank database in New File task pane	File | New		Ctrl + N
Database, open existing	6		File | Open		Ctrl + O
Database, rename	4		File | Rename (in My Computer)	In My Computer, right-click database file name, and then click Rename	
Delete, record	45	in Table Datasheet view	Edit | Delete Record, and then click Yes to confirm	Right-click selected record, and then click Delete Record	Delete
Delete, table field	39	In Table Design view, click record selector and then	Edit | Delete Rows Edit | Delete	Right-click a field name, and then click Delete Rows	Delete
Display, first record in form	84		Edit | Go To | First		Ctrl + Home
Display, last record in form	84		Edit | Go To | Last		Ctrl + End
Display, next record in form	21		Edit | Go To | Next		PageDown
Display, previous record in form	84		Edit | Go To | Previous		Page Up
Display, print preview of form	110		File | Print Preview	Right-click form name, and then click Print Preview	
Display, Total row in query design grid	201		View | Totals	Totals	
Display/close, field list	115	to close	View | Field List		

Access Task	Page	Mouse	Menu Bar	Shortcut Menu	Shortcut Keys
Display/hide report's page header/footer	124		View | Page Header/Footer	Page Header/Footer	
Display/hide report's report header/footer	124		View | Report Header/Footer	Report Header/Footer	
Display/hide, form header/footer	98, 110		View | Form Header/Footer	Form Header/Footer	
Edit, record	44	In Table Datasheet view, click in a field, and then type			Delete or Bksp to delete text
Exit, Access	54	in the Access window	File | Exit		Alt + F4
Field list, display/close	115	to close	View | Field List		
Field, add to table	41	In Table Design view, , and then type field name Click in first field of next available row, and then type field name	Insert | Rows (Design view)	Right-click a field name or blank row, and then click Insert Rows	
Form, add label	98	on Toolbox in Design view			
Form, add form footer	110	Add a label to Form Footer section (Design view)			
Form, add form header	98	Add a label to Form Header section (Design view)			
Form, add new record	90		Insert | New Record (in Datasheet view)		Ctrl + +
Form, close	21, 84	in form window	File | Close		Ctrl + F4 or Ctrl + W
Form, close AutoForm	89	in form window	File | Close		Ctrl + F4 or Ctrl + W
Form, close when maximized	110		Close (on form Program menu)	Right-click title bar, and then click Close	
Form, create AutoForm	87	On Objects bar, click Forms, and then click New and select an AutoForm Select a table, and then click on Database toolbar	Insert | Form, and then select an AutoForm		

Access Task	Page	Mouse	Menu Bar	Shortcut Menu	Shortcut Keys
Form, create with Form Wizard	96	On Objects bar, click Forms, and then click New, Form Wizard Double-click *Create form by using wizard*	Insert | Form, Form Wizard		
Form, delete record	91	on Formatting toolbar	Edit | Delete Record	Right-click record selector, and then click Cut	Delete
Form, display first	84		Edit | Go To | First		Ctrl + Home
Form, display last record	84		Edit | Go To | Last		Ctrl + End
Form, display next record	21		Edit | Go To | Next		PageDown
Form, display previous record	84		Edit | Go To | Previous		Page Up
Form, display print preview	110		File | Print Preview	Right-click form name, and then click Print Preview	
Form, display/ hide form header/footer	98, 110		View | Form Header/Footer	Form Header/Footer	
Form, display/hide rulers	98		View | Ruler (Design view)	Ruler	
Form, display/hide Toolbox	98	on Form Design toolbar	View | Toolbox	Toolbox	
Form, maximize window	98	Double-click title bar			
Form, move a field	103	Display , drag border (Design view)			
Form, move text box control separately from label	103	Display , drag large black handle (Design view)			
Form, open in Design view	21	Click form name and then Design		Right-click form name, and then click Design View	
Form, open in Form view	21, 84	Click form name and then Open Double-click form name		Right-click form name, and then click Open	

Access Task	Page	Mouse	Menu Bar	Shortcut Menu	Shortcut Keys
Form, print	110		File | Print	Right-click form name, and then click Print	Ctrl + P
Form, resize a field	103	Drag a selection handle (Design view)	Format | Size	Right-click field, and then click Size	
Form, save design	89	on Form design toolbar	File | Save		Ctrl + S
Form, switch to Design view	21, 98		View | Design View	Right-click form title bar, and then click Form Design	
Form, switch to Form view	21, 98		View | Form View	Right-click form title bar, and then click Form View	
Go to, first field of first record in datasheet	53	Click in first field			Ctrl + Home
Go to, first record in datasheet	53		Edit | Go To | First		Ctrl + Page Up and then Ctrl + Home
Go to, last field of last record in datasheet	53	Click in last field			Ctrl + End
Go to, last record in datasheet	53		Edit | Go To | Last		Ctrl + PageDown and then Ctrl + End
Go to, next record in datasheet	52, 53		Edit | Go To | Next		↓
Go to, previous record in datasheet	52, 53		Edit | Go To | Previous		↑
Move, field in form	103	Display , drag border (Design view)			
Move, query field	190	Drag column selector left or right			
Move, report field and label in different sections in Design view	117	Select using Shift, and then drag			→, ←, ↑, ↓

Access Task	Page	Mouse	Menu Bar	Shortcut Menu	Shortcut Keys
Open, existing database	6		File | Open		Ctrl + O
Open, form in Design view	21	Click form name and then Design		Right-click form name, and then click Design View	
Open, form in Form view	21, 84	Click form name and then Open Double-click form name		Right-click form name, and then click Open	
Open, query in Datasheet view	20, 162, 189	Click query name and then Open Double-click query name		Right-click query name, and then click Open	
Open, query in Design view	20, 162	Click query name and then Design and then click		Right-click query name, and then click Design View	
Open, report in Design view	23	Click report name and then Design		Right-click report name, and then click Design View	
Open, table in Datasheet view	14, 38	Click table name and then Open Double-click table name		Right-click table name, and then click Open	
Open, table in Design view	14	Click table name and then Design		Right-click table name, and then click Design View	
Page setup, check margins	42	In Print dialog box, click Setup	File | Page Setup		
Primary key, create	34	In Table Design view, click a field name, and then 	Edit | Primary Key	Right-click a field name, and then click Primary Key	
Print, table	42	 in Table Datasheet view	File | Print	Right-click table name, and then click Print	Ctrl + P
Print, form	110		File | Print	Right-click form name, and then click Print	Ctrl + P
Print, landscape/ portrait orientation	42	In Print dialog box, click Properties, Layout tab, and then Landscape or Portrait	File | Properties | Layout tab, Landscape or Portrait		
Print, query results	172		File | Print		Ctrl + P
Print, report	23	 on Print Preview toolbar	File | Print	Right-click on report, and then click Report	Ctrl + P

Access Task	Page	Mouse	Menu Bar	Shortcut Menu	Shortcut Keys
Query, add calculated field	196	Type expression in Field row, enclosing field names in brackets		Right-click in Field row, Field row, choose Zoom, type expression	
Query, add fields to design grid	156	Double-click field name in field list Drag field to grid Click in Field row, and then select from list			
Query, add table in Design view	156	, click Add	Query | Show Table, Add	Show Table	
Query, clear the design grid	180		Edit | Clear Grid		
Query, close	20, 161	in query window	File | Close		Ctrl + F4 or Ctrl + W
Query, create in Design view	156	On Objects bar, click Queries; click New; click Design View double-click *Create query in Design view*	Insert | Query, Design View		
Query, delete selected field(s)	163		Edit | Delete Columns	Cut	Delete
Query, display Total row	201	Σ	View | Totals	Totals	
Query, format calculated field	196		View | Properties	Properties	Alt + Enter
Query, group data	201	In Total row, click Group By			
Query, hide field from result	180	In the Show row under the field, clear the check box			
Query, move field	190	Drag column selector left or right			
Query, open in Datasheet view	20, 162, 189	Click query name and then Open Double-click query name		Right-click query name, and then click Open	
Query, open in Design view	20, 162	Click query name and then Design		Right-click query name, and then click Design View	

Access Task	Page	Mouse	Menu Bar	Shortcut Menu	Shortcut Keys
Query, print results	172		File | Print		Ctrl + P
Query, run	161	 in Design view			
Query, save design	161		File | Save		Ctrl + S
Query, save to new name	166		File | Save As	Right-click report name, and then click Save As	
Query, sort by multiple fields in Design view	190	Move fields in order of sort; in Sort row, select Ascending or Descending for each sort field			
Query, sort in Datasheet view	189	 or 			
Query, sort in Design view	190	In Sort row, select Ascending or Descending			
Query, specify * wildcard criteria	174	Type under field in Criteria row, substituting * for multiple characters			
Query, specify ? wildcard criteria	178	Type under field in Criteria row, substituting ? for single characters (Design view)			
Query, specify criteria using AND	187	Type under each field in Criteria row			
Query, specify criteria using comparison operators	184	Type under field in Criteria row with < > <= >= operators			
Query, specify criteria using OR	188	Type under field in Criteria and *or* rows			
Query, specify text or numeric criteria	166, 183	Type under field in Criteria row			
Query, switch to Datasheet view	20	 on Query Design toolbar	View | Datasheet View	Right-click query title bar, and then click Datasheet View	
Query, switch to Design view	20, 162	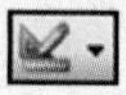	View | Design View	Right-click query title bar, and then click Query Design	
Query, use functions	203	In Total row, click Sum, Avg, Min, Max, etc.			

Access Task	Page	Mouse	Menu Bar	Shortcut Menu	Shortcut Keys
Record, add to table	36	In Table Datasheet view, , and then type Click in first field of next available record, and then type Click in last field of last record, and then press Tab and type	Insert | New Record (Datasheet view)	Right-click selected record, and then click New Record	Ctrl + +
Record, delete	45	in Table Datasheet view	Edit | Delete Record, and then click Yes to confirm	Right-click selected record, and then click Delete Record	Delete
Record, edit	44	In Table Datasheet view, click in a field, and then type			Delete or Bksp to delete text
Report, add page footer or report	124	, drag in Page Footer or Report Footer section			
Report, change setup	115	Setup on Print Preview toolbar	File | Page Setup		
Report, change width	117	Drag right edge of report , click Format tab, Width			
Report, close	23	in report window	File | Close		Ctrl + F4 or Ctrl + W
Report, create with Report Wizard	112	On Objects bar, click Report; click New, Report Wizard double-click *Create report by using wizard*	Insert | Report, Report Wizard		
Report, display/hide page header/footer	124		View | Page Header/Footer	Page Header/Footer	
Report, display/ hide report header/footer	124		View | Report Header/Footer	Report Header/Footer	
Report, maximize window	23	, Double-click title bar			
Report, move field and label in different sections in Design view	117	Select using Shift, and then drag			→, ←, ↑, ↓
Report, nudge object in Design view	117				Ctrl + (→, ←, ↑, ↓)

Access Task	Page	Mouse	Menu Bar	Shortcut Menu	Shortcut Keys
Report, open in Design view	23	Click report name and then Design		Right-click report name, and then click Design View	
Report, preview	23	Click report name, and then Preview or Double-click report name		Right-click report name, and then click Print Preview	
Report, print	23	on Print Preview toolbar	File | Print	Right-click on report, and then click	Ctrl + P
Report, save design	115	on Database toolbar	File | Save		Ctrl + S
Report, switch to Design view	23, 115		View | Design View	Right-click report title bar, and then click Report Design	
Report, switch to Print preview	23, 115	or	View | Print Preview	Right-click report title bar, and then click Print Preview	
Report, zoom to size	23	Fit on Print Preview toolbar	View | Zoom	Right-click on report, and then choose zoom setting	
Resize, column	46	Drag vertical line between column headings left or right	Format | Column Width	Right-click column heading, and then click Column Width	
Resize, column to fit widest entry	46	Double-click vertical line between column headings at right of field	Format | Column Width, Best Fit	Right-click column heading, and then click Column Width; choose Best Fit	
Resize, form field	103	Drag a selection handle (Design view)	Format | Size	Right-click field, and then click Size	
Resize, multiple columns	46	Select multiple columns; drag vertical line between column headings left or right	Format | Column Width	Right-click column heading, and then click Column Width	
Resize, multiple row heights	46	Select multiple rows; drag horizontal line between row headings up or down	Format | Row Height	Right-click row heading, and then click Row Height	
Resize, row height	46	Drag horizontal line between row headings up or down	Format | Row Height	Right-click row heading, and then click Row Height	
Resize, row height to default	46		Format | Row Height, Standard Height	Right-click row heading, and then click Row Height; choose Standard Height	
Save, form design	89	on Form Design toolbar	File | Save		Ctrl + S
Save, query design	161	on Query Design toolbar	File | Save		Ctrl + S

Access Task	Page	Mouse	Menu Bar	Shortcut Menu	Shortcut Keys
Save, query design to new name	166		File | Save As	Right-click report name, and then click Save As	
Save, report design	115	[Save button] on toolbar	File | Save		Ctrl + S
Save, table design	33	[Save button] on Table Design toolbar Switch views, and then click Yes	File | Save		Ctrl + S
Sort, query by multiple fields in Design view	190	Move fields in order of sort; in Sort row, select Ascending or Descending for each sort field			
Sort, query in Datasheet view	189	[Sort Ascending button] or [Sort Descending button]			
Sort, query in Design view	190	In Sort row, select Ascending or Descending			
Sort, records in ascending order	51	Select one or more adjacent columns, and then click [Sort Ascending button]	Records | Sort | Sort Ascending	Right-click anywhere in selected column(s), and then click Sort Ascending	
Sort, records in descending order	51	Select one or more adjacent columns, and then click [Sort Descending button]	Records | Sort | Sort Descending	Right-click anywhere in selected column(s), and then click Sort Descending	
Start, Access	6	[start button] on Windows taskbar, and then locate and click Microsoft Office Access 2003	Start | All Programs | Microsoft Office | Microsoft Office Access 2003		
Table, add field	41	In Table Design view, click [Insert Rows button], and then type field name Click in first field of next available row, and then type field name	Insert | Rows (Design view)	Right-click a field name or blank row, and then click Insert Rows	
Table, add record	36	In Table Datasheet view, click [New Record button], and then type Click in first field of next available record, and then type Click in last field of last record, and then press Tab and type	Insert | New Record (Datasheet view)	Right-click selected record, and then click New Record	Ctrl + +
Table, close	18	[Close button] in table window	File | Close		Ctrl + F4 or Ctrl + W

Access Task	Page	Mouse	Menu Bar	Shortcut Menu	Shortcut Keys
Table, create in Design view	29	On Objects bar, click Tables; double-click Create table in Design view or click New, and then click Design View	Insert | Table, Design View	Right-click Create table in Design view command, and then click Open	
Table, delete field	39	In Table Design view, click record selector and then 	Edit | Delete Rows Edit | Delete (Design view)	Right-click a field name, and then click Delete Rows	Delete
Table, deselect	46	Click anywhere in the table			
Table, enter description for field	29	In Table Design view, click a field's Description column, and then type text			
Table, hide columns	49		Format | Hide Columns	Right-click column heading, and then click Hide Columns	
Table, move down one screen	53	Click below scroll box in vertical scroll bar			PageDown
Table, move to first field in datasheet	53	Click in first field			Ctrl + Home
Table, move to first record in datasheet	53		Edit | Go To | First		Ctrl + Page Up and then Ctrl + Home
Table, move to last field in datasheet	53	Click in last field			Ctrl + End
Table, move to last record in datasheet	53		Edit | Go To | Last		Ctrl + PageDown and then Ctrl + End
Table, move to next record in datasheet	52, 53		Edit | Go To | Next		↓
Table, move to previous record in datasheet	52, 53		Edit | Go To | Previous		↑
Table, move up one screen	53	Click above scroll box in vertical scroll bar			Page Up
Table, open in Datasheet view	14, 38	Click table name and then Open Double-click table name		Right-click table name, and then click Open	
Table, open in Design view	14	Click table name and then Design		Right-click table name, and then click Design View	

Access Task	Page	Mouse	Menu Bar	Shortcut Menu	Shortcut Keys
Table, print	42	 in Table Datasheet view	File | Print	Right-click table name, and then click Print	Ctrl + PrtScr
Table, remove sort	51		Records | Remove Filter/Sort	Right-click anywhere in table, and then click Remove Filter/ Sort	
Table, save design	33	 on Table Design toolbar Switch views, and then click Yes	File | Save		Ctrl + S
Table, select column	14	Click column heading			
Table, select data type	29	In Table Design view, click a field's Data Type column, and then select from drop-down list			
Table, select row	14	Click row selector			
Table, sort records in ascending order	51	Select one or more adjacent columns, and then click 	Records | Sort | Sort Ascending	Right-click anywhere in selected column(s), and then click Sort Ascending	
Table, sort records in descending order	51	Select one or more adjacent columns, and then click 	Records | Sort | Sort Descending	Right-click anywhere in selected column(s), and then click Sort Descending	
Table, switch to Datasheet view	18, 33		View | Datasheet View	Right-click table title bar, and then click Datasheet View	
Table, switch to Design view	18		View | Design View	Right-click table title bar, and then click Design View	
Table, unhide columns	49		Format | Unhide Columns, and then select boxes for columns to unhide	Right-click table title bar, and then click Unhide Columns	

Glossary

Aggregate functions A function that groups and performs calculations on multiple fields.

Ascending order Sorts text alphabetically (A to Z) and sorts numbers from the lowest number to the highest number.

AutoForm A feature that creates a form, with minimal formatting, using all available fields from an existing table.

AutoNumber A data type that assigns a number to each record as it is entered into the table.

Compound criteria Two or more criteria in a query. Compound criteria are used to create more specific criteria and refine the query's results.

Control An object such as a label or text box in a form or report that allows you to view or manipulate information stored in tables or queries.

Criteria (1) The specifications that determine what records will be displayed. (2) The conditions specified to Access so it can find matching fields and records.

Data Facts about people, events, things, or ideas.

Data entry Typing data into the database.

Data type The type of data that can be entered in a field: text, memo, number, date/time, currency, AutoNumber, Yes/No, OLE object, and hyperlink. Specifies how Access organizes and stores data in a field.

Database A collection of data related to a particular topic or purpose.

Database window The window from which all database objects can be manipulated or accessed. The Database window displays when a database is open.

Datasheet view The view in which the information in a table or query can be viewed and manipulated. Datasheet view displays all the records in a table in a format of columns (fields) and rows (records).

Descending order Sorts text in reverse alphabetic order (Z to A) and sorts numbers from the highest number to the lowest.

Design The number and content of the fields in the table. Good design ensures that a database is easy to maintain.

Design grid The lower pane of the Select Query window.

Design view The view in which the structure of a table or query can be viewed and manipulated.

Detail In Design view of a form or report, the section that contains the fields and records that display in the form or report.

Extracting Pulling out specific information from a database based on the specified criteria.

Field An individual item of information that describes a record and is the same type for all records in the table. In Access, fields are located in vertical columns.

Fit An entire page of a report displays on screen at one time, giving an overview of what the printed pages will look like.

Form A database object used to enter, edit, and manipulate information in a table.

Form Footer Displays only at the end of a form when it is viewed in Form view or when the form is printed.

Form Header Displays only at the beginning of a form when the form is viewed in Form view or when the form is printed.

Form Wizard Creates a form in a manner that gives you much more flexibility in the design, layout, and number of fields included in the form. The Form Wizard asks the user questions and then creates a form based on the answers provided.

Information Data that has been organized in a useful manner.

Landscape orientation Refers to the printed page layout when the page is wider than it is high.

Logical operators Boolean operators. AND, OR, and NOT.

Nudge To move in small increments; especially useful in design view to move elements with precision.

Object The primary component of an Access database, such as a table, form, query, or report.

Objects bar Located on the left side of the Database window and contains the buttons to access the objects in the database.

Page Footer Contains information that displays at the bottom of every page of a form or report in Print Preview or when printed.

Page Header Contains information that displays at the top of every page of a form or report in Print Preview or when printed.

Populate Fill a table with data.

Portrait orientation Refers to the printed page layout when the printed page is taller than it is high.

Primary key One or more fields that uniquely identify a record in a table.

Primary sort field The field that Access sorts by initially during a sort operation.

Query (1) A database object that locates information based on specified criteria so that the information can be viewed, changed, or analyzed in various ways. (2) A question formed in a manner that Access can interpret.

Record All the items of information (fields) that pertain to one particular thing such as a customer, employee, or course. In Access, records are located in horizontal rows.

Record selector The gray bar along the left edge of a table or form, that when clicked, selects the entire record.

Report A database object that displays the fields and records from the table (or query) in an easy-to-read format suitable for printing or viewing on the screen.

Report Wizard Creates a report by asking a series of questions and then constructs the report based on the answers provided.

Row selector The small gray box at the left end of a row that, when clicked, selects all the cells in the row.

ScreenTip The button name that displays when the mouse pointer is positioned over the button.

Secondary sort field The field that Access uses to sort records that have matching primary sort fields during a sort operation.

Select query A query that retrieves data from one or more tables and then displays the results.

Sizing handles The small squares surrounding a control that indicate that the control is selected.

Sorting The process of rearranging records in a specific order. Records can be sorted either ascending or descending.

Table The database object that stores the data in a database. Data is organized in a format of horizontal rows (records) and vertical columns (fields).

Table area The upper pane of the Select Query window.

Table Design toolbar The toolbar that displays when a table is displayed in Design view.

Task pane A window within a Microsoft Office application that provides commonly used commands.

Text box control A control on a form or report where data from the corresponding table is displayed when the form or report is viewed.

Toolbox The toolbar that contains the controls that can be added to forms or reports.

View A view is a way of looking at something for a specific purpose, such as Design view or Datasheet view.

Wildcard characters A placeholder for an unknown character or characters in search criteria.

Zoom An option to make the page view larger or smaller.

Index

Symbols

A-B

C

D

E

F

T

U-V

W-Z